God Speaks Through His Word

God Speaks

THROUGH HIS WORD

A Daily Devotional Guide

by
A. F. Harper

Beacon Hill Press of Kansas City
Kansas City, Missouri

Permission to quote from the following copyrighted Scripture versions is acknowledged with appreciation:

The Bible: A New Translation (Moffatt), copyright 1954 by James A. R. Moffatt. By permission of Harper and Row, Publishers, Inc.

The *New American Standard Bible* (NASB), ©️ The Lockman Foundation, 1960, 1962, 1963, 1968, 1971, 1972, 1973, 1975, 1977.

The *Modern Language Bible,* the *New Berkeley Version in Modern English* (NBV), copyright ©️ 1945, 1959, 1969 by Zondervan Publishing House.

The *New English Bible* (NEB), ©️ The Delegates of the Oxford University Press and The Syndics of the Cambridge University Press, 1961, 1970.

Scripture quotations designated NIV are taken from *The Holy Bible, New International Version,* copyright ©️ 1978 by the New York International Bible Society. Used by permission of Zondervan Bible Publishers.

Four Prophets: A Modern Translation from the Hebrew (Phillips), by John B. Phillips. Copyright 1963 by the Macmillan Co.

The *New Testament in Modern English* (Phillips), Revised Edition ©️ J. B. Phillips, 1958, 1960, 1972. By permission of the Macmillan Publishing Co.

The *Revised Standard Version of the Bible* (RSV), copyrighted 1946, 1952, ©️ 1971, 1973.

The Bible: An American Translation (Smith-Goodspeed), J. M. Powis Smith, Edgar J. Goodspeed. Copyright, 1923, 1927, 1948 by The University of Chicago Press.

The Basic Bible: Containing the Old and New Testaments in Basic English (TBB), Copyright 1950 by E. P. Dutton and Co., Inc.

The *Good News Bible, Today's English Version* (TEV)—Old Testament ©️ American Bible Society, 1976; New Testament ©️ American Bible Society, 1966, 1971, 1976.

The Living Bible (TLB), ©️ 1971 by Tyndale House Publishers, Wheaton, Ill.

The Weymouth New Testament in Modern Speech (Weymouth), copyright 1929 by Harper and Brothers, New York.

10 9 8 7 6 5 4 3 2 1

Preface

God Speaks Through His Word has been written to help us meditate each day on some worthy truth from God's Word. It was also planned as a guided tour through the Bible.

The Plan

Beginning with Genesis, several chapters have been chosen to be read each day; they are titled "Scripture." From these chapters a shorter passage is selected as the focus for the meditation. This key scripture is called "The Story." The title and scripture text also reflect the theme for the day.

For a growing acquaintance with God's Word, one should read all of the several chapters chosen for the daily reading. Often this can be done in 10 or 15 minutes. An effective daily schedule might be to read the background chapters in the evening. Then the next morning for personal or family worship, read "The Story" and the meditation, and spend time in prayer. Such a commitment dedicates 20 to 30 minutes each day to knowing God better, and to nurturing one's spirit in Christian faith.

Your guided tour through God's great Book can be started at any time—at the beginning of the year or during the year. The meditations are undated. Start at your convenience, and spend a year with your heart and mind open to God's truth for you. Have a rewarding journey!

Translations

To help understand some of the more difficult passages of the Bible, quotations have often been chosen from one of the newer English translations. These are identified by the following abbreviations:

Moffatt   *The Bible, A New Translation*
NASB   *New American Standard Bible*
NBV   *Modern Language Bible, New Berkeley Version*
NEB   *New English Bible*
NIV   *New International Version*
Phillips   *New Testament in Modern English* and
       Four Prophets: A Modern Translation from the Hebrew

RSV *Revised Standard Version*
Smith-Goodspeed *The Bible: An American Translation*
TBB *The Basic Bible*
TEV *Good News Bible, Today's English Version*
TLB *The Living Bible*
Weymouth *New Testament in Modern Speech*

All unidentified passages, however, are from the King James Version.

The initials BBC refer to *Beacon Bible Commentary*, published by Beacon Hill Press of Kansas City, 10 vols., 1964-69.

Things You Have Always Wanted to Know

Are there some Bible questions that have puzzled you? I have tried to identify such problem passages and to give the best answers I have found. These answers are usually inserted under the scripture reference where the question occurs. I counted 199 of them. You will probably find some that I missed!

Personal Pronouns

In a few paragraphs of testimony, the personal pronouns refer to the writer.

However, in the prayers, confessions, and commitments the *I*, *me*, and *my* are designed to be words from the heart of the reader. Our deepest devotional experiences are moments of closest communion with God. Therefore, read these pronouns as your personal praise, thanks, or covenant. Let them express your own deep response to God.

My Prayer

It is my prayer that this guide through the Scriptures will help you develop a closer fellowship with the Heavenly Father. As you read His Word, practice opening your spirit to Him. Each day, may He speak some personal word to you and deepen your commitment to Him and to the truth of His Word.

A. F. HARPER

Genesis means beginning. If the first 11 chapters were lost, the rest of the Bible would be puzzling. Here God tells us about the beginning of the universe, the first people, the first children, the first sin, and God's plan for our salvation. Alexander Maclaren writes: "Genesis lifts us above the myths of the nations, some of them disgusting, many of them absurd, all of them unworthy."

Scripture: Genesis 1—2
The Story: Genesis 1:26-31
God blessed them (Gen. 1:22).

"In the Beginning God"

A new beginning always brings fresh excitement. Our scripture describes the excitement of a new world. At Christmas, through His Son, God gave us the gift of eternal life. But at His first New Year's party for man, God gave us natural life and the world in which we live.

Have you ever stopped to count how many good gifts from God are reported in these first two chapters of the Bible?

We must begin with God himself. In creating us He revealed His love and gave to us His companionship. It is His best gift, but it is by no means all. Where there was only an empty void, God filled it with the earth and sky. Where there was darkness, He gave us light. Where there was only an unending expanse of water, He raised the land to give the beauties of the shoreline, the lakes, and the oceans.

To all forms of life He gave the marvelous power of reproduction, each bearing seed according to its kind.

In the sky He placed the sun, the moon, and the stars. He planned fish for the sea and birds for the air. He made the cattle, wild beasts, and creeping things of the earth.

Into this life-support system God placed man—made in His image and after His own likeness. He gave us meaningful work to do; and in creating woman God brought to us companionship and completion.

What gifts on that first day of the new world!

Thank You, God. I'm glad to be alive on this first day of a new beginning. My spirit sings with the Psalmist,

"Bless the Lord, O my soul: and all that is within me, bless his holy name" (Ps. 103:1).

WEEK 1, MONDAY GENESIS

Scripture: Genesis 3—5
The Story: Genesis 5:18-29

And Enoch walked with God: and he was not; for God took him (Gen. 5:24).

A Father Who Died Young

Usually we do not expect devotional help from a genealogy—even when the list of ancestors and descendants is found in the Bible. But tucked away in these unpromising verses are some thoughts worth meditating on today.

Perhaps it is not accurate to speak of Enoch as a man who died, because the Bible says that "God took him." But it is true that his life on earth was relatively short. Compared to our life spans, he lived only about 30 years. His father, Jared, lived to be 862; his son, Methuselah, reached 969. Enoch was taken at only 365. But the worth of human life cannot be measured accurately by the years that we live.

Of every other man in the list, all that is recorded is that he lived a long time and fathered sons and daughters. Enoch did not live so long, and he probably had fewer children, but *he walked with God.* This devotion brought him personal reward; he was spared the struggle with death. But there is more. Enoch's great-grandson, Noah, also *walked with God* (Gen. 6:9). Thus we see fulfilled the Bible's universal promise that a godly life influences

8

those who come after us, even to "the third and fourth generation" (Deut. 5:9-10).

In Noah, mankind was to find mercy and salvation. His name means *relief* or *rest*. When this great-grandson of Enoch was born, his father prophesied, "Now we shall know 'a relief' from our labour and from our toil on the ground that the Eternal cursed" (v. 29, Moffatt).

Returning to the great-grandfather, we read: "Enoch was sixty-five years old when his son Methuselah was born. Afterwards he lived another 300 years in fellowship with God" (v. 24, TLB).

I would rather live 30 years walking with God, and have a great-grandson who saved a generation, than to live until 90 and be remembered only as a father of children.

▼

Scripture: Genesis 6—9
The Story: Genesis 6:17-22

Noah did this; he did all that God commanded him (Gen. 6:22, RSV).

The Justice and Mercy of God

We turn our attention today to this early epoch in the history of man. These chapters are often called the story of the Flood, but the main emphasis is on God's concern for man.

In the midst of destroying a world of evil, God took pains to save one good man and his family. He also allowed 120 years of mercy for all who were then alive. We believe that if others had heeded Noah's preaching and had entered the ark, they too would have been saved.

We are not told how long it took Noah to build the ark, but it must have been a long job. We may assume that he was ridiculed as a fool and fanatic. But Noah persisted. He is no fool of whom our text can be written, "Noah did this; he did all that God commanded him."

It is sad that innocent animals should perish because of man's sin. But in a world of interrelated influence such as ours, it can hardly be otherwise. Paul tells us, "We know that to this day the entire creation has been groaning and suffering agony together as if in childbirth" (Rom. 8:22, NBV).

And what shall we say of the deaths of the men and the women—and especially of their innocent young children? Our questions find hinted answers, and our minds find some rest when we remember that God is God. He has reserved to himself the power of life and death. We are awed by tragedies that snuff out the lives of hundreds in a plane crash or thousands in a single storm. But we remember that if these lives were not taken suddenly, still all of them would be taken one by one before many years had passed. From God's point of view, death must be some lesser evil than it appears to us.

Thought for today:

In the Flood, God visited the iniquity of the fathers upon the children. But through Noah and the ark He was showing mercy to a thousand generations yet to be born (Exod. 20:5-6).

▼

☐ WEEK 1, WEDNESDAY   GENESIS

Scripture: Genesis 10—12

From chapter 12 on, the stories in Genesis deal chiefly with the Hebrew people, but the viewpoint of the book is universal. Its themes and its characters speak to all of us, because in them we see the human spirit responding to God.

The Story: Genesis 12:1-8

By faith . . . he . . . obeyed; and he went out, not knowing whither he went (Heb. 11:8).

New Paths for a New Walk

How can we know where God wants us to go? How can we make right choices when we are uncertain? To help us with these decisions God reveals His will to us in the Bible, in Jesus, and through His Holy Spirit.

1. We read the Bible in order to learn the general direction of God's will for human life. But sometimes in our reading, a verse speaks so clearly and so forcefully that we know it is God's personal word to us for a decision today.

2. Sometimes God leads us through the open doors of circumstance. When an opportunity arises, we seek to find God's will for us. We ask ourselves: Is it an opportunity that fits into God's scheme of things? Can I better serve other people? Will I be able to contribute more to the kingdom of God?

3. In prayer we tell God that we belong to Him; we want to do what He wants us to do. As we think about the facts involved, His Holy Spirit gives us a growing conviction, "This is the way, walk ye in it" (Isa. 30:21).

4. We are sure that God always wants us to choose what we know to be right. In moral decisions we can usually be sure that the right way is the way that calls for courage.

5. In this new walk of faith, as we consciously seek to know and do God's will, we shall make good decisions one by one. When we look back along the paths that God has led us, our assurance will grow. As we face new decisions tomorrow, we can sing,

> *He leadeth me! Oh, blessed thought!*
> *Oh, words with heav'nly comfort fraught!*
> *Whate'er I do, where'er I be,*
> *Still 'tis God's hand that leadeth me.*
> —JOSEPH H. GILMORE

11

Scripture: Genesis 13—15
The Story: Genesis 13:2-18

Let there be no strife between you and me (Gen. 13:8, RSV).

How to Resolve Differences

Sometimes tensions between two people cure themselves with the passing of time; but not always. A leader in the church spoke out on an issue of policy. A colleague counseled him to "let sleeping dogs lie." He replied: "These dogs are not asleep; and besides, some of them are about to have pups!"

Some problems don't go away; they must be faced headon. To resolve this conflict of interests, Abram took the initiative. He went to Lot, laid out the problem that both of them knew was there, and then proposed a solution.

Conflicts yield easily when we do two things: (1) courageously take the initiative, and (2) offer to resolve the tension on the other man's terms. Abram said to Lot, "If you take the left hand, then I will go to the right; or if you take the right hand, then I will go to the left." That approach stops quarrels quickly. But to use this technique we must be close enough to God to really believe that peace is better than pastures. Abram understood the New Testament teaching, "Do nothing from selfishness or conceit, but in humility count others better than yourselves. Let each of you look not only to his own interests, but also to the interests of others" (Phil. 2:3-4, RSV).

Was Abram the loser in this unselfish settlement of their labor dispute? Is any man a loser when he settles any issue in God's way? "After Lot was gone, the Lord said to Abram, 'Look as far as you can see in every direction, for I am going to give it all to you and your descendants'" (vv. 14-15, TLB).

We do not believe that God always rewards spiritual faithfulness with material blessings. But we are sure that we cannot outgive God. No man ever regrets being generous. Jesus promised:

"Seek ye first the kingdom of God, and his righteousness; and all these things shall be added unto you" (Matt. 6:33).

▼

Scripture: Genesis 16:1—18:15 (Be sure to read the whole passage today.)
The Story: Genesis 17:15-22

Behold, my covenant is with you, and you shall be the father of a multitude of nations (Gen. 17:4, RSV).

Deferred Hopes

"Hopes long deferred make the heart grow faint" (Prov. 13:12, paraphrase). This was Abram's problem; and it is often ours. Some 24 years earlier God had said to Abram, "Get thee out of thy country . . . unto a land that I will shew thee: and I will make of thee a great nation" (Gen. 12:1-2). For 24 years Abram had prospered in God's land of promise; but there was agony along with the prosperity. He still had no heir through whom God could fulfill His promise of descendants—let alone "a multitude of nations."

What are we to do when our hopes are not realized, and when God's promises are not yet fulfilled? There is only one answer from heaven: "I am God Almighty; walk before me, and be blameless. And I will make my covenant between me and you" (Gen. 17:1-2, RSV).

It is well to remember that in our times of delayed answer, God gives us fresh courage. Hagar, who became deeply involved in Abram's struggle, discovered the reality of God. She called her son Ishmael, meaning "God hears." She named the messenger who appeared to her "a God of seeing." God thus gave to her a little insight into things as He sees them. She testified, "Have I even here seen after him who sees me?" (16:13, fn. reading).

13

In chapter 17 God also encouraged Abram ("exalted father") when He changed his name to Abraham ("father of a multitude"). When tempted to become discouraged it is a good thing to listen to God some more. When we are confronted by the Spirit of God, a bowed head and attentive heart are right responses. To commune with God is even better than to get the gifts that we desire.

And looking back on these experiences where God's delay has challenged our faith, we can joyfully sing:

> *He never has failed me yet.*
> *I have proven Him true;*
> *What He says He will do.*
> *He never has failed me yet.*
> —W. J. HENRY

▼

Scripture: Genesis 18:16—21:34
The Story: Genesis 19:12-20, or better, Genesis 18:16—19:29

Behold therefore the goodness and severity of God (Rom. 11:22).

God Spares the Obedient

God is in the business of destroying sin but saving sinners. Paul reminds us that in such an undertaking there is both kindness and judgment.

God will destroy sin, but if there is any chance to save men, He seeks to save them. As the two angels left Abraham and went on toward Sodom, God revealed to the patriarch that the city was to be destroyed. Abraham interceded, asking that the righteous element might avert the disaster. He began with 50, then 45, and 40. The bargaining went on for 30, and 20, and finally 10. But there were not 10 God-fearing people in the whole city. Only 4 persons believed God enough to flee from the impending judgment—and they almost had to be dragged from destruction. Behold the goodness of God!

But there is also severity. Those who will not believe will be destroyed. God has decreed it. "Lot went out and said to his sons-in-law, who were to marry his daughters, 'Up, get out of this place; for the Lord is about to destroy the city.' But he seemed to his sons-in-law to be jesting" (19:14, RSV). They did not believe; they stayed and died. "The Lord rained on Sodom and Gomorrah brimstone and fire from the Lord out of heaven; and he overthrew those cities, and all the valley, and all the inhabitants of the cities" (19:24-25, RSV). Why? "Because . . . their sin [was] very grave" (18:20, RSV).

Lot's wife believed God's message enough to let the angel lead her out of the city, but not enough to obey God's instructions. The angel said, "'Flee for your life; do not look back or stop anywhere in the valley; flee to the hills, lest you be consumed.' . . . But Lot's wife behind him looked back"—and she, too, died (19:17, 26, RSV).

Lot and his family were pretty sorry specimens, but three of them were saved. They were saved because they believed God's message of His judgment against sin; saved because they let God save them when He offered to do it. The conditions are still the same today.

▼

☐ WEEK 2, SUNDAY   GENESIS

Scripture: Genesis 22—24
The Story: Genesis 22:1-19

Now I know that thou fearest God, seeing thou hast not withheld thy son, thine only son from me (Gen. 22:12).

15

Giving What God Asks

Mark Twain once said, "It is not the things that I don't understand in the Bible that trouble me; it is what I do understand!" There is much in this story that we cannot grasp, but the message of complete obedience is clear enough to follow.

God's test stabbed Abraham at his most sensitive spot. The Lord called for a father's most cherished possession, "Thy son, thine only son Isaac, whom thou lovest."

For Abraham there must have been a terrible aloneness on the trip to Mount Moriah. How could he have told his plans to Sarah, the mother of his child? How could he return to her and to his family with the blood of Isaac staining his garments? With these desperate thoughts his tortured mind must have wrestled. How often must a cry have been stifled just short of a groan: "My God, my God, why have You forsaken me?"

At last the decisive hour has come. Abraham must go forward with his dread duty. He "bound Isaac his son, and laid him on the altar upon the wood." When God had first spoken, Abraham had replied with devotion: "Behold, here I am." The same readiness to give "the last full measure of devotion" to God must have also been in the heart of Isaac. He was a maturing young man at least 16 years of age, but there is only submission: Abraham does it, and God wills to have it done. We recall the spirit of God's own Son in Gethsemane, "Not my will, but thine, be done" (Luke 22:42).

The final awful moment has come. With fixed purpose and an eye lifted to heaven, Abraham stretches out his hand to give the fatal stab. But the knife does not fall. Just in time to accomplish His will and to strengthen our faith, God makes His purposes clear to us.

How are we to understand God's assertion, "Now I know"? Did He not know of Abraham's full faith even before this terrible test? Yes, God knew—but Abraham did not. Our tests come in order to demonstrate the truth both to God and to us. It is not only "Now I know"; it is also, "Now I know that you know how deep is your devotion to Me." After such a test God can trust His man— and a man can forever trust God.

What shall I give Thee, Master?
Thou hast given all for me.
Not just a part, or half of my heart—
I will give all to Thee!
                    —HOMER W. GRIMES

▼

Scripture: Genesis 25—27
The Story: Genesis 26:1-5, 19-25
Isaac built an altar there and called on the name of the Lord (Gen. 26:25; all quotes from NIV).

Like Father, like Son

A godly father is not always blessed with a God-fearing son—but the percentage is high. A man who obeys God does not get everything he wants from life—but he gets more than he could find any other way. These are the lessons we learn from Isaac.

Yesterday we saw Abraham under extreme pressure, but he remained obedient to God and he was rewarded by Jehovah. Isaac himself had lived through that miracle of faith, obedience, and reward. Could he ever forget it? Were there memories of Mount Moriah in his mind when "the Lord appeared to Isaac and said, 'Do not go down to Egypt; live in the land where I tell you to live. Stay in this land for a while, and I will be with you and bless you'"? (26:2-3). Was the faith and obedience of the father reproduced in the trust and obedience of his son? We read, "So Isaac stayed in Gerar" (26:6). Faithfulness in parents does encourage children to be faithful.

Isaac had his failures—he told a falsehood to protect his life (26:7-11), and showed favoritism toward one of his sons (25:28). His life also had its share of disappointments: resented because of his prosperity (26:16); conflict over grazing grounds (26:19-22);

17

disappointing marriages by his older son (26:34); blindness before he died (27:1); deceived by his wife and younger son (27:5-29); hatred to the point of intended murder between his estranged twin boys (27:41).

Can God bring fulfillment and happiness to a life with such a mixed bag? He did and He can. When we seek to do God's will, He adds His blessings.

Isaac obeyed God when it became clear what the Lord wanted him to do—and he built an altar for worship. He moved to new pastures rather than quarrel with unfair neighbors. Isaac loved God supremely and applied the golden rule in dealing with those around him. The Bible shows him to us as a man of God and a man of peace.

> *Lord, give us such faith as this;*
> *And then, whate'er may come,*
> *We'll taste e'en here, the hallowed bliss*
> *Of an eternal home.*
> —WM. H. BATHURST

▼

Scripture: Genesis 28—30
The Story: Genesis 28:10-22
Surely the Lord is in this place (Gen. 28:16).

Confronted by God

Sometimes we find God by seeking—but often He takes us by surprise. Jacob had just started a long journey. It was sundown and he was sleepy. He had left home and was lonesome. He had a rock for a pillow; it was hard. These do not seem like backgrounds for a life-changing experience; and Jacob did not expect anything unusual to happen. But God is not limited by our experiences; when He breaks through, the circumstances do not matter very much.

It is a great experience when we discover that there is a connection between earth and heaven. Life is changed when we see God at the top of our ladder, and when He speaks to us.

God spoke to Jacob in a dream—but when God speaks it is more than a dream. Dr. Sung Ming was imprisoned and persecuted during China's reign of terror under the "Gang of Four." Bibles and church services were forbidden; but God spoke to him, as to the prophets, in visions and dreams. He writes: "These are very different from ordinary dreams. Maybe the word should be capitalized as a proper noun. Such a Dream is no mere fiction of the mind unrelated to reality."

In whatever way God speaks to us, the life change comes when we recognize that it is He, and when we respond in worship and obedience. Whether He speaks in a church service, in a personal emergency, or in a dream—How do we respond? Good things begin to happen when we confess with Jacob, "Surely the Lord is in this place." All of life becomes different when we acknowledge, "This is . . . the house of God, and this is the gate of heaven." It is God's open door through which we enter into His presence.

Jacob vowed, "The Lord will be my God" (28:21, NIV). It was no trader's deal to buy material blessings. God had already promised that He would be with Jacob and bless him. Always it is God who makes the first offer: "Obey my voice, and I will be your God, and ye shall be my people" (Jer. 7:23). Because He freely offers so much, we can only respond with loyalty and love. Our awakened hearts sing:

> Thou, my everlasting portion,
> More than friend or life to me,
> All along my pilgrim journey,
> Saviour, let me walk with Thee.
> —FANNY J. CROSBY

Scripture: Genesis 31—33
The Story: Genesis 32:1-12

Save me, I pray, from the hand of my brother Esau
(Gen. 32:11; all quotes from NIV).

Jacob's Prayer—and Mine

Have I ever had to ask God for help when I didn't deserve it? Then I can identify with Jacob.

Twenty years earlier he had cheated a twin brother of his birthright; he had then left home to escape his brother's vengeance. For 20 years Jacob had made no effort to right that wrong. Now Esau, who had sworn to kill Jacob, was coming with a small army of 400 men. No wonder Jacob prayed in desperation, "O God . . . Save me, I pray, from the hand of my brother."

Many a man has been pushed to prayer when he has found his pressures greater than his resources. Jacob had previously found ways to outwit his opponents and to outmaneuver his problems. Now he faced a situation that was beyond him. In his prayer he gives us a pattern for finding aid when we are in the wrong but still need God's help.

✔ Jacob acknowledged his past experience of divine power: "O God of my father Abraham."

✔ He relied on the promises that God had given him: "O Lord who said to me, 'Go back to your country and your relatives, and I will make you prosper.'"

✔ A confession of humility always touches the Father's heart—and Jacob made that confession: "I am unworthy of all the kindness and faithfulness you have shown your servant."

✔ Gratitude is also a key that unlocks our spirits to the help of God. Gratefully Jacob acknowledged: "I had only my staff when I crossed this Jordan, but now I have become two groups."

✔ When we show concern for others, God finds in us something worth saving and strengthening. Jacob had more than a selfish interest in his prayer: "I am afraid he will come and attack me, and also the mothers with their children."

With these attitudes, the man presented his need: "Save me . . . from the hand of my brother Esau." God answered his prayer even though Jacob deserved Esau's retaliation. Our Father is always on our side when we confess our need for Him, and He is always interested in reconciling estranged brothers. The prayer was answered when "Esau ran to meet Jacob and embraced him; he threw his arms around his neck and kissed him. And they wept" (33:4).

Thank You, Father, for Your steadfast love. Thank You for helping me even when I have brought my problems on myself.

▼

Scripture: Genesis 34—36
The Story: Genesis 35:1-15

I will make there an altar unto God, who answered me in the day of my distress (Gen. 35:3).

God Comes to Us Through Remembering

How long has it been since my love for God burned at a fever pitch? Do I stand in need of spiritual revival? If so, our story reminds us of steps to renewal.

As when He first called us, God takes the initiative in our renewal. In His own way He confronts us and calls to memory the better days of the past. He told Jacob what he needed to do to repair the fellowship that had been broken: Move from where you are; move back to Bethel where you and I had closer communion— *and dwell there.* Renew your spiritual life by erecting again a place of true worship. The New Testament counsels us clearly, "Draw nigh to God, and he will draw nigh to you" (James 4:8).

21

God says, "Put away strange gods," and cleanse your life from all uncleanness. In this sense He is a jealous God; He will not give himself fully to us until we love Him supremely. He yearns to help us, but He cannot if we neglect or refuse to obey His leadings.

Have I put something else in first place? God says, Put it away. Have I allowed some sin to soil my spirit? He says, Clean it up. The Bible gives us the gracious promise, "Return unto me, and I will return unto you, saith the Lord" (Mal. 3:7).

Have I been afraid to break with some entangling hindrance or sin? Verse 5 reminds me that I need not fear. When I decide to obey God, He graciously removes the opposition that I feared would overwhelm me.

He reminds us in a hundred ways that returning to Him is wise and blessed. The old, selfish disposition is taken away, and a new nature is imparted. Jacob is a man who has seen God and struggled with Him. But God wins, and forever after the man bears His likeness.

Along with the joy of His presence, God gives us the material blessings needed for this life. As Paul put it, "He that spared not his own Son, but delivered him up for us all, how shall he not with him freely give us all things?" (Rom. 8:32).

When I remember God's promises of loving restoration, I repent of my failures and I renew my vows. I find a place of worship where my chastened spirit sings:

> *Take my love; my God, I pour*
> *At Thy feet its treasure store.*
> *Take myself and I will be*
> *Ever, only, all for Thee.*
> —FRANCES R. HAVERGAL

Scripture: Genesis 37—39
The Story: Genesis 37:1-36

**You intended to harm me, but God intended it for
good to accomplish what is now being done, the
saving of many lives** (Gen. 50:20, NIV).

God Guides a Responsive Teen

Bible biographies are the best mirrors in which we see reflected the
work of God in the spirit of men. And no Old Testament biography
reflects New Testament godliness as well as the life of Joseph.

From infancy the boy had three strikes against developing into
a worthy person—and normally three strikes puts the batter out!
He was at his birth (1) the youngest child in a large family, (2) a
favorite wife's only child, and (3) the son of his father's old age.
What child could survive that much spoiling and turn out well?

Joseph's brothers resented him, not only because he was his
father's pet, but also because he was a better person than they. At
17 his gentle spirit was shocked at the evil conduct he saw in his
brothers. The role of informer is never easy, but there are times
when to be silent is to share the guilt of evil. Joseph found himself
on that spot. He was right; his brothers were wrong. They could
not stand either his goodness or the exposing of their evil ways to
their father.

At worst, the teenage Joseph was unwise. But his father had
been even more foolish, and his brothers were downright malicious. At 17 the boy was not without mistakes—but he had four
points in his favor: (1) he had set his heart to do right; (2) he was
maintaining good poise between parental favoritism and resentful
older brothers; (3) he was beginning to glimpse God's plan for his
life; and (4) he was an obedient son even when sent on a difficult
assignment.

There is promise for mature years in such a youth. God give us
more teens like Joseph.

▼

Scripture: Genesis 40—41
The Story: Genesis 40:1-23

I will pour out of my Spirit upon all flesh . . . and your young men shall see visions, and your old men shall dream dreams (Acts 2:17).

Visions and Dreams

Does God communicate His truth to men through dreams? The Bible reveals that He has done so in the past; the text declares that He will do so in this age of the Holy Spirit.

Our scientific minds tend to raise questions or to challenge the possibility outright. But among Christians, Paul's query is appropriate: "Why should it be thought a thing incredible with you, that God should raise the dead?" (Acts 26:8).

Most dreams have no prophetic meaning, and not all of them come from God. But all dreams are functions of the mind—and God speaks to the mind. If He impresses a truth upon us in our semiconscious moments, why should it be thought a thing incredible?

To young Joseph, a dream brought intimations of God's future plans for his life (Gen. 37:5-11). In the jail God revealed to him the meaning of dreams that prepared the way for his deliverance from prison. Standing before Pharaoh, God showed Joseph dream interpretations that saved Egypt from famine, and Israel from destruction.

But does He reveal himself through dreams today? In *God Sets Prisoners Free*, Dr. Sung Ming testifies of his torture in a Chinese prison. "God knew that I could not bear my burdens alone. Just in time one night He showed me a vision. It was clear and powerful. Immediately after the vision disappeared a strong voice came from above to my spirit. The voice said: 'See no one, but Jesus only.' The vision and the voice awakened me and gave me peace of mind. I now knew that I was not alone in the prison. I knew that the Almighty God was with me and beside me. I heard His voice. I felt His presence. He was now teaching and protecting me."

Though dreams do not fit into our customary categories of rational communication, who would deny the divine origin of such a vision?

But the Bible says we must "try the spirits whether they are of God" (1 John 4:1). Does the dream move me toward God's plan for my life? Is my understanding of its meaning in line with Bible teaching? Does it reinforce my commitment to Christ and motivate me to more diligent efforts in His kingdom?

Surely such a dream comes from Him who sends "every good gift and every perfect gift" (James 1:17). For such a revelation, "Let us praise God together on our knees."

▼

□ WEEK 3, SUNDAY   GENESIS

Scripture: Genesis 42—44
The Story: Genesis 44:14-34

How shall I go up to my father, and the lad be not with me? (Gen. 44:34).

Selfless Intercession

In Judah's plea we see a complete turnaround in a human spirit. Twenty-two years earlier he had callously sold his brother into slavery; now he offers himself as a slave so that a brother can go free.

Once Judah had been so angered by teenage boasting that he was ready to kill his brother; now he can overlook and forgive an apparent theft. In the old days Judah was willing to lie to his father and let an aged parent suffer agony for 22 years believing that lie.

25

Now he chooses to be a slave for the rest of his life rather than to see Jacob's agony over the loss of Benjamin. Something had happened to Judah. He was not that many years older, but he had drawn nearer to God.

It was almost a capital offense to speak to an oriental despot in self-defense. But Judah took that risk. He put his life in jeopardy in a plea to the ruler of Egypt.

Judah appealed to the natural sentiments of sympathy implanted by God in the human spirit. He asked for mercy for a fragile old father whose life was bound up in the life of his youngest son: "When I come to my father and the lad is not with us, he will die, and your servants will be bringing the hoary head of your servant my father with sorrow to the grave" (v. 31, NBV).

With his new sense of spiritual values, Judah could not bear to see Benjamin condemned to a life of slavery. Nor could he bear the agony of his aged father when he learned that he had lost Benjamin. Slavery for the rest of Judah's life would be better than that. In a wholly selfless plea he offered to take Benjamin's place:

"I beg of you, therefore, to retain your servant in the lad's place, a slave to my master, and let the lad go up with his brothers: for how could I go up to my father and not have the lad with me, there to witness the grief my father must suffer!" (vv. 33-34, NBV).

Lord, I ask for Your spirit of intercession.

> *Give me a love that knows no ill;*
> *Give me the grace to do Thy will.*
> *Pardon and cleanse this soul of mine;*
> *Give me a heart like Thine.**
> —JUDSON W. VAN DEVENTER

Scripture: Genesis 45—50
The Story: Genesis 45:4-8; 50:15-21

Forgive us the wrongs we have done, as we forgive the wrongs that others have done to us (Matt. 6:12, TEV).

How Can I Forgive?

"If you have ever been guilty, and you knew it, and everybody else knew it, and you have then experienced forgiveness, you know why I call *forgiveness* the most beautiful word in the English language" (Leslie Parrott).

Forgiveness is also beautiful in Hebrew! Although Joseph's brothers could hardly believe it, he had already taken the first step toward full family reconciliation. The story is told in this moving passage:

"And Joseph said unto his brethren, Come near to me, I pray you. And they came near. And he said, I am Joseph, your brother, whom ye sold into Egypt. Now therefore be not grieved, nor angry with yourselves, that ye sold me hither: for God did send me before you to preserve life'" (45:4-5). What a flood of revenge and suffering was turned aside by a godly man's decision to forgive instead of to return evil for evil!

How could Joseph forgive his brothers when they had sinned against him so greatly? He had learned what we must learn: We forgive because God asks us to forgive, and because our brother needs reconciliation. It is God's love in us that moves us to seek restored relationships.

But how can I forgive? For an answer let us explore this man's experience. In his early years as a slave we read, "And the Lord was with Joseph" (Gen. 39:2). During prison years that acquaintance deepened: "The Lord was with Joseph, and shewed him mercy" (39:21).

How can I forgive? I learn forgiveness from the Heavenly Father. In a deepening fellowship with God I find nourishment for the spirit of reconciliation. When I reflect very long on how much God loves me—and blesses me in spite of my failures—it is difficult to continue to hate any fellowman. I lose all desire to seek revenge against him. Forgiveness flows from the Spirit of God. I find reconciliation easier as I open my spirit to Him.

Thank You, Father, for sharing Your spirit of love.

> *For the love of God is broader*
> *Than the measure of man's mind;*
> *And the heart of the Eternal*
> *Is most wonderfully kind.*
> —F. W. FABER

▼

□ **WEEK 3, TUESDAY**   **EXODUS**

The Book of *Exodus* is the story of God's power shown in delivering Israel from slavery in Egypt. Every faithful Israelite remembered that story and gave God glory. Centuries later Psalm 78, among others, recalled those miracles. In Acts 7 Stephen reminds his fellow New Testament Jews that the Exodus miracles were a preview of God's planned deliverance in Christ. The chapters of the book can be outlined:

    1—11   Oppression in Egypt
    12—18 Deliverance and Victories
    19—24 The Covenant at Mount Sinai
    25—40 Worship of God Established

Scripture: Exodus 1—4
The Story: Exodus 3:1-12

I will now turn aside, and see (Exod. 3:3).

When God Gives Me a Task

God is concerned for His people, but to help them He must find a concerned man. And to get us going He makes the first move.

At the time of the burning bush Moses had lived in Midian 40 years. There he had named his second son Eliezer; it means "the God of my father has been my help." This consciousness, coupled with a time of quiet meditation, is excellent preparation to hear God's voice.

It is a marvel the many ways God uses to get through to our human spirits. But however He does it, the experience always brings a conviction that it is something special to which I must give attention. My heart must say, "I will now turn aside and see." Such an encounter is as personal as if God had spoken my name. When it happens I know I am standing on holy ground.

It is a glad hour for the oppressed when we hear God say, "I have seen . . . and I have heard . . . I know their sorrows." Because God knows, He will not let me forget. When He disturbs me about some great need, He soon begins to show me what I can do—but it does not look easy. In verse 11 we see the struggle of an aroused man of God. He sees a need, he knows that God is concerned, but he doubts that he can do anything about it. Moses had faced his own limitations so long that it almost paralyzed his will.

The story reveals clearly that in a call to do some task (1) I must believe that God is sending me, (2) I must be willing to try, and (3) I must be prepared to face discouragements and setbacks.

When Moses agonizingly asked, How can I do this job? God replied: "Certainly I will be with thee." It would seem that such assurance would be enough—but our fearful hearts think up many excuses.

God rebuked Moses' fear, reminding him that if He calls us He will also qualify us. We do not have to be eloquent; it is enough to be obedient.

In 4:18 we read, "And Moses went." Here is the response that God wants. He confronts, reveals, explains, encourages, rebukes, adapts to our weakness—all in order to get us to act. Now that Moses was ready to go, God was in a position to deliver His people.

Lord, in view of the task You have been showing me, I now pray:

> *Take my life, and let it be*
> *Consecrated, Lord, to Thee.*
> *Take my hands, and let them move*
> *At the impulse of Thy love.*
> —FRANCES R. HAVERGAL

29

Scripture: Exodus 5—6
The Story: Exodus 5:1—6:8

"The Lord look upon you and judge, because you have made us offensive in the sight of Pharaoh and his servants, and have put a sword in their hand to kill us" (Exod. 5:21, RSV).

When Following God Gets Hard

Is it ever permissible for us to hesitate in obeying God? If so, when?

God had begun to deliver the people of Israel through the leadership of Moses and Aaron. But everything seemed to go wrong. Instead of immediate freedom from slavery, the burdens grew greater. Instead of loyally following Moses, the people blamed him for their growing burdens.

What shall I do when I'm obeying God to the best of my knowledge, but no progress is seen? What do we do when following God gets hard?

Moses gives us an answer by his example. When the Hebrew overseers brought faithless questions, this leader was wise enough to turn to God. If the Lord had really sent him to deliver Israel, why was the deliverance blocked, and why were the burdens of the people increased?

Who has ever attempted any task for God and not had occasion to ask these questions? But who has ever drawn closer to God and not found satisfying answers?

To a frustrated Moses, God replied with encouragement: "Now you shall see what I will do to Pharaoh; compelled by a mighty power he will not only let them go, but will drive them out of this land" (6:1, Smith-Goodspeed). God then renewed all of His previous promises to Israel. It is true, those promises were still only promises for the future—"I will bring you out." But the assurances were firm.

Moses encouraged the people, but his discouraged followers were not ready to rely on the promises of God: "They hearkened not unto Moses for anguish of spirit, and for cruel bondage" (6:9). With this added discouragement, Moses himself hesitated before going back to Pharaoh.

When is it permissible for me to hesitate? It is forgivable to falter—if I falter and then go. Moses went.

> *I would be true, for there are those who trust me.*
> *I would be pure, for there are those who care.*
> *I would be strong, for there is much to suffer.*
> *I would be brave, for there is much to dare.*
> — HOWARD ARNOLD WALTER

☐ WEEK 3, THURSDAY   EXODUS

Scripture: Exodus 7—11

How are we to understand 10:20, "The Lord hardened Pharaoh's heart, so that he would not let the children of Israel go"? (See also 10:1, 27; 11:10.)

In 8:15, 32, and 9:34 we are told that Pharaoh hardened his own heart. God has created the human spirit in such a way that when we resist Him we grow harder. Only in this sense does He harden the heart. The steps are:

1. A man resists God.
2. The laws of the mind begin to make that attitude firmer.
3. God allows His laws to take their course.

But even in His wrath, God's mercy is clear. Each plague was another opportunity to repent. After any one of the first nine, Pharaoh could have obeyed God and thus saved the life of his own son, as well as the lives of all the firstborn in Egypt.

The Story: Exodus 8:20-32 (The story selected is the plague of flies. The whole account of these plagues is told in chaps. 7—11. It will take about 45 minutes to read, but will be a rewarding time. Read the devotional first, checking the references given. Then read the entire account.)

In this thou shalt know that I am the Lord (Exod. 7:17).

God's Mercy and Wrath

What can we learn about God from this story of the plagues? Five truths come through clearly.

1. Here is a confrontation of powers—the power of God seeking to persuade a proud human spirit. God cannot help us until we recognize who He is and acknowledge our dependence on Him. In our text God declares: "In this thou shalt know that I am the Lord." In 8:10 Moses says to Pharaoh: "Be it according to thy word; that thou mayest know that there is none like unto the Lord."

2. God is merciful enough to give us a second chance if we refuse His first offer. He gave Pharaoh not only a second chance—but eight more. We must not, however, presume on God's mercy. If we refuse His will, even God must eventually give up on us and let His punishment fall.

3. When we resist God, He has a way of increasing the pressure on us. After the sixth plague God declared: "This time I will send the full force of my plagues against you . . . For by now I could have . . . wiped you off the earth" (9:14-15, NIV). It is God's mercy that seeks to persuade us with gentler pressure before He crowds us hard.

4. In the midst of general calamity the Heavenly Father has power to care for His own people. The first three plagues hurt the whole land. But none of the next seven devastating afflictions appeared in Goshen where God's people lived. Read 8:22; 9:4; 9:26; 10:23; and 11:7.

5. Even in our rebellion against God, He is merciful to man and beast. When the punishment of killing hail was announced, God gave a timely warning to save life. He said to Pharaoh: "Give an order now to bring your livestock and everything you have in the field to a place of shelter, because the hail will fall on every

man and animal that has not been brought in and is still out in the field, and they will die" (9:19, NIV).

Thank You, Father, for these gracious revelations of Your mercy. I join the Psalmist in his prayer:

"Oh that men would praise the Lord for his goodness, and for his wonderful works to the children of men!" (Ps. 107:8).

▼

Scripture: Exodus 12—15
The Story: Exodus 14:10-22

The Lord is my strength and song, and he is become my salvation (Exod. 15:2).

God's Man and God's Power

Yesterday we left Moses and the Israelites in the earliest hours of a great migration. At midnight the death angel had visited Egypt, and Pharaoh's resistance was broken. While it was yet dark the Exodus began.

But by the time the Hebrews reached the Red Sea, Pharaoh had recovered from the shock of the deaths of the Egyptian children. He determined to cut off this exodus and bring back his slaves. With the flower of Egypt's army he set out to do it.

When this word reached the Hebrew camp they were terrified. The sea was in front and Pharaoh's army behind. Like frightened children they cried to Moses: "Why have you brought us out here to get us killed? Didn't we tell you to leave us slaves in Egypt?" They didn't mean it. But like us, they were weak when frightened.

For such an hour God needs a man of faith and courage. Moses was that man. He said to the people: "Fear ye not, stand still, and see the salvation of the Lord . . . the Egyptians whom ye have seen today, ye shall see them again no more for ever. The Lord shall fight for you" (14:13-14).

Then it was time for some gentle chiding even for God's leader. The Lord said to Moses: "Wherefore criest thou unto me? speak unto the children of Israel, that they go forward" (v. 15). There is a time for prayer. But there comes a time for action, so Moses stretched out his rod over the sea. God sent a strong east wind that blew all night, and He set His protective cloud between Israel and the Egyptian army.

In the morning there was a dry pathway leading eastward across the seabed. Into the miraculous escape route the Hebrews marched. It took courage because there were walls of water on both sides. But whoever followed God very far without courage?

The Egyptians pursued, but in vain. The KJV says pictorially, God "took off their chariot wheels." They could not get on across, and they could not turn back. When the last Hebrew was safely over, God let the waters return to their place. Only by such an awesome measure could He accomplish His will against a determined leader with the power of a nation behind him.

It was time for a praise meeting. Moses led 600,000 men of Israel as they chanted: "I will sing to the Lord, for he has triumphed gloriously." Half a million women under Miriam's leadership sent back the strain:

"Thou hast led in thy steadfast love the people whom thou hast redeemed, thou hast guided them by thy strength to thy holy abode" (Exod. 15:13, RSV).

▼

☐ **WEEK 3, SATURDAY**   **EXODUS**

Scripture: Exodus 16—18
The Story: Exodus 18:8-27

Hearken now unto my voice, I will give thee counsel, and God shall be with thee (Exod. 18:19).

Giving and Taking Advice

The name Jethro means "excellence." Every part of his conduct proves him to have been a religious man and a true worshiper of God.

But Jethro was wise as well as religious. He first dug out the facts, then thought long enough to deal judiciously with them. All day he watched Moses judging the people who came to him. As a devout man he must have asked, "O God of wisdom, isn't there some better way for my son-in-law to serve these people?"

This wise leader knew that if you expect another to take your advice, you must understand his problem—and be able to suggest a better way to solve it. He asked Moses, "Why do you alone sit as judge, while all these people stand around you from morning till evening?" (18:14, NIV.)

Jethro listened attentively to the reply and discovered that Moses had good reasons. He accepted those facts wholeheartedly, but having reflected on them, he was ready to give his judgment: "The thing that thou doest is not good" (v. 17).

Living close to our problems, often we cannot see them in proper perspective. Jethro, in effect, said to Moses: "If you will look at this from a fresh viewpoint, you will see that your method is not the best way to manage the work." It is always good judgment to try to see our actions as they appear to others.

It is also sound procedure to take even our best judgments to the place of prayer. At no point does Jethro show himself so clearly the wise spiritual leader as when he says to Moses: "Pray about it, and if you find this plan to be God's will, adopt it." Our best decisions are those in which, with the leaders of the Early Church, we can say, "It seemed good to the Holy Ghost, and to us" (Acts 15:28).

When should we accept the Christian counsel of others? No absolute rule can be given, but our scripture suggests five guidelines. (1) Good counsel may come from unexpected sources. (2) It is wise to ask, Does the one who counsels us have at heart the interests of God's kingdom? (3) Does the advice make sense? Is it consistent with the best that we know? (4) Has the counselor prayed before giving his advice? (5) When we take the counsel to God in prayer, does His Spirit seem to say, "This is the way, walk ye in it"? (Isa. 30:21).

My prayer for today:
"Shew me thy ways, O Lord; teach me thy paths" (Ps. 25:4).

35

Scripture: Exodus 19—20

Mount Sinai is a key spot in Israel's history. The Bible sometimes refers to it as Horeb, which may indicate the whole range of mountains, with Sinai as the central peak.

Here God spoke to Moses from the burning bush. Here, only three months after leaving Egypt, Israel camped for a full year. During this year at Sinai God transformed Israel from a horde of ex-slaves into a nation of free people. Here He established His covenant with them. Here He gave them laws for their worship and for their relationships to each other (Exodus 19—24). Here God gave Israel the Tabernacle and their forms for worship (Exodus 25—40).

The Story: Exodus 20:1-17

All that the Lord hath spoken we will do (Exod. 19:8).

Thinking About God's Law

Today we think about the Ten Commandments. Thus far in the Exodus God had performed miracles generously for His people. Now, at Sinai, He reveals himself, not as a national Santa Claus, but as the God of righteousness. He is always ready to help His people, but He also places demands upon us. At Sinai we see what God asks of men who choose to follow Him—and what He promises to those who obey His commands.

The first four commandments reveal our responsibilities to God; the last six deal with our obligations to each other.

Sound thinking about these commandments begins with understanding the purpose for God's laws. Our Heavenly Father loves us; He has always loved us. His laws arise out of His concern for our welfare. These laws are what they are because our human

36

needs require them for our well-being. The Bible declares: "Thou shalt keep therefore . . . his commandments . . . that it may go well with thee, and with thy children after thee" (Deut. 4:40).

John Wesley once said, "The holy laws of God when viewed in a gospel light, are none other than so many great and precious promises"—promises assuring us that obedience to God's law is the certain pathway to fullness of life both here and hereafter.

God commands our loyalty, but He shows us that obeying Him is a reasonable service. He who made the bush to burn without being consumed imparts the continuing radiance to our sun, moon, and stars. He who sent manna, quails, and water still sends the returning seasons with their supply of food for our needs. He who divided the Red Sea and went before Israel in a pillar of cloud and fire still makes a way through every difficulty for His followers, He still provides guidance for the journey.

He demands our loyalty and obedience, but He gives good grounds for His demands.

Thank You, Father, for Your love and Your guidance for my life. With the Psalmist I sing: "O how love I thy law! It is my meditation all the day" (Ps. 119:97).

▼

Scripture: Exodus 21—24

Exod. 21:23-24 is often described as "the law of tooth and claw." In contrast to Christian forgiveness, an eye for an eye is evil revenge. But when God gave this law through Moses, it was a great ethical advance over then-current practices. The accepted rule was, If you destory my eye, I will kill you. God's law limited this spirit of vengeance to a fair exchange; His people were required to seek no more amends than an eye for an eye or a tooth for a tooth.

The Story: Exodus 21:12-19; 22:1-6

Be careful to do everything I have said to you
(Exod. 23:13; all quotes from NIV).

Blessed Are the Responsible

Our title is not one of Jesus' Beatitudes, but it shows one of God's requirements. The Heavenly Father expects us to observe the rights of others.

There is human behavior that God calls right—and misconduct that He calls wrong. We are responsible to do right and to teach it to our children.

Yesterday in reading the Ten Commandments we saw God's laws for worship, and also His general rules for living with each other. In today's study we find more detailed laws that show us our responsibilities.

God teaches us that human life is sacred; to destroy it is to violate God's plan; to deliberately take another's life is just cause to forfeit my own. God's high value on human life thus calls for extreme punishment for all crimes against life: murder, kidnapping, assault, and careless exposure of others to lethal danger. Personal violence against even a trespasser is limited: "If a thief is caught breaking in and is struck so that he dies, the defender is not guilty of bloodshed; but if it happens after sunrise, he is guilty of bloodshed" (22:2).

Intention is a key factor in our responsibility: "Anyone who strikes a man and kills him shall surely be put to death. However, if he does not do it intentionally . . . he is to flee to a place I will designate" (21:12).

Under God, personal property is a basic human right. To take it by force or to steal it is condemned by God: "If a man steals an ox or a sheep . . . he must pay back five head of cattle for the ox and four sheep for the sheep" (22:1).

Carelessness that destroys another's property is condemned by God: "If a fire breaks out and spreads . . . so that it burns shocks of grain or standing grain . . . the one who started the fire must make restitution" (22:6).

There is nothing in the New Testament that lessens these responsibilities to my neighbor's basic human rights. Jesus teaches us, however, that we are to be merciful when our rights have been infringed.

Father, help me to be Christlike. By Your grace, I shall respect my neighbor's rights—but teach me to forgive his wrongs. In Jesus' name I ask it. Amen.

Scripture: Exodus 25—27; 30; 40; also 37—38

The above chapters give us Moses' report of the instructions that God gave to him regarding the Tabernacle. Chapters 35—38 repeat the specifications as Moses passed them on to the men and women who were to build it.

The careful reader may wish to compare the two accounts. All should read 39:32—40:38 which tells the story of the erection and dedication of Israel's place of worship.

PLAN OF THE TABERNACLE IN THE WILDERNESS
30 Cubits Long, 10 Cubits Wide, 10 Cubits High (45' x 15' x 15')

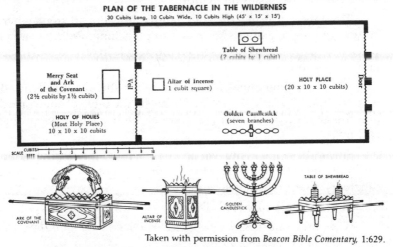

Taken with permission from *Beacon Bible Comentary,* 1:629.

The Story: Exodus 25:10-22

Let them make me a sanctuary; that I may dwell among them (Exod. 25:8).

The Tabernacle in the Wilderness

During the year at Mount Sinai God gave Israel her forms of worship as well as her laws for living. He said to them, as He says to us, Make Me a sanctuary, that I may dwell with you.

Coming into God's presence requires preparation on our part. Guides for devotional life suggest that our times of private prayer are usually more fruitful if we have a set time and place for coming to God. For public worship we gather in His house on His day.

For the Sunday morning prayer our local pastor kneels at the altar. He recalls this Old Testament scene by his invitation to the congregation: "I am going to the mercy seat. If any of you have occasions for praise or have special needs, I invite you to join me there."

The diagrams above picture Israel's place of worship in the wilderness. For 40 years they were a wandering people; therefore they needed a portable church. The building was a beautiful tent (tabernacle)—a wooden frame draped with gorgeous curtains and protected from the weather by an outer tent of tanned skins and an inner covering of goat's hair cloth.

The Tabernacle, like the later Temple, was not an arena where crowds of people gathered to listen to preaching. Rather it was a place where the priests represented the people in offering sacrifices and praises to God.

All of the equipment for worship, like the Tabernacle itself, was portable. The ark, the altar of incense, the table of shewbread, and the altar of burnt offerings were all built with carrying rings and poles.

Since Christ has come, we do not use these forms of worship. But the God who spoke to Moses still speaks to us, Make Me a sanctuary, that I may dwell with you.

My heart responds with David's:

When thou saidst, Seek ye my face; my heart said unto thee, Thy face, Lord, will I seek (Ps. 27:8).

Scripture: Exodus 28—29; 39
The Story: Exodus 28:1-3, 9-12; 29:27-28, 42-46
They shall know that I am the Lord their God
(Exod. 29:46).

God's Called Minister

Yesterday we saw that the worship of God needs an appointed place. But of yet greater importance is God's called minister.

Today's record of the Old Testament priests is the footage from which springs our Christian ministry. There are wide differences in our forms of worship between then and now—but the fundamental relationships are the same.

God chooses from among His people persons whom He designates to be spiritual leaders. He chose His priests then, and He calls His ministers today. He asks us to recognize His call and to give special regard to His minister: "Make sacred garments for your brother Aaron, to give him dignity and honor" (28:2, NIV).

Since Jesus came, we have laid aside the elaborate external garb of God's ministers. He taught us that "God is a Spirit: and they that worship him must worship him in spirit and in truth" (John 4:24). The external finery has been put away, but the essential role and ministry continues.

As did the priest in Israel, the minister today represents God to His people, and he represents his people before God. The names of the tribes of Israel were carried on Aaron's shoulders every time he went into the holy of holies (28:12). In a parallel ministry, every true pastor intercedes for his people when he kneels in the presence of God.

We are grateful that since the rise of the Protestant church, we recognize every man as his own priest. In this sense each of us can come to God in Christ; we need no official go-between. But all of us often need the help of another in our walk with God. The called minister is God's chosen instrument to provide this help.

Aaron wore a headpiece that proclaimed his ministry: HOLY

TO THE LORD (28:36, NIV). In a parallel relationship our pastor has also been chosen to devote his life and time to the purposes of a holy God.

God calls and appoints His ministers. But we ordain, honor, follow, and support those whom God gives to His Church in order that God may dwell among us.

Where God's people are led by God's faithful minister, there is God's promise fulfilled:

"I will meet with you and speak with you. And I will meet with the people . . . and the Tabernacle shall be sanctified by my glory. Yes, I will sanctify the Tabernacle and the altar and Aaron and his sons who are my ministers . . . And I will live among the people . . . and be their God, and they shall know that I am the Lord their God" (29:42-46, TLB).

▼

Scripture: Exodus 31; 35—36
The Story: Exodus 35:30—36:3

I have called by name Bezaleel . . . and . . . have filled him with the Spirit of God, in wisdom, and in understanding, and in knowledge, and in all manner of workmanship (Exod. 31:2-3).

God's Called Layman

The name Bezaleel means "in the shadow of God." This man's call to a lay ministry was just as clear as was Moses' call to be Israel's leader and prophet. Perhaps a year earlier at the burning bush in this same Sinai area, God had called His man by name, "Moses, Moses." Now Moses knew that God could speak just as clearly to others.

It was God who revealed this truth to His prophet: "The Lord spake unto Moses, saying, See, I have called by name Bezaleel"

(31:1-2). Perhaps until this revelation Moses had not fully realized that every man can hear the voice of God in his own soul.

The Lord could have told Moses to recruit Bezaleel for the job. But this would have left God in the background when He needs to be in the forefront of every man's consciousness. There can be no more moving experience in life than the conviction that God has called a man personally. When that happens life is lifted to a higher plane. We know that God himself has invited us to work under His direction and for the advancement of His purposes in the world.

Such a divine call is not limited to ministers. God has planned for this personal fellowship between himself and every human spirit. Bezaleel was a layman. So are we—assembly-line workers, teachers, housewives, salesmen, doctors, car-wash attendants. We are laymen, but every man and woman who chooses to live under the consciousness of God's call has something to contribute to the building of God's kingdom.

"The Lord . . . filled him with the Spirit of God." In creating us, God gives to every man and woman some qualities of His own spirit. But there is more. With all who open their lives wide to Him, He fills us with himself.

The last word we read of this man in the Bible is, "the brazen altar, that Bezaleel . . . made" (2 Chron. 1:5). Four hundred years after he slept with his fathers, the work of his hands was still being employed by God's people in their worship.

Prayer for today:

Lord, help me to find some work that I can do for You. Help me to do it with devotion and skill. And even when my work on earth is done, may men still worship You when they recall that I was Your servant. In Jesus' name I pray. Amen.

▼

□ **WEEK 4, FRIDAY**   **EXODUS**

Scripture: Exodus 32—34
The Story: Exodus 33:12-23

I beseech thee, shew me thy glory (Exod. 33:18).

"Shew Me Thy Glory"

The Bible gives us very little doctrine in neat theological defini-
tions. Rather, the great truths of God appear almost incidentally
out of the encounter of flesh-and-blood people with the living
Lord. It is so in this passage. Israel had flagrantly disobeyed God.
He had told them He would, therefore, not go with them into
Canaan. Moses interceded, asking God to reveal to him the divine
plan for Israel and the full glory of himself.

Moses prayed, "Shew me now thy way." Here was a man who
already knew something of God's nature and His will. Because he
was well acquainted with God, he desired to know all; he implored, "Shew me thy glory." It was a bold request—but a petition
that could not be granted completely. The Bible makes it clear that
we shall never fully understand the nature of God.

It is equally clear, however, that any man who earnestly desires to know more of God can count on his prayer being answered. God promised Moses, "I will proclaim the name of the
Lord before thee." This is the Hebrew way of saying, "I will show
you what I am like."

God sometimes reveals His power, but in this encounter He
promised to let Moses see His goodness. In spite of Israel's failure
and God's anger against them, they would see that He is a forgiving God. He would be gracious; He would show mercy. However,
He makes it clear, My mercy is given, not because men deserve it,
but because I am a God of kindness; I will show mercy, not only to
those who merit it, but also to all who need it.

When our prayers are unwise, God gives us as much as can be
helpful, but withholds what would hurt us. He said to Moses, "My
face you cannot see, for no mortal man may see me and live. . . .
Here is a place beside me. Take your stand on the rock and when
my glory passes by, I will put you in a crevice of the rock and cover
you with my hand . . . and you shall see my back, but my face shall
not be seen" (20-23, NEB).

Any man who has been filled with awe in the presence of God
does not find it hard to believe Moses' report. A modern child of
God knew something of that experience when she wrote:

> He hideth my soul in the cleft of the rock
> That shadows a dry, thirsty land.

He hideth my life in the depths of His love,
And covers me there with His hand.
                    —FANNY J. CROSBY

▼

Leviticus is the third of the five books of Moses
(The Pentateuch). It contains God's instructions to
guide His people in the Old Testament Levitical
system of worship. The name comes from the tribe
of Levi, chosen to administer Israel's worship. Our
nearest modern parallel to this book would be the
church *Manual,* outlining what we believe about
God, and how we express our faith and love in a
manner acceptable to Him.

Because some of the concepts in Leviticus are
difficult, reading from a modern-language version
will give a much clearer understanding.

Scripture: Leviticus 1—3

Sacrifice Concepts

1. *He shall put his hand upon the head* (1:4). The worshiper
identified himself with his sacrifice. With a firm gesture he thus
said to God, This that was mine, I give to You.

2. *Aaron's sons shall . . . sprinkle the blood round about upon
the altar* (1:5). The blood of animals was especially sacred to the
Hebrews. They were forbidden to eat it because the blood represented the life of the animal (17:10-12). The blood of their sacrifices was specifically designated as the medium of atonement.
The New Testament writer explains: "'This is the blood of the
covenant, which God commanded you to keep.' In the same way,
he sprinkled with blood both the tabernacle and everything used
in its ceremonies. In fact, the law requires that nearly everything
be cleansed with blood, and without the shedding of blood there
is no forgiveness" (Heb. 9:20-22, NIV).

3. *A sweet savour unto the Lord* (1:9). It would be foolish to imagine that God literally enjoys the odor of burning flesh or meal. What is clear is that He appreciates our devotion, and He is pleased when we worship according to His Word.

4. *When any will offer a meat offering* (2:1). Word meanings have changed since the King James translation of 1611. This was the one offering that did not consist of *meat*. It was a cereal offering made of finely ground grain.

5. *With all thine offerings thou shalt offer salt* (2:13). Salt indicated fellowship and fidelity. Ancient covenants were sealed with a common meal in which salt was an important part. To share a man's salt established a bond between host and guest.

6. *The fat that is on them* (3:4). The fat was considered the saved up riches of the animal; his store against any future need. Thus it represented the richest and best, which rightfully belongs to God. Having offered this to God, the remainder of the animal was for priest and people to enjoy.

The Story: Leviticus 1:1-9; 2:1-3

If his offering for a sacrifice ... be of the flock; male or female, he shall offer it without blemish (Lev. 3:6).

Bring an Offering

The Book of Leviticus begins where Exodus closes. In Exodus 40 we read of the dedication of the Tabernacle as the center of worship. Now in Leviticus God begins to speak to His people from the Tabernacle where He promised to meet with them.

The heart of Israel's worship lay in her sacrifices and in the worshiper's attitudes toward God when he brought his offering. The sacrifices reflected many moods—love, awe, obedience, joy, and a sense of security. The central idea, however, was nearness to God—not physical contact, but unity of spirit.

Sin is the one thing that separates man from God. We cut ourselves off from Him when we break His law and disregard His will. That separation is healed when we make a sacrifice of atonement. An offering that says, "I am sorry," brings at-one-ment with the Heavenly Father.

Nothing less than our best is a suitable offering to God. Hence the worshiper is told "he shall offer it without blemish" (3:6). The sacrifice is also to be complete—the whole offering was presented to the Lord; nothing was withheld for the worshiper until all was given to God.

In this Levitical system there is a beautiful blending of divine worship and human ministry. A part of the sacrifice, *the memorial,* was an offering of pure devotion; it was burned on the altar as an expression of love and obedience to God (2:9). The remainder was the worshiper's gift to the priests who ministered to the spiritual needs of God's people.

The requirements for sacrifices were exacting, as befits an offering to the eternal God; but those requirements were also flexible, as befits our human needs. If wealthy, one would bring a bull or a ram; if poor, he could satisfy God perfectly with a dove or a pigeon. The cereal offering could be of raw flour, or baked. When I bring my gift to God, He looks not so much at what I offer as the spirit with which I come to Him.

Since Christ came, we no longer offer material sacrifices at the place of worship, but God still looks for the spirit of love and obedience. Paul writes: "So then, my brothers, because of God's great mercy to us I appeal to you: Offer yourselves as a living sacrifice to God, dedicated to his service and pleasing to him" (Rom. 12:1, TEV).

> *Is your all on the altar of sacrifice laid?*
> *Your heart does the Spirit control?*
> *You can only be blest and have peace and sweet rest*
> *As you yield Him your body and soul.*
> —ELISHA A. HOFFMAN

▼

The Sacrifices of Israel

Israel's worship of God included solemn sacrifices, but the foundation principle of God's covenant with His people was obedience, not sacrifice.

The *burnt offering* (chap. 1) was the sacrifice of an animal or fowl on the altar in front of the sanctuary. It might be offered for an individual or for the nation as a whole. The name grew out of the fact that all of the animal except the skin was burned. Sometimes it is called "the whole burnt offering."

The *meal offering* (KJV, *meat offering,* chap. 2) was made of ground flour or meal. It represented the consecration to God of the fruit of one's labor.

The *peace offering* (chap. 3) indicated right relations with God; it expressed good fellowship, gratitude, and obligation. This offering was essentially a fellowship meal in which the priest and worshiper shared, after giving the choicest parts to God.

The *sin offering* (chap. 4) has special value as a sacrifice of atonement. It was probably unique to Israel, and indicates that salvation is based on sacrifice. The work of Christ is foreseen in this ritual.

The *trespass* or *guilt offering* (Lev. 5:14—6:7) was a special kind of sin offering. It was always an individual sacrifice and carried a fine with it. The sacrifice expressed atonement and restitution. The true penitent says not only, "I am sorry," but also, "What can I do about it?"

The *wave offering* (Lev. 7:30-34) was a part of the peace sacrifices. As an expression of joy and gratitude, the priest lifted the breast or the shoulder of the sacrificed animal and waved it before the Lord. The right shoulder and the breast, after being thus presented to God, were given to the priest for his part of the offering.

The *heave offerings* (Lev. 7:14, 32-34) seem to be similar to the wave offerings. They refer especially to the parts of the sacrifices that were lifted up, or separated to the service of God.

Drink offerings were required to be presented at all of Israel's set feasts. Wine and oil were customarily used.

Scripture: Leviticus 4—7
The Story: Leviticus 4:1-3, 13-14, 22-23, 27-28,
    32-35

If any one . . . sin through ignorance . . . if his sin . . . come to his knowledge: then he shall bring his offering (Lev. 4:27-28).

How Responsible Am I?

In chapters 4 and 5 God reminds us that ignorance of His law does not release us from responsibility. We are not guilty so long as we are ignorant of His commands and of the consequences of our acts. But when we come to understand our errors, we are responsible to God to make them right.

In these early times God made it clear that there are differences of responsibility, based upon the extent of our influence. But our text tells us that even the lowliest is not exempt: "If any one of the common people sin through ignorance . . . he shall bring his offering" (4:27-28).

The offering for the poor person could be a kid (2:28) or a lamb (4:32). For a ruler of the people, however, the sacrifice for ignorant transgression must be greater—only "a male without blemish" would be acceptable (4:23).

What is the measure of my influence? How great is my responsibility to know right and to do it?

Have I been called of God to teach or to preach? Then I bear a heavier responsibility because my ignorant actions bring more widespread failure and hurt. But fathers and mothers are also teachers; we, too, carry special responsibility. God's law states: "If the anointed priest sins, bringing guilt on the people, he must bring to the Lord a young bull without defect" (4:3, NIV). The New Testament reinforces this truth: "When we teachers of religion, who should know better, do wrong, our punishment will be greater than it would be for others" (James 3:1, TLB).

Every man is responsible to God for doing what he knows to be right. He is also responsible to make right any personal wrongs committed through ignorance. But is there more?

Yes. In Israel, community ignorance and community wrongs required the highest form of atoning sacrifice (4:13-14). In our world of interlocking influence we have at least some responsibility for every social evil. We are not fully responsible for these corporate wrongs, but we are responsible for what we can do to atone for them and to correct them.

What can I do about social evils? I can regret them; I can confess my part in them; I can use my influence to change them—and I want to do it.

To serve the present age,
  My calling to fulfill;
Oh, may it all my pow'rs engage
  To do my Master's will.
                    —CHARLES WESLEY

▼

Scripture: Leviticus 8—10
The Story: Leviticus 9:22—10:7
Behold, to obey is better than sacrifice, and to hearken than the fat of rams (1 Sam. 15:22).

How Important Is Obedience?

In a revival meeting, Dick felt that God wanted him to put $10.00 in the offering at each service. But on Friday, Satan suggested that for a pensioner to give that much was unreasonable. Dick faltered. He failed to put in his offerings at the next two services. Saturday night, however, he felt so convicted that he resolved to renew his promise. He wrote a check for $30.00 and put it in the plate Sunday morning.

I watched Dick weeping for joy during much of the morning service as the evangelist preached from the text, "When thou vowest a vow unto God, defer not to pay it" (Eccles. 5:4).

How precise are God's instructions? And how important is it to obey Him to the letter?

God is reasonable, and He is a God of mercy. He summons us to His best for us, but if we falter, He offers us a second best—and a third and a fourth. His mercy is great and His forgiveness is generous, but when His instructions are clear our obedience is essential.

In today's scripture we see God dealing with His most important concerns, and with His most responsible people. The choice of

Aaron and his sons was designed to give spiritual guidance to a whole nation for a thousand years of history. When the stakes are so high, leaders dare not fail.

At best, Nadab and Abihu were careless at a critical point. At worst, they deliberately substituted their own way for God's plan. If the ordained priest could publicly disobey God, what hope could there be for an obedient people? Faithfulness to God is sometimes more important than life itself. The Christian martyrs have proved that.

Disobedience is always disappointing—and sometimes tragic. Careful obedience to God is always rewarding—and sometimes glorious. When Moses and Aaron had done all that God asked them to do, "The glory of the Lord appeared to all the people. . . . and when all the people saw it, they shouted for joy and fell face-down" (9:23-24, NIV).

When God gives clear instructions, only careful obedience brings His blessing—but sincere obedience always does.

I will mind God, no matter what others do.
I will mind God, and do what He bids me do.
—WARREN ROGERS

▼

☐ WEEK 5, TUESDAY   LEVITICUS

Scripture: Leviticus 11—17

Leprosy (13:2). The Hebrew word translated *leprosy* in KJV, was used also for other skin diseases. More recent English translations use the term "infectious skin diseases" (NIV).

A *scapegoat* (16:8-10) is one who bears responsibility for the mistakes or sins of the true offender. The term is usually used in connection with a political leader who seeks to maintain public confidence in himself by blaming a subordinate. The word comes from 16:10 where a live goat symbolically carried Israel's sins out of the camp and was lost in the wilderness with those sins.

Although there are regulations in these chapters that we do not understand today, most of them are perfectly clear; there must have been good reasons for all of them at the time. God gave them to Moses, and He commanded His people: "Keep my decrees and follow them. I am the Lord who makes you holy."

> *The Story:* Leviticus 11:44-47; 12:6-7; 13:1-9, 45-46. (Today, read the devotional first, then examine the selected scriptures for better understanding and deeper appreciation.)
>
> **Ye shall be holy; for I am holy** (Lev. 11:44).

Read and Rejoice

As I read these chapters, I rejoice that Jesus came to reveal God's will for our lives more clearly than it was revealed to Moses.

Let us give thanks that the ceremonial law of the Old Testament was canceled when Christ came. We no longer need to remember scores of rules regarding foods that are displeasing to God. Jesus said, "'Nothing that goes into a person from the outside can really make him unclean, because it does not go into his heart but into his stomach and then goes out of the body.' (In saying this, Jesus declared that all foods are fit to be eaten)" (Mark 7:18-19, TEV).

Reading chapter 12, let us be glad that childbearing within marriage is recognized as a good gift from God. Bearing a daughter is equally honorable with giving birth to a son. And neither experience needs atonement or moral cleansing before the mother returns to the congregation for us to share with the parents in the joy of a new life.

Let us rejoice in the progress of health science with today's clearer understanding of the spread of contagious diseases. And we rejoice also that even in that distant day, God made clear our moral responsibility to isolate ourselves and so to protect others from infectious diseases (13:45-46).

Let us be glad that God has made us man and woman. A happy marriage is one of His most profound miracles. Within the protecting bonds of love and marriage, He has planned for sexual expression that enriches our lives and continues the race.

"Ye shall be holy" means, You are to live as I have planned for your best welfare and for your highest happiness. You are to honor Me and to live with one another as I have taught you.

God's guidelines for life come to us through the Bible, through Jesus Christ, and by listening to the Holy Spirit.

Let us read and rejoice. Let us

> Praise God, from whom all blessings flow;
> Praise Him, all creatures here below;
> Praise Him above, ye heav'nly host;
> Praise Father, Son, and Holy Ghost.
> —THOMAS KEN

Scripture: Leviticus 18—24

"The prohibition of mixing seed and fabric materials (19:19) illustrates the principle of separation. It was called *habdalah* by the Jews, and was to characterize all of life. What God separated, they were to keep separate. It may be that factors were involved, the importance of which is not known to us" (BBC).

Israel's Feasts

Chapter 23 describes Israel's holy days and the religious feasts that were observed before the Babylonian exile. The term translated *feasts* is the Hebrew word for "appointed times." It indicates designated days for Israel's worship of God. At these feasts, special sacrifices were offered in addition to the regular daily offerings.

1. The *Seventh Day* (23:3) was a distinctive Israelite observance. Giving one day to God acknowledged that all time was His, just as giving the tithe recognizes that He is the ultimate Owner of all things.

2. *Passover Week* in March-April (23:4-8) was one of Israel's three annual pilgrimage festivals when the people gathered at Jerusalem to give thanks to God. Passover was instituted to recall the Hebrews' deliverance from Egyptian slavery; it occurred at the time of the barley harvest.

3. *Firstfruits* (23:9-14) was an offering made at the beginning of the harvest. The worshiper brought the first sheaf of grain from his field, a lamb, and a cereal offering. On the day after the Sabbath, the priest waved the sheaf before God and sacrificed the lamb and the cereal offering. It was a reminder that God gives us our daily bread.

4. *Pentecost (Feast of Weeks)* in May-June (23:15-22). Fifty days after offering the firstfruits, Israel celebrated Pentecost. According to the rabbis, Pentecost falls on the day that the Law was given at Sinai. Among modern Jews it has become "confirmation day."

5. The *Feast of Trumpets* (23:23-25) was the first of three holy days of the seventh month (*Tishri,* September-October). *Trumpets* was a sacred celebration of the new year, calling attention to judgment for sin, and the need for penitence and forgiveness.

6. The *Day of Atonement* (23:26-32) was a preparation for the Feast of Tabernacles. It was to be a time of true repentance and faith.

7. The *Feast of Tabernacles* in September-October (23:33-36) commemorates the beginning of Israel's wilderness wanderings and God's care for His people. It was the most joyous season of the year.

> *The Story:* Leviticus 21:1-4, 8, 21-23; 22:1-3, 17-20, 31-33
>
> Note 21:17-24. Let us give thanks to God that He sent Jesus to teach us a better way. No physical defect puts a barrier between God and us; none disqualifies us from serving Him.

I must be acknowledged as holy . . . I am the Lord (Lev. 22:32, NIV).

"The Lord . . . High and Lifted Up"

The prophet caught a vision which all of us need to experience from time to time: "I saw . . . the Lord . . . high and lifted up" (Isa. 6:1).

Jesus taught us that God is our Heavenly Father who loves and cares for us. We may depend upon His love, and we may come to Him in every time of need. But God is still God—Creator, Sovereign, high and holy. The bottom line of chapters 21—22 is: God is Lord of our lives, and we must acknowledge that Lordship.

The priest in Israel and the Christian minister are set a little apart from other persons because they serve the sovereign God. This sacred calling is to be recognized by the minister himself; his work is God's work, and so it is special. Because the man of God is doing God's work, we must hold him in high esteem. The Scripture says, "Regard them as holy, because they offer up the food of your God. Consider them holy, because I the Lord, who makes you holy, am holy" (21:8, NIV).

The work of the priest was so important that he must not jeopardize it by making himself ceremonially unclean even "for his father, or for his mother" (21:11). Does not Jesus himself place this high and holy value on the things of God? "He that loveth father or mother more than me is not worthy of me" (Matt. 10:37).

In 22:4 and 6 the priest who was ceremonially unclean was not to eat even his own share of the people's offerings until he had cleansed himself and thus made his person acceptable to a holy God. Even the natural blessings that God provides for us are not to be enjoyed without our being consciously right with Him. This is the New Testament guideline for partaking of holy Communion. As we come into the presence of Christ in this sacred experience, Paul counsels, "Let a man examine himself, and so let him eat of that bread, and drink of that cup" (1 Cor. 11:28).

Father in heaven, I want to enjoy Your tender care and loving concern. But teach me also proper reverence. Let me sometimes stand in awe before You. Let me join in the adoration of Your servant:

> Most blessed, most glorious, the Ancient of Days,
> Almighty, victorious, Thy great name we praise.
> —WALTER C. SMITH

▼

☐ WEEK 5, THURSDAY   LEVITICUS

Scripture: Leviticus 25—27 (Today read the devotional first and then the scriptures.)
The Story: Leviticus 27:1-3, 8-10, 30-33

A tithe ... belongs to the Lord; it is holy to the Lord (Lev. 27:30, NIV).

Honest with God

To understand chapter 27 we must know the Hebrew practice of dedicating possessions and persons to God. These gifts were to be made without reservation; once made, they could not be withdrawn. The gifts represented complete devotion and unswerving loyalty. Sometimes such a gift was immediately destroyed to show that the worshiper laid no further claim to it. There was no turning back when one made a promise to God.

In Israel, the firstborn was always thus dedicated. But in the case of a child, he was to be redeemed by the parent paying a fixed redemption price. Some firstborn animals could also be redeemed.

There was a reasonable leniency in this law of making offerings to God. If a poor man could not pay the established redemption fee, the priest could set a lower figure which the man could afford. But the man himself was not permitted to make the exception; a disinterested party must determine what was just and right.

Also, in dealing with God a man was to penalize himself and give God the benefit of the doubt. If he dedicated a field and then wished to redeem it for his own use, he must add 20 percent to the market value as the price of redemption.

In all these transactions God's people were to keep honest accounts with Him. And He knows how easy it is to fool ourselves about our sincerity when personal interests and preferences are involved.

Lord, the tithe of my income is Yours. I will faithfully bring it to Your house. But Your blessings are so many that my grateful spirit yearns to give even more than You ask. And in my giving I give myself.

> *Take my love; my God, I pour*
> *At Thy feet its treasure store.*
> *Take myself and I will be*
> *Ever, only, all for Thee.*
> —FRANCES R. HAVERGAL

The Book of *Numbers* tells the story of God's care for His chosen people during their Exodus journey from Sinai to the crossing of the Jordan. The name comes from a census of the people, taken first at Sinai and later in Moab shortly before they entered the Promised Land. Moses is the human center of the story which covers most of the 40 years of his leadership of Israel.

Chapters 1—10 relate preparations made at Mount Sinai just before departure.

Scripture: Numbers 1—4

In 1:46 we are told that men of military age numbered more than 600,000. Adding women, children, and older men to this figure, we know that about 3 million Israelites made the journey from Egypt to Canaan.

Chapter 2 shows us Israel's order of march during their 40 years on the journey. Judah and two adjacent tribes marched in front, followed by Reuben, Simeon, and Gad. The Tabernacle and its equipment were carried by the Levites at the center of the line, followed by the other six tribes.

The Story: Numbers 1:1-4, 44-50

Aaron and his sons are to go into the sanctuary and assign to each man his work (Num. 4:19, NIV).

Meditating on Numbers

God pays close attention to the numbers when numbers affect people. Some persons in the church object to numerical goals as being less than Christian. But there is a right answer to that objection: "There are souls in those goals."

God is also concerned with national defense. He told Moses to number all the men in Israel who were "able to serve in the army"

(NIV). Military strength is not a nation's only business, usually not our first business. But when life is endangered, life must be protected or none of our other business can go on.

Verses 47-50 remind us, however, that physical survival is not everything. God exempts some persons even from national defense in order to lead His people in worship. One tribe out of 12 was designated to devote full time to the religious life of the people. In comparable ratio, the tithe commits $1.00 out of every $10.00 for the church and her ministries to our spirits.

Organization and division of labor are also a part of numbering. Moses and Aaron were to choose one assistant from each tribe to help them take the census. Also the Levites were organized to care for and transport the Tabernacle. Different families were assigned specific duties. It was God's command: "Aaron and his sons are to go into the sanctuary and assign to each man his work."

Numbers are not all, but wherever people live and work together, numbers and numbering are important to God's plan for human life.

Moses prayed, "So teach us to number our days, that we may apply our hearts unto wisdom" (Ps. 90:12).

I would join that prayer—and add to it. *Teach us to number the hours, and to reserve time for You each day. Teach us to number our dollars, and to lay aside what belongs to You and to Your work. Teach us to number our talents, and to find our place in Your work of ministering to the needs of men.*

"So teach us to number . . . that we may apply our hearts unto wisdom." Amen.

▼

☐ WEEK 5, SATURDAY   NUMBERS

Scripture: Numbers 5—9

When I read chapter 5 I am grateful for God's higher revelation in the New Testament. I am glad for Jesus' redemptive word: "Neither do I condemn thee: go, and sin no more" (John 8:11).

The Story: Numbers 9:15-23

At the Lord's command they encamped, and at the Lord's command they set out (Num. 9:23, NIV).

The Guiding Light

Most of us plan our journeys by sunrise and sunset, but Israel was to journey at God's command. Usually these two coincide because both have been given to us by God for our guidance: "Sometimes the cloud stayed only from evening till morning, and when it lifted in the morning, they set out" (v. 21, NIV).

But there are times when God's guiding light does not follow His usual schedule of morning for travel and evening for rest. For five years a friend has had to lay aside his evangelistic ministry to spend the days at the side of an invalid wife. He writes:

"We tearfully cry, There is no way this can possibly work out for my good and for the good of others involved."

But my friend knows the wisdom and the love behind the guiding light; he trusts that wisdom as confidently as did Moses and Israel. Sometimes the signal says, *Move at once.* Then again it says, *Wait here.* "When the cloud stayed over the Tent for a long time, they obeyed the Lord and did not move on" (v. 19, TEV).

Though we may not understand why, it is wisdom to obey. At the end of the long wait my friend testifies: "For the first time in my life I see the true meaning of Paul's testimony, 'All things work together for good to them that love God, to them who are the called according to his purpose' (Rom. 8:28). Verse 29 explains why—that we may 'be conformed to the image of his Son.'

"As I review the past years since illness came to our home, I am thankful to God for leading us this way. I can see that He is using it for His purpose and for our best good."

To a spirit thus conformed to the image of Christ, there always comes the blessed benediction from Numbers:

The Lord bless thee, and keep thee: the Lord make his face shine upon thee, and be gracious unto thee: the Lord lift up his countenance upon thee, and give thee peace (6:24-26).

Scripture: Numbers 10—12

The diagram below best explains the outline of the camp described in 10:14-28.

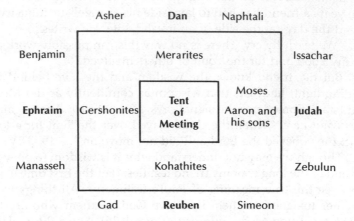

The Story: Numbers 11:4-17, 21-23, 31-32

Is the Lord's arm too short? You will now see whether or not what I say will come true for you (Num. 11:23, NIV).

What to Do When You're Down

In 12:3 we read, "Now the man Moses was very meek, above all the men which were upon the face of the earth." If God could say that about a man who had hit emotional bottom, perhaps there is recovery for us when we are down.

God does not leave us when we are discouraged—but He

wants us to rise above it. So, What do you do when you're down? The story suggests two things that you don't do, and two things that you do.

1. As Moses did in 11:11-15, talk to God about the problem—even if talking is only giving vent to our frustration. It helps to put the problem into words; and God won't toss us aside for our frailty nor gossip to others about our weakness. When we talk with Him it gives Him a chance to talk to us—and He always has the best answer to our dilemma.

2. Don't feel sorry for yourself. Moses did, but it only delayed his emotional recovery. God must somehow get our eyes off ourselves and fixed on Him before He can show us how to cope. And besides, when we feel sorry for ourselves we make rash statements. We blame God for our problems and may even ask to die. He is gracious to overlook our petulance and to remind us of His love. Nevertheless, it hurts when we look back and recall that we were so faithless and complaining.

3. Where God puts a period don't insert a question mark. Moses did, but soon learned that he had made a faithless mistake. God promised that the people would eat meat for a month. But Moses asked, How? He should have known better. He had seen the Red Sea rolled back, he had found water in the desert, and he had eaten manna for many months. But when discouraged, we don't think straight. We forget the love and the power of God.

4. Obey God. Moses told the people what God told him to tell them; there would be meat to eat (11:18-20). He called others to help him, as God had instructed him to do (24-25). Obedience is the key; say what God wants you to say, and do what He asks you to do. Moses obeyed, and the quail came in abundance; the least that any hunter bagged was 60 bushels! (32)

What do you do when you're down? Join in Johnson Oatman, Jr.'s, prayer:

> Lord, lift me up and let me stand,
> By faith, on heaven's tableland,
> A higher plane than I have found.
> Lord, plant my feet on higher ground.

Scripture: Numbers 13—15
The Story: Numbers 13:1-3, 26-33; 14:6-9
**If the Lord delight in us, then he will bring us into
this land, and give it to us** (Num. 14:8).

Caleb the Courageous

Life Begins at Forty. This book title may well have come from the
story of Caleb. He was just 40 when we first meet him in God's
Book of biographies. Israel was camped at Kadesh-barnea. There
God told Moses to choose a leader from each of the 12 tribes to spy
out the land of Canaan. Caleb, already a ruler in Judah, was chosen
to represent his tribe.

Of the 12 sent to spy out the land, 10 were only men, but
Caleb was a man of God. For 40 days they made their way secretly
about the country. It was a good land, figuratively flowing with
milk and honey. The fruit grew so large the spies were sure no one
would believe their story unless they brought the proof—a huge
bunch of grapes that took two men to carry it on a pole between
them. It was a good land; to that they all agreed, but that was all
they could agree upon. Ten of the spies had looked so long at the
giants that they had lost sight of God. But not Caleb.

There is a time to calculate one's strength and to count up the
opposition, but there is no help from those who can see only giants. The 10 carefully rehearsed the enemy forces. They could
count alright, but Caleb knew that when you count your opposition until you are ready to quit the task, it is time to quit counting
your opposition.

Disheartened by the majority report, the murmuring throng
became an angry mob. It was Caleb who checked them with a
declaration of faith. He had seen every threatening thing the other
spies had seen. But Caleb was able to measure the giants in the
light of God's power. Like Moses, he was "not fearing . . . for he
endured, as seeing him who is invisible" (Heb. 11:27). His courageous word was, "Let us go up at once, and possess it; for we are
well able to overcome it" (13:30).

God himself bids us note the attitude that gave Caleb his place in the great Bible biographies: "But my servant Caleb, because he had another spirit with him, and hath followed me fully, him will I bring into the land" (14:24).

Meditating on this life of courage, we would pray:

> *O for a faith that will not shrink,*
> *Though pressed by ev'ry foe,*
> *That will not tremble on the brink*
> *Of any earthly woe!*
> —WILLIAM H. BATHURST

▼

Scripture: Numbers 16—18
The Story: Numbers 16:1-7, 12-14
I will not put forth mine hand against my lord; for he is the Lord's anointed (1 Sam. 24:10).

Under God

Moses and Aaron, along with other men of God such as Paul, shared the same difficult assignments. They were called of God to be spiritual leaders; and there is no way for such leaders to stay out of deep involvement in the lives of other people. When their involvement displeases us, we call it meddling.

What is God's will for us when we don't trust our pastor, evangelist, or district superintendent?

Chapter 16 gives a tragic example of what not to do. We must not rebel against God's called servant, and we must not seek to displace or to destroy him. Does this mean that God's chosen leader is always right? No; he is human. But on the same basis, are we to assume that we are always right?

Korah and his followers felt deeply. They protested to Moses and Aaron: "You have gone too far! The whole community is holy, every one of them, and the Lord is with them. Why then do you set yourselves above the Lord's assembly?" (16:3, NIV).

We are always in danger if we let a rebellious spirit control us. We are wrong when we begin to feel and then to declare, "I am just as good as you." Because Korah was wrong and Aaron was right, God punished Korah and vindicated Aaron.

But sometimes the leader is wrong—even when he is a pastor or other elected church official. What is the right attitude then?

In the story of our text, David shows us the right way. Saul was Israel's anointed king but he was betraying his trust and persecuting innocent people. David had the opportunity to destroy him and to bring an end to Saul's evil acts. But David was a man under God. He knew the divine plan: "Vengeance is mine; I will repay, saith the Lord" (Rom. 12:19).

Today there are established church courts to which we may appeal. But we get ourselves into trouble when we try personally to determine justice and to assign penalties. It is better to trust God, to trust His called servant, and to trust His timing in righting what is wrong. God's way is better than permitting our spirits to fester with resentment, or trying to determine justice for another human being. He is under God, and we are under God.

Spirit of God, show me the way that I should take—always. Amen.

▼

☐ **WEEK 6, WEDNESDAY**   **NUMBERS**

Scripture: Numbers 19—21; 33; Deuteronomy
        2—3

Chapter 33 lists the stages of Israel's journey in three major movements: from Egypt to Sinai (vv. 1-15); from Sinai through the wilderness wandering (vv. 16-36; only a few of these places can be identified on today's maps); verses 37-49 list the movements included in the march from Kadesh to Canaan recorded in today's reading.

The Story: Numbers 20:1, 14-21; 21:10-13, 32-35

When we cried out to the Lord, he heard our cry and sent an angel and brought us out (Num. 20:16, NIV).

The God of History

God is Lord of the nations as well as the God of persons. "History is His story." Our scripture records God's care for His people as they moved from Kadesh to Canaan. For a clearer understanding read the story with a Bible map of the Exodus before you.

During the 38 years of wandering, Israel circled around in the Wilderness of Zin within 75 miles of Kadesh-barnea. Now the long delay was over; they were at last ready to begin the march to the Promised Land.

Instead of going directly north into Palestine, they planned to follow the King's Highway which lay east of them. The most direct path to this traveled route would have taken them east through Edom, but the Edomites refused them passage. Rather than give battle (because the Edomites were their cousins as descendants of Esau) Israel detoured south around the mountain range that runs to the Gulf of 'Aqaba (Ezion-geber). From here they came into Moab from the southwest. As they marched north, God gave them victories over the Amorites and over Og, king of Bashan, who had refused them a peaceful passage.

With these conquests completed, Israel descended into the valley of the Jordan River, opposite Jericho. Here they pitched their last camp before entering Canaan.

This is national history; but history involves people. God's work goes forward, even when in the process His leaders finish their earthly tasks. Miriam died and was buried in Kadesh. Aaron died also. The Bible tells the story in simple and moving words:

"While at Mount Hor, near the border of the land of Edom, the Lord informed Moses and Aaron: Aaron shall be reunited with his kindred, for he cannot enter the land which I have given to the nation of Israel, because both of you rebelled against my instructions at the waters of Meribah. Therefore take Aaron and his son Eleazar and bring them up to Mount Hor. . . . Moses did as the Lord had directed and they ascended Mount Hor, as the entire assembly looked on. After Moses had stripped Aaron of his robes and had put them on Eleazar his son, Aaron died there on the mountain top; after which Moses and Eleazar came down from the mountain. When the entire congregation saw that Aaron had passed away, the whole family of Israel mourned for Aaron thirty days" (Num. 20:23-29, NBV).

He had lived a long and useful life (123 years); God took him home; his own son carried on his father's work after him; a whole nation mourned his passing. Could any man ask for more?

To the God of history and of personal destiny we raise a prayer:

> O God, our Help in ages past,
> Our Hope for years to come,
> Be Thou our Guide while life shall last,
> And our eternal Home.
>
> —Isaac Watts

▼

□ **WEEK 6, THURSDAY** NUMBERS

Scripture: Numbers 22—26

Chapter 25 tells the story of Israel's first involvement in the idolatry and immorality of Canaanite worship. As in this instance, God often punished His people severely for their failure. But idolatry proved to be a recurring snare to Israel until after the Babylonian exile, 900 years later.

Chapter 26 gives the account of the second census, from which the Book of Numbers derives its name. The first was taken at Sinai (1:1) with a total of 603,550 (1:46). The second census of 601,730 showed only a slight decrease after 40 years of wandering (26:51). This second census was used to allocate territory to the tribes in Canaan.

The Story: Numbers 22:1-13

Must I not speak what the Lord puts in my mouth?
(Num. 23:12; all quotes from NIV).

When God Speaks

The story of Balaam is a puzzle in this otherwise historical book. Was he a fraud or a true prophet of God? Some things in his life would not pass the moral standards of the Bible. But, like Samson, he responded to the will of God when that will was made clear to him.

Balaam came from northeast of Palestine, near the Euphrates River (22:5). This had been the home of Abraham, and from here the wise men later came to honor the Infant Jesus.

God has unexpected ways of revealing himself to men who are open to Him. Here was a man of spiritual insight; and he looked to God for guidance. The messages are cast in poetic form, as were those of some of Israel's prophets of a later day. Let us hear what God says to us, though communicated by a man who was less than perfect.

We hear first the words of an obedient Balaam spoken to Balak's messengers: "Go back to your own country, for the Lord has refused to let me go with you" (22:13).

In Jude 11, Balaam is cited as a man who could be bribed to do wrong. But at this time his spiritual values were sound: "Even if Balak gave me his palace filled with silver and gold, I could not do anything great or small to go beyond the command of the Lord my God" (22:18).

This man could back down when he learned that God had different plans. He confessed: "I have sinned. I did not realize you were standing in the road to oppose me. Now if you are displeased, I will go back" (22:34).

In the first oracle to Balak, he cries: "How can I curse those whom God has not cursed? How can I denounce those whom the Lord has not denounced? . . . Let me die the death of the righteous, and may my end be like theirs!" (23:8, 10).

Balaam saw clearly God's sovereignty and the wisdom of man's conformity: "God is not a man that he should lie, nor a son of man, that he should change his mind. Does he speak and then not act? Does he promise and not fulfill? I have received a command to bless; he has blessed, and I cannot change it" (23:19-20).

In his third message Balaam courageously speaks directly contrary to the wishes of the man who had hired him: "How beautiful are your tents, O Jacob, your dwelling places, O Israel! . . . May those who bless you be blessed and those who curse you be cursed!" (24:5, 9).

Balaam's final word has been widely regarded as a prophecy of Christ's coming: "I see him, but not now; I behold him, but not near. A star will come out of Jacob; a scepter will rise out of Israel. . . . Edom will be conquered; Seir, his enemy, will be conquered, but Israel will grow strong. A ruler will come out of Jacob and destroy the survivors of the city" (24:17-19).

Thank You, Father, for every revelation of truth. Thank You for Your words spoken to us through Balaam. Without them we would forever be poorer.

▼

☐ **WEEK 6, FRIDAY**   NUMBERS

Chapters 28—29 describe again Israel's seasons of worship (see Leviticus 23). There had been a lapse of regular times of worship in the wilderness. Now the people needed to be reminded of God's requirements. See "The Sacrifices of Israel," page 47, and "Israel's Feasts," page 53.

"These laws may seem to us complicated and confusing. However one lesson should stand out—there is an offering to God appropriate in every time and place. . . . To the NT Christian this is the offering of a consecrated life lived every day, every week, every month, throughout all of our years" (BBC).

>   *Scripture:* Numbers 27; 30; 36
>   *The Story:* Numbers 27:1-7; 36:1-12 (If you find it hard to pronounce the names, call them by the first letter.)
>
>   **There is neither Jew nor Greek, slave nor free, male nor female, for you are all one in Christ Jesus** (Gal. 3:28, NIV).

68

Women's Rights and Social Responsibility

God is concerned about the practical problems of our lives. Any issue that affects us concerns Him. Any problem that affects two of us is to be resolved on the basis of what is right. In the Old Testament and in the New, God is on the side of what is fair and righteous. He asks us to join Him on that side.

Zelophehad's daughters and their family were about to be treated unfairly. What was happening was legal, but it was unfair. Because the existing law authorized an inheritance to sons only, the family was about to lose its inheritance in the Promised Land. These women asked for treatment that was outside of the law—and God granted it. He said to Moses, "What Zelophehad's daughters are saying is right. You must certainly . . . turn their father's inheritance over to them" (27:7, NIV). God rules on the basis of right rather than following any faulty legal code. He says, If the law is unfair to women, change the law.

But in chapter 36 fairness flows in the opposite direction. The law also provided that upon marriage, the wife's property became the property of her husband. If these daughters married men from other tribes, the whole future of Manasseh, their father's tribe, would be weakened through the loss of the land. In chapter 30 the woman's rights were limited by the rights of family—her father and her husband. Again God speaks for fairness and right; a woman may not, for personal interests, jeopardize the family or the community in the exercise of her rights.

God is on the side of right. Women's rights? Yes. But also family rights and community rights. We are a part of the larger human family. "None of us liveth to himself, and no man dieth to himself" (Rom. 14:7). We may need to be concerned about our rights, but God also requires that we be equally concerned about our responsibilities.

The Old Testament rule is still good for the New Testament Christian: "What doth the Lord require of thee, but to do justly, and to love mercy, and to walk humbly with thy God?" (Mic. 6:8).

With the Psalmist my heart responds:

Teach me your way, O Lord, and I will walk in your truth (Ps. 86:11, NIV).

More Information from Numbers

Chapter 31 gives an early illustration of wars of vengeance and extinction waged by Israel. How shall we understand a God of love giving such commands to His people? Perhaps the best answer is found in the principle of progressive revelation; God guided Old Testament persons in the light of their times—even as He guides us according to our knowledge. He allowed conduct in those dark days that is not consistent with the later revelations in the teachings of Jesus.

When we find Old Testament conduct that is sub-Christian, we simply declare our faith that the teachings of Jesus are God's highest revelation. We accept His teachings as the Christian's guide to conduct.

Chapter 32 relates how two and one-half tribes of Israel settled east of the Jordan River instead of being assigned territory in Canaan proper.

For the best understanding of chapter 34, examine in your Bible a map of Canaan as divided among the 12 tribes.

Chapter 35 explains arrangements for the tribe of Levi which had no single assigned tribal territory. The Levites were to be given 48 towns spread throughout the land. Each of these villages was to be located in a field more than half a mile square, thus providing pasture for the village flocks.

Among these Levitical cities, six were designated as cities of refuge to give protection to persons who had accidentally killed another. Here is underlined the importance of *intent* in determining the nature of a crime. Intent is also a determining factor in the biblical concept of sin. "It is 'willful transgression,' not the 'inadvertent slip,' which God judges as sin" (BBC).

▼

☐ **WEEK 6, SATURDAY**   **DEUTERONOMY**

The Book of *Deuteronomy* is made up almost entirely of Moses' farewell messages. We see Israel again standing at the borders of Canaan, as they had stood earlier at Kadesh-barnea. This time they stood on the plains of Moab east of the Jordan River, opposite the city of Jericho. The same enemies still inhabited Canaan; the same old battles must be fought. Nothing is ever gained by a delay in obeying God.

One thing was different. Moses was now an old man, a dying leader. God had told him that his work was finished; Joshua was to lead Israel across Jordan. In this book we have the last torrential outpouring of a great leader's heart and mind. Here is the deepest concern for the people he loved. Here is the highest devotion to the God he served. Again and again we see his thoughts, emotions, and prayers. Deuteronomy thus includes both the events of history and the attitudes of a man and of his God. It is these attitudes that determine the course of history.

Scripture: Deuteronomy 1—3
The Story: Deuteronomy 1:3-8, 21, 29-30; 2:2 3, 24-25, 31, 36

You have made your way around this hill country long enough; now turn north (Deut. 2:3; all quotes from NIV).

When God Says, Move!

In our journey there come times to rest, to listen, to draw strength from quiet communion with God. But there also come moments of decision when He says, Move!

Three times in our story God gave the command to press ahead toward the Promised Land. At Sinai, He gave the guidance: "You have stayed long enough at this mountain." At the end of 38 years of wandering in the desert, He encouraged: "You have made your way around this hill country long enough; now turn north." Again as Israel came to the borders of their promised inheritance, God spoke His word of exhortation: "Set out now and cross the

Arnon Gorge. . . . See, I have begun to deliver Sihon and his country over to you. Now begin to conquer and possess his land" (2:24, 31).

Sometimes God calls after months of preparation for a task, as when we must leave the security of school and face the uncertainty of a new job.

Again, the Spirit encourages us to new action after deep discouragement. In these hours He says: The past is past. I am God. I am still with you. Move ahead to the promised land to which I am leading you.

Our scripture reminds us not to listen to our fears in these critical moments. If fear defeats us, it is as bad as rebellion. To hold back because we are afraid robs us of God's blessing as surely as if we refuse to go. Three times God encourages us to conquer our fears: "Do not be discouraged" (1:21). "Do not be terrified" (1:29). "Do not be afraid of him" (3:2).

Is God asking me to move up? If so, He has already begun to give the victory that I seek. If I move when He speaks, I shall be able to testify with another man of God: "From . . . the rim of the Arnon Gorge . . . as far as Gilead, not one town was too strong for us" (2:36).

> Rise up, O men of God!
>   Have done with lesser things;
>   Give heart and mind and soul and strength,
>   To serve the King of Kings.
>   —WILLIAM PIERSON MERRILL

▼

☐ **WEEK 7, SUNDAY**   **DEUTERONOMY**

Scripture: Deuteronomy 4—6
The Story: Deuteronomy 4:1, 5-6, 9, 35, 39-40

Oh, that their hearts would be inclined to fear me and keep all my commands always, so that it might go well with them and their children forever! (Deut. 5:29, NIV).

Incline My Heart

Any man who has walked a lifetime with God knows that there is nothing—absolutely nothing—more important than faithfully following God. He yearns to see his children and his children's children find and follow this fulfilled life.

But to know the truth, and to desire and do it, are different ball games. We hear God sigh, "Oh, that their hearts would be inclined to fear me and keep all my commandments always!"

Do we really believe that God's way is the best way to live? Always? In every moral decision does this bedrock conviction undergird all of our thoughts? Does it shape all of our attitudes? Does He guide our actions?

When I do business with God the questions become intensely personal. Most of those to whom Moses spoke in the messages of Deuteronomy had not yet been born when God revealed himself at Sinai. But when God speaks, the issues are always up-to-date. Moses declares: "It was not with our fathers that the Lord made this covenant, but with us, with all of us who are alive here today" (5:3, NIV).

To know is good; but to sincerely desire and then to do the will of God is to find the fellowship with Him that our hearts crave. God's Spirit yearns, "Oh, that their hearts would be inclined to fear me!" Our spirits respond: "The Lord our God be with us, as he was with our fathers: let him not leave us or forsake us: that he may incline our hearts unto him, to walk in all his ways, and to keep his commandments" (1 Kings 8:57-58).

I do love God. I yearn to love Him with all my heart and with all my soul and with all my strength (6:5). In the power of His Holy Spirit I commit my life to Him.

"Teach me, O Lord, the way of thy statutes; and I shall keep it unto the end. Give understanding, and I shall keep thy law; yea, I shall observe it with my whole heart. Make me to go in the path of thy commandments; for therein do I delight. Incline my heart unto thy testimonies" (Ps. 119:33-36).

Scripture: Deuteronomy 7—10

In chapter 7, why was Israel commanded to ruthlessly destroy the nations that they were to conquer in their conquest of Canaan?

See the note on progressive revelation (p. 70). In addition, it helps to remember that God was dealing with nations rather than with individual persons. He was seeking to reveal himself to the world through a nation which knew and served Him. Israel was far from perfectly God-fearing, but she was greatly superior to any other people of the ancient world. The moral and religious life of the Canaanites was so far from God's plan that He could only appoint them to destruction, as once before He had destroyed most of the race in the Flood.

A second reason is simply that the Israelites were not strong enough to maintain their faith and win others to it. In the presence of Canaanite idolatry, the Israelites forsook God and bowed before idols. Living next door to heathen neighbors, they quit living as people of God and began living as heathen. Married to heathen husbands or wives, the Israelites were the weaker of the two. God knew that the heathen partner would "turn away thy son from following me, that they may serve other gods" (7:4).

The Story: Deuteronomy 8:6-18

Be careful that you do not forget the Lord your God, failing to observe his commands (Deut. 8:11, NIV).

Remember the Lord

Memory is short, and the human spirit tends to be self-sufficient. If we do not deliberately seek the fellowship of God, we soon lose vital contact with Him.

God's essential nature is the reason He forbids idolatry. He is real but He is not like any physical thing. Jesus reminds us, "God is a Spirit; and they that worship him must worship him in spirit and in truth" (John 4:24). If our hearts are to be raised in adoration we must always see God as Isaiah did, "high and lifted up."

Idolatry is forbidden because it is impossible to truly represent God in a physical form. Any material representation is less than God and therefore degrading to Him.

Perhaps our real modern danger is that the attempt to represent God by some physical object only increases our attachment to the material world and blinds us to the reality of the spirit. Maclaren writes: "The attempt to make the senses a ladder for the soul to climb to God is more likely to end in the soul going down the ladder instead of up."

The mirage of the material brings another hazard also. It is the danger that we shall become wholly children of this world, forgetting our divine Father and our heavenly citizenship. Because we are of the earth, earthy, we tend to become satisfied with food, family, entertainment, and money. What are the early warning signs of this spiritual illness?

- Finding excuses for staying away from God's house
- Giving attention to things but crowding out devotion
- Getting so busy at home that we cannot help at church
- Worrying about lack of money, but resting content with poor attitudes
- Thinking often of self but seldom of others

These are the modern idolatries. If they become first in our lives, it is usually not a deliberate decision. Rather, little by little they capture us. We become absorbed in this world and let the awareness of God's presence fade. We would never deliberately desert Him, but are we in danger of forgetting Him? My heart cries out for help.

> *More love to Thee, O Christ, More love to Thee!*
> *Hear Thou the prayer I make On bended knee.*
> *This is my earnest plea: More love, O Christ, to Thee;*
> *More love to Thee, More love to Thee!*
> —ELIZABETH PRENTISS

Scripture: Deuteronomy 11—15

Chapter 13 seems far removed from our lives, but it furnishes food for thought. As you read this chapter, how do you think God would answer the following questions? (Circle T for true, and F for false.)

Punishment does not deter evildoers.   T   F
Capital punishment is sometimes right.   T   F
Morality can be improved by right laws.   T   F
We should always be tolerant of persons who flout God and goodness.   T   F

The *Modern Language Bible, New Berkeley Version* helps us understand verse 9 and similar commands to Israel. "Executions . . . often had to take place, if innocent blood were not to rest upon the community, but no officer of the state ever performed it. Since it was community responsibility, the people stoned the guilty to death" (NBV, footnote at Deut. 19:10).

The Story: Deuteronomy 11:1-7, 16-19

It was your own eyes that saw all these great things the Lord has done (Deut. 11:7; all quotes from NIV).

Fair to My Family

Howard asked me, "I wonder if my children will grow up having the same excitement about the church that I received as a youngster?"

I had the same question about my children. Howard and I came from an era of intense revivals and summer camp meetings. We saw services where God's Spirit came in power. Sometimes the pastor did not get to preach. The people testified, wept, shouted, and sought God at the altars.

Our children have not seen as many of these outpourings as Howard and I experienced. Did our parents and their peers give us something more than we are giving to our children—and to our grandchildren?

Today's story comes from parents who lived in a distant day, but are not the situations parallel? Moses said: "Remember today that your children were not the ones who saw and experienced the discipline of the Lord your God . . . But it was your own eyes that saw all these great things the Lord has done" (11:2, 7).

God's leader could not send the new generation back through the Red Sea or across the Sinai desert. But he urged them to be faithful in the light of their own experience of God's presence. I may not be able to duplicate the miracles of my youth for my children, but I can be faithful to God.

To be fair to my family, I myself must experience enough of the reality of God's presence to have something to share with my children. God says: "Fix these words of mine in your hearts and minds" (11:18).

When God is real in my life I need to share that faith with my child. "Teach them to your children, talking about them when you sit at home and when you walk along the road, and when you lie down and when you get up" (11:19).

Like Israel, my children and I will find spiritual strength in public worship. The ancient advice is sound: "Seek the place the Lord your God will choose . . . there bring . . . your tithes . . . and your freewill offerings . . . There, in the presence of the Lord your God, you and your families shall eat and shall rejoice . . , because the Lord your God has blessed you" (12:5-7).

My heart responds, Help me to be fair to my family.

> *To serve the present age,*
> *My calling to fulfill;*
> *Oh, may it all my pow'rs engage*
> *To do my Master's will!*
> —CHARLES WESLEY

▼

Scripture: Deuteronomy 16—20
The Story: Deuteronomy 20:1-4, 8

Do not be afraid of them, because the Lord your God . . . will be with you (Deut. 20:1, NIV).

Facing My Fears

Tucked away in these five chapters of instruction for ancient peoples is a word to make my day.

In *Guideposts*, Jimmy Stewart tells of his experience as commander of an air squadron based in England during World War II.

"Tomorrow my squadron would face the enemy again. How could I give my crew confidence if I was so afraid? I slumped down at my desk.

"Fear is an insidious and deadly thing. It can warp judgment, freeze reflexes, breed mistakes. Worse, it's contagious. I knew my own fear, if not checked, could infect my crew members. And I could feel it growing within me.

"I thought of my . . . father who had served in the First World War. 'Were you afraid?' I'd asked as a youngster back in Pennsylvania, when we talked about Dad's experiences in France.

"I could remember the faraway look in his eyes as he nodded. 'Every man is, son,' he said softly. 'Every man is.' But then he would always add something else. 'Just remember that you can't handle fear by yourself, son. Give it to God; He'll carry it for you.'"

But most of us face our fears closer home. Mrs. Harper testifies:

"We had just moved to a large city. For several days our local paper had reported a bold intruder called 'Sockfoot,' who was entering homes and terrorizing women.

"On this fall morning our children had left for school, and my husband was out of town. I was upstairs making the beds when I heard the sound of footsteps on the floor below. My thoughts flew to 'Sockfoot' and I froze, paralyzed with fear.

"But after only a few seconds I heard an inner Voice saying: 'Why are you afraid? I am here.' I relaxed, and with tears in my eyes said, 'Thank You, Lord. That's all I need.'

"I don't know what caused those muffled sounds that day. I also know there have been times since when I have been afraid. But I do not panic. I remember that special day when my Heavenly Father whispered, 'Why are you afraid? I am here.'"

I would join Mrs. Harper in her testimony of confidence:
"When I am afraid, I will trust in you. . . . in God I trust; I will not be afraid" (Ps. 56:3-4, NIV).

▼

Scripture: Deuteronomy 21—25

In chapters 21—25 there are some things that seem irrelevant to our lives. Is it worthwhile to read such sections of the Bible? Try this exercise in understanding and appreciation.

Read these five chapters again. Beside ideas where you need to know more about the concept in order to understand it, place a question mark (?); beside ideas where you see no relevance for today, place a minus sign (-); beside every idea that seems worthy and right, place a plus mark (+).

My personal score was five question marks, 22 minuses, and 29 pluses. Not bad for a difficult five chapters.

The Story: Deuteronomy 24:14-22

Blessed are the merciful: for they shall obtain mercy (Matt. 5:7).

Give Me Compassion

God asks His people to be fair, to be concerned for others, to watch out for their welfare, to be compassionate, to be generous. In Israel there was much that fell short of Christlikeness, but God was pointing them—and us—to His better way.

✔ Be fair to the girl you marry. "When you . . . see among the captives a beautiful girl you want as your wife, take her home with you. . . . you may marry her. However, if after marrying her you decide you don't like her, you must let her go free—you may not sell her or treat her as a slave" (21:10-14; all quotes from TLB).

✔ Watch out for the welfare of your guests. "Every new house must have a guardrail around the edge of the flat rooftop to prevent anyone from falling off" (22:8).

✔ Protect your neighbor's property. "If you see someone's ox or sheep wandering away, don't pretend you didn't see it; take it back to its owner. If you don't know who the owner is, take it to your farm and keep it there until the owner comes looking for it, and then give it to him" (22:1-2).

✔ Treat another as you would like to be treated. "If a slave escapes from his master, you must not force him to return; let him live among you in whatever town he shall choose, and do not oppress him" (23:15-16).

✔ Never knowingly take away a man's living. "It is illegal to take a millstone as a pledge, for it is a tool by which its owner gains his livelihood" (24:6).

✔ Always be considerate of the needy. "Never oppress a poor hired man . . . Pay him his wage each day before sunset, for since he is poor he needs it right away" (24:14-15).

✔ Be honest with every man and woman. "In all your transactions you must use accurate scales and honest measurements" (25:13-14).

✔ Among God's people, compassion extends to all God's creatures. "If you see someone trying to get an ox or a donkey onto its feet when it has slipped beneath its load, don't look the other way. Go and help!" (22:4).

Father in heaven, my heart cries:

> *Oh, to be like Thee! full of compassion,*
> *Loving, forgiving, tender and kind,*
> *Helping the helpless, cheering the fainting,*
> *Seeking the wand'ring sinner to find!*
> —THOMAS O. CHISHOLM

☐ **WEEK 7, FRIDAY**   **DEUTERONOMY**

Scripture: Deuteronomy 26—28
The Story: Deuteronomy 26:1-11

**He brought us to this place and gave us this land
. . . and now I bring the firstfruits of the soil that
you, O Lord, have given me** (Deut. 26:9-10, NIV).

I Am Grateful, Lord

Thanksgiving is best shown by thanksliving. At harvesttime God
instructed His people to express their gratitude by bringing offerings to His house. He has appointed these times of thanksgiving to
nourish our spirits and to make us like himself.

Has God done something good for me in recent months for
which I am grateful? Is my heart moved to say, "Thank You," and to
draw closer to Him? Perhaps the Psalmist can help me say just how
I feel.

"Give thanks to the Lord, because he is good,
    and his love is eternal. . . .
In my distress I called to the Lord;
    he answered me and set me free.
The Lord is with me, I will not be afraid . . .
I was fiercely attacked and was being defeated,
    but the Lord helped me. . . .
Open to me the gates of the Temple;
    I will go in and give thanks to the Lord! . . .
I praise you, Lord, because you heard me,
    because you have given me victory. . . .
You are my God, and I give you thanks;
    I will proclaim your greatness.
Give thanks to the Lord, because he is good,
    and his love is eternal"
        (Ps. 118:1, 5-6, 13, 19, 21, 28-29, TEV).

▼

Scripture: Deuteronomy 29—31
The Story: Deuteronomy 30:11-20
        See Rom. 10:6-8 where Paul quotes
        verses 11-14.

Now choose life, so that you and your children may live and that you may love the Lord your God, listen to his voice, and hold fast to him (Deut. 30:19-20; all quotes from NIV).

Decision and Destiny

Decisions for good or evil become choices for life or death. Living for God is more than knowing—it is choosing. To serve Him means to listen to what He says, and then to obey. When God makes His will known to us, we are forced to make a decision. To evade or to delay is to say no.

God here declares plainly, "I call heaven and earth as witnesses against you that I have set before you life and death, blessings and curses. Now choose life, so that you and your children may live and that you may love the Lord your God, listen to his voice, and hold fast to him." Because the Bible makes God's will known to me, it requires me to make decisions—and those decisions are the hinges upon which my destiny turns.

God is concerned with good and evil. My responses, therefore, involve life or death. To choose evil in a world where goodness is the goal puts me in opposition to my Creator. I cannot fight Him and win. The Bible declares to all: If you continue to disobey God, "you will certainly be destroyed." But the Word affirms just as surely, "Love the Lord your God . . . then you will live and increase, and the Lord your God will bless you" (30:16).

It is an awesome choice that God sets before me. I win all or lose everything by the decision that I make. But this choice becomes even more moving when I remember that through my influence I involve my children also. Every child must choose for himself when he reaches the age of accountability, and when the

Spirit of God confronts him. But by my example, I encourage or discourage his obedience to God. My choices also involve my innocent child in the tragedies that my sin brings to the home; or I surround him with the blessings that Christian faith brings to family life.

O Father, I hear Your call, and I choose today.

> *Take my love; my God, I pour*
> *At Thy feet its treasure store.*
> *Take myself and I will be*
> *Ever, only, all for Thee.*
> —FRANCES R. HAVERGAL

▼

☐ WEEK 8, SUNDAY   DEUTERONOMY

Scripture: Deuteronomy 32—34
The Story: Deuteronomy 3:24-28; 32:48-52; 34:1-8

At that time I pleaded with the Lord. . . . "Let me go over and see the good land beyond the Jordan" (Deut. 3:23-25; all quotes from NIV).

Joy in Place of Sorrow

A veteran missionary commented to me: "I have always felt God was not quite fair to Moses. I wish He had let him cross Jordan into the Promised Land."

Moses' disappointment has been called "one of the saddest stories in Hebrew history." It was disappointing; but when we walk with God the last word is always good. He sometimes allows us to suffer, but He *never* is unloving or unfair.

After Moses' failure at Meribah God told him, "Because you did not trust in me enough to honor me . . . you will not bring this community into the land I give them" (Num. 20:12). Moses never quite believed that God meant it. Some time later in camp at the borders of Canaan he prayed: "Let me go over and see the good land beyond Jordan." But it was not to be.

The events are not recorded in the Bible, but in the Bible we see the character of God. I think He came to Moses' tent one afternoon and called his name. Entering, He sat with Moses in silence for a while, then said gently: "You're disappointed."

Moses replied, "I am. For 40 years I have lived for this moment."

God answered, "I know. But come and take a walk with Me."

Arm in arm they walked through the camp and climbed the slopes of Mount Nebo. At some high point God said, "Let's sit on this rock and rest awhile."

As they rested together, God said: "Look across the river, Moses." The view stretched away 50 miles west to the Mediterranean Sea and 90 miles north. Here was the land of Moses' dreams and the goal of his life's labors. With a deep sigh he pressed his case:

"I want to go over with the people. It has been my dream for 40 years."

God knows our deepest disappointments, and He knows how to heal them. Once again He spoke.

"I know, Moses. But turn and look to the east."

As Moses lifted his eyes, there streamed from beyond the peaks of Pisgah the glory of an eternal city. After a few moments of silence God said:

"I know how much you want to cross Jordan with your people. But you have seen My home. In a little while I am going there tonight, and I invite you to go with Me. You may go back to camp and into Canaan with the people, or you may go home with Me."

When you make that offer to a man who has walked a lifetime with God, you really give him no choice!

Moses replied: "I thought I wanted more than anything else to cross Jordan into Canaan. But I would rather go home with You."

God reached out His hand and Moses took it. Together they rose and slowly climbed the mountainside. Israel went on across Jordan with Joshua. They had Canaan, but Moses had God—and no man can ask for more.

God doesn't plan to take us to heaven disappointed. His last word is always good. My spirit testifies:

He gives me joy in place of sorrow,
He gives me love that casts out fear;
He gives me sunshine for my shadow,
And "beauty for ashes" here.
                                    —J. G. CRABBLE

▼

The Book of *Joshua* tells the story of the Israelite
invasion of Canaan. It includes the record of three
successful military campaigns led by Joshua; also
the allotment of the territory to the different tribes.

The closing chapters recount the renewal of
the covenant between God and His people, including Joshua's moving testimony: "Choose you
this day whom ye will serve . . . but as for me and
my house, we will serve the Lord" (24:15).

Scripture: Joshua 1—4
The Story: Joshua 1:1-9

**I will be with you; I will never leave you or for-
sake you** (Josh. 1:5, NIV).

A New Day and a New Task

I recently visited with a friend in middle life. With his wife and two
younger children Walter had come to a Catholic country to establish the Church of the Nazarene. He came to people in a secular
culture, with a foreign language, and an alien theology. I asked
him, "How do you begin to win such folk to Christ and nurture
them in a holiness church?"

He answered: "We do not know, but God will help us."

Most of us do not face such dramatic assignments, but all of us
awaken some mornings knowing that we have not gone this way
before.

85

We may not know how to meet today's challenge, but we do not face the task alone. When God's man needed God's help, "the Lord spoke to Joshua."

But even with divine reassurance, a new task calls for initiative. God said to Joshua, "Now therefore arise, go over this Jordan, thou, and all this people" (1:2). Act. Begin. Get going!

And to support our initiative God gives His promise of success. "Every place that the sole of your foot shall tread upon, that have I given unto you . . . There shall not any man be able to stand before thee all the days of thy life: as I was with Moses, so I will be with thee: I will not fail thee nor forsake thee" (1:3, 5).

But new land is not conquered easily. Even with God's promise, new tasks call for human courage—lots of it. Three times in our story the Lord reminded His man, "Be strong and of good courage."

I am glad that in new ventures of the spirit we are not left without dependable guidelines: "This book of the law shall not depart out of thy mouth; but thou shalt meditate therein day and night . . . for then thou shalt make thy way prosperous, and then thou shalt have good success" (1:8).

Thank You, Father, for this new day and for Your help with its new tasks. Thank You for Your gracious promise, "I will be with you; I will never leave you or forsake you." Amen.

▼

Scripture: Joshua 5—7
The Story: Joshua 6:6-7, 14-16, 20-21, 27
It is not the will of your Father which is in heaven, that one of these little ones should perish (Matt. 18:14).

Why?

I was teaching at our European Nazarene Bible College in Switzerland. When we studied this story in our Old Testament class, Mariella, a young wife from Sicily, had a question about verse 21. In her limited but beautifully accented Italian-English she asked, "Vy deed dey have to keel all dee veemens and dee cheeldern?"

We have to answer this question more than once as we read the historical books of the Old Testament. Our Christian conscience is troubled until we find an answer that satisfies a devout but inquiring mind. We believe that God is good, that He loves all persons. Jesus tells us, "It is not the will of your Father which is in heaven, that one of these little ones should perish." How do we reconcile this with verse 21?

Students of the ancient world tell us the people of Jericho were so sinful that God must let them die out in order to make himself known to the world through the people of Israel—and we believe it. But still our troubled minds ask Mariella's question: Why did they have to kill all the women and the children?

We do not know the full answer, but we are sure of this: Jesus would not want innocent and helpless people destroyed. Much of God's will is clearly revealed in the Old Testament, but we occasionally find attitudes and actions that seem to contradict teachings of the New Testament.

Because this is true, we hold to the principle of *progressive revelation*. We believe that God revealed as much of His will as He could make known to Old Testament men of God. But even His chosen people were often limited in their understanding of what God wanted. That is why He sent Jesus into this world as the perfect revelation of himself.

When we find Old Testament records that do not agree with the teachings of Jesus, we accept the New Testament as God's will for today.

Mariella, we believe that God does not want innocent women and children to die. We believe it because Jesus taught it.

Thank You, Father, for all that You revealed to men of the Old Testament, and for their readiness to obey You. But thank You most of all for the final revelation of yourself in Jesus. We are glad that we can always obey and follow Him. In His name. Amen.

Scripture: Joshua 8—11
The Story: Joshua 11:1-8, 16-17

Joshua captured all the land—the hill country and foothills, both north and south, all the area of Goshen . . . as well as the Jordan Valley (Josh. 11:16, TEV).

Where Did It Happen?

The Bible breathes the air of Palestine. Most of its 66 books were written there. They contain almost countless references to the geography of the country. It is a small land 150 miles from north to south—from Dan to Beersheba—and varying from 20 to 60 miles east to west. It is bounded on the west by the Mediterranean Sea. The Philistines, who gave Israel trouble in the days of Samuel and David, lived on the southern coastal plains. In the north are Tyre and Sidon, from whence Solomon secured timbers for building the Temple.

Palestine's eastern boundary is in the vicinity of the Jordan River. Its headwaters are near Mount Hermon—mentioned as the northern limits of Joshua's conquests. Just south are "the waters of Merom" where Joshua defeated a coalition of the northern kings. This today is Lake Hule, center of a rich farming area in modern Israel. Ten miles farther south lies the Sea of Galilee, where so much of Jesus' earthly ministry was carried on.

The Jordan River flows out of the Sea of Galilee and due south for about 60 miles, where it empties into the Dead Sea. Near this spot Joshua and the Israelites crossed Jordan to enter Canaan. A few miles north of here is "the city of Adam" where the waters of the Jordan stood still and rose as a wall, giving the Israelites time enough to cross on dry land (Josh. 3:15-16).

Palestine is divided by the deep chasm of the Jordan Valley— an ancient geological fault continuing into the Dead Sea. The southern half of the Jordan River and all of the Dead Sea are below sea level—the bottom of the Dead Sea being 2,600 feet lower than the surface of the Mediterranean.

Much of central Palestine is a waterless, desert plateau. But its mountains, rising to heights of 3,000 feet, are filled with springs. The slopes are suitable for cultivation of grapes, figs, and olives. This was "the hill country of Judea" which the 12 spies explored for Moses and which Caleb claimed 45 years later.

Of Palestine's geography Daniel Twohig wrote:

> I walked today where Jesus walked . . .
> A sweet peace fills the air.
> I walked today where Jesus walked,
> And felt His presence there.*

*Copyright G. Schirmer, Inc. Used by permission.

▼

☐ **WEEK 8, THURSDAY** JOSHUA

Scripture: Joshua 12—15

For most helpful reading of chapters 12—19 you will want a Bible map of Canaan as divided among the 12 tribes. From these descriptions in the Bible the mapmakers drew their maps. Joshua gave careful instructions for the tribal borders, thus enabling us to visualize their boundary lines. He also gave lists of the cities and towns, so that we can pinpoint many of those places on our maps (see 15:20-62).

Not all locations listed by Joshua are known today, but you will find enough of them to visualize the tribal territories. You will thus identify enough places to help make your reading of the Old Testament come alive.

The Story: Joshua 14:6-14; 15:13-19

I wholly followed the Lord my God (Josh. 14:8).

A Good Old Age

Caleb was semiretired but not ready to quit. What is it that brings an old man to the edge of the grave ready for war instead of the rocking chair?

It is a good old age when a man's spiritual insight is as keen as his eyesight. Caleb credited God for his strength. Such vibrant faith both gives life and preserves it. This faith delivers us from worry that wears life down; it keeps us from sin that destroys life; and it constantly replenishes the springs that nourish life.

Age has its distinctive tasks and triumphs. In advanced years we must normally adjust to a quieter life. But our limitations need not mark the end of usefulness. There are ministries that can be accomplished best by those who are rich in experience and grace.

It is the vision to see and the courage to try that gives verve at every age. To a little boy trying to move a table his father said, "Son, don't try to move the table; it is as big as you are." The lad's reply challenges us: "But, Daddy, I am as big as the table!"

Even in old age Caleb was a child of the future. He knew that it takes no more strength to plan what we shall do tomorrow than to recall what we did yesterday. At 85 he laid plans to take on giants—and by God's help "Caleb drove thence the three sons of Anak, Sheshai, and Ahiman, and Talmai."

Because he was still busy in old age he had something to give to his children. When Othniel won the hand of Caleb's daughter, the girl asked her father for a blessing. From the territories recently conquered, Caleb gave her a southern slope of the mountains, and added for good measure upper and lower springs of water.

Father, let me testify with Caleb, "I have wholly followed the Lord my God." Give me some resources to pass on to my children and to my children's children. In Christ's name. Amen.

▼

Scripture: Joshua 16—19
The Story: Joshua 17:14—18:10

As the Lord commanded by the hand of Moses
(Josh. 14:2).

Faith and Action

Truth is found in the strangest places! Buried in these accounts of tribal geography we discover God's plan for divine cooperation.

He does not tow us through life like a trailer behind a tractor. Nor does He wish us to attempt the journey without His presence and power. Twenty-four times in the Old Testament we are told that God accomplished His purpose "by the hand of Moses." He desires that our lives shall be ventures in divine-human partnership.

Joshua reminded the tribes of Ephraim and Manasseh that nothing really good comes to us without effort. When they complained that their territories were too small, he said, "Go north, young men, go north!" Wooded mountains and productive valleys lay just beyond their borders. Territory was there for the taking When they complained about the opposition, God's man replied: "Though the Canaanites have iron chariots and though they are strong, you can drive them out" (17:18, NIV).

When the seven remaining tribes needed territory allotted, Joshua did not pray for a vision. First there was work to do: "Appoint three men from each tribe. I will send them out to make a survey of the land and to write a description of it . . . After you have written descriptions . . . bring them here to me and I will cast lots for you in the presence of the Lord our God" (18:4, 6, NIV).

To merely cast lots is to rely on chance. But Joshua knew that to cast lots "in the presence of the Lord" is to trust Him and to commit the outcome to His decision. This is His plan for us: to do all that we can—and then to trust Him.

Thank You, Father, for the joy of partnership with You.

Scripture: Joshua 20—22
The Story: Joshua 22:9-16, 21-22, 26-34
This day we perceive that the Lord is among us
(Josh. 22:31).

How to Resolve a Misunderstanding

When we studied this 22nd chapter at our European Nazarene Bible College, Jan Van Otterloo from Holland made a class report. He said in his accented English, "I theenk these story tells us that we must not make preyudiced yoodgments." The Holy Spirit gave Jan a clear spiritual insight.

Here is a story that has been repeated at least 1,097 times in the lives of God's people. A misunderstanding occurs between persons, both of whom love God and are seeking to serve Him. Both feel deeply about the issue because both are trying to do God's will. Somebody jumps to a wrong conclusion that what the other is doing cannot please God. How do we resolve these conflicting opinions between opposing groups in the church? This story from God's Word gives us some important clues.

Let us first confide in the wisest leaders in the church. The children of Israel went to Phineas, their spiritual leader. With him they chose 10 other godly men in whom they had confidence. If a right solution to this divisive difference of opinion could be found, they would trust the wisdom of their leaders to find it.

The second rule for clearing up sharp differences is to reach a clearer understanding. This procedure solved the problem for Israel—and will often resolve our current problems. In verses 16-20 Phineas explained why their delegation had come, and how very deeply they felt about the issue. In response, the eastern tribes carefully explained why they had built their altar. Understanding the motive behind the action fully satisfied the fears of Phineas and his colleagues.

Rule three is that when both sides have been heard, someone must take the lead in stating what course should be taken in view of the new facts uncovered. Phineas took this initiative. He voiced the feelings of the entire group when he said, "This day we perceive that the Lord is among us."

The blessed outcome of a God-guided effort to resolve a misunderstanding was a spirit of joy and praise. "The Israelites were satisfied and praised God. [They said] 'This altar is a witness to all of us that the Lord is God'" (v. 34, TEV).

Prayer for today:

Lord, with Francis of Assisi, I pray, Help me to understand more than to seek to be understood.

☐ WEEK 9, SUNDAY   JOSHUA

Scripture: Joshua 23—24
The Story: Joshua 23:1-8

We will serve the Lord our God. We will obey his commands (Josh. 24:24; all quotes from TEV).

When We Say Farewell

Mrs. Harper and I have not lived 110 years as Joshua had, but we have lived long enough to reflect seriously on the future of our children and their children. Everyone who walks a lifetime with God finds the way so good that he yearns to see those he loves also walk that way.

Joshua had spent his life with these people. He had loved them and led them. Together they had fought their battles, suffered their failures, and shared their victories. Now it was time to say farewell.

How do we persuade those whom we love to follow the Lord

as we have tried to do? We must persuade—because we cannot compel them.

✔ We can remind them of our experiences and of their own. "Every one of you knows in his heart and soul that the Lord your God has given you all the good things that he promised. Every promise he made has been kept; not one has failed" (23:14).

✔ We can advise and urge the paths that we have found good. "Be careful to obey and do everything that is written in the book of the Law . . . Do not neglect any part of it . . . Instead, be faithful to the Lord as you have been till now. . . . Be careful, then, to love the Lord your God'" (23:6, 8, 11).

✔ We can remind them of God's past blessings. "I gave you a land that you had never worked and cities that you had not built. . . . you are . . . eating grapes from vines that you did not plant, and olives from trees that you did not plant" (24:13).

✔ We can walk so close to God that our children and friends will be moved by our example. The writer tells us, "As long as Joshua lived, the people of Israel served the Lord, and after his death they continued to do so as long as those leaders were alive who had seen for themselves everything that the Lord had done for Israel" (24:31).

Prayer for today:

Lord, help me to live so that my children and my church shall see in my life some miracles of Your grace. Let them see in me some manifestations of Your love and power that shall encourage them to maintain their commitment to You.

▼

☐ **WEEK 9, MONDAY**   **JUDGES**

Scripture: Judges 1—3
The Story: Judges 2:8-17; 21:25

You have disobeyed me. Why have you done this?
(Judg. 2:2, NIV).

Our Faithful God

The Book of *Judges* tells the story of God's people during 300 years from the death of Joshua to the crowning of King Saul. It is a sad story of Israel's backsliding, but the glad story of God's mercy and forgiveness.

In 2:10 we read, "There arose another generation after them, which knew not the Lord." What will be the faith of our children? It is a searching question that challenges every parent and Christian worker. If our children are less devoted to God than their fathers, if the church means less to them than to their parents, we are backsliding. We are already going downhill to "another generation after them which knew not the Lord." Unless genuine revival occurs, each generation moves still further from vital faith.

In our neighbor's family the grandfather and grandmother were Spirit-filled Christians. The son and his wife were good, clean-living people—leaders in a neighborhood church. But they had abandoned the high level of holy living maintained by their parents. In the third generation the children are only casual church attenders; and two of them married Catholics. The grandchildren in the fourth generation are being reared in the Catholic church. Only 60 years from Wesleyan holiness to Roman Catholicism!

We cannot choose Christ for our children. Each generation must kindle for itself the fires of faith upon its own altars. But we have a responsibility to them. Do our children see as much of God in our homes and in our church services as we saw in the homes of our fathers, and in the churches in which we grew up? If not, are we being faithful to them?

I am glad that God is not entirely limited to our influence. Where we may fail, He remains faithful. He does not permit us or our children to wander from Him, or to lose our souls easily. In mercy, God chastises us when we forget Him. He seeks to save us from the sadness of sin's consequences. Above all, He seeks to save us from the eternal tragedy of losing our souls.

Today my chastened heart sings:

> *Judge not the Lord by feeble sense,*
> *But trust Him for His grace;*
> *Behind a frowning providence*
> *He hides a smiling face.*
> —WILLIAM COWPER

95

Scripture: Judges 4—5 (Be sure to read all today)
The Story: Judges 4:4-8; 5:1-7

Be strong and of a good courage; be not afraid, neither be thou dismayed: for the Lord thy God is with thee whithersoever thou goest (Josh. 1:9).

A Woman of Courage

Israel was weak and struggling. God had a future for her, but no one could see that future. Then, when the men were no use at all, a woman, under God, turned the tide of history. That woman was Deborah, a prophetess and the judge of Israel.

The great French general, Marshal Foch, once said, "A leader is, above all things, an animator. His thought and faith must be communicated to those he leads." Deborah was a leader.

In Shaw's *Saint Joan* we find a perfect illustration of the Spirit which moved Deborah. Joan of Arc had a vision that she was to drive the English out of France. In trying to inspire the prince to take his rightful part in the project, Joan says: "I tell thee, Charles, it is God's business we are on, not our own. I have a message to thee from God, and thou must listen to it, though my heart break with the terror of it!"

Deborah also had courage because she was sure she had heard from God. "Hath not the Lord God of Israel commanded, saying, Go and draw toward mount Tabor, and take with thee ten thousand men of the children of Naphtali and of the children of Zebulun? And I will draw unto thee to the river of Kishon Sisera, the captain of Jabin's army, with his chariots and his multitude; and I will deliver him into thine hand" (4:6-7).

Woman of God, and inspirer of armies, Deborah also composed soul-stirring poetry. As she reflected on God's help she wrote:

"My heart is with the commanders of Israel, with the people who gladly volunteered. Praise the Lord! . . . The stars fought from the sky; as they moved across the sky, they fought against Sisera. A flood in the Kishon swept them away—the onrushing Kishon River. I shall march, march on, with strength!" (Judg. 5:9, 20-21, TEV).

Lord, I do not have the talents of Deborah, but all the talents I have, I lay at Your feet. Use me today in any way that You can.

▼

Scripture: Judges 6—9
The Story: Judges 6:11-16, 36-40; 7:9-15

Go in this thy might . . . have not I sent thee?
(Judg. 6:14).

"Surely I Will Be with Thee"

How do we find courage when God asks us to do a hard job? Gideon discovered that confidence can be a growing experience.

In his hometown of Ophrah, he was threshing grain secretly in order to hide from the plundering Midianites. Appearing in human form, the angel talked with him about the plight of his people. But Gideon's circumstances were not conducive to an easy faith. He raised an understandable question: If God is anywhere around, "Why then is all of this befallen us?"

In reply the angel encouraged him, If you will have faith enough to obey my word, God will prove that He is with you. "Go in this thy might, and thou shalt save Israel."

This reassurance should have been enough, but when God answers one objection, weak faith always raises another. From doubting God, Gideon turned to questioning his own ability. "Wherewith shall I save Israel? . . . my family is poor . . . and I am the least in my father's house" (6:15).

97

It is well that God knows how human we are. With patient urging He presses us into the way we ought to go. He answered, You can't do it in your own strength, but "Surely I will be with thee."

This gave Gideon enough faith to muster his army but not enough to send them into battle. When 32,000 men had assembled, he again asked for assurance. A fleece was spread on the ground and Gideon asked the Lord to make it wet with dew while the ground remained dry. It was a strange test, but God is patient with a man who wants to be sure.

Thus encouraged, perhaps Gideon would have made the attack, but God voluntarily offered one last boost to his faith. He said, "If you are fearful, go down to the enemy camp with your servant Phurah." There they heard a soldier tell his dream. A barley loaf came rolling down the hill and flattened their tent. Another fearful soldier interpreted the dream as a sign that the sword of Gideon would destroy Midian.

It was enough. God thus breathed assurance into the soul of His servant. Gideon hurried back to his valiant 300 to order the attack. The venture required faith, and God gave what was needed. He always does.

When we stray too far in depending on our own intelligence and strength, He checks us. It is "not by might, nor by power, but by my spirit, saith the Lord of hosts" (Zech. 4:6). When we fail to act because we are paralyzed by indolence or fear, He says, "Go in this thy might . . . Surely I will be with thee" (Judg. 6:14-16).

Today I want the center of His will. With Haldor Lillenas I pray:

> Lord, I am pleading; hear Thou my prayer.
> Let me Thy blessed fellowship share.
> From day to day Thy servant I'd be.
> Grant me a closer walk with Thee.*

Scripture: Judges 10—12
The Story: Judges 11:29-40
Thou, O God, hast heard my vows (Ps. 61:5).

Zeal Not According to Knowledge

Caroline is the young wife of the pastor where I was holding revival services. At the table one day she said, "Walt and I got sucked in at a Bible conference. We pledged ourselves to read 10 chapters from the Bible every day." Both her words and her tones showed that she regretted making the promise. She had often found it difficult to read her 10 chapters; she felt guilty and condemned when she failed.

Did God require Caroline to keep that promise? Did He want her to feel condemned when urgent responsibilities in the parsonage made keeping her promise difficult?

Such vows are personal transactions between ourselves and God. Only the Holy Spirit can show each of us what is His continuing will for us under our circumstances. From correspondence it is clear that Caroline has at times felt the pressure of conscience to keep the vow she made. But she also testifies that her time with God's Word is usually more rewarding than difficult. Sometimes doing God's will can be both difficult and blessed!

Keeping her promise may be God's will for Caroline. But surely Jephthah's vow and the keeping of it was not the will of our God whom we see revealed in Jesus. Honesty in dealing with God is always good, but it is not the only good. Paul writes of his fellow Jews, "They are deeply devoted to God; but their devotion is not based on true knowledge" (Rom. 10:2, TEV).

If Jephthah knew, he had forgotten that God regards human life more highly than keeping some enthusiastic but unwise promise. God does not want us to be careless in our devotion to Him. But neither does He want us to be bound by vows that deny His love and bring suffering or tragedy to another human being.

Show me, Father, what is Your will for me. Give to me both a full devotion and a wise understanding of who You are and what You want from those who serve You. Then shall I be doing Your will "in earth, as it is in heaven" (Matt. 6:10).

▼

Scripture: Judges 13—16
The Story: Judges 13:2-5, 24-25; 16:4, 15-30

O Lord God, remember me, I pray thee, and strengthen me . . . only this once (Judg. 16:28).

Howbeit

Lost opportunity is the tragedy of every man or woman who fails to follow the Lord fully. Samson was such a man.

Alexander Maclaren has written: "Nobody could be less like the ordinary idea of an Old Testament saint than Samson. . . . He had no moral elevation or religious fervour. He led no army against the Philistines. When he does attack them, it is because he is stung by personal injuries; and it is only with his own arm that he strikes. . . . A strange champion for Jehovah!"

But God sometimes uses strange men in ways that baffle our understanding. Samson's decision to violate the law of Israel and marry a Philistine wife was "of the Lord," because he sought an occasion against the Philistines. We may understand by this, not that God planned a man's disobedience, but only that He permitted it. Even out of Samson's willfulness God found a way to bring some good to Israel.

The man's final failure came from his besetting sin; "he loved a woman in the valley of Sorek." With no true love for Samson, Delilah betrayed him. But it was his own disloyalty to God that cost him his strength, his liberty, his eyes, his leadership among his people, and his sense of God's presence.

Even from this sad story we may learn to be thankful for one thing—the howbeits of God. Verse 22 says, "Howbeit the hair of his head began to grow again." No matter how great our failure, God's mercy is extended to all who will turn again to Him. To the penitent, God's last word is always forgiveness and mercy.

The final scene is tragic, but it was not failure. Samson's death was not suicide in the usual sense. In his last hour he called on God for help; and he was ready to sacrifice himself in order to serve his people.

Maclaren writes: "Nothing in his life became him like the leaving of it. The penitent heroism of its end makes us lenient to the flaws in its course; and we leave Samson to sleep in his grave, recognizing in him, with all his faults and grossness, a true soldier of God, though in a strange garb."

Thank You, Father, for every man whose life You can use even in some small measure. Amen.

*   *   *

Optional Reading

Judges 17—21 tells several dark stories from the history of the tribe of Dan. These strange episodes reflect the anarchy of a land where "there was no king . . . every man did that which was right in his own eyes" (21:25).

▼

☐ **WEEK 9, SATURDAY**   **RUTH**

Scripture: Ruth 1—4
The Story: Ruth 1:1-18

Thy people shall be my people, and thy God my God (Ruth 1:16).

A Decision of Destiny

Why is the story of *Ruth* included among the biographies of Old Testament worthies? She was foreign-born, led no armies, made no prophecies, and was unknown outside the village of Bethlehem. Perhaps her story is given to remind us again that it is not leadership or position or fame that counts in God's records; rather it is love for God and concern for our fellowman.

Ruth was a girl who stood true to God and faithful to her responsibilities in ordinary affairs. She lived in the times of the judges when violence abounded. But even in the midst of turmoil, life must go on. Young people grow up and marry; a living must be made; adjustments must be worked out with our in-laws; death leaves us bereft. In these affairs Ruth excelled. She stands as a shining example of the loyalty and love that make life worthy.

God came to Orpah in the same way that He came to Ruth; yet Orpah is forgotten while Ruth's name is immortal. What makes the difference? A decision.

At the borders of Israel the girls were confronted with a choice. They could go with Naomi or return to their mothers; they could go over to Israel or remain in Moab; they must accept Naomi's God or cling to Chemosh, the god of Moab.

These choices are the hinges of destiny. In the hour of decision Orpah turned back but Ruth pressed on. She seemed to be giving up security for poverty, married happiness for lonely widowhood, a known religion for an untried faith, her own family for strangers. It was a difficult choice but Ruth loved Naomi, and through her she had learned to love Naomi's God.

Ruth's commitment of immortal beauty has been repeated most often at the marriage altar, when the heart seeks to express life's most sacred bond of human affection: "Entreat me not to leave thee, or to return from following after thee: for whither thou goest, I will go; and where thou lodgest, I will lodge: thy people shall be my people, and thy God my God: where thou diest, will I die, and there will I be buried" (1:16-17).

God confronted Ruth, and she responded to His call. For her it was a decision of destiny, the beginning of a new life. It always is—and I thank God for those choices.

▼

First Samuel tells about the life and work of Samuel, Israel's judge and prophet. It also records the story of King Saul and the story of David until the time of Saul's death.

Scripture: 1 Samuel 1—3
The Story: 1 Samuel 1:1-3, 9-11, 17-18; 3:1-10

Train up a child in the way he should go: and when he is old, he will not depart from it (Prov. 22:6).

How Does God Prepare a Leader?

Kagawa, a great Christian leader from Japan, once said. "In my gospel work I was advised to begin with the children and to grow up with them. But I was too impatient and thought the process was too slow. So I went out to preach to harlots and to convicts. Some of them were saved—but they didn't make good judges!"

When God gets ready to prepare a leader He starts with the child's parents. Samuel's father was no genius but he was a good man, devoted to God and concerned for the welfare of his family. He represents many a Christian layman from whose home God calls a preacher of the gospel. His name, Elkanah, means "God has possessed." We read of him, "This man went up out of his city yearly to worship and to sacrifice unto the Lord of hosts in Shiloh" (1:3).

Samuel's mother, like his father, was devoted to God. Even though the women of Israel were not required to do so, Hannah went with Elkanah to Shiloh for sacrifice and worship. As she faced life's disappointments, Hannah took them to God in prayer: "And she was in bitterness of soul, and prayed unto the Lord . . . And she vowed a vow, and said, O Lord of hosts . . . give unto thine handmaid a man child, then I will give him unto the Lord all the days of his life" (1:10-11).

This mother, chosen of God to cradle a prophet, was also a

woman of quiet and radiant faith. When she had made her petition and received her assurance, she "went her way, and did eat, and her countenance was no more sad."

God found parents who would nurture the child, and a priest in Shiloh who would instruct the youth. God also found a child and later a youth who yielded himself to the divine influences. When God spoke, this young man listened and obeyed. From such devotion, and from responses of obedience, God shapes the lives of His followers.

Today, Father, I thank You for the influence of my own Christian parents. Help me to minister to my children as Samuel's parents ministered to him. Thus may "thy kingdom come, thy will be done in earth, as it is in heaven." In our Savior's name. Amen.

▼

Scripture: 1 Samuel 4—7
The Story: 1 Samuel 7:5-6, 10-17
Hitherto hath the Lord helped us (1 Sam. 7:12).

Failure and Forgiveness

God does not bless us when we are careless of our obligations to Him. But if we repent and turn to Him, in mercy He saves us.

The Philistines had conquered Israel, but they were not permitted to think they had defeated Israel's God. The ark was taken to Ashdod. There it was placed in the heathen temple of Dagon. But the next morning the idol had fallen on its face. The second morning the idol had fallen again and was broken. Also the plague broke out among the Philistines.

After seven months of misfortune they loaded the ark on a cart and sent it home to Israel. It was finally located at Kirjath-jearim, the nearest place of importance on the road from Philistia to Shiloh.

For 20 years Israel was so little concerned with God that no one bothered to return the ark to the Tabernacle in Shiloh. But at last they began to seek God.

Samuel sent word of a gathering to be held at Mizpeh. Here the people gave themselves to earnest repentance. With one voice they cried, "We have sinned against the Lord."

Samuel offered a sacrifice "and cried unto the Lord for Israel." But even as that sacrifice was burning, "the Philistines drew near to battle." When men truly seek the Lord, enemies may be permitted to draw near, but they are not allowed to do real harm. The Lord heard Samuel and sent a great storm that broke upon the Philistine army.

So complete was the victory that the Philistines never attacked Israel again during the days of Samuel. In memory of this victory they set up a monument and called it Ebenezer. Samuel knew and Israel knew that it was God who had given the victory. From grateful hearts they shouted, "Hitherto hath the Lord helped us."

Today I join thousands of devoted spirits who have sung:

> *Here I raise my Ebenezer;*
> *Hither by Thy help I'm come;*
> *And I hope, by Thy good pleasure,*
> *Safely to arrive at home.*
> —ROBERT ROBINSON

▼

☐ **WEEK 10, TUESDAY**   **1 SAMUEL**

Scripture: 1 Samuel 8—11
The Story: 1 Samuel 8:4-7, 19-22; 10:25-27;
    11:12-13

Forgive, if ye have ought against any: that your Father also which is in heaven may forgive you (Mark 11:25).

Gracious Under Pressure

What is the right attitude when friends in the church disagree with us and disappoint us? Our story for today includes two men who show us God's answer to that question.

Israel's request for a king was a personal blow to Samuel, as well as a departure from God's best plan for the government of His people. The old prophet sought to dissuade them from their purpose, but the elders were insistent. In prayer, God told Samuel to grant their wishes. He then eased the ache in the aging leader's heart by reminding him, "They have not rejected thee, but they have rejected me, that I should not reign over them" (8:7).

With dignity and grace Samuel bowed to the inevitable. He continued to serve the people the best he could under conditions as they were. The monarchy was not God's first choice for Israel. But He is a God of mercy, and He often offers a second best to those who do not accept His best. Even when God's people make unwise moves, they still need guidance from God's leaders. And always, all of us need to be as helpful as possible under conditions as they exist. Samuel knew that God's servant must not forsake a people whom God is still trying to help.

Our second example is seen in the generous spirit of the new king. When Samuel dismissed the people, Saul went to his own home in Gibeah. Although the people had shouted, "God save the king," there were still dissatisfied factions. They grumbled, "How shall this man save us?"—and offered no support. The new king wisely refrained from attacking his opposition. He was willing to let time prove that he was God's man for that hour.

After the first great military victory, some of Saul's associates were in favor of purging the opposition. But Saul showed a godly spirit when he graciously declared: "No one will be put to death today, for this is the day the Lord rescued Israel" (11:13, TEV).

Thought for today:

"I have often regretted acting too severely, but I have never had occasion to regret being too kind" (John Wesley).

Scripture: 1 Samuel 12—15
The Story: 1 Samuel 13:5-13; 15:17-22

**To obey is better than sacrifice, and to hearken
than the fat of rams** (1 Sam. 15:22).

The Tragedy of Disobedience

In his guidance for devotional Bible reading F. B. Meyer suggests
that we ask, "Is there here any danger for me to avoid?" This is our
clue for today. In our scripture we see the disintegration of a man
who refused the will of God and turned away from the spiritual
influences of his life.

The heartbreaking part of Saul's failure is that it came in spite
of such great opportunities. He began well. God's Spirit was upon
him; he was changed into another man; he had the counsel of
God's prophet, Samuel. Early proofs of God's power had been
given to him in Israel's victory over her foes. But in spite of all
these, Saul failed.

The final collapse of his house did not take place for another
25 years, but the quicksands upon which It stood were apparent as
early as this second year of his reign. At Gilgal Saul showed an
impetuous, self-willed spirit. He took things in his own hands,
showing disregard for God's will. The offense of offering the sacrifice himself instead of waiting for Samuel may seem unimportant
to us. But Saul disobeyed the clear instructions of God; and he
considered that disobedience as not important. God knows if He
cannot depend on a man to obey Him in small things, there is no
assurance of obedience at all. He cannot trust us if we will not obey
Him.

Again in the battle with the Amalekites, Saul disobeyed God's
instructions. Pride kept him from obedience. He had brought
home the conquered king and the cattle to enhance his victory
celebration.

At this point Saul had so little regard for God that he practically renounced the Lord. It was "the Lord thy God" for whose

sacrifice the people had saved the animals. Not really Saul's God—only Samuel's.

To one so disobedient and so unresponsive to God, only condemnation and judgment are of any avail. "Samuel said, . . . Behold, to obey is better than sacrifice, and to hearken than the fat of rams. . . . Because thou hast rejected the word of the Lord, he hath also rejected thee" (15:22-23).

Prayer for today:

Father, save me from the sin of Saul. "For thy name's sake lead me, and guide me" (Ps. 31:3).

▼

Scripture: 1 Samuel 16—19
The Story: 1 Samuel 16:1; 19:9-12; 2 Samuel 5:1-5
Rest in the Lord, and wait patiently for him (Ps. 37:7).

God Can Sometimes Wait

As the Lord works out His plans for my life, have I ever said, Hurry up, God? It is a common temptation; but if we yield, we find only problems and unhappiness. David teaches us the wisdom of God's timing. We must learn to follow the Lord—not push Him.

When King Saul died, Israel seemed to be left without a leader. But God had His man ready. There had been 13 years of gaining experience—and there were yet 7 years of delay before the entire nation was ready to accept God's nominee; but God can wait.

David had his heart turned toward the Lord from his youth. And God had His eye on this lad from Bethlehem. When Jesse and his sons gathered for the feast, the Lord said to Samuel, "Arise, anoint him: for this is he" (16:12).

But men of God must often be patient while they seem to be denied their God-given assignments. Moses was 40 years herding sheep while the Israelites suffered under Pharaoh. David spent unhappy years as a hunted fugitive while Israel languished. Delays chafe the spirits of vigorous men, but they always "work together for good to them that love God, to them who are the called according to his purpose" (Rom. 8:28).

Eventually God's plan was realized: "And they anointed David king over Israel." He was now 37 years of age, and 20 trying years had passed since Samuel had anointed him as a lad in Bethlehem. The delay was difficult, but through it God did something for Israel's great king. In the words of Alexander Maclaren: "It deepened his unconditional dependence upon God. By the alternations of heat and cold, fear and hope, danger and safety, it tempered his soul and made it flexible, tough, and bright as steel. It evolved the qualities of a leader of men, teaching him command and forbearance, promptitude and patience, valor and gentleness."

Israel at long last had a king whose heart was true to God; and God at long last had a king who would lead Israel in the way she ought to go. God's day had come for Israel and for David.

> *Be still, my soul; the Lord is on thy side.*
> *Bear patiently the cross of grief or pain;*
> *Leave to thy God to order and provide.*
> *In ev'ry change He faithful will remain.*
> —KATHARINA VON SCHLEGEL

▼

Scripture: 1 Samuel 20—23
The Story: 1 Samuel 18:3-4; 23:15-18

A friend loveth at all times, and a brother is born for adversity (Prov. 17:17).

Spendthrift of Love

"There is no man so poor that he is not rich if he has a friend; there is no man so rich but he is poor if he has no friend."

Jonathan was a brave warrior, but God would have us remember him as "the greatest friend in the Old Testament." He first met David in the presence of King Saul after David had killed Goliath. In David, the young prince found a courage to admire, a common concern for Israel's welfare, a faith to share, and a friend who called out his utmost love and loyalty. In that hour "the soul of Jonathan was knit with the soul of David" (18:1). In a surge of deep affection, Jonathan stripped himself and gave to David the emblems of his leadership—his armor, his sword, his bow, and his belt.

As David grew in favor with the people, Jonathan knew the truth of his father's savage assertion: "As long as the son of Jesse liveth upon the ground, thou shalt not be established, nor thy kingdom" (20:31). Jonathan knew it, but because he loved God and loved David, he did not resent it.

Insane with jealousy, Saul was later fiercely pursuing David. But the new pressures only strengthened Jonathan's faithfulness to his friend. From Saul's court he made his way to David's wilderness hideout, bringing a message of divine reassurance. They have been called "the most unselfish words ever uttered." "Fear not: for the hand of Saul my father shall not find thee; and thou shalt be king over Israel, and I shall be next unto thee" (23:17).

Jonathan was "a spendthrift of love." He died fighting for a lost cause in loyalty to a power-crazed father. When the news reached David, his anguished heart poured itself out in a sob:

"O Jonathan! by your death I am mortally wounded,
I am distressed for you my brother Jonathan!"
(2 Sam. 1:25, Smith-Goodspeed)

Today I, too, am grateful for a friend. At the most critical point in my ministry he took a week for a hunting trip with me so that he could know his ground when he presented my case to his colleagues.

And since I have no gold to give,
    And love alone must make amends;
My only prayer is, while I live,
    God, make me worthy of my friends.
—AUTHOR UNKNOWN

110

Scripture: 1 Samuel 24—27
The Story: 1 Samuel 26:2-12

The Lord rewards every man for his righteousness and faithfulness (1 Sam. 26:23, NIV).

"A Heart like Thine"

In her daily devotions Caroline had just finished reading 1 Samuel 24—27. She commented: "I don't think David was so great!"

Judged by New Testament standards, his conduct can be faulted. In chapter 25 he set out on a mission of revenge and murder. In 27 he raided innocent peoples, stole their cattle, killed whole families to cover up the raids, and lied to King Achish. How could God say of this man, "I chose David to be over my people Israel" (1 Kings 8:16)?

For the true answer, we must evaluate David—and every man—in the light of his own times, and in view of his commitment to God.

These stories come from David's fugitive days when he fled from an insanely jealous King Saul. He was making a desperate effort just to stay alive until God opened the kingship to him.

When boorish Nabal was unfair and disdainful to him, David started to seek revenge. Other men would have persisted in their evil purpose, but David could be swerved. When confronted by claims of mercy for innocent men, he was moved. God can use any man who will do that.

In chapters 24 and 26 Saul was seeking to kill his own son-in-law. Twice the king was in David's power. Others thanked God for the opportunity and were ready to kill Saul. But because David was God's man he held back. He was willing to trust God's appointments and to wait for God's timing. David was a man after God's own heart.

Even in those days when God's will was not so clear, David knew when he had sinned. But he also knew of God's forgiveness and grace. David could testify: "He hath not dealt with us after our sins; nor rewarded us according to our iniquities. For as the heaven is high above the earth, so great is his mercy toward them that fear him" (Ps. 103:10-11).

Am I a man after God's own heart? Are my attitudes being shaped by His Spirit? When another needs mercy, do I give it? When the Holy Spirit shows me that my intended action will bring regret, do I turn from it? These are the marks of God's man.

Father in heaven:

> *Give me a love that knows no ill;*
> *Give me the grace to do Thy will.*
> *Pardon and cleanse this soul of mine;*
> *Give me a heart like Thine.** *
> —JUDSON W. VAN DEVENTER

*Copyright 1920 by Homer A. Rodeheaver. © Renewed 1948, The Rodeheaver Co. Used by permission.

▼

☐ **WEEK 11, SUNDAY**   **1 SAMUEL**

Scripture: 1 Samuel 28—31
The Story: 1 Samuel 28:4-16; 31:1-5

God is departed from me, and answereth me no more (1 Sam. 28:15).

Disobedience and Death

God is long-suffering. He forgives us when we ask to be forgiven. He helps us to salvage our lives by giving us second bests even when we have rejected His first plans for us. But the time comes in an unrepentant life when God himself must give up on us.

Because of Saul's continuing disobedience God determined to give the kingdom to another (1 Sam. 15:28). Saul had chosen to

112

run his own life and to rule Israel without accepting God's guidance. The king had made his choice, and God could only let him suffer the consequences.

Twenty years slipped by, and Saul continued to fight against God. But now he was again face-to-face with Israel's ancient and deadly enemy. When the king saw the armies of the Philistines he was terrified. He needed God and he knew it. But Saul had forgotten the language of humility and confession. He had rejected God so long that now when he turned toward Him, the Lord answered him not, "neither by prophets nor by dreams" (28:15).

Saul had once abolished witchcraft, but now, in desperation the king turned to the evils which he had earlier condemned. We can never know to what depths we may sink when we deliberately turn from God.

Out of the blackness of despair there came only the echo of God's judgment: "God hath departed from me, and answereth me no more."

Saul went out the next day to fight a battle already lost. Dangerously wounded and unable to escape, he still stubbornly sought to determine the course of his destiny. Thwarted by an armor-bearer who refused to take the king's life, he fell upon his own sword. Saul died as he had lived, self-willed and contending against God.

It is tragic enough to read, "So Saul died," but that is not the end of the tragedy. For there also died "his three sons, and his armor-bearer, and all his men." We cannot sin alone. Our wrong doing always involves others; and those who suffer most are our loved ones. Disobedience is sin—and "the wages of sin is death" (Rom. 6:23).

> Dear Lord and Father of mankind,
> Forgive our foolish ways!
> Reclothe us in our rightful mind;
> In purer lives Thy service find;
> In deeper rev'rence, praise.
> —JOHN GREENLEAF WHITTIER

▼

Second Samuel tells the story of David's 40-year reign as king of Judah and Israel.

Scripture: 2 Samuel 1—4
The Story: 2 Samuel 1:17—2:4*b*

The meek will he guide in judgment: and the meek will he teach his way (Ps. 25:9).

Finding God's Guidance

In a recent theology class we were discussing the work of the minister. Our textbook said that a minister must be prepared to lead his congregation in administrative decisions. Ewe's question was, "How does one know what to do?" It is a question that faces each of us as we seek to know God's will for our lives.

Today we see David at one of life's turning points. King Saul was dead. Israel was without a leader. A dozen years earlier God had spoken through Samuel declaring that David was to be the king of Israel.

But now in an hour of grief one must first work through his sorrow and pay tribute to the dead. From an agonizing spirit David sobs, "Saul and Jonathan were lovely and pleasant in their lives . . . they were swifter than eagles, they were stronger than lions. . . . I am distressed for thee, my brother Jonathan: very pleasant hast thou been unto me: thy love to me was wonderful, passing the love of women" (1:23, 26).

Such deep grief lingers, but life must go on. "After this . . . David inquired of the Lord . . . Shall I go up into any of the cities of Judah?" (2:1).

A decision must be made. But when our lives are dedicated to God we make no important decision without asking, "Lord, what shall I do?"

What answer shall we expect to that kind of inquiry? We believe that God's reply can be just as specific as our questions. David asked, "Shall I go up?" God answered, "Go up." Then David asked, "Whither shall I go?" and God replied, "Unto Hebron."

God's guidance can be clear and specific, but it is normally within the context of our previous experience. David was already acquainted with the people of southern Judah. The people of Hebron knew and loved this young leader. When, in Hebron, David was anointed king of Judah, it was a next step that led him toward God's ultimate plan for his life.

Will God speak as clearly to me? We do not know how God may make His will known to us. We are sure, however, that if we sincerely want to know God's will for our lives, He will not let us down. And so we pray in confidence:

"Shew me thy ways, O Lord; teach me thy paths" (Ps. 25:4).

▼

☐ **WEEK 11, TUESDAY**   **2 SAMUEL**

Scripture: 2 Samuel 5—7
The Story: 2 Samuel 7:18-29

O Lord God, why have you showered your blessings on such an insignificant person as I am? (2 Sam. 7:18, TLB).

When God Says No

No godly man with a sensitive spirit is ever content when he is doing more for himself than he is doing for God. David was disturbed because he lived in a palace while the ark of the covenant was housed in a tent of animal skins. Calling the prophet, the king laid bare his heart; he told Nathan of his desire to build a house of God.

Though David's desire was wholly commendable, and though his purpose came from a heart filled with devotion, the divine answer was no. Sometimes God must thwart our most cherished dreams even when those dreams are meant well for the advancement of His kingdom.

How does He help us to accept His will in these hours of disappointment? David wanted to build a house for God; but instead, Nathan declared, "The Lord telleth thee that he will make thee an house." Nor was David's dream of building a temple to be forgotten. God promised: "I will set up thy seed after thee. . . . He shall build an house for my name."

Though deeply disappointed, King David made his way into the presence of the Lord and prayed the prayer that we have read. His disappointment was turned into glad acceptance even though he could not know all that God was promising to him. And is this not true of every man or woman whose life is wholly given over to God? It is heartening to remember that when we make plans for the good of men and for the kingdom of God, we always do better than we know.

God reminded David that spiritual concerns and influences go beyond our earthly lives. What we do here counts for eternity.

O Master, teach me to live my life in You. Inspire me to deeper concern for the spiritual welfare of my family and my friends. May Your life in me draw others closer to You. Grant that I may live so that when life's sunset comes I may with David turn to You with this song of thanksgiving:

"Who am I, O Lord God? and what is my house, that thou hast brought me hitherto?"

▼

Scripture: 2 Samuel 8—10
The Story: 2 Samuel 9:1-13

Is there anyone . . . to whom I can show loyalty and kindness, as I promised God I would? (2 Sam. 9:3; all quotes from TEV).

The Grace of Gratitude

In a moment of profound spiritual insight Lady Clara Vere deVere wrote:

Kind hearts are more than coronets,
And simple faith than Norman blood.

Today we see a king who was kind. Sometimes we are nice to people because they can do something nice for us. But David was kind to Mephibosheth because he was grateful to God, and because Mephibosheth needed kindness.

At this time David had been king for 20 years. For a little while his mind was free from pressing affairs of war and state. As he reflected on God's goodness to him he recalled a day 25 years earlier when in the field with Jonathan they had exchanged their sacred vows: "God be with you. The Lord will make sure that you and I, and your descendants and mine, will forever keep the sacred promise we have made to each other" (1 Sam. 20:42).

A man of action, David was not content simply to feel good emotions. He wanted to know, Is there something I can do? It is a good piece of advice: When you see someone in trouble, do not ask, Is there something I can do? Rather, think up something—then go and do it.

It was a trembling Mephibosheth who came to Jerusalem. In David's day the custom was for a new king to put to death all the family of his predecessor—all who might have legal claim to the throne. But God's man was breaking a heathen tradition. "Don't be afraid," David replied. "I will be kind to you for the sake of your father Jonathan . . . and you will always be welcome at my table" (9:7).

Undeserved kindness is a mystery to those who do not understand the love of God. Mephibosheth bowed and said, "I am no better than a dead dog, sir! Why should you be so good to me?" (9:8).

David did not answer; he only acted. From that time on "Mephibosheth, who was crippled in both feet, lived in Jerusalem, eating all his meals at the king's table" (9:13).

Have you had a kindness shown?
Pass it on.

'Twas not meant for thee alone.
  Pass it on.
Let it travel down the years.
Let it dry another's tears.
Till in heav'n the deed appears,
  Pass it on.
                    —HENRY BURTON

▼

Scripture: 2 Samuel 11—14
The Story: 2 Samuel 12:7-17

Blessed is he whose transgression is forgiven, whose sin is covered (Ps. 32:1).

Sin and Forgiveness

No man, apart from the power of God, is free in this life from the danger of sin. Even David, after years of devotion, found his life blighted by gross sin when he was past 50 years of age.

When Uriah died the king eased his conscience, saying, These things happen in war—"the sword devoureth one as well as another." But David deceived only himself. Temptation, adultery, fear of exposure, deceit, and murder—this was the tragic course of his sin.

Those dark stains seemed well hidden, but God knew about them—and David could not forget them. When the right time came, "The Lord sent Nathan unto David." With rapierlike thrust, the prophet pointed a finger at the king and said, "Thou art the man."

Other monarchs would have ordered Nathan killed on the spot. But One greater than Nathan had spoken. It was a prophet's word, but the voice was God's. Always sensitive to the divine will, David forgot he was the king; he remembered only that he was a sinful man standing in the presence of God. All the agonizing hours of remorse and inner repentance were concentrated in that one swift moment of confession, "I have sinned against the Lord."

Here was a man weak enough to commit adultery, fearful enough to attempt a lie, desperate enough to commit murder—but repentant enough to confess his sin. The cry of that anguished heart has given words to thousands who have sinned and who seek forgiveness. With David every sinner may plead:

"Have mercy upon me, O God, according to thy lovingkindness: according unto the multitude of thy tender mercies blot out my transgressions. Wash me throughly from mine iniquity, and cleanse me from my sin. For I acknowledge my transgressions: and my sin is ever before me. . . . Purge me with hyssop, and I shall be clean: wash me, and I shall be whiter than snow. . . . Create in me a clean heart, O God; and renew a right spirit within me. Cast me not away from thy presence; and take not thy holy spirit from me. Restore unto me the joy of thy salvation; and uphold me with thy free spirit" (Ps. 51:1-3, 7, 10-12).

▼

☐ **WEEK 11, FRIDAY**   **2 SAMUEL**

Scripture: 2 Samuel 15—17
The Story: 2 Samuel 16:5-13; 19:18-23

Forgive us the wrongs that we have done, as we forgive the wrongs that others have done to us (Matt. 6:12; all quotes from TEV).

Forgiven and Forgiving

In one pungent sentence Jesus tells us how we ought to respond to God's grace of forgiveness. He asks us to forgive in the measure that we have been forgiven.

Ah! That is a high standard. But David was a man ahead of his times. When the king was forced to leave Jerusalem to save his life in Absalom's rebellion, he fled east from Jerusalem across the Jordan. In this hour of humiliation, Shimei seized the opportunity to add insult to the king's injury. As the helpless royal party passed near his town, Shimei reviled them, throwing stones and clods of dirt at the king.

This despicable person was one of Saul's relatives. For years he had nursed jealousy and hatred toward David, but dared not express it. Now that the king seemed down, Shimei was ready to vent his hatred.

The insult was doubly vexing because it was hurled at the king within hearing of all the subordinates who journeyed with him. Abishai, one of the king's bodyguards, begged David, "Let me go over there and cut off his head!" But David had known the grace of God's forgiveness. His heart responded with the spirit of Jesus who teaches us to pray, "Forgive us . . . as we forgive the wrongs that others have done to us."

David's generous spirit is seen again after his victory, when he returned, absolute master in Israel. Shimei came cringing. He knew that ordinarily he would have been marked for death. Indeed, Abishai was ready to kill him on the spot as he knelt fawning before the king.

But David had been forgiven much. Now that Shimei acknowledged, "I have sinned," the king was forgiving as well as forgiven. Great soul that he was, he risked the enmity of his friends to spare the life of his enemy.

From this side of Calvary we remember what God has done, and our forgiven spirits respond:

> *Oh, dearly, dearly has He loved,*
> *And we must love Him, too;*
> *And trust in His redeeming blood,*
> *And try His works to do.*
> —CECIL F. ALEXANDER

Scripture: 2 Samuel 18—21
The Story: 2 Samuel 18:24-33

O my son Absalom, my son, my son Absalom! would God I had died for thee, O Absalom, my son, my son! (2 Sam. 18:33).

A Father's Grief

Emotions run deep when duty conflicts with a father's love. In the tank battles for southern Europe the commanding general sat in his tent, face buried in his hands. When an aide asked if he were ill, he replied: "I have just sent men to their deaths in the battalion that I have ordered to advance."

"But," replied the aide, "that is the daily work of a commander."

"I know," replied the general. "But today my son commands the lead tank."

In today's story David was the king but he was also a father—father of a proud and rebellious son. The king knew what he must do, but the father's heart drew back.

When battle plans were laid and he reviewed the troops as they went into battle, the father-heart spoke its yearning: "For my sake don't harm the young man Absalom." However, because of his rebellion Absalom died, and that tragic news was brought to an anxious father.

When the first runner appeared, the father's mind affirmed what his heart desired, "If he is alone he is bringing good news." Then came the quest for reassurance: "Is the young man Absalom safe?" Ahimaaz could not bring himself to break the news to the king. Only when the second runner came was the father forced to face the truth of his son's untimely death.

With breaking heart he sobbed, "O my son Absalom, my son, my son Absalom! would God I had died for thee, O Absalom, my son, my son!"

Are there not here echoes from the heart of the Eternal? Jesus assures us, "It is not the will of your Father which is in heaven, that one of these . . . should perish" (Matt. 18:14). When a soul is lost there must be in heaven the sob of anguish, My son! My son! My son!

On a gray, granite tombstone in Australia one may read God's epitaph for the lost: "If love could have saved him, he would not have died." We know that

> *. . . the love of God is broader*
> *Than the measure of man's mind;*
> *And the heart of the Eternal*
> *Is most wonderfully kind.*
> —FREDERICK W. FABER

▼

☐ **WEEK 12, SUNDAY** 2 **SAMUEL**

Scripture: 2 Samuel 22—24
The Story: 2 Samuel 22:2-33

You, Lord, are my light; you dispel my darkness (2 Sam. 22:29, TEV).

A Song of Praise

The 22nd chapter of 2 Samuel is the same as the 18th psalm. It was written by David when he remembered how God had helped him through the struggles of life. Verse 1 says, "David sang this song to the Lord." Let us join him in his chorus of praise.

"The Lord is my protector; he is my strong fortress. My God is my protection, and with him I am safe. He protects me like a shield; he defends me and keeps me safe. He is my savior; he protects me and saves me from violence. I call to the Lord, and he saves me from my enemies. Praise the Lord!

"The waves of death were all around me; the waves of destruction rolled over me. The danger of death was around me, and the grave set its trap for me. In my trouble I called to the Lord; I called to my God for help. In his temple he heard my voice; he listened to my cry for help. . . .

"The Lord reached down from above and took hold of me; he pulled me out of the deep waters. . . . He helped me out of danger; he saved me because he was pleased with me. The Lord rewards me because I do what is right; he blesses me because I am innocent. I have obeyed the law of the Lord; I have not turned away from my God. I have observed all his laws; I have not disobeyed his commands. . . .

"O Lord, you are faithful to those who are faithful to you, and completely good to those who are perfect. . . . You, Lord, are my light; you dispel my darkness. . . .

"This God—how perfect are his deeds, how dependable his words! He is like a shield for all who seek his protection. The Lord alone is God; God alone is our defense. This God is my strong refuge; he makes my pathway safe" (22:2-7, 17, 20-23, 26, 29, 31-33, TEV).

Praise for today:

"Surely goodness and mercy shall follow me all the days of my life: and I will dwell in the house of the Lord for ever" (Ps. 23:6).

▼

☐ **WEEK 12, MONDAY**   **1 KINGS**

First Kings continues the story of the Israelite monarchy begun in the Books of Samuel. Here we find (1) the story of Solomon's accession to the throne; (2) the record of his reign and achievements, especially the building of the Temple; (3) the division of the nation into the Northern and Southern kingdoms, and the stories of the kings who ruled those nations until about 850 B.C.

Scripture: 1 Kings 1—4
The Story: 1 Kings 3:5-15

**Give me the wisdom I need to rule your people
with justice and to know the difference between
good and evil** (1 Kings 3:9, TEV).

Prayer That Pleases God

Do my waking thoughts create a climate in which God can make
himself real to me in my dreams?

God came to Solomon in the night hours, but we must believe
the content of his dream came from the young king's wakeful and
serious thoughts concerning the task ahead. The Lord comes to us
when our minds are open to Him. He fulfills our requests when our
deep desires are in accord with His own.

God is pleased with a grateful spirit. Solomon showed gratitude when he gave thanks for a godly father: "Thou hast shewed
unto thy servant David my father great mercy, according as he
walked before thee in truth and righteousness" (3:6).

In verse 7, a young man who might have been proud of his
office, bows before God in a spirit of humility. "O Lord my God,
thou hast made thy servant king instead of David my father: and
I am but a little child: I know not how to go out or to come in." The
Heavenly Father is pleased with this spirit. He "resisteth the proud,
but giveth grace unto the humble" (James 4:6).

Good judgment is more important than great knowledge. The
young king knew it and prayed for this gift of God's Spirit: "Give
me the wisdom I need to rule your people with justice and to know
the difference between good and evil" (3:9, TEV).

We are always in tune with the divine will when we recognize
that the people of God are important to Him and to His plans for
our world. Solomon sets us an example when he prays: "Here I am
among the people you have chosen to be your own" (3:8, TEV).

Gratitude, humility, wisdom to advance God's cause, prosperity for the Kingdom—this is the prayer that pleases God.

*Father, I too need this concern. Let me give Your kingdom tasks
priority. I pray today, "Thy kingdom come. Thy will be done in earth, as
it is in heaven"* (Matt. 6:10).

▼

Scripture: 1 Kings 5—7
The Story: 1 Kings 5:5-6; 6:11-15, 27-30
**I purpose to build an house unto the name of the
Lord my God** (1 Kings 5:5).

Is Anything Too Good for God?

In our Old Testament class, we had just finished this story of build-ing the Temple. Ananda, who came from a culture not saturated with our concept of simple worship, asked:

"Don't you think we build our churches too cheaply and too plainly? Shouldn't we make them the most beautiful buildings in the community so that people will know how great God is?"

I explained that God is more concerned with the spirit of our worship than with elaborate buildings. But the more I thought about his question, the more I was impressed with his desire to give to God the very best. His spirit was like the spirit of David when he prayed: "See now, I dwell in an house of cedar, but the ark of God dwelleth within curtains" (2 Sam. 7:2). In the New Testa-ment, our Lord commended Mary's spirit of prodigal love when she "took . . . a pound of ointment of spikenard, very costly, and anointed the feet of Jesus" (see John 12:3-8).

Nothing is too good for God if it is mine to give. I can hardly give too much of my money when it advances God's work. I cannot give too much time when I keep in mind all the good things God is seeking to get done in the lives of men.

Of course I have personal obligations, and I owe time to my family and friends. But the Christian spirit of "all out for God" seldom works hardships on my creditors or my family. God has ways of making it up to every man or woman who serves His cause with unstinted love.

He says to us as He said to Solomon: "Concerning this house which thou art building, if thou wilt walk in my statutes, and exe-cute my judgments, and keep all my commandments to walk in them; then will I perform my word with thee . . . And I will dwell

among the children of Israel, and will not forsake my people"
(6:12-13).

*Father, give me a spirit of reckless devotion. Save me from the fear
of doing too much for You.*

▼

Scripture: 1 Kings 8
The Story: 1 Kings 8:10-11, 22-23, 27-28, 33,
    36-39, 54-58

**May the Lord our God be with us . . . may he
never leave us or abandon us; may he make us
obedient to him, so that we will always live as he
wants us to live** (1 Kings 8:57-58, TEV).

A Prayer for God's People

With the leaders of the nation gathered in Jerusalem, Solomon
arranged to move the ark of the covenant from its temporary quar-
ters into the most holy place of the new Temple. God was there in
a way that He could be seen.

"As the priests were leaving the Temple, it was suddenly filled
with a cloud shining with the dazzling light of the Lord's presence,
and they could not go back in to perform their duties. . . .

"Then in the presence of the people Solomon went and stood
in front of the altar, where he raised his arms and prayed,

"'Lord God of Israel, there is no god like you in heaven above
or on earth below! You keep your covenant with your people and
show them your love when they live in wholehearted obedience to
you. . . .

"'But can you, O God, really live on earth? Not even all of
heaven is large enough to hold you, so how can this Temple that I
have built be large enough? Lord my God, I am your servant. Listen
to my prayer, and grant the requests I make to you today. . . .

"'When your people . . . have sinned against you, and then when they turn to you . . . humbly praying to you for forgiveness, . . . listen to them in heaven. Forgive the sins of the king and of the people . . . and teach them to do what is right. . . .

"'When there is disease or sickness among them, listen to their prayers. If any of your people . . . out of heartfelt sorrow, stretch out their hands in prayer . . . hear their prayer. Listen to them in your home in heaven, forgive them, and help them.' . . .

"After Solomon had finished praying to the Lord, he stood up in front of the altar . . . In a loud voice he asked God's blessings on all the people assembled there. He said,

"'Praise the Lord who has given his people peace, as he promised he would. He has kept all the generous promises he made'" (TEV).

We can only say a fervent Amen, and echo the king's benediction:

"Blessed be the Lord, that hath given rest unto his people . . . according to all that he promised: there hath not failed one word of all his good promise, which he promised" (8:56).

▼

Scripture: 1 Kings 9—11
The Story: 1 Kings 9:1-7; 11:1-4, 9-10

If thou wilt . . . do according to all that I have commanded thee . . . I will establish the throne of thy kingdom . . . for ever (1 Kings 9:4-5).

Middle Life Malaise

Why do some who are devoted to God in early years grow careless in middle life?

If ever a youth had every spiritual advantage, it was this young man. His father named him Solomon, *The Peaceful;* Nathan called him Jedidiah, *Beloved of the Lord.* He was brought up in the king's palace at Jerusalem and probably tutored by Nathan, the prophet. A godly father gave him this encouraging counsel: "Be strong and of good courage . . . fear not, nor be dismayed: for the Lord God . . . will be with thee; he will not fail thee, nor forsake thee" (1 Chron. 28:20).

How could a young man who started so well in his 20s drift so far in his 40s? Perhaps his story can alert us to our parallel dangers.

Wealth can lull us into self-security and lure us away from the Lord. It was God himself who gave honor and riches to Solomon. But such gifts from God do not relieve us from the responsibility to use those gifts wisely and unselfishly. God's counsel is still sound: "If riches increase, set not your heart upon them" (Ps. 62:10). Wealth hoarded or used for display destroys the soul. That same wealth used to honor God and to bless others enriches the spirit.

Sensuality indulged has destroyed men of God. One of middle life's temptations is the impulse to recover the waning sexual excitement of youth. The story of the king's tragic spiritual failure opens with the words, "But . . . Solomon loved many strange women." Doubtless some were married for political advantage, but others came into Solomon's household as a result of unrestrained passion. A sensual man sought to satisfy a flame of desire aroused by the sight of an attractive and available woman. For more than one man it has been the occasion for disobedience and divorce.

To the end of life it is possible to miss God's way and to stray from Him. If I find myself at that point, is there a road back? Yes. It is in following the path of repentance that first led me to Him:

> *Just as I am, and waiting not*
> *To rid my soul of one dark blot,*
> *To Thee whose blood can cleanse each spot,*
> *O Lamb of God, I come! I come!*
> —CHARLOTTE ELLIOTT

Scripture: 1 Kings 12—15

In chapter 12 we have the story of Jeroboam's rebellion and the beginning of the divided kingdom. From 1 Kings 12:1 to 2 Kings 17:41 the writer records parallel accounts from the histories of Israel and Judah. Israel, founded in 931 B.C., had 19 kings in 210 years; not one of them was faithful to God. This Northern Kingdom disappeared after the fall of Samaria in 721 B.C.

Judah continued 135 years longer. In 345 years she had 20 kings, some of whom worshiped God faithfully. This Southern Kingdom came to an end with the fall of Jerusalem in 586 B.C.

In 14:19 and 29 reference is made to "the book of the chronicles of the kings of Israel" and to "the book of the chronicles of the kings of Judah." These historical documents are referred to repeatedly in the Books of Kings and Chronicles. They were known to, and used by, the biblical writers but have been lost to us.

The Story: 1 Kings 12:25-33; 13:33-34

If you obey me completely . . . I will always be with you (1 Kings 11:38, TEV).

Lessons from History

Can selfishness ruin a life of high promise? It did for Jeroboam. God chose him, made him leader of a nation, and gave him a promise of lifelong support. But God's choices and promises are always premised on obedience.

It is possible for a man who has known God to backslide and to reject God by putting Him in second place. How does it happen?

It begins in self-interest: in using God or the church to bolster one's personal projects. Jeroboam set out to use God instead of to serve Him. "In his every move he schemed to promote the cause of 'Jeroboam the son of Nebat' rather than the cause of God."

Backsliding is often accompanied by evasion and self-deception. When we want the wrong thing badly it is easy to find reasons to call it good. Jeroboam excused his disobedience to God by persuading himself that he was helping the people. Appealing to the desire for an easy religion, he said, "It is too much for you to go up to Jerusalem . . . O Israel" (12:28).

The road downhill is steep. Selfishness and self-deception soon take us further from God. This new king built shrines like those used in Canaanite worship—shrines that God had told Israel to destroy. Jeroboam also ordained priests contrary to God's plan, established a worship day to compete with Israel's Feast of Tabernacles—and in a month of the king's "own choosing." His final act of backsliding was to worship personally at a heathen shrine. It was a deliberate example planned to lead his people into similar sin.

Probably in the beginning Jeroboam never intended to go that far. He only wanted to protect himself. But self-seeking is self-destructive when it puts my wishes ahead of God's known will. The sad climax was the death of Jeroboam's child and the loss of the kingdom that he sought to preserve. Even after God's warnings, "Jeroboam did not change his evil ways. . . . This was the sin of the house of Jeroboam that led to its downfall and to its destruction from the face of the earth" (13:33-34, NIV).

Father, save me from self-seeking.

> *Search me, O God, and know my heart today.*
> *Try me, O Saviour; know my thoughts, I pray.*
> *See if there be some wicked way in me;*
> *Cleanse me from ev'ry sin, and set me free.*
> —J. EDWIN ORR

▼

☐ WEEK 12, SATURDAY   1 KINGS

Scripture: 1 Kings 16—18

In Israel, God's prophets were often as important as the kings in determining the destiny of the people. Thirty-six years after Jeroboam's death, Israel's strong but wicked King Ahab came to the throne. During the 21 years of Ahab's reign it was Elijah who kept alive the awareness of God in the Northern Kingdom. The Elijah accounts in chapters 17—21 include some of the best-loved stories in the Bible.

The Story: 1 Kings 17:1-16

Fear not. . . . for thus saith the Lord God of Israel, the barrel of meal shall not waste (1 Kings 17:13-14).

A Mother Dares to Trust

Has God ever asked me to do something that seemed unreasonable and impossible? When He does, I need to remember this widowed mother in Zarephath.

Elijah's request to be fed first was not what we expect from a man of God; nor was the woman's agreement an easy human response. But on this occasion both of them were under the direct guidance of God. When we are convinced that the Lord is leading us, the only right response is, *Fear not—and do it!*

In this famine God needed someone to care for His servant Elijah. When God's work is in need, He asks His people to help, He sometimes asks us to do what seems unreasonable. It is for these crucial hours that Jesus gives His guideline and His promise for Christian decision: "Seek ye first the kingdom of God, and his righteousness; and all these things shall be added unto you" (Matt. 6:33).

Have you ever felt you just didn't have what it would take to do what God was asking? This mother did: "I swear by the Lord your God that I haven't a single piece of bread in the house. And I have only a handful of flour left and a little cooking oil in the bottom of the jar. I was just gathering a few sticks to cook this last meal, and then my son and I must die of starvation" (17:12, TLB).

The Heavenly Father, however, never says, "Do it," without pledging His resources to back us up. To this desperate mother He declared, "Thus saith the Lord God of Israel, The barrel of meal shall not waste, neither shall the cruse of oil fail, until the day that the Lord sendeth rain upon the earth" (17:14).

Will I dare to trust God's promise? She did. First "she went and did according to the saying of Elijah." Then "she, and he, and her house, did eat many days."

Thank You, Father, for this example of trust, obedience, and blessing. When You challenge me with a difficult task, give me courage to tackle it because You ask me to do it, and because with me You promise to see it through.

▼

Scripture: 1 Kings 19—22
The Story: 1 Kings 19:1-19

The Lord is my shepherd . . . He restoreth my soul (Ps. 23:1, 3).

What Are You Doing Here?

How does God lift us above a burned-out spirit? In Elijah's experience we see the picture clearly painted.

We can expect an emotional low soon after we have been flying high. On Mount Carmel, Elijah stood alone against 450 false prophets. He exulted in God's victory and thrilled at God's power.

But no mortal can fly that high without coming back to earth with a thud. The very next day with Queen Jezebel threatening him, "Elijah was afraid and ran for his life" (NIV)—never stopping until he reached Beersheba, 60 safe miles from Jezebel. Too exhausted to go farther, he collapsed in the shade of a desert bush and prayed:

"God, let me die."

He didn't really mean it. If he had wanted to die he could have stayed in Jezreel where the queen had promised to take care of that little chore! It wasn't an honest prayer; he was discouraged.

But God is still with us even when our courage fails. He often lifts the spirit by restoring the body. He let His prophet sleep before the angel roused him for breakfast. Again, God let him take a nap before lunch. The physical renewal was real, but the scared prophet kept running 40 days longer. He finally reached Mount Sinai and there hid in a cave.

Now he could feel safe, but God can't use us when we are running and hiding. As soon as Elijah was relaxed enough to listen, God asked:

"What are you doing here, Elijah?"

The prophet answered in complaint and fear. "I have been very zealous for the Lord God Almighty. The Israelites have rejected your covenant . . . and put your prophets to death with the sword. I am the only one left, and now they are trying to kill me too" (19:10, NIV).

He was complaining, but he was talking to God again. If we will talk to Him, God helps us to see past our problems to His power. After the wind, the earthquake, and the fire, God spoke to His man in the still small voice:

"Go back the way you came. I have work for you to do." And the man obeyed: "So Elijah went from there and found Elisha."

Father, thank You for Your healing ministry to hurting spirits. Today I testify with David:

"The Lord is my shepherd; I shall not want. He maketh me to lie down in green pastures: he leadeth me beside the still waters. He restoreth my soul" (Ps. 23:1-3).

▼

☐ Week 13, Monday   2 Kings

Second Kings continues the histories of the Northern and Southern kingdoms from where 1 Kings closes. Chapters 1—17 record the parallel stories of the two nations until the fall of Samaria and the disappearance of Israel in 721 B.C. Chapters 2—14 include the stories of Elisha who followed Elijah as the prominent prophet in Israel.

From 18:1 to the end of the book we follow

Judah's history from Hezekiah's reign to the fall of
Jerusalem in 586 B.C.

Scripture: 2 Kings 1—3
The Story: 2 Kings 2:1-15
   In verses 3 and 5, "Take away thy master
from thy head" means "the Lord is going to
take your master from you today" (NIV).

Let a special measure of your spirit be on me (2
Kings 2:9, TBB).

The Double Portion

How can a man be filled with the Spirit of God? Jesus' answer is
clear: "Blessed are they which do hunger and thirst after righteousness: for they shall be filled" (Matt. 5:6). Old Testament experience
is not always a New Testament road map, but there is good guidance for us in Elisha's search for the power of God in his life.

The young prophet's request was not for twice as much of
God's Spirit as Elijah had. Rather, the "double portion" was the
recognized right of all firstborn sons in Israel. God offers His fullness to every born-again child. But how?

1. The first step is to sense my need for resources that flow
from a deeper commitment to God (vv. 1-3). When my heart says,
"I hunger," and my spirit echoes, "I thirst," I am on my way.

2. I must put my whole self into this search for the fullness of
God. Elijah seemed to test the genuineness of the young prophet's
concern. Three times on the journey he suggested, "Stay here"; but
every time Elisha replied, "I will not leave you" (vv. 2-6). When I
earnestly desire the baptism with the Holy Spirit I can claim Jesus'
promise, "Seek, and ye shall find" (Luke 11:9).

3. Elisha's hunger was deepened when he saw God's power
manifested in Elijah (v. 8). As I recall Spirit-filled Christians whom
I have known, my own heart yearns, "Fill me now, fill me now."

4. Elisha knew his need and asked God to supply it: "Let a
special measure of your spirit be on me." Is my need today to be
filled with God's Spirit? Then I must seek Him as definitely as did
the 120 who waited for His coming in the Upper Room. He will

come if we obey Jesus' instructions, "Tarry ye . . . until ye be endued with power from on high" (Luke 24:49).

5. God gives the witness of His presence and the evidence of His power in the lives of those whom He fills. Elisha asserted his faith, used his master's mantle, and the waters divided as they had done for the man of God before him.

Today my heart joins in the yearning of Elisha:

> Let Thy Spirit fall on me;
> Let Thy Spirit fall on me.
> The promised blessing—may it be outpoured.
> Let Thy Spirit fall on me!*
> —FLOYD W. HAWKINS

▼

□ **WEEK 13, TUESDAY**   **2 KINGS**

Scripture: 2 Kings 4—6:23
The Story: 2 Kings 5:1-19

Now I know that there is no God in all the earth, but in Israel (2 Kings 5:15).

Lessons from Naaman

The Bible teaches us what we need to know about God and our relationships to Him.

God is available. The story of Naaman teaches us that a man can serve God in any generation and in whatever circumstances life places him. All that God requires is that we hear His voice and respond to His will.

Our witness can be a blessing. It was so in Syria. A servant girl, perhaps still in her teens, remembered what God had done for her and for her people. Because she had experienced the power of God she had faith to believe that God was the answer to her master's need. She opened the door for a great new lease on life for Naaman

135

in one earnest sentence of witness: "Would God my lord were with the prophet that is in Samaria! for he would recover him of his leprosy" (5:3).

Pride can rob us of God's blessing. A man can stand on the threshold of a miracle and still miss God's help. It almost happened to Naaman. His battle was with personal pride and with the mood to dictate the way that God's blessings were to come. "Naaman wished to be treated like a great man who happened to be a leper. Elisha treated him like a leper who happened to be a great man" (Alexander Maclaren). He who would receive help from God must accept help in the way that God chooses to send it.

Wise counsel may come from humble persons. Under the pressure of anger a man never thinks as clearly as he ought to think. Naaman was in a foolish mood, ready to die from leprosy rather than to humble himself under the hand of God. Fortunately there were friends nearby who helped him come to his senses. His servants counseled him: "If the prophet had told you to do something great, would you not have done it? How much rather, then, when he tells you only to wash and be clean?" (5:13, Moffatt).

> If I am right, Thy grace impart
> Still in the right to stay;
> If I am wrong, oh, teach my heart
> To find the better way!
> —Life's Journey

▼

☐ WEEK 13, WEDNESDAY   2 KINGS

Scripture: 2 Kings 6:24—10:36

In 9:6-10 as elsewhere in these historical books, serious questions arise concerning the moral character of God. How could He direct Jehu to murder all of Ahab's family—even innocent children?

We do not know all of the answers, but we do know that Jesus is God's final revelation of himself. In Jesus we see a God of absolute goodness and love. If the Old Testament does not agree with the New, we accept Jesus' teaching as true and right. In *A Song of Ascents,* Dr. E. Stanley Jones writes: "The Old Testament was God's preparation for Christianity, but it was not Christianity ... The Old Testament is pre-Christian and sub-Christian. Jesus made his own word final, even in Scripture. ... His word was the last word and the final word. I would bring everything to the bar of his person."

The Story: 2 Kings 6:24-30; 7:1-16

We shouldn't be doing this! We have good news, and we shouldn't keep it to ourselves (2 Kings 7:9, TEV).

The Beauty of Goodness

It is Thanksgiving morning as I reflect on this passage. I am moved to thank God for goodness, for conscience, for compassion, and for concern. I am grateful for the spirit of unselfishness, generosity, and gratitude. I am glad that God teaches His people, "Thou shalt love thy neighbour as thyself" (Lev. 19:18). Goodness is beautiful, and I am grateful for it.

I am thankful for the voice of conscience—that gift of God which reminds me when I do wrong, makes me feel bad when I am selfish, and persuades me that I ought to do better.

I am grateful for compassion—the ability to see myself in the misfortunes of my brother man. Compassion is the spirit of concern and helpfulness that Jesus pictured in the story of the Good Samaritan. It was beautiful in His life. I yearn for more of it in mine.

I am glad that goodness is not confined to the comfortable. The four men of our story were desperately ill, socially outcast, caught between starvation and being shot on sight. If ever men had reason to be angry at God and to be set against their fellows, these men did. But from somewhere deep in the human spirit the voice of goodness spoke and moved them to be generous.

I am glad that conscience and compassion can prevail over temptations to do wrong. The first impulse of hungry men is to eat. The first reaction of the destitute is to take for themselves, to hide it from others, and to think only of their own future. But it was in facing these temptations to selfishness that the voice of God and goodness prevailed: "We shouldn't be doing this! We have good news, and we shouldn't keep it to ourselves."

Thank You, God, for the beauty of goodness.

> *How e'er it be, it seems to me*
> *'Tis only noble to be good.*
> *Kind hearts are more than coronets,*
> *And simple faith than Norman blood.*
> *—TENNYSON*

▼

□ WEEK 13, THURSDAY   2 KINGS

Scripture: 2 Kings 11—12

David wrote, "Happy is that people, whose God is the Lord" (Ps. 144:15). Although Judah was often as unfaithful as the Northern Kingdom, she had some righteous kings who turned the people back toward God. In the midst of terrible times, we find in chapters 11—12 a story of these good days. Under the boy-king, Joash, and the regency of the high priest, Jehoiada, Judah experienced nearly 40 years of renewed faithfulness to God.

The Story: 2 Kings 11:1-4, 12, 17-18; 12:1-5

Wilt thou not revive us again: that thy people may rejoice in thee? (Ps. 85:6).

When God Gives Revival

Our church sponsored a recent prayer-life seminar. In one session we looked at 15 hindrances to prayer. Later in a testimony service, Margaret confessed: "All 15 had frustrated my fellowship. Oh, I'm so glad for God's new touch on my life!" She had found revival.

What helped in Margaret's life? What brought revival to Judah? If we can discover and follow those steps we shall find the answer to our heart's deep desire.

Charles Finney writes: "A revival is nothing else than a new

138

beginning of obedience to God." In Judah's revival, two faithful women began it. Jehosheba knew that God wanted Judah's rightful heir on the throne. At the risk of her life she hid the baby prince, Joash. Then for six years an unnamed but faithful nurse cared for him in hiding.

As with these women, some revival obedience is personal and secret, but some involves public initiative. Jehoiada knew what was needed to advance God's purposes among His people. The priest laid careful plans and courageously recruited others. Again, unnamed persons, the captains and Temple workers, helped bring revival by loyalty to God and by following their spiritual leader.

Every revival of religion involves renewed commitments to God. "And Jehoiada made a covenant between the Lord and the king and the people, that they should be the Lord's people" (11:17).

Revival always means tearing down the idols that have kept us from God's full will for our lives. In Judah, "All the people of the land . . . smashed the altars and idols to pieces." In our family, teenage Chuck broke and burned his records and tapes of unchristlike music.

Revival also brings renewal of our gifts to God, and renewed concern for public worship. King Joash commanded: "Collect all the money . . . received from personal vows and the money brought voluntarily . . . let it be used to repair whatever damage is found in the temple" (12:4-5, NIV)

Father, "Wilt thou not revive us again: that thy people may rejoice in thee?" I pray today for revival—and begin it in me.

▼

☐ **WEEK 13, FRIDAY**   **2 KINGS**

Scripture: 2 Kings 13—17
The Story: 2 Kings 13:14-20

Righteousness exalteth a nation: but sin is a reproach to any people (Prov. 14:34).

Optional Reading

Chapters 13—17 include some of the more difficult reading in the Bible. In six pages the author scans alternately nearly 100 years of the history of two nations. He sketches in encyclopedia style the reigns of nine kings of Israel and four rulers of Judah.

The names are strange, and the language for each sketch is similar. Unless I am paying close attention, I don't know whether I am reading about a king of Israel or of Judah. If my mind wanders for a moment, when I come back to the page I can't tell where I stopped reading. If you struggle with these chapters, you have lots of company! So, unless you are a teacher of Bible history, don't let it worry you.

In these difficult chapters, however, there are some items of high interest. In 13:14-20 we read the story of Elisha's death. In 14:25 we learn that Jonah was a prophet from Gath Hepher in northern Israel. Without this note we would not know Jonah's origin or nationality.

Chapter 17 is important history because it describes the fall of Samaria in 721 B.C., signaling the end of the Northern Kingdom. During the 209 years of Israel's history not one godly king sat on the throne. Under such leaders, the author describes the sad course of the nation: "They worshiped worthless idols and became worthless themselves . . . The Lord was angry with the Israelites and banished them from his sight, leaving only the kingdom of Judah" (17:15, 18, TEV).

Oliver Goldsmith might well have been writing Israel's epitaph in *The Deserted Village:*

> *Ill fares the land, to hastening ills a prey,*
> *Where wealth accumulates, and men decay.*

We must never forget it: "Righteousness exalteth a nation: but sin is a reproach to any people" (Prov. 14:34).

▼

Scripture: 2 Kings 18—19

In 19:2, 20, we read of "Isaiah the prophet." Isaiah's ministry covered about 40 years, from 740 to 700 B.C. He was familiar with the reigns of Judah's kings Amaziah (Uzziah), Jotham, Ahaz, Hezekiah, and Manasseh—recorded in chapters 14—21. Under Hezekiah he was a revered court counselor in Jerusalem. Tradition says Isaiah was killed by being sawed asunder (see Heb. 11:37) by order of the evil King Manasseh.

The Story: 2 Kings 18:1-6; 19:14-19

He did that which was right in the sight of the Lord ... He trusted in the Lord God of Israel (2 Kings 18:3, 5).

Gratitude for Godly Leaders

I was glad when President-elect Eisenhower, in his inaugural address, said to the nation, "I would like to offer a little prayer of my own." I felt good when Jimmy Carter openly acknowledged his Christian faith and identified himself closely with the church during his presidency. I rejoice in every sincere man of God who comes to a place of public leadership.

Because "he trusted in the Lord God of Israel," King Hezekiah brought 30 years of honor and prosperity to Judah. A godly man in a place of political power can do much to suppress outbroken evil and to discourage flagrant immorality. It is always good for a community when unrighteousness is curbed and when low morals feel the pressure of negative public opinion. I thank God and support those who throw their weight against wrongdoing.

We are hero worshipers. It is therefore good when any popular hero is a man of integrity and a servant of God. We may be grateful for every idolized public figure who casts his influence for good.

God alone knows when one man's faith may determine the destiny of a nation. In the face of a foreign invasion, Hezekiah went to prayer. Today, as we wrestle with the issues of increased military defense versus disarmament, I would feel safer if I knew that those who make the decisions were praying, "Now, O Lord our God, deliver us . . . so that all kingdoms on earth may know that you alone, O Lord, are God" (19:19, NIV). I pray for our leaders as they honestly seek the best way for all of us.

Even godly men are still human; they will make mistakes. In 20:12-18, Hezekiah made a wrong decision that brought suffering to his people. But even in their errors, our leaders need the support of God's people.

Prayer for today:

Father, today I follow the admonition of Your Word to pray for "all that are in authority." I give thanks for my country. Give us, I pray, leaders of wisdom, honor, courage, and faith. In our problem-filled world, show them how to lead our nation for the good of all our people. Give them courage to assign us some difficult tasks to help make life better for the needy in our land—and for those beyond our borders.

Make me a strong supporter of every move that is prompted by compassion or that calls for courage. May Thy kingdom come and Thy will be done in all the earth as it is done in heaven. Through Christ our Lord. Amen.

▼

☐ **WEEK 14, SUNDAY**   **2 KINGS**

Scripture: 2 Kings 20—21
The Story: 2 Kings 20:1-6, 21; 21:1-6, 19—22:2

I have heard your prayer, and seen your tears; I will heal you (2 Kings 20:5, NIV).

Father, Teach Me What to Ask

As I read chapters 20—21, my prayer life is improved. I am deeply persuaded never to ask God for healing, or for any other gift, without honestly adding Jesus' ultimate request, "Thy will be done."

If Hezekiah had known in chapter 20 what would happen in chapter 21, would he have asked God to extend his life?

Manasseh was Judah's most wicked king. For most of his 55 years he undid and destroyed every good thing that his father had struggled to build. If God had not given Hezekiah what he pled for in chapter 20, Manasseh would never have been Judah's king. He was only 12 years old when he began to reign—so he was born during the 15 years of extended life that God gave to Hezekiah.

And the wisdom of divine providence is seen again in 21:19—22:2. We would not condone murder to try to prevent evil. But as we look back, was not the early death of King Amon a blessing to God's cause? He was Manasseh's son, and during his two years as Judah's king he walked in the evil ways of his father. Had he lived longer, how much would he have corrupted his young son, Josiah?

Amon's death permitted Josiah's mother to mold Judah's boy-king into a man after God's own heart. Her name, Jedidah, means "Beloved"; her father's name, Adaiah, meant "Jehovah has adorned"; she named her son Josiah, "Jehovah supports him."

O God, I am not wise enough to know what to ask. Guide me in my petitions. When I ask wrongly, in love and mercy deny my requests. Give me only what You know is best for Your kingdom—because that will be best for me also. In Jesus' name I ask it. Amen.

◆

Scripture: 2 Kings 22—23
The Story: 2 Kings 22:3-13; 23:1-3

Thy word is a lamp unto my feet, and a light unto my path (Ps. 119:105).

Thank God for the Bible

Rediscovery of Bible truth brought revival to Judah; it gave to us the Protestant Reformation. Bible truth brings light to every man who will open himself to it. With William How we sing:

We praise Thee for the radiance
That from the hallowed page,
A Lantern to our footsteps,
Shines on from age to age.

Like the sun, the Bible radiates light for all men. But like the sun, it gives light only to those who have eyes to see. How shall I come to the Scripture in order to find light for my way? Josiah gives me some clues.

A recent book is titled *I Would Like to Know God.* It is this openness to the divine will that we see in Josiah. He was repairing God's house, and thus already doing what he understood to be "right in the sight of the Lord" (22:2). An intense desire to know God's will opens my mind to the truth of His Word.

Anselm, a Christian teacher of the Middle Ages, reminds us of another basic guide to discovery of God's truth. He writes: "I believe in order that I may know." Josiah accepted the book of the law (probably our Book of Deuteronomy) as the Word of God. The Lord then promised good to the king, because "your heart was responsive and you humbled yourself before the Lord when you heard what I have spoken" (22:19, NIV). It is this attitude of acceptance that makes Scripture the Authority for my life.

But God's Word is not primarily truth to know—it is truth to be obeyed. Josiah acted. He "made a covenant before the Lord . . . to keep his commandments and . . . to perform the words . . . that were written in this book" (23:3).

Father, I thank You for Your Word. As I read it, give me a teachable mind. Enable me to receive its truths not as the words of men, but as the very Word of God. Keep me ready to read, open to understand, and quick to obey. Then I shall know the joy of walking with You.

*   *   *

Important History

Chapters 24—25 tell the sad story of Judah's last years under three weak and wicked kings. Babylon was the dominant power in the Near East, and all lesser states were tributaries to her. These were the last years of Jeremiah's prophecies. We read a parallel account in Jer. 52:1-34. A thumbnail sketch with approximate dates may help fix the important facts.

144

598 B.C.—King Jehoiakim revolted against Babylon; he died the same year.

597—Nebuchadnezzar's Babylonian (Chaldean) army marched against Jerusalem, forcing 18-year-old King Jehoiakin to surrender. The Babylonians took 10,000 captives and much of Judah's treasure. Zedekiah was placed on the throne as a puppet king.

589—Against the counsel of Jeremiah (Jer. 27:12-13), Zedekiah revolted, and Nebuchadnezzar launched an all-out campaign to destroy Judah.

586—After a siege of 18 months, Zedekiah and Judah's army escaped from Jerusalem, but the army was scattered and Zedekiah was captured, blinded, and taken to Babylon.

586—One month later, Nebuchadnezzar's army returned to destroy the Temple and the city. All but the poorest people were exiled. Jeremiah was permitted to remain in Judah (Jer. 40:1-6).

586—Gedaliah was appointed governor to represent the king of Babylon in control of the land.

585—Gedaliah was murdered by Ishmael, who then fled to Egypt, forcing Jeremiah to go with him, along with the remnant who had been left in Judah.

It was the end of national life for that period.

The historian writes: "So Judah went into captivity, away from her land" (2 Kings 25:21, NIV).

▼

☐ **WEEK 14, TUESDAY**   **1 CHRONICLES**

The name *Chronicles* means narrative, or history. In these books we have the story of God's people from the time of Samuel to the fall of Jerusalem and the exile to Babylon.

The Chronicles were probably written by Ezra after the Jews returned from the Babylonian exile.

But Chronicles is more than history—it is history with a purpose. (1) The author reminds us that God was keeping His promises to His people in spite of the disasters that had fallen upon them. (2) Chronicles bids us remember the place of worship in our service for God.

First and Second Chronicles largely retell the events of the Books of Samuel and Kings. We shall therefore look at events and truths that could not be included during our meditations of the past month.

Scripture: 1 Chronicles 1—5

My niece, Virginia, is an avid student of our family history. If, like her, you are interested in your relatives' roots and keep records of your family tree, you will revel in these early chapters of Chronicles. Read the first five chapters verse by verse to discover how many names have some meaning for you. It will be an enjoyable half hour.

However, you may be like me. The Beatitudes of Matthew are great—but the begatitudes of Chronicles are a pain! If so, read only the following 19 verses: 1:1-4, 34; 2:1-2, 11-15; 3:10-16. Check as many names as you recognize from Bible history.

The Story: 1 Chronicles 5:1-2; 4:9-10; 5:23-26, 18-22 (Read in this order)

Oh that thou wouldest bless me indeed . . . and that thou wouldest keep me from evil . . . ! (1 Chron. 4:10).

God and His People

There is more to Chronicles than lists of names. Tucked away in these endless genealogies you will discover truths as exciting as finding a nugget of gold in a jillion grains of sand.

In 5:1-2 is the sad story of a favored child. Reuben, firstborn son of Jacob, would have inherited honor and wealth. But sin robbed him of his happiness and his inheritance.

In 4:9-10 the chronicler gives us a glad contrast. Jabez was

146

born under such hard circumstances that his mother named him *Pain.* But his spirit was drawn to God, and in the prayer of our text, he reached out for divine help: "Oh that thou wouldest bless me indeed . . . and that thou wouldest keep me from evil." The Bible, even in bone-dry Chronicles, brings to us this message of hope: "God granted his request."

What is true for individuals is true also of communities. God's face is set against us when we do wrong: "The people of . . . Manasseh were numerous . . . They were brave warriors . . . But they were unfaithful to the God of their fathers . . . So . . . God . . . stirred up the spirit of Pul king of Assyria . . . who took . . . Manasseh into exile" (5:23-26, NIV).

But God also blesses and helps groups who follow Him. In an earlier, happier time we read of this same tribe: "They were helped in fighting . . . and God handed the Hagrites and all their allies over to them, because they cried out to him during the battle. He answered their prayers, because they trusted in him" (5:20, NIV).

Thank You, Father, for these life-building object lessons from Chronicles:

"The way of the ungodly shall perish" but *"The Lord knoweth the way of the righteous"* (Ps. 1:6).

▼

□ **WEEK 14, WEDNESDAY**   **1 CHRONICLES**

Scripture: 1 Chronicles 6—9
The Story: 1 Chronicles 9:1-3, 20-34

These are the men David put in charge of the music in the house of the Lord (1 Chron. 6:31, NIV).

To All Who Help Us Worship

Chronicles was compiled 600 years after David appointed musicians to lead Israel's worship (6:31-47), and 1,000 years after Aaron and his sons were designated by God to serve as priests for His people (6:49).

About 400 B.C. Ezra led the Jewish exiles back from Babylon to Jerusalem. There, in order to reestablish the community, he had to build on God's earlier guidance, so he compiled the record of Israel's heritage. This sacred history was to provide dependable guidelines for a new government under God.

Chronicles is thus a book of history, but in these early chapters there is little about battles and victories. There is much about the worship of God and social organization. On these ancient foundations God would rebuild His nation.

For their religious music, the Jews looked with gratitude to Heman, Asaph, and Ethan as we look to Charles Wesley, Fanny Crosby, and Haldor Lillenas. The early musicians from the tribe of Levi were specially chosen to serve the people—and their ministry was music. Examine the titles to Psalms 50 and 73—83. Who gave these songs to Israel? Psalm 88 is credited to Heman, and Psalm 89 to Ethan. Korah (6:37) must have passed along his gift of music to his children: Psalms 44—49; 84—85; and 87—88 were written by "the sons of Korah."

There were also other less prominent ministries necessary to the worship in the congregation of Israel. Some were "gate-keepers," and others "in charge of articles used in the temple service." Still others cared for "the furnishings and all the other articles of the sanctuary." When I read today about those who cared for the "wine and oil" and for "baking the offering bread," I recalled with love the Allens and Golitkos, who prepared the elements for our Communion service last Sunday.

For all who minister to public worship, I give my heartfelt thanks and support. They are Your servants, O God; and they are my ministers when I come to Your house of prayer. With them I join in Your praise:

> *O God, our Help in ages past,*
> *Our Hope for years to come,*
> *Be Thou our Guide while life shall last,*
> *And our eternal Home.*
> —ISAAC WATTS

Scripture: 1 Chronicles 10—12

The Story: 1 Chronicles 10:13—11:9

We are yours, O David! We are with you, O son of Jesse! Success . . . to you . . . for your God will help you (1 Chron. 12:18, NIV).

A Nation's Leader—Under God

One example is worth 1,000 words. Six hundred years after David's reign, Ezra recalled this great and godly leader as a model to rally his people for the rebuilding of Judah.

The Chronicles story is condensed (see 2 Samuel 2—5 for the full account). After Saul's death, the leaders of Judah came to David and made him king over their people. Between 11:2 and 11:3 is a lapse of seven years. At the end of that time "all the elders of Israel," leaders of the northern tribes, came to Hebron and anointed David king over all Israel.

In earlier years under Joshua, Jerusalem had been surrounded but never fully conquered. The original inhabitants still controlled this strategic height at the center of the Promised Land. With a shrewd challenge to aspiring leaders, David inspired his men: "Whoever leads the attack on the Jebusites will become the commander-in-chief" (NIV). His valiant nephew, Joab, responded; they took the city and established a national capital.

By all human standards the son of Jesse was a skillful leader of men. But those talents were exercised under God. "David knew that the Lord had established him as king over Israel and had exalted his kingdom for the sake of his people Israel" (2 Sam. 5:12, NIV).

Here was a leader who sought the guidance of God in his military ventures—and won victories. He also followed the rules of righteousness in civil administration: "I look out for the faithful in the land, to have them at my court; men of integrity shall be my ministers. . . . I will be active . . . to root out every evildoer from the Eternal's city" (Ps. 101:6-8, Moffatt).

Ezra gives the verdict of history: "David became more and more powerful, because the Lord Almighty was with him" (NIV).

Is it any wonder that this man won the love of his people? Is it any wonder that his men shouted their loyalty: "We are yours, O David! We are with you . . . for your God will help you"?

Praise for today:

Lord, I thank You for leaders who know and follow You. Bless every man in high office who seeks to serve You in his place of responsibility. I ask it in the name of Jesus. Amen.

▼

Scripture: 1 Chronicles 13—16

In 13:9-10, why was God's judgment against Uzzah so serious?

David and his followers had forgotten God's divinely appointed means for transporting the ark (by carrying-poles resting on the shoulders of four Levites, Exod. 25:10-14). They had carelessly imitated the heathen Philistines, setting the ark on a bullock cart. Uzzah also forgot God's instructions not to touch this symbol of His holy presence. It was a natural thing to do, but therein lay the sin of his act. We may not treat the worship of God just as we deal with other concerns. The things of God are sacred. They are holy.

The Story: 1 Chronicles 13:1-14

Look to the Lord . . . seek his face always (1 Chron. 16:11; all quotes from NIV).

Seeking God's Guidance

When I wrote to Mark, in his second year at college, I closed with a word of counsel: "Above all, Mark, when you face important decisions, find a quiet place and ask, 'Lord, what do You want me to do?'" There is no surer path to right decisions and to a fulfilled life.

It was this deep desire to know and do the will of God that made David Israel's greatest leader. When the enemy threatened national security, "David inquired of God: 'Shall I go and attack the Philistines? Will you hand them over to me?'" (14:10).

Now, in the effort to enhance the spiritual life of his people, the king wrote, "If it seems good to you and if it is the will of the Lord our God . . . Let us bring the ark of our God back to us, for we did not inquire of it during the reign of Saul" (13:2-3).

Following the will of God always involves some risk. We do not know everything, and we are not given perfect judgment. We shall sometimes make mistakes. But it is better to err in trying to obey God than to sin through fear and failure to follow Him. When Uzzah touched the ark and died, "David was afraid of God that day and asked, 'How can I ever bring the ark of God to me?'" (13.12).

Fear and temporary failure may give us pause, but they must not frustrate our obedience. Those three months while the ark remained at the house of Obed-Edom helped David see what his failure had been. Also God's blessing upon the family of Obed-Edom encouraged the king to try again.

Persistence in carrying out God's plans for us always brings His promised blessings to us: "They brought the ark of God and set it inside the tent that David had pitched for it . . . That day David first [sang] this psalm of thanks to the Lord: . . . 'Sing to him, sing praise to him; tell of all his wonderful acts. Glory in his holy name; let the hearts of those who seek the Lord rejoice'" (16:1, 7-10).

At this point, read aloud to your family group—or for yourself if worshiping alone—David's prayer of praise, 1 Chron. 16:8-36. This passage quotes Pss. 105:1-15; 96:1-13; 106:1, 47-48.

▼

☐ WEEK 14, SATURDAY   1 CHRONICLES

Scripture: 1 Chronicles 17; 22; 28—29 (David's
  hopes and plans for the Temple)
The Story: 1 Chronicles 17:1-27

There is no one like you, O Lord, and there is no God but you (1 Chron. 17:20, NIV).

God's Promise and My Prayer

God's promises and David's prayer of thanksgiving were very personal experiences—but they have universal meaning. In the face of life's greatest disappointments we, too, find healing for our hurts, and place our hope in God's promises for the future. The details of our stories are different, but God's ministry is the same. Today we may join David in his prayer of praise and love as we come to sit before the Lord.

"Who am I, O Lord God, and what is my family, that you have brought me this far? And as if this were not enough in your sight, O God, you have spoken about the future of the house of your servant." I believe what You said to David, "The mercy of the Lord is from everlasting to everlasting upon them that fear him, and his righteousness unto children's children" (Ps. 103:17). I accept that promise. "What more can [I] say to you for honoring your servant? For you know your servant, O Lord. For the sake of your servant and according to your will, you have . . . made known all these great promises.

"There is no one like you, O Lord, and there is no God but you. And who is like your people—whose God went out to redeem a people for himself, and to make a name for yourself, and to perform great and awesome wonders before your people, whom you redeemed? You made your people your very own forever, and you, O Lord, have become our God.

"And now, Lord, let the promise you have made concerning your servant and his children's children be established forever. Do as you promised, so that it will be established and that your name will be honored. Then men will say, 'The Lord Almighty is God!' And the house of your servant will be established before you.

"You, my God, have revealed to your servant that you will build a house for him. So your servant has found courage to pray to you. Lord, you are God! You have given this good promise to your servant.

"Now you have been pleased to bless the house of your servant, that it may continue in your sight; for you, O Lord, have blessed it, and it will be blessed forever" (1 Chron. 17:16-27, NIV, adapted).

▼

Scripture: 1 Chronicles 18—21 (Military victories; spiritual defeat)
The Story: 1 Chronicles 21:1-26

I have sinned greatly . . . I beg you, take away the guilt of your servant (1 Chron. 21:8; all quotes from NIV).

Steps to Restoration

What shall I do when I discover that I have displeased God?

In this vignette from the life of David, God gives clear answers. First, we need to understand the *elements of disobedience:* (1) "Satan . . . incited David"—we are never exempt from his plans to defeat us. (2) The sin of self-dependence—"that I may know how they are." (3) Stubborn persistence in wrong—"The king's word overruled Joab." When any of these forces gets the upper hand in our lives, the result is "evil in the sight of God."

After recognizing our failure, what is the road back?

Confess, and ask forgiveness—"I have sinned greatly by doing this. Now, I beg you, take away the guilt of your servant. I have done a very foolish thing" (v. 8).

Cast ourselves upon the mercy of God—"Let me fall into the hands of the Lord, for his mercy is very great; but do not let me fall into the hands of men" (v. 13).

Accept full responsibility; don't make excuses—"Was it not I who ordered the fighting men to be counted? I am the one who has sinned and done wrong" (v. 17).

Intercession for persons whom our failure has injured—"These

153

are [innocent]. What have they done? O Lord my God, let your hand fall upon me and my family, but do not let this plague remain on your people" (v. 17).

Obey what God shows us to do—"So David went up in obedience to the word that Gad had spoken in the name of the Lord" (v. 19).

Make things right—"I insist on paying the full price. I will not . . . sacrifice a burnt offering that costs me nothing" (v. 24).

Draw close to the Lord—"David built an altar . . . and sacrificed burnt offerings and fellowship offerings. He called on the Lord" (v. 26).

When God's repentant man has taken these steps, the Lord will "answer him with fire from heaven."

Today my restored spirit sings with H. H. Heimar:

> *Oh, the joy of sins forgiv'n!*
> *Oh, the bliss the Blood-washed know!*
> *Oh, the peace akin to heav'n,*
> *Where the healing waters flow!*

*　　*　　*

Optional Reading: 1 Chronicles 22—27

These six chapters have historical rather than devotional value. During the closing days of David's life he called a national convocation to affirm Israel's governmental organization, and to arrange for transfer of leadership from himself to his son Solomon.

David had become king of a scattered and unorganized people. After 40 years of leadership he would leave them greatly enlarged, and well organized in religious life, military power, and civil government. Six hundred years later, as Ezra sought to rebuild the nation, he wanted his people to be aware of this structure.

Chapters 23:1—26:19 describe plans for the religious life of the nation. In 23:25-26 David had pointed out that a large part of Levi's original assignment, carrying the Tabernacle and its furnishings during the wilderness wandering, was no longer relevant. But he knew the worship of a people, then as now, needs skilled and full-time ministers.

Chapter 24 outlines the assignment of Aaron's descendants to prepare the sacrifices offered in worship, and to care for the Tabernacle itself. These Levites were organized into 24 groups; each group served one week at a time, approximately twice a year. This plan still prevailed in Jesus' day when Zechariah, father of John the Baptist, was visited by an angel while on his tour of priestly duty in the Temple (Luke 1:5-23).

Chapter 25 is another account (see chap. 6) of David's plan for trained musicians in Israel's worship. The *gatekeepers* (chap. 26) were guards for the Tabernacle, and later for the Temple. It was the Temple guards, called *soldiers*, who later came with Judas to arrest Jesus in Gethsemane (Luke 22:52). Still other Levites were assigned as *treasurers* responsible for the care of monies and materials that David and the people had given for building the Temple.

Chapter 27 describes Israel's military organization—12 armies of 24,000 men; each army serving one month of the year. Chapter 27 also lists the civil administrators, leaders of each tribe, comparable to state governors. Finally, 27:25-34 records the administrators personally responsible to the king—perhaps comparable to the president's cabinet.

▼

☐ **WEEK 15, MONDAY**   **2 CHRONICLES**

Scripture: 2 Chronicles 1—3
The Story: 2 Chronicles 2:1-16

Praise be to the Lord . . . who made heaven and earth! (2 Chron. 2:12; all quotes from NIV).

Cultivating Friends for God

Yesterday I rode along with a superintendent who was preaching for a nearby congregation. En route we discussed the work of a fellow minister. My friend said, "Some folk can help us more in a marginal ministry than if they had a regular assignment." It set me to thinking.

How do we solicit assistance from friends who are not members of the church? Perhaps the wisdom of Solomon can help us, as reflected in his approach to his neighbor, King Hiram.

Go to persons who are in a position to help, and let them know the need. Solomon sent this message to the king of Tyre, his neighbor to the north: "Send me cedar logs as you did for my father David."

Let them know how important you feel the project is. "I am about to build a temple for the Name of the Lord my God and dedicate it to him. . . . The temple I am going to build will be great, because our God is greater than all other gods."

Enlist cooperation. Solomon was specific in naming his needs: "Send me . . . a man skilled to work in gold and silver. . . . Send me also cedar, pine and algum logs from Lebanon."

Compliment their competence. Solomon was wise enough to know that an honest compliment is one way to win friends and influence people: "I know that your men are skilled in cutting timber there. My men will work with yours."

Be fair in offering remuneration. "I will give your servants, the woodsmen who cut the timber . . . wheat . . . barley . . . wine and . . . olive oil."

Solomon's five-point approach won cooperation from the king and secured the help needed to build the house of God.

Was the experience a convincing witness to this neighbor? We do not know how deeply Hiram felt the impact. But we would be grateful for an unsaved neighbor who, from a business contact with us, was moved to testify, as did King Hiram, "Praise be to the Lord, the God . . . who made heaven and earth."

Lord, teach me to cultivate friends for You.

▼

☐ **WEEK 15, TUESDAY**   **2 CHRONICLES**

Scripture: 2 Chronicles 4—7
The Story: 2 Chronicles 5:1-14

There, above the cover between the two cherubim that are over the ark of the Testimony, I will

meet with you and give you all my commands (Exod. 25:22; all quotes from NIV).

The Presence of God

The most sacred room in the Tabernacle and in the Temple was the holy of holies. The heart of the room was the ark of the covenant, with its cover known as the mercy seat. That room was called the most holy place, because there God promised to meet with His people. He made this clear to Moses in our text:

"There, above the cover between the two cherubim that are over the ark of the Testimony, I will meet with you and give you all my commands."

We know, as Solomon knew, that God is not confined to one room or to one location. But we also know that God meets with us when we set aside a time and a place to come into His presence. That is why, in our Sunday morning service, the pastor invites us to an open altar during the pastoral prayer. His invitation is: "I am going to the mercy seat, and I invite you to join me there."

Coming reverently into the presence of God, confessing our love for Him, telling Him of our needs, listening to His response and guidance—this is the heart of all genuine Christian experience of God.

We join in Solomon's prayer: "Now, my God, may your eyes be open and your ears attentive to the prayers offered in this place. Now arise, O Lord God, and come to your resting place, you and the ark of your might. . . . May your saints rejoice in your goodness" (6:40-41).

We worship in the glow of God's reassuring answer:

"If my people, who are called by my name, will humble themselves and pray and seek my face and turn from their wicked ways, then will I hear from heaven and will forgive their sin and heal their land. Now my eyes will be open and my ears attentive to the prayers offered in this place" (7:14-15).

Scripture: 2 Chronicles 8—12

At this point one unique feature of Chronicles becomes apparent. There is only a brief reference to the division of the kingdom (10:1—11:17); and there is no history of the Northern Kingdom, as recorded in 1 Kings 12—2 Kings 17. The writer of Chronicles is concerned only with the history of Judah, the remnant of God's chosen people through whom the nation would be continued after the Babylonian Exile.

The Story: 2 Chronicles 10:1-19

A gentle answer turns away wrath, but a harsh word stirs up anger (Prov. 15:1; all quotes from NIV.)

Be Considerate

Solomon knew the truth of our text. He knew it well enough to write the proverb, but he failed to teach it to his son.

How different might the history of Israel have been if only Rehoboam had been considerate! His wise counselors faithfully advised him: "If you will be kind to these people and please them and give them a favorable answer, they will always be your servants" (10:7).

But Rehoboam rejected that counsel. In self-centered pride the king refused to listen to the deeply felt concerns of others. In foolish arrogance he spoke the harsh words: "My father made your yoke heavy; I will make it even heavier. My father scourged you with whips; I will scourge you with scorpions" (10:16).

Harsh words are not the wise way; they are not a good way; they are not God's way. Why does a man permit such a wrong attitude, and commit such a great sin? The Bible answers: "He did evil because he had not set his heart on seeking the Lord" (12:14).

Father in heaven, save me from the twin evils of a callous spirit and harsh words. Set my heart to seek Your ways.

Oh, to be like Thee! Full of compassion,
Loving, forgiving, tender and kind.
—THOMAS O. CHISHOLM

▼

Scripture: 2 Chronicles 13—16

Asa (chaps. 14—16) was the third king of Judah, the grandson of Rehoboam. He ruled for 41 years in Jerusalem, and did much to encourage his people to be faithful to God.

In 14:3, "the groves" were Asherah poles, symbols of the heathen goddess Asherah.

The Story: 2 Chronicles 14:1-5; 15:1-2, 7-15

Be strong and do not give up, for your work will be rewarded (2 Chron. 15:7; all quotes from NIV).

Courageous for God

You cannot legislate morality. True or false? How does the answer influence my efforts as a Christian? How does it affect my vote as a citizen? If King Asa had believed this currently popular slogan and had based his actions on it, there would have been no reform among his people.

You cannot legislate morality? It is a half-truth and therefore a dangerous concept. There are difficulties in answering either yes or no.

If we believe we can make persons good without their personal choice to do good, we are wrong. If we believe too strongly in legislating righteousness, and have the power to enforce our will, we may follow the path of the religious inquisitions. Asa at least started in this direction: "All who would not seek the Lord, the God of Israel, were to be put to death, whether small or great, man or woman" (15:13). We can be thankful that the plan was

159

never carried out; but even to consider it was wrong. We do not win people to God by killing them—we do not win them, or their children, or their neighbors. You cannot force righteousness. That is half the truth. But is it the important half for us as Christians in today's permissive society?

Can our children be helped to accept right values and form good habits by maintaining rules in the home? Can life be improved by compulsory school attendance? Can some young people be guided past drug abuse and addiction by laws that make drugs more difficult to get? Can lives be saved by enforcing laws against murder? To ask these questions is to answer them. Good laws do help make better persons.

We cannot force people to be good, but by indifference to wrong we encourage evil. By making wrong choices difficult, we help guide young and old toward right choices. We cannot win people to God by force, but by standing for righteousness we can remind them of right, and influence them toward it.

God's prophet gives God's guidance to all of us who seek to encourage goodness and godliness:

"Be strong and do not give up, for your work will be rewarded."

▼

☐ **Week 15, Friday**   **2 Chronicles**

Scripture: 2 Chronicles 17—20
The Story: 2 Chronicles 17:1-9: 19:4-7; 20:5-12

The Lord was with Jehoshaphat because ... he ... sought the God of his father and followed his commands (2 Chron. 17:3-4; all quotes from NIV).

A God-guided Life

"Once is not enough." I have forgotten what this TV ad was promoting, but the message is right on when we serve the Lord. One obedience is not enough to satisfy God. One prayer is not enough to fulfill my life and guarantee my influence for good. Jehoshaphat reminds us that God helps those who consult Him in all of life's important decisions.

Obedience to God in childhood and youth lays foundations for later life. "The Lord was with Jehoshaphat because in his early years he walked in the ways his father David had followed. . . . His heart was devoted to the ways of the Lord" (17:3, 6).

The king's father, Asa, had passed laws to promote godly living. In addition, Jehoshaphat relied on teaching: "In the third year of his reign he sent his officials . . . throughout Judah, taking with them the Book of the Law of the Lord; they went around to all the towns of Judah and taught the people" (17:7, 9).

Jehoshaphat did not trust himself to the advice of secular men. When 400 of Ahab's counselors prophesied success in a battle, he asked, "Is there not a prophet of the Lord here whom we can inquire of?" (18:6).

God's man knew that our Lord is concerned with justice. He told his judges: "Consider carefully what you do, because you are not judging for man but for the Lord, who is with you whenever you give a verdict. . . . Judge carefully, for with the Lord your God there is no injustice or partiality or bribery" (19:6-7).

In the face of overwhelming odds Jehoshaphat turned to prayer: "O our God . . . we have no power to face this vast army that is attacking us. We do not know what to do, but our eyes are upon you" (20:12).

Here was a man who lived by his faith, and testified to the rightness of God's way. Here is 20/20 spiritual vision: "Have faith in the Lord your God and you will be upheld; have faith in his prophets and you will be successful" (20:20).

Prayer for today:

> O for a faith that will not shrink,
> Tho' pressed by ev'ry foe,
> That will not tremble on the brink
> Of any earthly woe!
> —WILLIAM H. BATHURST

Scripture: 2 Chronicles 21—23
The Story: 2 Chronicles 23:1-16

Jehoiada ... made a covenant that he and the people and the king would be the Lord's people (2 Chron. 23:16, NIV).

God's People in Politics

Many good Americans are in a turmoil over the Moral Majority, headed by a Christian minister, Jerry Falwell. I, too, am in some turmoil. I don't agree with all of his goals, and I cannot subscribe to some of his methods—but I send him a small check each year to support the movement. He fights for righteousness, and I believe he is on God's side.

Jehoiada, the priest, was a kind of Jerry Falwell. He found his nation in moral chaos and set out to improve it.

When King Jehoshaphat died, Judah almost died with him. For eight years his son Jehoram ruled so badly that "he passed away, to no one's regret" (21:20, NIV). His equally evil grandson, Ahaziah, ruled for one year and was murdered (22:6-9). The queen mother was Athaliah, the daughter of the Northern Kingdom's most evil rulers, Ahab and Jezebel. When her son Ahaziah was killed, she seized power and set out to murder all of Judah's royal family. She would have succeeded had it not been for Jehoiada and his devoted wife, Jehosheba. They rescued Judah's infant crown prince from his murderous grandmother and hid him for seven years.

When the time was right, Jehoiada, the priest, got into politics. He recruited the religious people and laid plans to win the struggle against evil influences in the government. Jehoiada won that victory and saved Judah for the cause of God and right.

What lessons should we learn from Jehoiada? Are not these truths biblical and self-evident?

★ It is better to fight for right than to ignore evil.

★ Flagrant wrongs should be checked rather than permitted to go on.

★ Wicked persons should not be allowed places of influence in government or in the media.

★ There are values higher than individual liberty.

★ One evil person should not be allowed to corrupt and destroy a whole community.

★ It is better to oppose wrong than to remain indifferent and inactive.

Prayer for today:

Lord, let me join Jehoiada and enter into his covenant that I and my people shall be the Lord's people.

Scripture: 2 Chronicles 24—27
The Story: 2 Chronicles 24:1-14

All the officials and all the people brought their contributions gladly (2 Chron. 24:10; all quotes from NIV)

Cooperation Does It

When progress is needed in God's work, what human principles assure success? This slice of life from the Old Testament gives some answers.

Verse 7 tells why the project was needed. The family of Queen Athaliah had neglected and desecrated God's Temple. They had taken the objects of divine worship and prostituted them in the religion of Baal. Heroic effort was needed to restore God's house to a place of public respect and national pride.

God begins by planting *a dream in a man's spirit.* "Joash did what was right in the eyes of the Lord." Out of that faithfulness came the dream and decision: "Joash decided to restore the temple of the Lord."

But no man can do it alone; *leadership must be added to vision.* The king "called together the priests and Levites and said to them, 'Go to the towns of Judah and collect the money due annually from all Israel, to repair the temple of your God'" (24:5).

Responsible persons must be accountable. Jehoiada should have pressed for action. When he failed to do it, the king called him to give an accounting: "Why haven't you required the Levites to bring in . . . the tax . . . ?" (24:6).

When one method fails, try another. The king himself ordered a collection chest placed at the Temple gate. The plan captured Judah's imagination and gained wide support: "All the officials and all the people brought their contributions gladly, dropping them in the chest until it was full" (24:10).

Cooperation does it. Even the laggard Levites were kept involved in the project. They, with the king's officials, counted the money.

Every talent was employed. All gave; some counted; some supervised. The carpenters, masons, and metal workers used their skills for God's work.

Action does it. "The men in charge of the work were diligent, and the repairs progressed under them. They rebuilt the temple of God" (24:13).

Prayer for today:
Do it again, Lord!

▼

☐ **WEEK 16, MONDAY**   **2 CHRONICLES**

Scripture: 2 Chronicles 28—31
The Story: 2 Chronicles 29:1-11

Return to the Lord . . . that he may return to you (2 Chron. 30:6; all quotes from NIV).

"Revive Us Again"

We were made to live in the image of God. If competing influences have drawn us away from Him, we need to return. We need to be renewed and revived.

When Ezra sought to rebuild spiritual life in Jerusalem, he remembered Hezekiah's revival 250 years earlier. Those revival principles had brought the people back to God. The same steps will bring revival to us and to our churches.

Take the initiative. When one person sets out to seek God's will he brings example and encouragement to others. This revival began when a man testified, "It is in my heart to enter into a covenant with the Lord, the God of Israel" (29:10, NBV).

Begin to obey God. Nothing but disobedience keeps God at a distance. When we begin to order our lives after His pattern He draws near again. In 29:16, the priests "brought out . . . of the Lord's temple everything unclean that they found." These unclean obstacles were simply objects that God had said did not belong in His presence. If there is in our lives some forbidden act or attitude, revival begins when we determine to throw it out.

Begin to praise God. When we think about the goodness and power of God, our spirits are drawn to Him. In the Jerusalem revival, "King Hezekiah and his officials . . . sang praises with gladness and bowed their heads and worshiped" (29:30).

Renew your giving. God becomes real when we put His work high in our budgets. Hezekiah knew our gifts to God should come from gratitude: "You have now dedicated yourselves to the Lord. Come and bring sacrifices and thank offerings" (29:31). He also knew that giving is obedience: "He ordered the people . . . to give the portion due." So "they brought a tithe of everything. . . . a tithe of their herds and flocks and a tithe of the holy things dedicated to the Lord their God" (31:4-6).

These four steps brought revival and gladness—they always do. "There was great joy in Jerusalem . . . The priests and the Levites stood to bless the people, and God heard them, for their prayer reached heaven, his holy dwelling place" (30:26-27).

Prayer for today:

> *Revive us again; Fill each heart with Thy love;*
> *May each soul be rekindled With fire from above.*
> —WILLIAM P. McKAY

165

Scripture: 2 Chronicles 32—36

For the background of chapter 36, read the note on 2 Kings 24—25, "Important History." Here in Chronicles, Ezra briefly recounts the last 25 tragic years of Judah's history, and explains why God permitted the fall of Jerusalem and the Exile to Babylon (36:12-20). Compiling this history after the Exile, Ezra adds the concluding note of hope (36:22-23), showing how God was still helping His people.

The Story: 2 Chronicles 34:1-3, 8-10, 29-33; also 2 Kings 21:25—22:2

While he was still very young, he began to worship the God of his ancestor King David (2 Chron. 34:3, TEV).

The God of Hope

The story of Josiah brings encouragement and hope to the Christian parent, and to children in every spiritually divided home.

Looking at his father's side of the family, we would never have expected to meet Josiah in this story of deep personal faith and spiritual leadership. His grandfather, Manasseh, was Judah's most evil king. His father, Amon, "forsook the Lord God of his fathers, and walked not in the way of the Lord" (2 Kings 21:22).

But Josiah followed God in spite of his father and grandfather. We can thank God for the other side of the family. His mother's name, Jedidah, meant "beloved," and she came from a godly home. Her father's name, Adaiah, means "Jehovah hath adorned." It was surely this devout mother who named her baby Josiah, meaning "Jehovah supports him." It was her influence that molded the life of the boy from his infancy. There is Christian hope where a mother faithfully follows the Lord.

However good a boy's spiritual heritage, the time comes when he must seek God for himself; and Josiah did. "In the eighth year of his reign [he was 16 years old] he began to seek the God of his father David" (24:3, NIV).

Was it the influence of the church, through the prophet Jeremiah, that turned the mind and heart of this young man to God? We are not sure, but we know that Jeremiah was active at this time (Jer. 1:2). We also know that the prophet's call to salvation was clear: "Then shall ye call upon me, and ye shall go and pray unto me, and I will hearken unto you. And ye shall seek me, and find me, when ye shall search for me with all your heart. And I will be found of you, saith the Lord" (Jer. 29:12-14).

Alexander Whyte writes: "If a boy has a good mother and a good minister he is all but independent of his father."

I thank God for the combination of devout mothers and concerned pastors. I am also grateful that God can reach past all hindering circumstances. From the worst environments, God can save every child who will seek Him. I rejoice that I have known redeemed children who, in turn, have led their unsaved parents to Christ. *I glory in the God of hope!*

☐ **WEEK 16, WEDNESDAY**   **EZRA**

The Exile and Return

Yesterday in the last chapter of 2 Chronicles, Ezra's thoughts went back 125 years as he retold the story of Jerusalem's fall in 586 B.C., and the final Exile to Babylon. Today, in the book that bears his name, he reports the happier events that still lived in the memories of his countrymen after they had returned to their homeland.

History requires dates. To help us visualize this whole period of 175 years, the key events and their dates are listed.

606 B.C.	The first captivity	516	Temple re-built and dedicated
586	Jerusalem destroyed	485-465	Ahasuerus and Esther
550-535	Daniel's prophecies in Babylon	458	Second return—Ezra
538	Fall of Babylon	444	Third return— Nehemiah Walls rebuilt
537	Decree of Cyrus		
536	First return— Zerubbabel	440-430	Prophecies of Malachi
520	Haggai and Zechariah prophesy		

Scripture: Ezra 1—3

The leaders of the first return were Sheshbazzar, the governor (1:8), also called Zerubbabel (2:2); and Jeshua, the religious leader (2:2), also called Joshua (Hag. 1:1; Zech. 3:1).

The Story: Ezra 1:2-4; 3:1-3, 10-11

When seventy years are completed for Babylon, I will come to you and fulfill my gracious promise to bring you back to this place (Jer. 29:10; all quotes from NIV).

I Know God's Promise Is True

William Cowper wrote:

> *God moves in a mysterious way*
> *His wonders to perform;*

Because of this glorious truth he exhorts God's people:

> *Ye fearful saints, fresh courage take.*
> *The clouds ye so much dread*

Are big with mercy, and shall break
In blessings on your head.

Because God cares for His people, He gave the loving promise through Jeremiah:

"This is what the Lord Almighty, the God of Israel, says to all those I carried into exile from Jerusalem to Babylon: . . . 'When seventy years are completed for Babylon, I will come to you and fulfill my gracious promise to bring you back to this place. For I know the plans I have for you,' declares the Lord, 'plans to prosper you and not to harm you, plans to give you hope and a future. Then you will call upon me and come and pray to me, and I will listen to you. You will seek me and find me when you seek me with all your heart'" (Jer. 29:4, 10-13).

Fifty-six years later God kept that promise:

"In the first year of Cyrus king of Persia, in order to fulfill the word of the Lord spoken by Jeremiah, the Lord moved the heart of Cyrus king of Persia to make a proclamation throughout his realm and to put it in writing: . . .

"'The Lord, the God of heaven, has given me all the kingdoms of the earth and he has appointed me to build a temple for him at Jerusalem in Judah. Anyone of his people among you—may his God be with him, and let him go up to Jerusalem in Judah and build the temple of the Lord, the God of Israel, and the God who is in Jerusalem. And the people of any place where survivors may now be living are to provide him with silver and gold, with goods and livestock, and with freewill offerings for the temple of God in Jerusalem'" (Ezra 1:2-4).

I know God's promise is true!

Today I join those other people of God, who when they had seen His answers to their prayers:

"With praise and thanksgiving . . . sang to the Lord: 'He is good; his love . . . endures forever.'"

▼

Scripture: Ezra 4—6

Ezra 4:6-23 appears to be a misplaced record; it reports events that occurred in 465-424 B.C. This was later than the days of Zerubbabel. Ezra probably used the account here as a third illustration of opposition to the Jews returning to Jerusalem. These three challenges to the Jews occurred over a period of 51 years, during the reigns of three foreign kings: Cyrus, 536 B.C.; Darius, 520 B.C.; and Artaxerxes, 485 B.C.

The Story: Ezra 4:1-5; 5:3-10

The eye of their God was watching over the elders of the Jews, and they were not stopped (Ezra 5:5; all quotes from NIV).

Persistence Pays

It was not the U.S. Marines who first immortalized persistence. Jerome was the first to declare, "The only difference between the difficult and the impossible is that the impossible takes longer."

In the spring of 537 B.C., Sheshbazzar (Zerubbabel) with his caravan of nearly 50,000 returning exiles left Babylon. The journey covered 900 weary miles on foot. On arrival in Judah, the first months were spent building houses and clearing long-neglected fields for planting.

But the central purpose of these returning colonists was to reestablish the worship of God. They had returned to build "a temple for the Lord, the God of Israel." Just 14 months after arriving in Jerusalem they began the foundations (3:8).

Have you ever undertaken a task for God and found it all easy? Governor Zerubbabel and the Jews did not. No sooner were the foundations laid than foes tried to stop the project.

These "enemies of Judah" were foreign colonists settled in Samaria by the king of Assyria 50 years earlier. Perhaps some were remnants of Israel who had drifted into idolatry. Zerubbabel was sure their offer of help was a trick. The enemies were only seeking to infiltrate Judah's ranks and disrupt the work. With steadfast purpose the governor replied, "We alone will build it for the Lord, the God of Israel."

The opposition of Tattenai (chap. 5) occurred 17 years later. The prophets Haggai and Zechariah had challenged the people to action. As a result, the work on the Temple was resumed and progressed rapidly.

Fearing a serious threat to the interests of the king of Persia, the territorial governor, Tattenai, came to investigate and then sent a red-flag letter to King Darius. Tattenai supposed his letter would halt the project, but God overruled this opposition also. Chapter 6 tells the story of Darius' reply. He not only reaffirmed Cyrus' permission to build the Temple, but also ordered the governor to give full aid to the Jews.

Faith and persistence had won the day. When we persist in some task for our Lord, we too can testify with the people of Jerusalem, "The eye of their God was watching . . . and they were not stopped."

▼

Haggai

Haggai was the first prophet of the Restoration. He was probably among the exiles who returned with Zerubbabel in 536 B.C. The reference to the "former glory" of the Temple (Hag. 2:3) suggests that Haggai was one of the few returnees who had been born in Judah before the Temple was destroyed. If so, he was an old man at the time of this prophecy.

We read Haggai and Zechariah here in the historical context of their work.

Scripture: Ezra 5:1-2; Haggai 1—2
The Story: Haggai 1:1-15

My house . . . remains a ruin, while each of you is busy with his own house (Hag. 1:9; all quotes from NIV).

"Seek Ye First the Kingdom of God"

We often do better repelling great foes than conquering small attitudes. A friend with keen insight commented about a mutual acquaintance: "He is great when fighting lions, but mosquitoes worry him to death."

It was true of Zerubbabel, Joshua, and the Jews. The foundations of the Temple were laid, but for 14 years the work stood still and the site was covered with rubble. The causes lay in the attitudes of the leaders and the people. The chief obstacle was a lack of will to do the work. They just didn't care enough.

Verse 2 lays bare their self-centered spirit and worldly lifestyle. An indifferent people sighed, "The time has not yet come for the Lord's house to be built." But a holy God challenges our human negligence: "Is it a time for you yourselves to be living in your paneled houses, while this house remains a ruin?" (v. 3).

Then with a ringing challenge, God's prophet warned: "This is what the Lord Almighty says: 'Give careful thought to your ways. Go up into the mountains and bring down timber and build the house, so that I may take pleasure in it and be honored'" (vv. 7-8).

Our Lord himself challenges us to the same spirit and Christian life-style: "Seek ye first the kingdom of God, and his righteousness; and all these things shall be added unto you" (Matt. 6:33).

Question for today:

Since I am a follower of Christ, does God's work occupy as much of my planning and my time as is pleasing to Him?

▼

172

Zechariah

The second prophet of Judah's restoration was Zechariah. He was probably a young man when he wrote these prophecies, having come to Jerusalem 17 years earlier as a child in the caravan from Babylon. Just two months after Haggai's vision, God also spoke to Zechariah. It was November of 520 B.C.

Like the writer of Revelation, Zechariah often uses figures of speech instead of literal language. The "horns" of chapter 1 are the world powers that ravished Judah. The "two olive trees" of chapter 4 were Judah's two leaders, Joshua and Zerubbabel. The "flying scroll" of chapter 5 symbolized God's righteous law for His people; the "woman in a basket" stood for evil that must be repressed and removed from the community.

Also, like John in Revelation, Zechariah himself needed to be told the meaning of some of the visions that God gave him (see Zech. 1:8-9; 4:11-14; Rev. 7:13-17).

Scripture: Zechariah 1—4
The Story: Zechariah 3:1-7; 4:1-9

Not by might, nor by power, but by my Spirit, says the Lord Almighty (Zech. 4:6; all quotes from NIV).

The Ministry of Encouragement

Among the New Testament gifts of the Spirit, Paul lists "those able to help others" (1 Cor. 12:28). This was God's gift to Zechariah.

Haggai's preaching had inspired the people to quick action. Within 24 days after he began to preach, they began to work (Hag. 1:1, 15). It was left to Zechariah, Haggai's younger contemporary, to bring the task of Temple building to completion. His great contribution was to encourage Joshua, the priest, and Zerubbabel, the governor.

Zechariah writes: "He showed me Joshua the high priest standing before the angel of the Lord, and Satan standing at his right side to accuse him. The Lord said to Satan, 'The Lord rebuke you, Satan!'" (3:1-2). Then came this moving message of encouragement:

"This is what the Lord Almighty says: 'If you will walk in my ways and keep my requirements, then you will govern my house and have charge of my courts'" (3:6). In 6:11, 13 God commands the prophet: "Take . . . silver and gold and make a crown, and set it on the head of the high priest, Joshua . . . It is he who will build the temple of the Lord."

Young Zechariah also brought God's message of encouragement to the hard-pressed governor:

"This is the word of the Lord to Zerubbabel: 'Not by might nor by power, but by my Spirit,' says the Lord Almighty." Are there mountains of difficulty in the governor's office? Well, God says to the mountain, "You will become level ground." Are there those who say the work will never be finished? God's answer to a faithful servant is: "The hands of Zerubbabel have laid the foundation of this temple; his hands will also complete it" (4:6-8).

When we are earnestly seeking to do God's will, there is no greater strength than to hear such assurance from the Lord. Having heard it, we can sing with Ira Stanphill:

> *Many things about tomorrow*
> *I don't seem to understand;*
> *But I know who holds tomorrow,*
> *And I know who holds my hand.**

Scripture: Zechariah 5—8; 10
The Story: Zechariah 8:1-17

They will be my people, and I will be faithful and righteous to them as their God (Zech. 8:8; all quotes from NIV).

God of the Nations

I can understand God's dealings with individuals because I have experienced them personally. It has been harder for me to grasp His control and concern for the nations. But the prophets knew how great God is. Zechariah saw Him as God of the nations— indeed, as "Lord of the whole world" (6:5).

He is the sovereign God, and He gives guidelines to the nations. For their welfare and continuance, He requires obedience from them. Chapter 5 tells us that nations, like individuals, must observe God's moral law or perish. Dishonesty and falsehood destroy the very foundations of a society. Where those evils persist, God's judgment "will remain in his house and destroy it, both its timbers and its stones" (5:4).

But our righteous God yearns for a full life for His people in every land. In Zechariah's time there were few old people and children in Judah. To an obedient nation Jehovah gave His promise: "Once again men and women of ripe old age will sit in the streets of Jerusalem . . . The city streets will be filled with boys and girls playing there" (8:4-5).

God offers His love and forgiveness to repentant people— whether individuals or nations. The songwriter puts it truly:

> *Tho' we have sinned, He has mercy and pardon,*
> *Pardon for you and for me.*
>   —WILL L. THOMPSON

It is God himself who closes Zechariah's plea to the nation: "O Judah and Israel, so will I save you, and you will be a blessing. Do not be afraid, but let your hands be strong" (8:13).

To that appeal our glad hearts respond:

> *Thy love divine hath led us in the past.*
> *In this free land by Thee our lot is cast.*
> *Be Thou our Ruler, Guardian, Guide, and Stay,*
> *Thy Word our law, Thy paths our chosen way.*
> —DANIEL C. ROBERTS

☑ WEEK 17, MONDAY   ZECHARIAH

Scripture: Zechariah 9; 11—14
The Story: Zechariah 9:8-10

"Shout and be glad, O Daughter of Zion. For I am coming, and I will live among you," declares the Lord (Zech. 2:10; main quotes from NIV).

"Hosanna to the Son of David"

Among the Old Testament prophets only Isaiah foretold more than Zechariah about the coming of the world's Redeemer.

Before the Exile, Isaiah had seen Israel's Messiah as the "righteous Branch." Now Zechariah picks up the theme: "I am going to bring my servant, the Branch. . . . I will remove the sin of this land in a single day" (3:8-9). And again, "Here is the man whose name is the Branch . . . and he will be clothed with majesty and will sit and rule on his throne" (6:12-13).

From Zechariah came the shouted hosannas at Jesus' triumphal entry: "Rejoice greatly, O Daughter of Zion! Shout, daughter of Jerusalem! See, your king comes to you, righteous and having salvation, gentle and riding on a donkey, on a colt, the foal of a donkey" (9:9).

Over 400 years before our Lord's betrayal by Judas, Zechariah wrote: "So they paid me thirty pieces of silver. And the Lord said to me, 'Throw it to the potter'—the handsome price at which they priced me! So I took the thirty pieces of silver and threw them into the house of the Lord to the potter" (11:12-13).

Our prophet also clearly reveals the atonement and crucifixion of Jesus: "I will pour out on the house of David and the inhabitants of Jerusalem a spirit of grace and supplication. They will look on me, the one they have pierced . . . On that day a fountain will be opened to the house of David and the inhabitants of Jerusalem, to cleanse them from sin and impurity" (12:10; 13:1).

In his last vision, Zechariah was shown that distant day when the kingdoms of this world shall become the kingdoms of our Lord and of His Christ. "A day of the Lord is coming . . . I will gather all the nations to Jerusalem to fight against it . . . Then the Lord will go out and fight against those nations . . . On that day his feet will stand on the Mount of Olives, east of Jerusalem . . . Then the Lord my God will come, and all the holy ones with him" (14:1-5).

With John, our expectant hearts respond: *"Amen. Even so, come, Lord Jesus"* (Rev. 22:20, KJV).

☑ **WEEK 17, TUESDAY**   **EZRA**

Scripture: Ezra 7—10; Nehemiah

See page 168 for the date of Ezra's ministry.

Ezra's handling of forbidden marriages (chaps. 9—10) was an Old Testament action. It does not provide a Christian pattern for today. To persons unscripturally married, the church says: "Christ can redeem. . . . Where the scriptural ground for divorce did not exist and remarriage followed, the marriage partners, upon genuine repentance for their sin, are enjoined to seek the forgiving grace of God and His redemptive help in their marriage relation" (*Manual,* Church of the Nazarene).

The Story: Ezra 7:1, 6-10; Nehemiah 8:1-10

Administer justice to all the people . . . who know the laws of your God. And . . . teach any who do not know them (Ezra 7:25, NIV).

The Power of Teaching

Knowledge is power—and knowledge of God is power with God. Ezra was a strong leader, a skillful administrator, and a devout servant of God. In addition to all of these, he was a committed teacher. He had "devoted himself to the study and observance of the Law of the Lord, and to teaching its decrees and laws in Israel" (7:10, NIV).

The story of Ezra's Scripture seminar is given in Neh. 8:1-10. Probably the request of the people (v. 1) had been made before the gathering; a high platform (v. 4) had been built for the public reading of the Law.

This renewed knowledge of God's Word was the seedbed from which Ezra expected to nurture new spiritual life among the people. It was—and is—a dependable nurturing ground. The Psalmist testified, "Thy word have I hid in mine heart, that I might not sin against thee" (Ps. 119:11).

The knowledge of God that stimulates love and obedience in our lives will bear the same fruit in the lives of our children and our neighbors. It is God himself who teaches us how to pass our faith along to others: "Be careful, and watch yourselves closely so that you do not forget the things your eyes have seen or let them slip from your heart as long as you live. Teach them to your children and to their children after them" (Deut. 4:9, NIV).

We cannot guarantee faith in the life of another, but we can faithfully follow God's formula. Let our prayer for today be twofold—a petition and a commitment.

> *Oh, teach me, Lord, that I may teach*
> *The precious truths Thou dost impart;*
> *And wing my words, that they may reach*
> *The hidden depths of many a heart.*
> —FRANCES R. HAVERGAL

Nehemiah

Nehemiah was born in or near Babylon. Like Daniel before him, Nehemiah had risen to prominence in the Persian court. As cupbearer to the king he was a trusted palace officer and leading minister. Shushan (Susa) was the summer palace of Persia. Here the story of Queen Esther and Mordecai had occurred 25 years earlier.

Nehemiah arrived at Jerusalem in 444 B.C. to rebuild the city walls. The story of his work gives us four lessons in leadership for anyone who has a job to do for God. That person may be any concerned Christian—a committee chairman, class president, teacher, board member, or me!

Scripture: Nehemiah 1—3
The Story: Nehemiah 1:1—2:8

The God of heaven will give us success. We his servants will start rebuilding (Neh. 2:20, NIV).

Prayer and Initiative

How can I best serve God when He has a job for me to do? Nehemiah's example in Shushan gives us three guidelines to follow.

✔ No work is done for the Lord until some Christian sees a need and is stirred. The Bible reminds us, "Where there is no vision, the people perish" (Prov. 29:18). Nehemiah was in touch with heaven, and he was open to the prompting of God's Spirit. When the need became known, his heart responded. Here was a prominent layman in humanly comfortable circumstances, but he could not remain comfortable in spirit while God's work and God's people were in need. That concern sent him to his knees.

✔ In his prayer, Nehemiah reminded God of the promise to His people: "If you return to me and obey my commands . . . I will gather them . . . and bring them to the place I have chosen as a dwelling place for my Name." He also prayed for the favor of the

179

king: "Give your servant success . . . in the presence of this man."
He prayed for courage and wisdom as he talked to the king: "Then
I prayed to the God of heaven, and I answered . . . 'If it pleases the
king . . . send me to the city in Judah where my fathers are buried
so that I can rebuild it'" (1:9, 11; 2:4-5, NIV).

✔ Nehemiah saw a need; he prayed earnestly about it—and
then he acted.

> There are strong men of fact,
> There are wise men of tact.
> There are those who think carefully through it.
> But God waits for men who both think and pray—
> And after their prayers—go do it!
>
> —ADAPTED

Father, teach me to follow Nehemiah, Your model doer. Tune my
heart to the needs of people. Talk to me about those needs—then send
me out to rebuild some broken walls for You. Amen.

▼

☑ WEEK 17, THURSDAY   NEHEMIAH

Scripture: Nehemiah 4—7
The Story: Nehemiah 4:1-23

We prayed to our God and posted a guard day
and night to meet this threat (Neh. 4:9, NIV).

Pray and Plan

How much opposition can I take and still persevere in God's work?
Nehemiah is our model.

He confronted open opposition from the enemies of God's
people: anger, ridicule, physical force, intrigue, blackmail, and
threats against his life. He also faced internal weakness among his
colleagues: discouraged spirits, faint hearts, and outright traitors.

How does a man continue when threatened by these foes?
Nehemiah's first secret was the sense of a divine partnership. In

Shushan he had prayed for guidance before he began the task. Then in the midst of the difficulties, he relied on God. When enemies ridiculed him, he prayed: "Hear us, O our God, for we are despised." When attack threatened, he said, "We prayed to our God and posted a guard." When colleagues grew discouraged and fainthearted, this man of God exhorted: "Don't be afraid of them. Remember the Lord, who is great and awesome" (Neh. 4:4, 9, 14, NIV). With God as our Partner, we have adequate resources.

This layman was an early Arminian. He placed full confidence in the power of God—but he knew that God calls for courageous effort from His men. He both prayed to God "and posted a guard day and night to meet this threat." Nehemiah and his men literally slept in their clothes during the 52 days that the walls were going up. He testifies: "So we laboured in the work" (4:21). *The Living Bible* translates it, "We worked early and late, from sunrise to sunset."

Thanks for your model, Nehemiah. By God's help we shall follow your example.

> Then forward still, 'tis Jehovah's will,
> Tho' the billows dash and spray.
> With a conqu'ring tread we will push ahead;
> He'll roll the sea away.
> —H. J. Zelley

☑ WEEK 17, FRIDAY   NEHEMIAH

Scripture: Nehemiah 9—10
The Story: Nehemiah 9:1-8 (If names are difficult, call them by their first letters)

In all that has happened to us, you have been just; you have acted faithfully, while we did wrong (Neh. 9:33, NIV).

Confession and Praise

It is not enough for God's leader to be a leader—he must first of all be God's man. Nehemiah was a layman with spiritual insight and the devotion of a true pastor. After the walls were rebuilt, he joined Ezra and Israel in confession of their sins and in praise for God's faithfulness. Let us join them in their worship:

"They stood in their places and confessed their sins and the wickedness of their fathers. They stood where they were and read from the Book of the Law of the Lord their God . . . Standing on the stairs were the Levites . . . who called with loud voices . . . 'Stand up and praise the Lord your God, who is from everlasting to everlasting.'

"Blessed be your glorious name, and may it be exalted above all blessing and praise. You alone are the Lord. You made the heavens, even the highest heavens, and all their starry host, the earth and all that is on it, the seas and all that is in them. You give life to everything, and the multitudes of heaven worship you. . . . You have kept your promise because you are righteous. . . .

"In [Israel's] hunger you gave them bread from heaven and in their thirst you brought them water from the rock; you told them to go in and take possession of the land you had sworn with uplifted hand to give them. . . .

"But they were disobedient and rebelled against you; they put your law behind their backs. . . . They sinned against your ordinances, by which a man will live if he obeys them. . . .

"But you are a forgiving God, gracious and compassionate, slow to anger and abounding in love. . . . Because of your great compassion you did not abandon them in the desert. By day the pillar of cloud did not cease to guide them on their path, nor the pillar of fire by night to shine on the way they were to take. You gave your good Spirit to instruct them. . . .

"When they were oppressed they cried out to you. From heaven you heard them, and in your great compassion you gave them deliverers, who rescued them from the hand of their enemies" (9:2-6, 8, 15, 26, 29, 17, 19-20, 27, NIV).

With the Psalmist my heart responds today:

"Bless the Lord, O my soul: and all that is within me, bless his holy name" (Ps. 103:1).

Scripture: Nehemiah 11—13

The genealogies in 11:4—12:26 may be omitted without great loss.

If Nehemiah's prayers in 13:14 and 22 seem self-righteous, remember he lived in Old Testament times. Perhaps Jesus would say to him and to us, "When you have done everything you were told to do, [you] should say, 'We are unworthy servants: we have only done our duty'" (Luke 17:10, NIV).

The Story: Nehemiah 13:1-12

I purified the priests and the Levites of everything foreign, and assigned them duties, each to his own task (Neh. 13:30, NIV).

Zealous for God

The city walls and the new Temple helped to accomplish God's work—but they were not enough. God needs men loyal to His law and zealous for His work.

Read 11:1-2. Jerusalem was once again a walled city, enclosing the rebuilt Temple. The government officials lived there; but men, women, and children were needed if the city of Jerusalem was to be the city of God. Nehemiah led the people in casting lots. Every 10th family thus chosen agreed to move inside the city walls.

There is cause for appreciation even in the dreary genealogies of these chapters. Here are the names of men known to God and recorded in His Book. They were people willing to suffer the strain of relocation in order that God's work might go forward. Such loyal servants are worthy of human appreciation and divine remembering.

In chapter 13 the focus shifts back to Nehemiah in his zeal for God. Perhaps today we would not use his methods, but his goals were right. He read the Scriptures and determined to be guided by them (13:1-3). He refused to allow God's house to be used for selfish privilege (13:4-5, 8-9). When others grew careless, Nehemiah faithfully called them back to the loyal service of God (13:10-13). From those who scorned God's day he demanded at least outward observance (13:15-22). Men who had married heathen wives and thus allowed ungodly influences on their children, he rebuked and disciplined (13:23-28).

The ways of God and man have not changed since the days of Nehemiah. The principles that he followed with such success in rebuilding Judah will build the church today. Give us leaders of vision and devotion who trust God and fear no opposition; give us people who are willing to change life-styles and, if necessary, move to another city to achieve the purposes of God; give us a hatred of evil and a love for good; give us a profound faith in God and in His plans for our lives—give us these attitudes, and God's kingdom shall prosper.

> I love Thy kingdom, Lord,
> The house of Thine abode,
> The Church our blest Redeemer saved
> With His own precious blood.
> —TIMOTHY DWIGHT

▼

☑ WEEK 18, SUNDAY   ESTHER

The Book of *Esther* belongs to the period of the Babylonian Exile. The name Ahasuerus is a Hebrew variant for Xerxes who ruled Persia from 485 to 465 B.C. The events thus occurred at the Persian court in Shushan between Zerubbabel's return to Jerusalem in 536 B.C. and Ezra's return in 458.

Scripture: Esther 1—2
The Story: Esther 2:5-20

Esther won the favor of everyone who saw her (Esther 2:15; all quotes from NIV).

184

Beauty, Goodness, and Courage

When beauty is combined with courage and character, we feel like applauding. Here is the fascination of the story of Esther.

But first, let us honor those who have the courage of their convictions and suffer for it. Queen Vashti was probably right in refusing to allow her physical beauty to be exploited in a banquet hall full of intoxicated men. Because of her courage she lost her crown, but our world is better for it. Every hard decision to do right ennobles the one who makes the choice—and encourages others who waver. Without Vashti's steadfastness, God could not have later saved His people through Esther's influence. Thanks, Vashti, for your moral courage.

James Russell Lowell writes:

> Truth forever on the scaffold,
> Wrong forever on the throne—
> Yet that scaffold sways the future,
> And behind the dim unknown
> Standeth God within the shadow
> Keeping watch above His own.

The story of Esther's early years teaches us that *it is better to be kind than to be heartless.* God's purpose for His people was accomplished because Mordecai accepted responsibility for an orphaned child.

It is better to make friends than to antagonize associates. Because Esther became a favorite with Hegai, she was better prepared to win the favor of the king and to come to a place of influence for righteousness.

It is better to be obedient than rebellious. Esther "continued to follow Mordecai's instructions as she had done when he was bringing her up" (2:20).

It is better to be wise than foolish. She listened to the counsel of her guardian and concealed her Jewish ancestry. What she concealed, she later acknowledged openly at the right time for God to save His people. To know thus when to speak and when to be silent is the gift of wisdom. Mordecai had it; Esther honored it; God used it.

It has been said: "God's name is not mentioned in the Book of Esther, but His hand is perfectly evident in the events." Let us praise Him for His providences.

▼

Scripture: Esther 3—6
The Story: Esther 4:1-17

Who knoweth whether thou art come to the kingdom for such a time as this? (Esther 4:14).

The Risks of Righteousness

For Esther there was no way to avoid the high hazard of appealing to the king to change his decree. For us also, serving God sometimes brings dangers that must be braved.

This beautiful young woman was not tempted to commit outbroken sin. Her option was simply to remain silent while tragedy came to others. But she knew that to speak up might avert the tragedy.

In these circumstances God presents us with only two alternatives; we cannot remain neutral. To seek to avoid the struggle by remaining silent is sin. He asks us to choose the right and run the risks. If we decline, we choose the wrong and must suffer the consequences. And in our interrelated world of personal influence we always involve our families and friends for good or for evil.

Esther's gift was physical beauty and personal charm. These qualities had attracted the king and thus opened for Esther her door of opportunity. Such gifts often spoil us through pride or selfish privilege. But Esther courageously dedicated her talent to the service of God for the good of her people.

In the last analysis, doing God's will comes down to a personal decision. Nevertheless, in such choices we are reinforced by knowing that others share with us in the struggle. When Esther faced the supreme test, she asked Mordecai to call the Jews together and proclaim a fast for three days. Before she put her life on the line, she would pray.

There are no more moving words in Scripture than the simple and grandly heroic stand of this young woman. When she saw her duty clearly, she declared with deep commitment: "And so will I go in unto the king, which is not according to the law: and if I perish, I perish" (4:16).

In the presence of such courage we can only pray for ourselves:

> Lord, give us such a faith as this;
> And then, whate'er may come,
> We'll taste, e'en here, the hallowed bliss
> Of an eternal home.
> —WILLIAM H. BATHURST

▼

☐ **WEEK 18, TUESDAY**   **ESTHER**

Scripture: Esther 7—10
The Story: Esther 8:3-13

Grant me my life—this is my petition. And spare my people—this is my request (Esther 7:3; all quotes from NIV).

"The Wrong Shall Fail, the Right Prevail"

In light of Jesus' teachings, how shall we view the destruction of 75,000 Gentiles from India to Ethiopia (9:16)? How shall we explain the request of Esther that the fighting in Susa be continued for a second day, and that the bodies of Haman's sons be publicly displayed on the gallows (9:13)?

We do not feel good about these choices. Of such Old Testa-

187

ment attitudes Jesus declared, "You have heard that it was said, 'Love your neighbor and hate your enemy.' But I tell you: Love your enemies and pray for those who persecute you, that you may be the sons of your Father in heaven" (Matt. 5:43-45). Love and forgiveness are Christian; hate and revenge are wrong.

We must, however, be fair to Esther and the Jews of the Persian Empire. They were fighting for their lives. Haman intended to exterminate God's people. His order was "to destroy, kill and annihilate all the Jews—young and old, women and little children" (3:13). In contrast, Mordecai's decree was designed to provide for self-defense. The Jews were permitted "to assemble and protect themselves; to destroy, kill and annihilate any armed force . . . that might attack them and their women and children" (8:11). Most of us feel that force is justified in defense of our nation and the lives of our loved ones.

But beyond these less-than-Christian human responses, we are here viewing the hand of God. The main truth of this story is God's purpose to protect His people from their sworn enemies. Here is the overruling providence of a just God in heaven. We rejoice in the assurance that He is against evil. We are confident that "the Lord watches over the way of the righteous, but the way of the wicked will perish" (Ps. 1:6). When evil seems to triumph, we rest back on our Christian faith in a righteous and all-powerful God. With Longfellow we sing:

> Then pealed the bells more loud and deep:
> "God is not dead, nor doth He sleep;
> The wrong shall fail, the right prevail,
> With peace on earth, goodwill to men."

▼

☐ WEEK 18, WEDNESDAY   JOB

> If you have a philosophical mind that asks *why,*
> you will enjoy *Job.* Here the unanswered question
> is, Why do good men suffer?

The book is a drama in which the themes are developed in dialogue. The first scene introduces God, and also Satan who appears as His adversary. Job, the hero, is a wealthy citizen of Uz. He is joined by three friends: Eliphaz, Bildad, and Zophar. They come to comfort their old friend.

The three counselors are certain that Job's suffering is caused by some sin he has committed. They are sure that humility and repentance will clear up the matter. Job, however, insists that he has committed no sin that would cause his misfortunes.

At the end of the book, Job's repeated requests that God would appear and give meaning to his suffering are answered. God, however, does not address himself directly to the problems Job has raised. Rather, the Lord makes clear who He is and points out the confidence that a person must place in Him.

We do not know the author of the book nor its date. Scholars generally agree that it was written about Job rather than by him.

Scripture: Job 1—2
The Story. Job 1.6-12, 2.1-7
The Lord gave, and the Lord hath taken away; blessed be the name of the Lord (Job 1:21).

"Thou God Seest Me"

We could begin the study of the book by looking at Job, but in difficult circumstances of life is it not better to look first at God?

Have we recently been going through some deep trial? Then let us reflect on where God has been and what He has been doing about it.

The author of this drama wants us to know that even the best of men and women suffer—and they suffer with God's full knowledge and permission. In the opening dialogue God asks Satan, "Have you considered my servant Job? ... He is blameless and upright, a man who fears God and shuns evil" (1:8, NIV). Thus in Job's dark hour God knew where His man was and what he was suffering.

In the Lord's dialogues with Satan about us, can He raise the same question? And with the same confidence?

The Heavenly Father lets us suffer only because He believes we can stand firm against the pressure. God gave permission to Satan, but He also set protective limits: "Very well, then, everything he has is in your hands, but on the man himself do not lay a finger" (1:12, NIV).

Our Father is proud of His children who persevere in spite of pressure. In the first encounter God expresses confidence in the outcome, but in the second test He brags on Job's victory: "He has kept faith in me despite the fact that you persuaded me to let you harm him without any cause" (2:3, TLB).

The Bible assures us: "God keeps his promise, and he will not allow you to be tested beyond your power to remain firm; at the time you are put to the test, he will give you the strength to endure it, and so provide you with a way out" (1 Cor. 10:13, TEV). In trust, my heart replies with God's servant Hagar, "Thou God seest me" (Gen. 16:13).

Thank You, Father. I am sure that You know when I am tested. I know that You care for me. Even now I feel the flow of strength You are giving me for this day. Through Jesus Christ. Amen.

▼

☐ WEEK 18, THURSDAY   JOB

Today's reading introduces the poetic form of this book. From chapter 3 through 42, except for half a dozen short paragraphs of prose, the thoughts and feelings are expressed in poetry. This poetic language is especially suited to Job's cries of distress because poetry is the language of emotion.

Scripture: Job 3—6
The Story: Job 3:1-4, 11-13, 16-17; 6:11-12

Teach me, and I will be quiet; show me where I have been wrong (Job 6:24; all quotes from NIV).

A Wounded Spirit

Our pastor recently said: "Wounded spirits, like wounded bodies, require time for healing—and often healing for the spirit takes longer than for the body."

As we share today in Job's agony we may enlarge our understanding of wounded spirits and our compassion for those who suffer. As we give ourselves to God's ministry to the wounded, we may find healing for our own deep hurts. Three methods of therapy come from these scriptures.

Remember your best thoughts before your mind was clouded by pain.

"Think how you have instructed many,
     how you have strengthened feeble hands.
Your words have supported those who stumbled;
     you have strengthened faltering knees.
But now trouble comes to you, and you are discouraged;
     it strikes you, and you are dismayed.
Should not your piety be your confidence
     and your blameless ways your hope?" (4:3-6).

Talk with God about the suffering.

"If it were I, I would appeal to God;
     I would lay my cause before him.
He performs wonders that cannot be fathomed,
     miracles that cannot be counted.
He bestows rain on the earth;
     he sends water upon the countryside.
The lowly he sets on high,
     and those that mourn are lifted to safety" (5:8-11).

Accept what God permits to come your way.

"Blessed is the man whom God corrects;
     so do not despise the discipline of the Almighty.

191

For he wounds, but he also binds up;
  he injures, but his hands also heal" (5:17-18).

Thank You, Father, for Your words of quiet counsel:
"Teach me, and I will be quiet; show me where I have been wrong."

▼

Scripture: Job 7—8
The Story: Job 7:1-3, 6-11, 16
Surely God does not reject a blameless man or strengthen the hands of evildoers (Job 8:20; all quotes from NIV).

Keep Your Thinking Straight

In discussing failures of faith, Dr. J. B. Chapman declared that three intellectual anchors will keep one from drifting: (1) There is an intelligent Ruler of the universe, (2) He desires to communicate His will to us, (3) God is righteous and good. As we commit ourselves tenaciously to these bedrock truths we find meaning to life, and satisfying answers in our faith.

Job complained about the hard lot of the day laborer. But hard work and low pay were not Job's real frustration; many day laborers find life good and maintain firm faith in God. Job's problem was that he had lost his No. 3 anchor; he no longer believed that God was good.

With this anchor gone, he had also lost his faith in God's promise of life beyond the grave. In that dark mood he could only despairingly say:

"My days are swifter than a weaver's shuttle,
  and they come to an end without hope" (7:6).

How do we find our way out of this morass of self-pity and gloom? In Bildad's counsel we find at least one sound answer: Get anchor No. 3 in place again. Begin to reaffirm faith in the goodness of God. Sound thinking asks, "Does God pervert justice? Does the Almighty pervert what is right? . . . Surely God does not reject a blameless man or strengthen the hands of evildoers" (8:3, 20). With this anchor holding firm, the storms may blow but they cannot destroy us.

If we are not certain, it may be because we are living at too low a level. If we live for pleasure or for money or fame, then the spiritual realities must of necessity become nebulous and vague. To feel that we are immortal we must live like immortals. Gazing constantly into the trivial blinds the eyes to the splendor of the eternal, and working always for fading wreaths robs the heart of its belief in the crown of glory. God breathes assurance only into hearts which are open to him. To those who give themselves wholeheartedly to the service of mankind in the spirit of his Son, he communicates not only peace and joy, but an unconquerable conviction that when work here is finished, to die is gain *(Dean C. Dutton)*.

Thank You, Father. In my darkest hours I cling to the truth of Your Word:
"If you will look to God and plead with the Almighty . . . even now he will rouse himself on your behalf" (8:5-6).

▼

Scripture: Job 9—11
The Story: Job 9:1-4, 11-12, 14-18, 22-24
Can you fathom the mysteries of God? . . . Their measure is longer than the earth and wider than the sea (Job 11:7, 9; all quotes from NIV).

"True Wisdom Has Two Sides"

When desperation has pushed us to think only of God's naked power, we need to remember the counsel of Eliphaz: "Are God's

193

consolations not enough for you, words spoken gently to you? Why has your heart carried you away, and why do your eyes flash, so that you vent your rage against God and pour out such words from your mouth?" (15:11-13).

There are two sides to the divine action. God is more than supreme power; He is also unlimited love. Even an angry Job confesses: "You gave me life and showed me kindness, and in your providence watched over my spirit" (10:12).

Through Isaiah God appeals to us: "'Come now, let us reason together,' says the Lord. 'Though your sins are like scarlet, they shall be as white as snow; though they are red as crimson, they shall be like wool. If you are willing and obedient, you will eat the best from the land'" (Isa. 1:18-19).

Zophar also adds his testimony of faith: "True wisdom has two sides. Know this: God has even forgotten some of your sin. . . . If you devote your heart to him and stretch out your hands to him, if you put away the sin that is in your hand and allow no evil to dwell in your tent, then you will lift up your face without shame; you will stand firm and without fear.

"You will surely forget your trouble, recalling it only as waters gone by. Life will be brighter than noonday, and darkness will become like morning. You will be secure because there is hope; you will look about you and take your rest in safety. You will lie down with no one to make you afraid" (11:6, 13-19).

Thank You, Father, for Your other side. You are all-powerful, but You are more. With Frederick Faber I sing:

> *There's a wideness in God's mercy*
> *Like the wideness of the sea;*
> *There's a kindness in His justice*
> *Which is more than liberty.*

▼

☐ **WEEK 19, SUNDAY** **JOB**

Scripture: Job 12—16
The Story: Job 12:1-2; 13:1-5; 16:1-5

To every thing there is a season . . . a time to keep silence, and a time to speak (Eccles. 3:1, 7).

A Time to Keep Silence

Job's friends were not the world's wisest counselors. Their great mistake was pushing logic when Job needed love. On one occasion I, too, was tempted to set a man straight, but the Holy Spirit checked me. As I listened to his complaint I discovered that he had not come to criticize but to share his pain.

Wisdom bids us learn where a man hurts, and share his suffering. To understand this ministry we need to read it from the heart of one who has lived through it. Sharon Marshall writes of the support her friends gave in the early days of agony when she learned that their child was hopelessly defective.

"Handicapped! Brain damaged! Mentally retarded! Deformed! Birth defect! Enormous head size! What a nightmare of words! What a blow! Those awful words rang in my ears and haunted me as I tried to sleep. . . .

"Our friends immediately began to respond to our hurt with phone calls and notes of encouragement. My heart reached out and touched theirs as they groped for words. Several years before I had been in their shoes. My college roommate's first baby had been hydrocephalic, stillborn—and I had to comfort her. Words were just so inadequate, and I felt helpless to ease her pain.

"As I looked back, I realized it was she who eased my pain; now it was my turn. God gave me peace and power to respond to what I heard, and the calls of my friends warmed my heart and spoke to me of His love. Someone in the midst of tragedy needs your person, not your words.

"Those who gave advice were truly messengers of God—the advice came at my hour of need and rang true in my heart. Most, however, simply said, 'I'm sorry,' reaffirming their love and support. I desperately needed that, even more than I needed the best advice available" (Justin, *Heaven's Baby*).

Father, teach me something of Your compassion: "A bruised reed shall he not break, and the smoking flax shall he not quench" (Isa. 42:3).

Scripture: Job 17—19
The Story: Job 17:13-16; 19:23-27
I know that my Redeemer lives . . . I myself will see him with my own eyes—I, and not another (Job 19:25, 27; all quotes from NIV).

The God of All Hope

When some sin separates us from God, we must find our way around it, or through it, or over it. Somehow we must recover our faith in God, or life never comes out right.

In the beginning of the book, Job was a God-fearing man. But through attacks of Satan and testing by God he began to entertain faithless thoughts and to develop wrong attitudes. We learn from Job that loss of faith cuts us off from God. We must somehow recover that faith and find our way back to Him.

We can never think clearly nor respond rightly to God's plan for our lives unless we believe that we are meant to live forever. Job himself soon came to realize how essential faith in immortality is for a wholesome understanding of human destiny: "If the only home I hope for is the grave, if I spread out my bed in darkness, if I say to corruption, 'You are my father,' and to the worm, 'My mother' or 'My sister,' where then is my hope? Who can see any hope for me?" (17:13-15).

In the closing service of a revival campaign Dr. Ross Price brought hope to the still struggling when he said: "No soul will ever be lost who keeps open to the Holy Spirit." Job must have sensed that profound truth. In all of his doubts and arguments his heart was seeking for God. He prayed: "If only you would set me a time and then remember me! . . . I will wait for my renewal to come. You will call and I will answer you; you will long for the creature your hands have made" (14:13, 15).

Even a little faith added to such a yearning for God brings the joy of discovery and the sense of reestablished fellowship with Him. Job's rekindled faith rises to a triumphant shout: "I know that my Redeemer lives." His faith had once again put him in living touch with the God of all hope. Here is the saving faith reflected in the lines from Handel's *Messiah*:

I know that my Redeemer liveth,
*   and that he shall stand at the latter day upon the earth.*
And though worms destroy this body,
*   yet in my flesh I shall see God.*
For now is Christ risen from the dead,
*   the first fruits of them that sleep.*

▼

Scripture: Job 20—21
The Story: Job 20:4-9, 21:7-15

The mirth of the wicked is brief, and the joy of the godless lasts but a moment (Job 20:5, NIV).

Which Do I Really Believe?

God's Word declares, "The Lord knoweth the way of the righteous: but the way of the ungodly shall perish" (Ps. 1:6). In chapters 20—21 Job and Zophar debate this issue. Shall we listen to the arguments and weigh the evidence?

We are sometimes tempted to believe Job's negative assertions, but will his witness stand up under cross-examination?

"The wicked live on to a good old age, and become great and powerful. [Always _____ or only sometimes _____] They live to see their children grow to maturity around them, and their grandchildren, too. Their homes are safe from every fear [True _____ or False _____], and God does not punish them. Their cattle are productive, they have many happy children, they spend their time

197

singing and dancing. They are wealthy [All of them ____ or only some of them ____] and need deny themselves nothing; they are prosperous to the end. . . .

"Look, everything the wicked touch has turned to gold! . . . the wicked get away with it every time [Yes ____ No ____]. They never have trouble [Agree ____ Disagree ____], and God skips them when he distributes his sorrows and anger" (21:7-13, 16-17, TLB).

Now let us hear the summary of God's spokesman:

"Don't you realize that ever since man was first placed upon the earth, the triumph of the wicked has been short-lived, and the joy of the godless but for a moment? Though the godless be proud as the heavens, and walk with his nose in the air, yet he shall perish forever . . . Those who knew him will wonder where he is gone. He will fade like a dream. Neither his friends nor his family will ever see him again. . . . The heavens will reveal his sins, and the earth will give testimony against him. . . . This is what awaits the wicked man, for God prepares it for him" (20:4-9, 27, 29, TLB).

The arguments are finished, the evidence is in. What are the facts? I must render the verdict. With all my heart I really believe:

God's way is the best way,
God's way is the right way,
I'll trust in Him alway,
He knoweth the best. *
—LIDA SHIVERS LEECH

*Copyright 1911, © Renewed 1939 by The Rodeheaver Co. (A Div. of WORD, INC.) All Rights Reserved. International Copyright Secured. Used by Permission.

▼

☐ WEEK 19, WEDNESDAY   JOB

Scripture: Job 22—24
The Story: Job 22:21-30; 23:3-7

Submit to God and be at peace with him (Job 22:21, NIV).

"Just as I Am . . . I Come"

What actions or attitudes keep us from fellowship with God?

Eliphaz accuses Job of the besetting sins of the wealthy—robbing the poor, cheating the widow, and exploiting the orphan (22:1-11). But Job knew he was innocent of these gross sins. He testified: "I rescued the poor who cried for help . . . The man who was dying blessed me; I made the widow's heart sing. . . . I was eyes to the blind and feet to the lame. I was a father to the needy; I took up the case of the stranger" (Job 29:12-13, 15-16, NIV). But in spite of these good works God seemed far away.

The second charge came closer to the problem in Job's spirit. Because God allowed good men to suffer, Job denied God's knowledge of the world and His compassion for its needs "God is so great—higher than the heavens . . . 'That is why he can't see what I am doing! . . . He is way up there, walking on the vault of heaven'" (22:12-14, TLB).

The Bible says, "If I regard iniquity in my heart, the Lord will not hear me" (Ps. 66:18). To exploit my neighbor is to commit sin; but to deny God's loving involvement in my life is also to "regard iniquity in my heart."

Does God seem far away today? Am I yearning to feel His presence and approval in my life? Eliphaz gives me right counsel: "Submit to God and be at peace with him." Even if I am confused about the reasons for my lostness, the advice is right. The Bible promises, "Draw nigh to God, and he will draw nigh to you" (James 4:8).

God's Word reminds me, when I need guidance, I can listen to His voice (22:22). If there is sin in my life, I can put it away (22:23). If I have been selfish with my money, I can begin using it for His glory (22:24-25). If I have questioned His providence, I can reaffirm my love and begin to do what I know He is asking of me.

Job was making progress when he declared his faith in God's goodness: "If I only knew where to find him . . . I would find out what he would answer me. . . . There an upright man could present his case before him."

Today, Father, I move toward You even though I am not exactly sure what You want me to do.

199

Just as I am, tho' tossed about
With many a conflict, many a doubt,
Fightings and fears within, without,
O Lamb of God, I come! I come!
                    —CHARLOTTE ELLIOTT

Scripture: Job 25—28
The Story: Job 26:7-14; 27:1-6, 13-19
**Behold the fear of the Lord, that is wisdom; and
to depart from evil is understanding** (Job 28:28).

Right Thinking About God

We may know much about God without enjoying His fellowship
and approval. Knowledge without fellowship is the snag where Job
was hung up for so long. Is that my problem?

In a beautiful description of God's plan for the weather, Job
acknowledges the Creator's power: "He spreads out the northern
skies over empty space; he suspends the earth over nothing. He
wraps up the waters in his clouds, yet the clouds do not burst
under their weight. He covers the face of the full moon, spreading
his clouds over it. . . . By his breath the skies become fair; . . . And
these are but the outer fringe of his works" (26:7-9, 13-14, NIV). So
far, so good; but this much "the devils also believe, and tremble"
(James 2:19).

Job's theology is straight at a second point, too; God is against
unrighteousness. He will not let the wicked prosper forever: "Here
is the fate God allots to the wicked, the heritage a ruthless man
receives from the Almighty . . . Though he heaps up silver like dust
and clothes like piles of clay, what he lays up the righteous will
wear . . . The house he builds is like a moth's cocoon, like a hut
made by a watchman. He lies down wealthy, but will do so no

more; when he opens his eyes, all is gone" (27:13, 16-19, NIV). God wants us to be righteous, but if we trust in our own goodness we have little contact with the Heavenly Father. He wants us to love Him as well as to obey Him.

If for any reason I am teed off against God, I do not enjoy His fellowship. This is where Job stumbled, and this is where he fell on his face once more near the end of his struggle: "I vow by the living God . . . who has embittered my soul, that . . . I will never, never agree that you are right; until I die I will vow my innocence" (27:2-3, 5, TLB). Like Job I may feel justified in my attitude—but self-justification wins no friends and brings no healing help from God.

Father, I thank You that Your law and Your grace have kept me from many of the outbroken sins. Now I pray that Your love shall save me from an embittered spirit. Teach me that You are too good to do wrong. Fill my mind with Your spirit of understanding, and fill my heart with Your love. In my loving Savior's name. Amen.

▼

Scripture: Job 29—31
The Story: Job 29:2-3; 14:13-17

How I long for . . . the days when God watched over me . . . and by his light I walked through darkness! (Job 29:2-3; all quotes from NIV).

Give Me God's Smile

In these three chapters we come to Job's final speech. There is no new argument and no conversation. Rather, we have a 103-verse monologue in which Job summarizes his position.

Chapter 29 reflects a time of fulfillment in his life when he knew the heights of human happiness. He had enjoyed walking with his Creator: "God's intimate friendship blessed my house, when the Almighty was still with me and my children were around me" (29:4-5).

Chapter 30 contrasts Job's unhappy present with those joyful days of the past. Friends who once honored him now mock him. Enemies who formerly feared him now brazenly attack. Health that undergirded his strength "vanishes like a cloud. And now my life ebbs away" (vv. 15-16).

The frustrating part is that Job knows God is somehow behind all of the trouble that has befallen him. He cries, "God has unstrung my bow and afflicted me" (30:11). "In his great power God . . . throws me into the mud, and I am reduced to dust and ashes. I cry out to you, O God, but you do not answer; I stand up, but you merely look at me" (30:18-20).

Locked in what seems to be a hopeless conflict of wills with the Almighty, Job still shouts his self-justification: "Oh that I had someone to hear me! I sign now my defense—let the Almighty answer me; let my accuser put his indictment in writing" (31:35).

It is as far as a man can go in any stubborn controversy with God. There is no more to be said: "The words of Job are ended" (31:40).

Why does God appear to maintain the role of adversary when a man longs for His smile but refuses to accept what his mind does not understand? The answer of Eliphaz is the only answer we know: "He wounds, but he also binds up; he injures, but his hands also heal" (Job 5:18). The more stubborn our demands, the more deeply God must wound us to try to bring us to himself. Blind Fanny Crosby testifies: "He took away my eyes that my soul might see."

Father, if I have contended to some bitter end for my own way, forgive me. You know my deep need—and my heart's cry: "How I long for . . . the days when God watched over me . . . and by his light I walked through darkness!" I give up my demands. I accept Your love. Your light shall show me the way through the darkness.

▼

Scripture: Job 32—34
The Story: Job 33:12-30

The Lord is . . . not willing that any should perish, but that all should come to repentance (2 Pet. 3:9).

God's Love Is from Everlasting

Whatever attitudes separate us from God, He goes a third mile to remove the barriers and to win our love.

In chapters 32—37 we hear a new voice. Elihu, a younger counselor, reminds us of God's deep concern and His steadfast love. Verses 23-24 in the story are understood as Messianic prophecies. In them we foresee that "God was in Christ, reconciling the world unto himself" (2 Cor. 5:19). This message of Elihu can best be communicated in the words of Scripture itself.

"God is greater than man. Why should you fight against him just because he does not give account to you of what he does?

"For God speaks again and again, in dreams, in visions of the night when deep sleep falls on men as they lie on their beds. He opens their ears in times like that, and gives them wisdom and instruction, causing them to change their minds, and keeping them from pride, and warning them of the penalties of sin, and keeping them from falling into some trap.

"Or, God sends sickness and pain, even though no bone is broken, so that a man loses all taste and appetite for food and doesn't care for even the daintiest dessert. He becomes thin, mere skin and bones, and draws near to death.

"But if a messenger from heaven is there to intercede for him as a friend, to show him what is right, then God pities him and says, 'Set him free. Do not make him die, for I have found a substitute.' Then his body will become as healthy as a child's, firm and youthful again. And when he prays to God, God will hear and answer and receive him with joy, and return him to his duties. And he will declare to his friends, 'I sinned, but God let me go. He did not let me die. I will go on living in the realm of light.'

"Yes, God often does these things for man—brings back his soul from the pit, so that he may live in the light of the living" (Job 33:12-30, TLB).

Today I join the prayer of David:

"Bless the Lord, O my soul . . . who forgiveth all thine iniquities" (Ps. 103:2-3).

▼

Scripture: Job 35—37
The Story: Job 36:1-16
I will ascribe justice to my Maker (Job 36:3, NIV).

What Is God Like?

We seldom respond rightly to God until we think correctly about Him. Wrong concepts bring wrong attitudes; right understanding moves us to right response. Jesus said, "Ye shall know the truth, and the truth shall make you free" (John 8:32).

In chapter 35 Elihu points out some concepts that were frustrating to Job. In chapter 36 he outlines truths from Scripture that undergird faith. Today let us probe our foundations and rejoice in their strength. The following statements about God's character are attributed to Job by Elihu. Do you believe the assertions to be true or false? Circle your answer. (A modern translation will reflect these truths more clearly.)

T   F   There is no profit to me in keeping free from sin (35:1-3).

T   F   God does not know or care if I sin (35:5-6).

T   F   For a man to live a righteous life means nothing to God (35:7-8).

T   F   Men are more inclined to thank God in good times than to complain in hard times (35:9-11).

T F God never answers when we cry out against oppression by the wicked (35:12).

T F God does not even hear when we protest against evil (35:13).

T F God pays no attention when we are perplexed by His silences (35:14-15).

In contrast to Job's false arguments, Elihu makes the following assertions about God. Do you believe them to be true or false?

T F God holds firmly to His purposes, but He never despises the needs of a man (36:5).

T F God does not allow the wicked to prosper in order to encourage their wickedness (36:6).

T F God remembers and loves the righteous in their times of suffering and perplexity (36:7).

T F When we commit sin, God is faithful to remind us (36:8-9).

T F When we have sinned, God commands us to repent (36:10).

T F When we repent, God forgives and blesses us (36:11).

T F If we refuse to obey and serve God, we shall perish (36:12).

Thank You, Father, for a right understanding of both Your righteousness and Your love. "I will ascribe justice to my Maker."

▼

☐ **WEEK 20, MONDAY** JOB

Scripture: Job 38—39
The Story: Job 38:1-7, 24-33

To God belong wisdom and power; counsel and understanding are his (Job 12:13; all quotes from NIV).

The Greatness of God

The author of Job wants us never to lose sight of God's concern and of the intricate design of the world that He created for us.

Verses 24-30 probe for an explanation of the marvelous weather patterns of the earth: "What is the way to the place where the lightning is dispersed or the place where the east winds are scattered over the earth?" We know it is the Lord who planned these forces and makes them mesh to provide rain for men and animals.

God created this earth as a home for us and planned its intricate resources to supply our needs. But there is more. God is concerned for the needs of animal life, and perhaps for inanimate resources also. He provides valleys for watercourses on the earth, and rain for plant life even "where there is no man."

From these detailed provisions for our life on the earth, God turns our thoughts to the heavens: "Can you bind the beautiful Pleiades? Can you loose the cords of Orion? Can you bring forth the constellations in their seasons: or lead out the Bear with its cubs? Do you know the laws of the heavens?"

With a subdued and reverent Job, we can only answer no to God's query. When we see our own limited knowledge and power in true perspective, we cry with David: "When I consider your heavens, the work of your fingers, the moon and the stars, which you have set in place, what is man that . . . you care for him?" (Ps. 8:3-4).

We cannot fathom how any power can be strong enough or any mind wise enough to create the immense and complex physical world. But we believe it is so. In the Apostles' Creed we confess our faith: "I believe in God the Father Almighty, Maker of heaven and earth."

Based on that faith we joyfully sing with F. S. Pierpoint:

For the beauty of the earth,
For the glory of the skies,
For the love which from our birth
Over and around us lies,
Lord of all, to Thee we raise
This our hymn of grateful praise.

Scripture: Job 40—42
The Story: Job 40:1-5; 42:2-6

**My ears had heard of you but now my eyes have
seen you. Therefore I . . . repent in dust and ashes**
(Job 42:5-6; all quotes from NIV).

Surrender with Honor

God loves us too much to let us stray from Him easily. He sometimes takes strong measures to call us back to clear thinking and
devoted loyalty to Him.

Job vacillated between rebellion and loyalty, but it is clear he
had not come through his trial unscarred. His own attitude had
become his greatest problem. In defending his integrity he had cast
aspersions on the integrity of God.

Now God says to Job: "Will the one who contends with the
Almighty correct him? Let him who accuses God answer him!"
(40:2). The Lord had to jolt His man hard enough to clear his mind.
In such a controversy we must finally acknowledge that we are no
match for God—either in power, or knowledge, or wisdom.

In any confrontation God will crowd us, but He never forces
our agreement or acceptance. He respects the thinking mind and
the free will that He has given us. God's argument here is an appeal
to reason. He asks us to respond because it is right. It is a wise
decision in view of the facts under consideration.

If God be real, and if He is a wise and good God, it makes
sense for us to reverence Him, to love Him, to try to live the way He
asks us to live. To reject these facts and to fly in the face of God's
revealed will for life brings only further confusion and chaos.

Faith in the God of the Bible does not answer all of the mind's
questions; but faith answers more of them, and faith answers them
better than any alternative open to us. Surely to find the most

answers and to reach the best answers is the path of wisdom for a thoughtful human being.

In any struggle with God the bottom line reads, *Surrender*— because surrender to our Heavenly Father is always to surrender in wisdom and with honor.

Father, "I know that you can do all things; no plan of yours can be thwarted. . . . Surely I spoke of things I did not understand, things too wonderful for me to know. . . . My ears had heard of you but now my eyes have seen you. Therefore I despise myself and repent in dust and ashes" (42:2-3, 5-6).

▼

☐ WEEK 20, WEDNESDAY   PSALMS

The *Psalms* are poems, and poems are usually written to express our feelings. To get the message we must try to feel what the writer felt. This calls for deliberate reading and sympathetic understanding.

We get the most value from reading the psalms if we take the poems one at a time. But we have a reading schedule to keep, so we must cover several chapters each day.

Try reading one psalm in the morning, one later in the day, and one in the evening. Read the psalm containing "The Story" at the time when you have the most leisure to read both the psalm itself and the related meditation.

Scripture: Psalms 1—3
The Story: Psalm 1:1-6

The Lord knoweth the way of the righteous (Ps. 1:6).

We Are on the Right Track!

This is my Father's world.
Oh, let me ne'er forget
That though the wrong seems oft so strong,
God is the Ruler yet.

In these words Maltie Babcock affirms the heartfelt faith of the Psalmist. In these poems we feel a profound commitment to God and to His plan for our lives. Here is the faith of men and women who have walked with God; they have proved Him faithful in a thousand circumstances of life.

This attitude of trust sets the mood for the whole Book of Psalms. Life is greatly simplified and our choices are made easier when, with the Psalmist, we recognize that there are only two roads for one to travel. We must choose the way of the righteous, or we find ourselves on the way of the ungodly.

But choosing God's way is the wise way. It is best for us. It is what we really want most from this life. The philosopher talks about the *summum bonum*—life's highest good; we are sure it is found only in God's will.

Every man and woman desires happiness; but we find it only when we are related rightly to God, to persons around us, to truth, and to God's world of nature. These right relations bring an increasing and all-pervasive kind of contentment. We call it personal fulfillment. He who finds this deep satisfaction is indeed the blessed man. Such fulfillment comes from walking with God. It comes from standing firm against sin's encroachment on our lives. We find fulfillment in meditating often upon God's Word as we open our spirits to His Holy Spirit.

Oh, I know it is true! His Spirit witnesses with our spirits "that we are the children of God" (Rom. 8:16).

We are on the right track!

▼

Scripture: Psalms 4—6

In verses 2 and 4 we encounter the word *Selah.* It was not intended to be read, but seems to have been a musical notation similar to the rest sign (⦚) that we sometimes see on the staff in our songbooks. It meant "stop." When we encounter *Selah* in the Psalms we should take it to mean "pause and reflect." Try out this practice on verse 4: "Stand in awe, and sin not: commune with your own heart upon your bed, and be still." *Stop and think about that!*

The Story: Psalm 4:1-8

The Lord hath heard my supplication; the Lord will receive my prayer (Ps. 6:9).

An Evening Prayer

In these psalms David assures us,
> *There's a blessing in prayer, in believing prayer;*
> *When our Savior's name to the throne we bear.*
> *Then a Father's love will receive us there;*
> *There is always a blessing, a blessing in prayer.*
> —E. E. Hewitt

Our scripture reminds us of experiences in which our lives are enriched by communion with God. Psalm 6 describes finding His help when life is hard. Psalm 5 shows us a man seeking God's guidance at the beginning of the day. But Psalm 4 encourages us to remember God's goodness at evening time. As we learn to pray, we find ourselves testifying in all of our circumstances, "The Lord hath heard my supplication; the Lord will receive my prayer" (6:9).

At the close of this day as I draw near to Him, what does God encourage me to remember?

First, I am always welcome in His presence. Even if I have failed Him during the day, He wants me to talk with Him about it. But how much easier to come to Him if, through His grace, I have tried faithfully to serve Him. In 4:3 I am reminded, "The Lord has set apart the redeemed for himself. Therefore he will listen to me and answer when I call to him" (TLB).

In 4:1 David remembers God's blessings of the past but knows that he needs further help tonight. "You have always cared for me in my distress; now hear me as I call again" (TLB). There is a kind of repeated "againness" in our coming to God. But the Father welcomes it.

The quietness of the evening hour often opens our lives to God's Spirit. In the excitement of the day's activities conscience may not be heard or may go unheeded. But when the lights are out and only His gentle voice is heard, we are inclined to renew our commitments to Him. That is why David writes, "Lie quietly upon your bed in silent meditation. Put your trust in the Lord, and offer him pleasing sacrifices" (4:4-5, TLB).

After I have discussed the day with Him, I can say, *Good-night, Lord.*

"I will lie down in peace and sleep, for though I am alone, O Lord, you will keep me safe" (4:8, TLB).

▼

□ **WEEK 20, FRIDAY** **PSALMS**

Scripture: Psalms 7—10
The Story: Psalm 8:1-9

What is man, that thou shouldst think of him . . . ?
Yet thou hast made him but little lower than God
(Ps. 8:4-5, Smith-Goodspeed).

Under God, I'm OK—You're OK

One of the current books written to help us understand ourselves carries the encouraging title *I'm OK—You're OK* (by Thomas A. Harris, M.D.) If the author means that in myself I can make it, he is wrong. But if he means what the Psalmist meant, he is right. David was ready to bet his life on the proposition, Under God, I'm OK—you're OK.

211

God has given us the ability to think, to ask questions, to reason, and to reach conclusions. It is natural that we should reflect on our existence. We need God's answers to our questions: Who am I? From whence did I come? Why am I here? What is my destiny?

Our confidence in a good meaning for human life rests upon our faith in a sovereign and loving God. That is where David begins: "O Lord our Lord, how excellent is thy name in all the earth!" We are OK in this universe because God has all of it under His control.

Who am I? I was created by God when in the council chambers of eternity He said, "Let us make man in our image, after our likeness" (Gen. 1:26). I am similar to God because He gave me intelligence and a spiritual nature. He created me to make responsible choices between good and evil, and to live forever. He wanted me to be like Him, and to have fellowship with Him. That is indeed high destiny!

The Bible view of man is a high view. With David we sing our praise because God has crowned our lives "with glory and honour."

Within the Christian faith we find God's answer to our need for a wholesome and adequate self-image. God knows our needs and He knows how to balance accounts. For evil men with a false ego complex, He has a day of reckoning. But for His people, tempted at times to be weak and fearful, He gives assurance. I stand tall when I remember, "The helpless man commits himself to you; you have always helped the needy" (Ps. 10:14, TEV).

Today, let us close our meditation where David closed his: "O Lord our Lord, how excellent is thy name in all the earth!"

▼

☐ **WEEK 20, SATURDAY**   **PSALMS**

Scripture: Psalms 11—13
The Story: Psalms 11:1—13:6

If the foundations be destroyed, what can the righteous do? (Ps. 11:3; all other quotes from NIV).

Hang In There

A newspaper carried this thought for the day: "You cannot climb the ladder of success with the cold feet of fear." We don't know who said it—but we know it is true.

If the question of our text be taken out of its setting, it leaves us with a great sense of uncertainty and fear. The faint heart cries, "Oh, dear, what shall the righteous do now?" But we must not take the verse out of its context. David was not expressing fear; he was talking faith.

Look again carefully at 11:1, 3. God's man declares, "In the Lord I take refuge. How then can you say to me: 'Flee like a bird to your mountain. . . . When the foundations are being destroyed, what can the righteous do?'"

When the foundations seem to be destroyed, hang in there! God himself is beneath those foundations, and He will keep them firm.

With David we can declare, "In the Lord I take refuge." With him we reaffirm our confidence that "the Lord is on his heavenly throne." We know that God still watches men; that His soul hates wickedness and violence; that He loves justice, and that upright men will see His face.

In Psalm 12 we can recognize the presence of evil men; we can even acknowledge their temporary success without losing our faith. We affirm confidently, "O Lord, you will keep us safe and protect us from such people forever" (v. 7).

With David in Psalm 13, we may cry out at God's delay, "How long? How long? How long?" But our faith shall triumph. We, too, can sing with all the believing saints:

"Give light to my eyes . . . I trust in your unfailing love; my heart rejoices in your salvation. I will sing to the Lord, for he has been good to me."

213

Scripture: Psalms 14—16
The Story: Psalm 15:1-5

I have set the Lord always before me: because he is at my right hand, I shall not be moved (Ps. 16:8).

What Does God Ask of Me?

A prosperous young businessman came to Jesus with the question, "Good Master, what shall I do that I may inherit eternal life?" (Mark 10:17). It is the same query that concerned David: "Lord, who shall abide in thy tabernacle? Who shall dwell in thy holy hill?" (15:1).

God's answer always requires something from us, but the conditions are never complex or overwhelming. David's spirit heard the answer in six simple assertions.

✔ God's man is "He whose walk is blameless and who does what is righteous" (15:2, NIV). To be *blameless* describes God's acceptance of us—He does not charge us with failure. To be *righteous* describes our attitudes toward God. When we honestly seek to do His will, we are given His full approval.

✔ The next couplet reflects the inward quality of true religion. The man of God "speaks the truth from his heart and has no slander on his tongue" (NIV). Elsewhere the Psalmist understands this full devotion to God when he prays, "Let the words of my mouth, and the meditation of my heart, be acceptable in thy sight, O Lord, my strength, and my redeemer" (19:14).

✔ Jesus put answer No. 3 very simply: "Thou shalt love thy neighbour as thyself" (Matt. 19:19). In the Old Testament David heard God's word: "Do your neighbor no wrong and cast no slur on your fellow man" (author's paraphrase).

✔ He who walks with God reacts to right and wrong as God responds to them. Does my spirit revolt against the sin of the vile person? Do I feel like applauding and supporting those who fear the Lord?

✔ God's man doesn't weasel. Do I keep my promise even when it costs me more than I had expected?

✔ Finally, God asks me to use my money to further His business. Usury is the interest you have to pay when your need is greatest and your collateral is lowest. The worldly lender takes advantage of a man's need to make a greater gain. God's lender knows that fair treatment is always more important than bigger returns.

Six things God asks of me—and promises, "He who does these things will never be shaken" (15:5, NIV).

Thank You, Lord.

"I will bless the Lord, who hath given me counsel . . . because he is at my right hand, I shall not be moved" (16:7-8).

▼

Scripture: Psalms 17—18
The Story: Psalm 17:1-8, 15

Hear, O Lord . . . Give ear to my prayer—it does not rise from deceitful lips (Ps. 17:1, NIV).

"Draw Near . . . in Full Assurance"

In these two psalms an Old Testament saint has discovered some New Testament theology. The writer of Hebrews encourages Christians: "Let us draw near with a true heart in full assurance of faith, having our hearts sprinkled from an evil conscience, and our bodies washed with pure water. Let us hold fast the profession of our faith without wavering" (Heb. 10:22-23).

David based his confidence on righteous living. In this there is nothing wrong; it is only human self-righteousness that is like filthy rags. God's man here testifies to the confidence that springs from integrity when we come into the presence of God. We know that God is righteous, and that God asks us to live righteous lives.

Therefore the man prays: "Hear, O Lord, my righteous plea; listen to my cry. Give ear to my prayer—it does not rise from deceitful lips" (NIV).

But this man's deep regard for holy living is not a self-righteousness. He knows that all he is and all he has comes from God: "I call on you, O God, for you will answer me; give ear to me and hear my prayer. Show the wonder of your great love, you who save by your right hand those who take refuge in you" (17:6-7, NIV).

When we walk with God in faith and obedience, we find assurance not only for the present but also for the life to come. This psalm gives us one of the clearest Old Testament witnesses to faith in immortality: "As for me, my contentment is not in wealth but in seeing you and knowing all is well between us. And when I awake in heaven, I will be fully satisfied, for I will see you face to face" (TEV).

From such deep assurance comes overflowing joy:

"The Lord lives! Praise be to my Rock! Exalted be God my Savior! ... Therefore I will praise you among the nations, O Lord; I will sing praises to your name" (18:46, 49, NIV).

▼

☐ **WEEK 21, TUESDAY** **PSALMS**

Scripture: Psalms 19—23

Why not memorize Psalm 19 for your own spiritual enrichment?

Psalm 22 is a Messianic psalm. On the Cross Jesus quoted the first verse. Also verses 6-8, 13, and 16-18 seem to describe His bodily condition and emotional experience during the Crucifixion.

The Story: Psalm 19:7-14

Your word is a lamp to my feet and a light for my path (Ps. 119:105, NIV).

The Book That Changes Our Lives

How does the Bible change lives and bring us strength today? In 19:7-8 we find four couplets that explain why we treasure the Word of God. In each couplet a fundamental characteristic of the Bible is described. These are followed by blessed results that we discover as we read and obey the Scriptures.

The law of the Lord is perfect, converting the soul. It is a sound and good law, exactly suited to God's purpose. That purpose is to make us good and godly persons.

When a man obeys this law of God he finds himself converted, turned around. Sin turns our faces away from God and sets our feet on the downward path. Therefore God has revealed himself in the Bible in order that we may find our way back to Him. Peter writes, We are "born again . . . by the word of God, which liveth and abideth for ever" (1 Pet. 1:23).

God's Word *is sure, making wise the simple.* A sure testimony is a clear and true one. When the Bible predicts the outcome of a course of action, we can be sure it will happen that way.

The man described here as simple is the open-minded, teachable person. The more readily we accept the sure guidance of the Bible, the wiser we become.

The truths of God found in Scripture are *right, rejoicing the heart.* As we shape our lives by the Bible's instructions we discover just how right God is. He gives no arbitrary requirements. None are imposed upon us apart from God's desire for our good.

When we discover this, our hearts rejoice. After a few disappointing experiences of going contrary to Bible teachings, and after several radiant results of obeying God, we gladly testify with the Psalmist, "The judgments of the Lord are true and righteous altogether."

The commandment of the Lord is pure, enlightening the eyes. Moffatt translates these words, "The Eternal's command is clear, a light to the mind." The further we go in the Christian life, the clearer we see our way. Indeed, "The path of the just is as the shining light, that shineth more and more unto the perfect day" (Prov. 4:18).

Thank You, God, for the Book that is transforming our lives.

Scripture: Psalms 24—27

Psalm 25 is one of nine acrostic psalms in which each verse begins with a successive letter of the 22-letter Hebrew alphabet.

The Story: Psalm 27:1-14

The one thing I want from God, the thing I seek most of all, is the privilege of . . . living in his presence every day of my life . . . There I'll be when troubles come (Ps. 27:4-5, TLB).

Living in His Presence

Psalm 27 breathes a sense of deep peace and assurance. "The Lord is my light and my salvation; whom shall I fear? The Lord is the strength of my life; of whom shall I be afraid?" (v. 1).

God is always available, but we do not always appropriate His grace. David had learned the lesson that if he came regularly into the presence of God, he would be there in his hours of emergency.

Our younger son and his wife have two boys and a girl. When the children were still young, George and Jodie were confronted with the doctor's diagnosis of Jodie's breast cancer and the need for immediate surgery. Here is the kind of family threat where each member needs all the help that his faith can bring. And God did not fail them.

After the surgery George testified that God gave him assurance and support through the words of our psalm: "The Lord is my light and my salvation; whom shall I fear? . . . The one thing I want from God, the thing I seek most of all, is the privilege of . . . living in his presence every day of my life . . . There I'll be when troubles come."

The surgery was successful, and in a blessed ripple effect, the

218

power of God flowed out beyond the immediate family. Jodie's dad, who had not yet come to know Christ, acknowledged, "Jodie had something more than medicine going for her."

Today I testify with David:

"When thou saidst, Seek ye my face; my heart said unto thee, Thy face, Lord, will I seek" (27:8).

▼

Scripture: Psalms 28—30
The Story: Psalm 29:1-11

The Lord will give strength unto his people; the Lord will bless his people with peace (Ps. 29:11).

When God Speaks

What voice do I hear in the thunder? Do I respond with terror or with a feeling of joy at the greatness of God?

In this psalm David's mood was set by a crashing storm. It originated in the *waters* of the eastern Mediterranean Sea; moved inland over the hills of *Lebanon;* rumbled across *Sirion* (Mount Hermon), and on northeast bringing rain to the deserts of *Kadesh* (see a map of northern Palestine in your Bible).

In such an awesome display, some see only brute power and human terror. But David bids us see and hear as men of God. William Cowper could write:

> *God moves in a mysterious way*
> *His wonders to perform;*
> *He plants His footsteps in the sea,*
> *And rides upon the storm.*

How can we thus see beyond twisted trees, shaking hills, and forked lightning? In these it is easy to understand that He who controls the elements is a God of strength. If we fight against Him,

219

the battle is lost before it begins. But if He is on our side, and if His strength is at our disposal, we can only shout for joy at this language of power.

Psalm 29 reminds us that God is first of all, the God of His people. It is addressed to *ye mighty ones,* literally, "ye sons of the mighty one." This God of all power is also the God of peace. He is "The Lord [who] gives strength to his people; the Lord [who] blesses his people with peace" (NIV).

The psalm begins with the assurance that we are God's people, and closes with God's purpose of peace. Within this framework there is no room for fear; only for a song of glad praise.

"Ascribe to the Lord, O mighty ones, ascribe to the Lord glory and strength. Ascribe to the Lord the glory due his name; worship the Lord in the splendor of his holiness. . . . The Lord sits enthroned over the flood; the Lord is enthroned as King forever. The Lord gives strength to his people; the Lord blesses his people with peace" (29:1-2, 10-11, NIV).

▼

☐ WEEK 21, FRIDAY   PSALMS

Scripture: Psalms 31—34

Psalm 34 is worthy of programming into your spiritual memory bank. Read this psalm thoughtfully and prayerfully twice a day for a month—once in the morning and again before going to bed. At the end of the month you will find your faith in God deepened—and a great spiritual resource on deposit for the rest of your life.

The Story: Psalm 33:8-22

Blessed is the nation whose God is the Lord (Ps. 33:12).

Can God Control Nations?

Today we wrestle with a Christian issue that has been hard for me to resolve. I believe I am ready to live my personal life on the basis of Christ's teaching that love is more powerful than hate. But should I place unqualified faith in God's power and assume my country's leaders can guide national policy on the basis of returning good for evil?

One of our presidents built his foreign policy on the premise that peaceful negotiation is better than all-out preparation for war. In this he met with frustration. For example, a political opponent attacked this policy on national television. He charged the president with incompetence, declaring, "It has taken him three years to learn that he cannot trust the Russians."

Do I want my president to trust in all-out physical force in order to keep our nation secure? Is such trust a viable solution in today's world? If David were living today, would he write: "The bomb is a vain thing for safety: neither shall it deliver any people by its great power"? (see 33.17).

Government leaders are sure that Russia has enough rockets and enough hydrogen bombs to wipe out many American cities in one attack. It has been estimated that 40 million Americans would die in that first all-out nuclear strike against the United States.

We are told that current national defense policies are based upon the premise that in the event of such an attack the United States could inflict equal destruction upon Soviet cities. No one could win such a war of annihilation.

But I am sure God does not want a national defense policy based only on fear of our own destruction and death. I believe He wants a policy based on trust in His power to overrule the plans of evil men.

I thank God that I do not have to make those policy decisions. Yet in a democratic society I cannot escape responsibility for them; I vote to support or to reverse the decisions.

Today, with Paul, I pray "for all that are in authority; that we may lead a quiet and peaceable life in all godliness and honesty" (1 Tim. 2:2).

With the Psalmist I declare:

"In him our hearts rejoice, for we trust in his holy name. May your unfailing love rest upon us, O Lord, even as we put our hope in you" (33:21-22, NIV).

▼

Scripture: Psalms 35—37
The Story: Psalm 37:1-8

Do not fret—it leads only to evil (Ps. 37:8, NIV).

God's Cure for Fretting

Psalm 37 is one of the wisdom psalms. This wisdom literature of the Bible tells us that to follow God's plan for our lives is just good common sense.

Here God's Word warns that fretfulness is a snare of the devil. If this bad attitude takes control, we lose spiritual strength and jeopardize the life that is nourished by faith in God. Our text counsels us, "Do not fret—it leads only to evil."

The cure for worry over our earthly problems is to seek their solution in the power and the promises of God. David gives us the fourfold formula that strengthened him.

Trust in the Lord (v. 3). Do I believe that God knows about my concern? Do I believe that His Holy Spirit will guide me if I ask Him? Do I believe that His love wants to resolve my problem in the best possible way for me and for others who are involved? *Lord, these convictions are the foundations of my faith. I trust You.*

Delight thyself in the Lord (v. 4). Having placed my trust in God, I shall think less about my problems and more about His love and power. I praise Him for what He has done for me. As I turn my thoughts to Him my spirit grows calm, and I can think more clearly.

Commit thy way unto the Lord (v. 5). This is my act of intelligent and deliberate choice. My trust is based on my past experience of God's love and care. He never has failed me yet, and this assures me that He will not fail me now. He knows the best possible resolution of this problem. I can commit it to Him. *I do turn this problem over to You, Lord. Lead me to the right decisions to bring about Your will in this issue.*

Rest in the Lord, and wait patiently for him (v. 7). Having committed my concern to God, I will not pick it up again and try to solve it in my own way. *I continue to trust You, Lord. I continue to thank You for the help You have given.*

I trust and refuse to fret. I praise and feel more confident. I rest and find a clearer mind and a stronger spirit as I move forward—"not somehow, but triumphantly."

▼

Scripture: Psalms 38—40; 70

Read Ps. 40:13-17 and then Psalm 70. They are practically identical. Both are ascribed to David. For this reason it is often assumed that Psalm 40 is a combination of two other shorter poems, verses 1-12 being one poem, and verses 13-17 the second.

Read 40:6-8 and then Heb. 10:5-9. Because of this New Testament use, the psalm is called Messianic, referring at least in part to Christ.

The Story: Psalm 38:1-10

I am about to fall, and my pain is ever with me. I confess my iniquity, I am troubled by my sin (Ps. 38:17-18, NIV).

The Blessing of a Miserable Conscience

Do I feel an identity with this man who wrote, "My guilt has overwhelmed me like a burden too heavy to bear"? (v. 4, NIV). Can I recall hours in my life when conscience has condemned me for some wrong that I have done? These are the hours in which there is left in the human spirit only "the white cold ashes of moral defeat."

Whence comes this feeling of devastation? Why is it a part of our human experience? How can we cope with it?

We believe that conscience is the voice of God sounding in our souls to save us from sin. Sometimes the psychiatrist seeks to remove the symptoms, urging us to forget our feelings of guilt. But this is superficial treatment. Most of the time we feel guilty because we are guilty. We have broken some law of God; we have hurt some fellow human brother. When this happens we ought not to feel comfortable; we ought not to forget it easily.

But conscience is not designed just to make us feel depressed. God wants us to feel our sins deeply in order that we may turn from them completely, in order that we may find forgiveness, restoration, and a better way of life. The Bible tells us, "Being punished isn't enjoyable while it is happening—it hurts! But afterwards we can see the result, a quiet growth in grace and character" (Heb. 12:11, TLB).

How do we cope with the misery of a bad conscience? David shows us God's way: "I confess my iniquity." The hurt is God's reminder that He wants to forgive and to heal.

> *And when sometimes on the downward way*
> *Your heart grows sick with a sudden fear,*
> *If you breathe His name it will be enough,*
> *For the ear of the Lord is quick to hear.* *
> —ANNIE JOHNSON FLINT

*Used by permission of Evangelical Publishers, a Division of Scripture Press Publications, Ltd.

▼

Scripture: Psalms 41—43
The Story: Psalm 42:1-11

As the heart panteth after the water brooks, so panteth my soul after thee, O God (Ps. 42:1).

The Insatiable Craving

Man's deep thirst for God is the gift of divine love and grace. Just as He created in our bodies hunger for food, He placed a yearning for himself in our spirits. Augustine writes, "Thou hast made us for thyself, and our heart is restless until it finds its rest in Thee."

Of all our deep human needs, the craving for God is the greatest; finding satisfaction for that need is life's most urgent business. But our normal spiritual hunger is not often an overwhelming consciousness. It is more like a dull ache in the body that tells us something is wrong, and we ought to see the doctor.

Often in the teenager's verve for life and in the absorbing interests of early adulthood we may be barely aware of the vague discomfort. But at times this hunger for God becomes as acute as a burning fever. Sooner or later we recognize that something is seriously wrong; something is missing from life. Particularly after about age 40 we know it. Without recurring personal fellowship with God we find little satisfaction from our activities; we feel vaguely disconnected, rootless, purposeless.

It is in these hours that we identify with our early American statesman Daniel Webster. He was once asked, "What is the most profound thought that has ever occupied your mind?" He hesitated for a reflective moment and then replied, "My personal responsibility to God."

In our moments of hunger and thirst, how do we find Him for whom our spirits yearn? In verse 5 the man of God speaks of "the help of his countenance." What are we to understand by this phrase? Is it not this, that whatever my need today, if I but lift my face toward God, I find Him there? Is it not that He has been looking in my direction? That He has been there all of the time? That He is paying attention to my need? That He is prepared to help me now?

Today I join this other yearning pilgrim and cry to my thirsty spirit:

"Hope in God; for I shall again praise him, my help and my God" (42:5-6, RSV).

Scripture: Psalms 44—46
The Story: Psalm 45:1-17

Psalm 45 is called a *Maschil* or teaching poem. The same title is given to 12 other psalms (32; 42; 44; 52—55; 74; 78; 88; 89; and 142).

This psalm is also classified as Messianic because Heb. 1:8-9 makes these quoted Old Testament words an unqualified statement of the deity of Christ.

My heart is stirred by a noble theme (Ps. 45:1; all quotes from NIV).

An Ode to an Ideal Marriage

At first Psalm 45 seemed out of place in the Psalter. When singing the praises of God, why introduce a poem exalting a man, a woman, and marriage?

It seemed inappropriate. But then I remembered that "this holy estate of marriage Christ adorned and beautified with His presence and first miracle that He wrought in Cana of Galilee." And I recalled that marriage between a godly man and woman signifies to us "the mystical union that exists between Christ and His Church."

Then it seemed right for this inspired author to begin his psalm: "My heart is stirred by a noble theme." Here we are invited to reflect on the fitness of a young man dedicated to truth, humility, and righteousness. By his side stands a young woman devoted to her husband, her home, and to the welfare of her children.

Verses 2-9 describe one of Israel's kings at the time of his marriage. He was young, talented, a wise and fluent leader; the blessings of God rested upon him. The Lord promised to give him victory over his enemies because the young man was committed to God's concerns of righteousness, meekness, and truth. So right was this combination of leader and people that the New Testament writer applies the words to describe Christ and His kingdom (Heb. 1:8-9).

Verses 10-17 advise and honor the young woman chosen to be the companion and queen of this home. In God's plan, her husband and her home must now come first. In this sense she is admonished to "forget your people and your father's house." Her beauty and attractiveness are foundations of marriage and strong ties to her husband. Through her children she exercises an influence for good over generations not yet born. God promises her: "Your sons will take the place of your fathers: You will make them princes throughout the land. I will perpetuate your memory through all generations; therefore the nations will praise you for ever and ever."

Prayer for today:
Lord, let it be so in our home; let it be true of our children.

▼

Scripture: Psalms 47—49
The Story: Psalm 49:1-20

God will redeem my soul from the grave; he will surely take me to himself (Ps. 49:15, NIV).

We Know, but We Are Not Afraid

In Psalm 49 a man of God reflects on life and death. He knows that the certainty of death changes the value a wise man places on wealth. Every man who depends on material possessions becomes bankrupt at the edge of his grave. The man of God puts generous investments in things eternal because he knows that beyond death there is a better life.

I, too, have been reflecting on death and life. I have passed my "threescore years"—and 17. I have fewer years left than I have already lived. I do not know when my time will come. It may be today with an unexpected heart attack; it may be 20 years from now after a gradual decline or a lingering illness.

At best, we senior citizens know that we are not far from the close of our earthly journey. We know, but we are not afraid. We are not told when our time will come, but we know that it is God who will call us; and we know that through His grace we shall be ready.

He called us from sin to righteousness, and it was a good change. He called us to the high country of holy living; and walking with Him has been glorious. He has sometimes called us to walk through dark valleys, but the wonder of His presence has gone with us. Every summons from Him has looked good as we look back. And so we look forward with confidence.

We know that someday soon He will bid us come home. Men call the journey death. We know it awaits us, and soon; but we are not afraid.

My pastor recently ministered daily to a dying saint. On one visit, after prayer the pastor said, "Howard, I have come to be at peace about you." To which the dying man replied, "I, too, am at peace."

With another I give glad testimony:

"Surely goodness and mercy shall follow me all the days of my life: and I will dwell in the house of the Lord for ever" (Ps. 23:6).

▼

☐ **WEEK 22, THURSDAY** PSALMS

Scripture: Psalms 50—52
The Story: Psalm 51:1-19

The sacrifices of God are a broken spirit; a broken and contrite heart, O God, you will not despise (Ps. 51:17, NIV).

I Ask Forgiveness

Forgive me. They are two of the most important words in our language. Here are great healers of broken relationships in the family; and they always reestablish fellowship with God.

David wrote this psalm when God's Spirit convicted him after he had committed adultery with Bathsheba, tried to deceive her husband, and then sent him to his death. Here is the deep agony of a man who sees clearly that he has sinned against God and has been grossly unfair to other persons. Such a spirit of remorse and repentance is always redemptive.

God loves us too much to let us lose our souls easily. If He cannot woo us to himself with love, He sometimes pressures us with pain. The mental agony of having failed Him is like the pain of broken bones and a crushed body. The godly sorrow that works repentance (2 Cor. 7:10) comes from the knowledge that God knows how sinful I have been. I cannot endure the continued pain of His disappointment and sorrow. I can only pray, *Forgive me.*

We have said that this prayer always establishes renewed fellowship with God. It does. No matter what our failure or sin, all that God requires for restoration is our prayer of repentance. With David, we can always come praying, "Have mercy on me, O God, according to your unfailing love; according to your great compassion blot out my transgressions. Wash away all my iniquity and cleanse me from my sin" (51:1-2, NIV).

Is there some failure or sin between God and me? Do I yearn for Him to "restore to me the joy of your salvation"? Then I simply ask sincerely, *Forgive me.* Charlotte Elliott wrote it, and thousands have come back to God singing it:

> *Just as I am, without one plea*
> *But that Thy blood was shed for me,*
> *And that Thou bidd'st me come to Thee,*
> *O Lamb of God, I come! I come!*

Scripture: Psalms 53—55
The Story: Psalms 53—54

Surely God is my help; the Lord is the one who sustains me (Ps. 54:4, NIV).

What Makes a Man Deny God?

Psalms 53 and 54 paint contrasting pictures. In 53 a man turns away from God in rejection. In 54 he turns to God in trust.

What kind of thinking causes a man to deny the reality of a Supreme Being? The Psalmist answers, "Only a fool says, 'There is no God.'" Such a man surely overlooks a lot of evidence when he makes this declaration. He denies the promptings of his own spirit; he forgets the evidence in the world around us; and he rejects the revelation of God in Christ. David declares that only a warped mind can go so far wrong.

But many young atheists are hurt believers. Somewhere in life they have been disappointed in what they expected God to do. Failing to achieve faith in spite of disappointment, they have found a low level of intellectual consistency. When they failed to find in God a solution to their problem, they have said, There is no God. In such an emotional impasse we can be helped only by finding a bigger God than the one who seemed to let us down.

But the context in Psalm 53 makes it plain that the Psalmist is not talking about the intellectual atheist. This fool is not one who says honestly, My mind is not convinced. This is the practical atheist; he denies a righteous God because he chooses to live a sinful life. Most of Ps. 53:1-3 is quoted by Paul in Rom. 3:10-12. Read these verses to see how the Apostle describes the universal depravity of the human heart. This practical atheist is the man foolish enough to decide, There shall be no God for me.

The issue thus becomes rejection of God's will for a man's life. Men decide to do their own thing instead of obeying God; they reject the divine will as it is made known through the Bible. Of these God-rejecters the Psalmist writes: "Depraved their lives are and detestable, not one of them does right. God looks down from heaven upon mankind, to see if any have the sense to care for God" (Ps. 53:2, Moffatt).

How much wiser and better is the man who turns to God with the cry:

"Hear my prayer, O God; listen to the words of my mouth. . . . Surely God is my help; the Lord is the one who sustains me. . . . I will sacrifice a freewill offering to you; I will praise your name, O Lord, for it is good" (54:2, 4, 6, NIV).

▼

Scripture: Psalms 56—60

We were reading the Psalms in our daily family worship. On the day that we read Psalm 58 Mrs. Harper prayed, "We won't criticize David, but, Lord, give us more love for sinners." Here is a natural Christian response to six imprecatory psalms where the writer calls for vengeance on his enemies (35; 58; 69; 83; 109; 137).

Parts of these psalms appear to fall far short of the standards of forgiveness set by Jesus in the Sermon on the Mount. We may be helped to understand these scriptures if we remember the following facts.

1. These are Old Testament writings; God gave a higher revelation in Jesus.

2. The Jews have traditionally understood that destruction of the wicked means that God will destroy, not sinners, but sin itself.

3. It is difficult to determine grammatically whether a Hebrew writer is saying, "Let this happen," or "This will happen."

4. The Psalmist's words do not necessarily reflect personal spite or cruelty. These men identified their enemies as enemies of God.

5. Even the New Testament makes it clear that evil men must ultimately reap the consequences of their evil deeds.

The Story: Psalms 56—57

In God I trust; I will not be afraid (Ps. 56:4; all quotes from NIV).

231

A Shelter in the Time of Storm

The cynics have charged that religion is only a crutch for the cripple. The man of faith replies, God is more than solace in trouble—but He is there to help us in our trouble when we need Him.

Psalms 56 and 57 are songs of lament. When, as a young man, David's life was being sought by King Saul he took refuge in the Philistine territory of King Achish (1 Sam. 21:10-15). A fugitive from his own people, and scarcely tolerated in this foreign city, David poured out his heart to God in these psalms.

Hardly any man escapes serious trouble on at least a few occasions during a lifetime. It is then that our prayers become pleas for help. With David we cry: "Have mercy on me, O God, have mercy on me, for in you my soul takes refuge. I will take refuge in the shadow of your wings until the disaster has passed" (57:1).

We are grateful when God stirs himself on our behalf. Sometimes He intervenes to remove the threat to our lives. Sometimes He reveals himself to us in ways that leave us no longer afraid. In either case our hearts join the glad praise of the Psalmist: "When I am afraid, I will trust in you. In God, whose word I praise, in God I trust; I will not be afraid. What can mortal man do to me?" (56:3-4).

When He answers our call, our hearts gladly sing:

"Be exalted, O God, above the heavens;
let your glory be over all the earth" (57:5).

▼

☐ **WEEK 23, SUNDAY**   **PSALMS**

Scripture: Psalms 61—64

About two-thirds of the psalms have titles; there are five types. (1) Some describe the character of the psalm: a song, a prayer, or praise. (2) Others, like Psalm 61, describe the musical setting: "to the chief musician," or "set to Muthlabben" (a tune). (3) A third type refers to the use of the psalm: "for the Sabbath," or "songs of ascent." (4) Other titles refer to authorship: "of David," "the sons of Korah." (5) The last type, like Psalm 59, refers to the occasion on which the psalm was written: "When Saul had sent men to watch David's house in order to kill him."

The Story: Psalm 62:1-12

Find rest, O my soul, in God alone; my hope comes from him (Ps. 62:5; all quotes from NIV).

My Soul Finds Rest in God

Recently we sang with David, "You, O God, are my fortress" (Ps. 59:9). But having a fortress and using it are two different things. David knew this also, and prayed, "Lead me to the rock that is higher than I." When God leads, we must follow if we are to find our safety in Him.

David knew what we must learn: Our divine resources are not found once for all. God is always present and ready to help us, but again and again we must flee to the fortress and climb to the security of the high tower.

Read Ps. 62:1-2. David here shows us clearly the ever-present resources of God. But he hastens to remind us in verses 3-4 that the enemies of our souls are never far away—and they are unceasing in their efforts to destroy us.

In verses 5-6 the man of God sings, "God alone . . . is my fortress, I will not be shaken." But when we get out of the fortress we are vulnerable again. From the safety of full dependence on God, we tend to drift back to reliance on money, on friends, or other purely human resources. When this happens we must find our way back to a full reliance on God. The Psalmist exhorts us once again to center our trust in eternal values: "Find rest, O my soul, in God alone."

David learned that he could keep his feet firmly on the earth but at the same time fasten his faith to God in heaven. We do not deny the importance of temporal values. But we must remember again and again that nothing of this world is more valuable than trust in God and walking with Him.

This recurring persuasion comes through prayer and contemplation. If we gaze on the attractions of the world and only glance at the realities of God, we do not find the safety that He promises. To find security we must abide in Him.

> Turn your eyes upon Jesus;
> Look full in His wonderful face;
> And the things of earth will grow strangely dim
> In the light of His glory and grace.*
> —HELEN HOWARTH LEMMEL

▼

☐ **WEEK 23, MONDAY** **PSALMS**

Scripture: Psalms 65—67
The Story: Psalm 65:1-13

Come and see what God has done . . . in man's behalf! (Ps. 66:5, NIV).

"Praise God from Whom All Blessings Flow"

The Book of Psalms is a book of prayers. As we read it thoughtfully, we encounter every situation in which our spirits feel the urge to commune with God.

Last Sunday our pastor discussed five forms of prayer that should often be in our hearts and on our lips.

Praise to God for who He is and what He does.

Thanksgiving for personal blessings and answered prayer.

Confession of failure, shortcoming, or sins.

Intercession for the concerns of others.

Petitions for personal needs.

In a balanced prayer for the day, we should come round full circle to close as we begin—with a prayer of praise.

Thanksgiving and praise are prayer paths that run parallel, but they are different. Thanksgiving is the expression to God of

234

our appreciation for personal blessings and for answered prayers. In expressions of praise we are less conscious of ourselves and more conscious of God who has blessed us. We are also joyfully aware of God's universal gifts. We praise Him who sends "rain on the just and on the unjust" (Matt. 5:45).

This prayer of praise is the dominant note of our three psalms for today. Let us join David in his Psalm 65 praise for these universal blessings.

For being a God who hears prayer, we praise You (v. 2).

For Your forgiveness of sins, we come in glad worship (v. 3).

For being God who shares Your fellowship with us, we love You (v. 4).

For the Church and public worship, we are grateful (v. 4).

Before the Creator of mountains and seas, we stand in awe (vv. 6-7).

At sunrise and sunset we adore You for giving us beauty (v. 8).

For clear, cool water, we bless You (vv. 9-10).

For crops and flocks, we join the meadows and valleys as "they shout for joy and sing" (vv. 11-13).

Truly our praise is proper.
"Shout with joy to God, all the earth! Sing to the glory of his name; offer him glory and praise" (Ps. 66:1, NIV).

▼

☐ **WEEK 23, TUESDAY**   **PSALMS**

Scripture: Psalms 68—70
The Story: Psalm 69:1-3, 13-18, 30-34

I will pray to you, Lord; . . . Answer me because of your great love (Ps. 69:13; all quotes from TEV).

A Prayer for Urgent Need

Howard Paris quips, "We get too impatient with God. We ask for something and want it by Monday morning. *I'm not going to push, God. Tuesday will be OK.*"

But when we are hurting as badly as David hurt, God welcomes an urgent cry. Yesterday we shared in a prayer of praise; today we offer a prayer of petition for a deep personal need.

Let us try to overlook the imprecations of verses 22-28 and feel the heartthrob of a devout man in deep need.

"Save me, O God! The water is up to my neck;
I am sinking . . . and there is no solid ground;
I am out in deep water,
    and the waves are about to drown me.
I am worn out from calling for help,
    and my throat is aching.
I have strained my eyes, looking for your help. . . .
But as for me, I will pray to you, Lord;
    answer me, God, at a time you choose.
Answer me because of your great love,
    because you keep your promise to save.
Save me from sinking in the mud; keep me safe . . .
    safe from the deep water.
Don't let the flood come over me; don't let me
    drown in the depths or sink into the grave.
Answer me, Lord, in the goodness of your constant love;
    in your great compassion turn to me!" (69:1-3, 13-16).

At this point our prayer turns appropriately to thanksgiving.

"I will praise God with a song;
    I will proclaim his greatness by giving him thanks.
This will please the Lord more than offering him cattle . . .
The Lord listens to those in need
    and does not forget his people . . .
Praise God, O heaven and earth,
    seas and all creatures in them" (69:30-31, 33-34).

Scripture: Psalms 71—72
The Story: Psalm 71:5-24

Your righteousness, God, reaches the skies. You have done great things (Ps. 71:19; all quotes but one from TEV).

The Joys of Looking Back—and Forward

The *Good News Bible, Today's English Version,* titles Psalm 71 "An Old Man's Prayer." At 77, I prefer to call it "The Joys of Looking Back." Let me share in the testimony of this unnamed psalmist and of the wise man who wrote: "The path of the just is as the shining light, that shineth more and more unto the perfect day" (Prov. 4:18, KJV).

The Psalmist spoke from a lifetime of walking with God: "Lord, I put my hope in you; I have trusted in you since I was young. I have relied on you all my life; you have protected me since the day I was born. I will always praise you" (vv. 5-6).

Because God had been with him, he had satisfying memories of a good influence: "My life has been an example to many, because you have been my strong defender. All day long I praise you, and proclaim your glory" (vv. 7-8).

One of the great joys of a life of faith is the spiritual verve it brings to the present: "I will always put my hope in you; I will praise you more and more. I will tell of your goodness; all day long I will speak of your salvation, though it is more than I can understand" (vv. 14-15).

He who has walked with God has a testimony to share: "You have taught me ever since I was young, and I still tell of your wonderful acts. . . . Be with me while I proclaim your power and might to all generations to come" (vv. 17-18).

Fellowship with God here stimulates faith for the life to come. "Your righteousness, God, reaches the skies. You have done great things . . . you will restore my strength; you will keep me from the grave. . . . you will comfort me again" (vv. 19-21).

Looking back on a lifetime of God's gracious ministries to us brings a joyful affirmation:

"I will praise your faithfulness, my God. . . . with my whole being I will sing because you have saved me. I will speak of your righteousness all day long" (vv. 22-24).

▼

Scripture: Psalms 73—75

Psalm 73 is the first of 17 that make up Book III. Of the 17, "[six are] psalms of lament; five of adoration, worship, praise, and thanksgiving; three wisdom psalms; and one each of the imprecatory, liturgical, and Messianic psalms. Some of the finest and most dearly loved pieces in the Psalter are found in this section" (BBC).

The Story: Psalm 73:1-28

When I tried to understand all this, it was oppressive to me till I entered the sanctuary of God (Ps. 73:16-17, NIV).

Saved from Bitterness

A dear friend who came into the blessing of perfect love a year ago writes, "The Holy Spirit is showing me that feeling pain is not a sin; but that I must honestly take the pain to the Great Physician, before bitterness sets in to rot my soul."

It was bitterness of spirit that caused the Psalmist nearly to lose his faith in God. Moffatt translates the dilemma: "I almost slipped, I nearly lost my footing, in anger at the godless and their arrogance, at the sight of their success" (73:2-3). The New Testament also cautions us against this danger: "Follow peace with all men, and holiness . . . lest any root of bitterness springing up trouble you, and thereby many be defiled" (Heb. 12:14-15).

How does a man recover firm footing when he feels his feet slipping? The Psalmist tells us how he found help: "I went into the sanctuary of God." What we cannot understand in isolation, begins to make sense when we come into the presence of the Lord, and when we allow Him to talk to us. As the Psalmist made God his daily Companion (v. 23), the pieces of his life began to fit into place. When he felt his feet slipping, he then felt God holding "me by my right hand." When he couldn't see ahead what might happen tomorrow, he could confidently declare, "Thou shalt guide me with thy counsel." Even if the worst happens in life here, with the Psalmist I am upheld by knowing: "Thou shalt . . . afterward receive me to glory."

The faith that this man almost lost and then recovered is affirmed in verse 1: "Surely God is good to Israel, to those who are pure in heart."

Bitterness somehow evaporates in the experienced sunshine of God's love and care for us. When we follow the Psalmist into the presence of God, we too can sing his song:

"Whom have I in heaven but thee? and there is none upon earth that I desire beside thee. My flesh and my heart faileth: but God is the strength of my heart, and my portion forever. . . . it is good for me to draw near to God: I have put my trust in the Lord God" (73:25-26, 28).

▼

☐ **WEEK 23, FRIDAY**   **PSALMS**

Scripture: Psalms 76—78
The Story: Psalm 78:1-7

I will remember the works of the Lord (Ps. 77:11).

Our Charter for Christian Teaching

Psalms 77—78 tell us about the importance of religious teaching in the home and in the church.

Here in 78:7 we find the clearest statement of the purpose for Christian education to be found anywhere in the Bible. We teach in order that our children may "set their hope in God, and not forget the works of God, but keep his commandments."

Also, in this psalm we have the most effective methods of passing our faith to the next generation. We are to share with others our personal experiences with God—we pass along what "we have heard and known, and our fathers have told us" (78:3).

We tell our children about our faith—and we tell them while they are young. We do not hide these life-giving truths by silent lips or careless lives. Let us ask God to help us show "the generation to come the praises of the Lord, and his strength, and his wonderful works that he hath done" (78:4).

Also, we are to put clear content into our teaching. In 78:1 *my law* means "my teaching, my guidance." Our children must know what God expects of them as well as the blessings that He promises. The *testimony* and *law* refer to the Ten Commandments and the stone tablets on which God wrote them.

Those commandments are negative as well as positive—and there are penalties for disobedience. The Psalmist tells us, "In spite of all [that God had taught them and the ways He had blessed them] they kept on sinning . . . So he ended their days in futility and their years in terror" (78:32-33, NIV).

It is often through faithful living and clear teaching by us that God saves our children and fulfills His promises to them. Through this ministry of sharing, "the generation to come" learns the truth and finds God. Through our faithfulness, their children, yet unborn, will arise and declare God's grace to our great-grandchildren.

> Oh, teach me, Lord, that I may teach
> The precious things Thou dost impart;
> And wing my words, that they may reach
> The hidden depths of many a heart.
> —FRANCES HAVERGAL

Scripture: Psalms 79—81
The Story: Psalms 79:1; 80:1-2, 7-15

O God Almighty! Look down from heaven and see! Watch over this vine . . . your right hand has planted (Ps. 80:14-15, NIV).

Beyond Ourselves

God's purpose is to make us like himself. He wants to kindle in us flames of holy love for himself and for others.

The natural man thinks first of himself. God's desire is to change this—to turn us around. The Christian puts God first, others second, and himself last. Thus God seeks to lead us beyond our narrow selves to a broad concern for others. This is love—His kind of love.

When we focus on God in our prayers, we offer praise and thanksgiving; when we think of ourselves, we offer petitions; when we focus on others, we pray the prayer of intercession. It is this prayer that we hear from God's Word today. The Psalmist was not thinking of himself but of his people. Thirty-eight times in Psalm 80 he speaks of *we, us, our,* or of the *vine* as a name for his people. Not once is the prayer focused on himself as an individual.

A member of my adult Sunday School class reminded us that a wholesome Christian life is like a triangle. Our love for God places Him and His will at the top; we are at the lower left corner; others are on our own level at the right corner—we love them as we love ourselves.

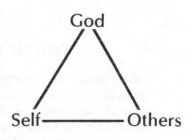

As God fills us with His loving Spirit, our prayers often turn to our neighbors, to our church, to our nation. When we thus intercede for others we find ourselves becoming involved in their lives and needs. We begin to see our church and our world from God's point of view. In this we are lifted beyond ourselves. The vision and mood of the Psalmist was the inspiration for Timothy Dwight's devotion to the Church. Today I join him in that commitment:

> For her my tears shall fall;
> For her my pray'rs ascend;
> To her my cares and toils be giv'n
> Till toils and cares shall end.

▼

Scripture: Psalms 82—84

Psalm 83:9-18 is imprecatory—the Psalmist prays for the destruction of the wicked. But it is not a selfish prayer. He prays with a high purpose: "That men may know that thou ... art the most high over all the earth" (83:18). His prayer also places the decision for punishment in the hands of God where it belongs: "Arise, O God, judge the earth" (82:8).

The Story: Psalm 84:1-12

I long to be in the Lord's Temple. With my whole being I sing for joy to the living God (Ps. 84:2, TEV).

Longing for God

In my study Bible I have written in the margin, "Psalm 84 is to be read when you feel deeply the blessings of knowing God and the fellowship of His Church." Such communion with God is the highest fulfillment to the human spirit.

It was soul hunger that brought the Jews on their pilgrimages to the Temple; it was this longing that drew the Psalmist to "the courts of the Lord"; it was intense desire for the place of worship that inspired the exiles to return to Jerusalem and build again the house of God. The cry of the human heart in its deepest longing is universally the same—we yearn to find fellowship with God.

If our desire is dim and weak, we can encourage it. We need the house of God. In order that its ministry may be regularly ours, we must have a deep inner urge to come and worship. Jesus assures us, "Blessed are they which do hunger and thirst after righteousness: for they shall be filled" (Matt. 5:6). When we seek righteousness with the intensity of a hunger long denied, we will discover it. When we seek God with the eagerness of an unslaked thirst, we shall find Him. When our desire for God's house disturbs us as the desire for food and drink, we shall cry with the Psalmist, "I long to be in the Lord's Temple."

Today my heart is drawn to God. With the Psalmist, my spirit sings:

"How lovely is your dwelling place, O Lord Almighty! My soul yearns, even faints for the courts of the Lord; my heart and my flesh cry out for the living God" (84:1-2, NIV).

▼

Scripture: Psalms 85—88
The Story: Psalm 88:1-18

Shall thy lovingkindness be declared in the grave? or thy faithfulness in destruction? (Ps. 88:11).

Thinking About Dying

The Psalmist was facing death; it is a confrontation that none of us finally escapes. Here is one of life's sobering experiences, but it need not be depressing for us who walk with God. This man knew God but he did not know Him well enough; he did not understand God's deep involvement with us in death.

Verses 10-12 reflect an Old Testament view: "Soon it will be too late! Of what use are your miracles when I am in the grave? How can I praise you then? Can those in the grave declare your lovingkindness? Can they proclaim your faithfulness? Can the darkness speak of your miracles? Can anyone in the Land of Forgetfulness talk about your help?" (TLB).

Is death indeed a place of darkness where no light from God shines? Is it the "Land of Forgetfulness" where we are no longer in God's thoughts and in His loving care? The New Testament answers no. Paul testifies, "We are confident . . . [that] to be absent from the body . . . [is] to be present with the Lord" (2 Cor. 5:8). Jesus assures us, "In my Father's house are many mansions: if it were not so, I would have told you. I go to prepare a place for you" (John 14:2).

Death is a great enemy; but it is a conquered foe. In Christ we are victors even over death: "We believe that Jesus died and rose again, even so them also which sleep in Jesus will God bring with him. . . . Wherefore comfort one another with these words" (1 Thess. 4:14, 18).

The fear of the Old Testament asks, "Shall the dead arise and praise thee?" The faith of the New Testament sings in glad reply: "I heard as it were the voice of a great multitude . . . saying, Alleluia: for the Lord God omnipotent reigneth" (Rev. 19:6). "Therefore are they before the throne of God, and serve him day and night . . . and he . . . shall dwell among them" (Rev. 7:15).

Thank You, Lord, for Your promise of eternal life. Thank You for our full New Testament faith.

▼

□ **WEEK 24, TUESDAY**   **PSALMS**

Scripture: Psalms 89—92
The Story: Psalm 91:1-16

I will say of the Lord, He is . . . my God; in him will I trust (Ps. 91:2).

Freedom from Fear

Whatever special help Christians find in overcoming fear is found in our saving contact with God. "He who dwells in the shelter of the Most High will rest in the shadow of the Almighty" (91:1, NIV). He who lives in God, finds rest in God.

This psalm is filled with promises of God's protection from the weather, from war, from disease, and from dangers that lurk in the dark. How shall we interpret these gracious assurances?

G. Campbell Morgan reminds us: "We shall understand God's dealings with us and get to the throbbing heart of such promises . . . if we start from the certainty that . . . it does *not* mean . . . that we are going to be God's petted children, or to be saved from the things that fall upon other people. No! No! We have to go a great deal deeper than that."

In the face of life's evils we succeed best in overcoming fear by understanding the power of God and the love of God. No ultimate harm can come to me when I am under the "shadow of the Almighty." I am at peace because I know that "in everything God works for good with those who love him" (Rom. 8:28, RSV).

Are we then to say that God never spares His child from suffering in answer to prayer? No. This would deny the truth of the Bible and the testimony of our own experience. God does at times intervene to save His child from physical harm. He who made the world of natural law stands above it and controls it. With John W. Peterson our faith sings: "I believe in miracles, for I believe in God." But our ultimate freedom from fear rests not only in God's control of circumstances; it rests also in His ministry to our spirits.

It is God himself who promises: "Because he loves me . . . I will rescue him . . . I will be with him in trouble, I will deliver him and honor him" (91:14-15, NIV).

With this assurance we triumphantly sing:

"Who then can ever keep Christ's love from us? . . . Death can't, and life can't. The angels won't, and all the powers of hell itself cannot keep God's love away. Our fears for today, our worries about tomorrow . . . nothing will ever be able to separate us from the love of God" (Rom. 8:35-39, TLB).

Scripture: Psalms 93—95
The Story: Psalm 95:1-11
Come, let us sing for joy to the Lord (Ps. 95:1, NIV).

Our Prayer of Praise

Psalm 95 is used by the Jews for morning prayer on the Sabbath. It is repeated by Christians in the Sunday morning service to prepare our minds for worship. Its mood ought often to be a part of private and family devotions. Here is a prayer in which we express our adoration and praise to God.

Verses 1-2 invite us to recall who God is, and to sing our praise and thanksgiving. Verse 3 reminds us of God's power—the ultimate force in the universe. In verses 4-5 we recall that He is Creator of valleys and mountains, sea and land. Then when the physical world was finished, He made us; He gave us the earth to use and to enjoy.

God not only created us—He loves us. "He is our God; we are the people he cares for, the flock for which he provides" (95:7, TEV).

In view of all that God has done;

"Come, let us sing for joy to the Lord;
Let us shout aloud to the Rock of our salvation.
Let us come before him with thanksgiving
and extol him with music and song.
For the Lord is the great God,
the great King above all gods.
In his hand are the depths of the earth,
and the mountain peaks belong to him.
The sea is his, for he made it,
and his hands formed the dry land.
Come, let us bow down in worship,
let us kneel before the Lord our Maker;
for he is our God
and we are the people of his pasture,
the flock of his care" (95:1-7, NIV).

Scripture: Psalms 96—102

Psalm 96 is found also in 1 Chron. 16:23-33, where it is credited to David.

Psalms 95—100 are liturgical, that is, they were often repeated in unison in public worship. Two other groups, 113—118 and 146—150, were also used in this way. Psalm 100 was probably sung by the procession of worshipers as they approached the Temple with their thank offerings.

The Story: Psalms 98:1-6; 100:1-5

Sing unto the Lord a new song (Ps. 98:1).

My Song

In the college chapel service a visiting pastor, Frank McConnell, testifed: "Sometimes when I can't pray through, I can sing my way through." I have found that to be true.

Poetry is the language of emotion—and music is her twin sister. When words that express our thoughts about God are set to music that stirs our emotions, we have a perfect voice for our praise.

Our text invites us, "Sing unto the Lord a new song." That new song is *my* song. No one else in the world can offer to God my adoration; that is the new song. No song that I have sung before can express today's joy in my fellowship with Christ; an old song cannot speak my gratitude for today's blessings. That is why I need my new song.

Of what blessings do these scriptures remind us? God has provided salvation; He walks with us in daily fellowship; His righteousness is known even among the heathen; to all men He offers steadfast love; and "his faithfulness continues through all generations" (NIV).

247

Which songs of the Church best express your love for Christ? As you recall one, let it sing itself in your heart all day. Two themes from P. P. Bliss express the way I feel:

> *I will sing of my Redeemer*
> *And His wondrous love to me.*

And another:

> *Sing them over again to me,*
> *Wonderful words of life!*
> *Let me more of their beauty see,*
> *Wonderful words of life!*

▼

☐ **WEEK 24, FRIDAY**   **PSALMS**

Scripture: Psalms 103—107

Psalms 105—107 are historical psalms. Lessons from the past are recalled in order to correct and encourage God's people. Psalm 105 recounts God's blessings under the patriarchs (7-12), in Egypt (23-36), and during the Exodus (37-45). Psalm 106 repeats these epochs and adds Israel's sad history in Canaan through the period of the Judges and in the Exile. Psalm 107 is a more general history. The experience of Jonah seems to be reflected in 23-30.

The Story: Psalms 105:1-8; 106:40-48

Give thanks to the Lord for his unfailing love and his wonderful deeds for men (Ps. 107:8, NIV).

    This text is a congregational response repeated after each recitation of God's steadfast love—see 107:8, 15, 21, 31.

Learning from History

President Harry S. Truman often repeated, "He who will not learn from history must repeat history." It is as true in the life of faith as in the pursuit of politics. Let him who would walk with God remember the works of God.

As we reflect on the divine power and love, the only appropriate response is praise. The Psalmist cries, "O give thanks unto the Lord; call upon his name: make known his deeds among the people" (105:1). Here are three right responses: (1) thanks for what God has done, (2) calling on Him for the help that we need, (3) telling others about Him.

In 106:40-46 we see both God's discipline and His love. Because of His discipline, He allows us to suffer when we sin. He allows us to be punished by pain. But the pain He sends is intended to be redemptive. If He can turn us from our evil way by raising a roadblock of suffering, God raises the roadblock. He does it because He loves us. He allows us to suffer in order, if possible, to turn us from our error.

But this God of discipline is also a God of mercy: "He regarded their affliction, when he heard their cry" (106:44).

As we recall the history of God's grace in our own lives, let us unite our voices with the Psalmist:

"Praise be to the Lord, the God of Israel, from everlasting to everlasting. . . . Praise the Lord" (106:48, NIV).

▼

☐ WEEK 24, SATURDAY   PSALMS

Scripture: Psalms 108—112

Each of today's psalms calls for special comment. Psalm 109 contains perhaps the strongest of the imprecatory sections. Some translations put verses 6-20 in quotation marks to indicate that they were the vindictive prayers of David's enemies against him. See the note on imprecatory passages, page 231.

Psalm 110 is one of the outstanding Messianic passages in the Old Testament. It is quoted 21 times in the New Testament in relation to Christ and His kingdom. See Matt. 22:44; Mark 12:36; and Heb. 10:12-13.

Psalms 111—112 are a pair of wisdom poems. Each contains

10 verses, and in the Hebrew each is an acrostic, having 22 lines that begin with a successive letter of the Hebrew alphabet. Both are psalms of praise. In 111 the poet praises God for His kindness and bountiful provision for our needs. In 112 he thanks God for the ways His presence transforms our spirits.

Psalm 108 is almost the same as Ps. 57:7-11 and Ps. 60:5-12. All three are attributed to David. G. Campbell Morgan suggests that some occasion prompted David to pick up parts of two earlier poems and put them together in this chapter as a special psalm of praise.

The Story: Psalm 108:1-13

I will praise you, O Lord, among the nations; I will sing of you among the peoples (Ps. 108:3, NIV).

"I Will Praise You, O Lord"

As king of Israel, David had opportunities to witness for his Lord "among the nations." But even we can talk about Him "among the peoples."

We can witness by the life that we live. True. But the Psalmist pledges himself to be vocal—"I will sing of you among the peoples." The quiet witness of a godly life is beautiful, but it is strengthened when we give it a voice.

Our best witness is a glad testimony to personal experience. We want to tell someone else the good news when, in our walk with God, we discover that "great is your love, higher than the heavens; your faithfulness reaches to the skies" (NIV).

Perhaps talking to others about God's goodness would be easier if Satan did not battle so hard to keep us quiet. In this situation we must choose whose counsel we shall follow. Jesus says, "Ye shall be witnesses unto me" (Acts 1:8). He commissions us, "Go and make disciples" (Matt. 28:19, NIV).

Lord, in my own way—or, rather, in Your way for me—I want to be Your witness today. By Your guidance and help, "I will sing of you among the peoples."

Scripture: Psalms 113—118

These six short psalms are often called "The Egyptian Hallel." The exhortation "Praise the Lord" translates the Hebrew *Hallelu-Yah*— our Hallelujah. These psalms praise God for His deliverance "when Israel came out of Egypt" (114:1, NIV). They were sung by the Hebrews after the Passover was finished. These probably were the very words used by Jesus and His disciples where we read, "And when they had sung an hymn, they went out into the mount of Olives" (Matt. 26:30).

The Story: Psalm 118:1-6, 21-24, 28-29

The Lord is my strength and my song; he has become my salvation (Ps. 118:14, NIV).

Today Is a Good Day

I sat one morning in an upstairs bedroom at our son's home. On page 218 I have related God's ministry to him at the time of his wife's surgery. Today I recall the Spirit's ministry to his wife, Jodie.

Four years ago she sat at that east window. It was the fear filled day of her surgery for cancer. The sun was shining, the lawn was green, and the flower garden was a riot of color. But she saw none of the beauty; it was blocked out by fear of the future.

Later she testified, "Suddenly there came to my mind the scripture, 'This is the day which the Lord hath made; we will rejoice and be glad in it.' It was so neat! God gave it to me, because I never would have thought of it by myself." On the strength of that word she went to her surgery with confidence and courage.

Martin Luther said of this chapter: "It is a psalm that I love . . . for it has often served me well and has helped me out of grave troubles, when neither emperors, kings, wise men, clever men, nor saints could have helped me" (BBC, 3:385).

Each day comes to us fresh from the hand of God. Today is a good day because God made it. I do not know what the day holds for me. I may harbor some unknown illness, but I do not fear tomorrow. God is in control, and I know that He loves me. I live for today with its opportunities, its responsibilities, its sunshine or cloud.

Thank You, Father, for all the joys of life that You have given. Today is a good day. It is the day that You have made.

▼

Scripture: Psalm 119

This psalm is the longest in the Psalter. It is an acrostic poem, having a stanza beginning with each of the 22 letters of the Hebrew alphabet. Each stanza is composed of 8 verses. The theme is the wonderful law of the Lord, and our wholehearted observance of that law. Our story includes the first two stanzas.

As you read this psalm, how many of the prayers express your own deep desires?

The Story: Psalm 119:1-16

Teach me, O Lord, the way of thy statutes; and I shall keep it unto the end (Ps. 119:33).

A Prayer for Bible Readers

Man's life under God is more than learning. To serve God means to listen to what He says, and then to obey Him. Thus we read the Bible in order to know God's will. But it is even more important that we read the Scriptures intending to do all the will of God that He makes known to us. For this we pray.

"Holy, most mighty, and most merciful God, we thank Thee for the written records which tell us what kind of people Thou wouldst have us to be. Bless those engaged in furthering the use of Thy Holy Scriptures. Let Thy hand of divine favor rest upon those who break the Bread of Life, those who teach the eternal Word.

"Thy Word is before us. While we read and study it, give us

humble, reverent, and teachable minds. Open to us its sacred truths and enable us to receive them, not as words of men, but as the Word of God, which liveth and abideth forever. Be Thou, O Blessed Spirit, our Teacher! Enlighten our minds and prepare our hearts. Shine forth, O Lord, upon Thine own sacred pages, and make Thy messages clear to us.

"Thou givest of Thy Spirit freely to all who will partake. Where we are wrong, correct us; what we do not see, show us. Bring home to our souls the truths that shall make us wise unto salvation. Keep us ready to read, quick to learn, alert to 'go where You want me to go, dear Lord, to be what You want me to be.'

"May we treasure the Bible through life without dimming the luster of its teachings or soiling the purity of its truths. In our Savior's name, for His sake, we pray. Amen" (*Advanced Bible School Quarterly*).

▼

□ **WEEK 25, TUESDAY**   **PSALMS**

Scripture: Psalms 120—122

Our three psalms are the first of 15 which bear the title "A song of ascents." The title probably refers to going up to Jerusalem on an annual pilgrimage of worship.

The time sequence of Psalm 122 begins some place away from Jerusalem. Companions said to the writer, "Let us go to the house of the Lord." In verse 2 the worshipers have arrived in Jerusalem, and the writer speaks to the city as to a person: "Our feet are standing in your gates, O Jerusalem." In verses 3-5 the poet sings his eulogy to the city of God. Then in verses 7-9 he exhorts the people to pray for God's work—and he joins in that prayer.

The Story: Psalm 122:1-9

For the sake of my brothers and friends, I will say, "Peace be within you" (Ps. 122:8; all quotes from NIV).

A Prayer for My Church

In one week's list of prayer requests from our church family I read: "Pray with the family of Marilyn for the church in Ohio where three generations of her family have grown up. The church is experiencing tremendous turmoil at this time with a negative vote for the pastor, and losing members." In these circumstances the Psalmist would urge all involved: "Pray for the peace of Jerusalem."

We have a God-given responsibility to promote peace in the work of the church: "For the sake of my brothers and friends, I will say, 'Peace be within you.'"

Such praying assures that our attitudes will be right and helpful. We cannot genuinely pray for peace among our brethren and then mount a campaign of criticism or opposition. When we pray for their prosperity, we are likely to begin to work toward that goal. Prayer is thus God's appointed way to begin action in His kingdom.

The peace for which we pray is not a mere feeling of tranquility. Peace means the existence of right relationships; then tranquility follows naturally. When relationships are wrong within the church, there is tension and unrest. When through prayer and love those relationships are made right, tension is relieved and tranquility comes. That is a blessed peace. In its glow we sing with John Fawcett:

> Blest be the tie that binds
> Our hearts in Christian love;
> The fellowship of kindred minds
> Is like to that above.

▼

☐ **Week 25, Wednesday**   **Psalms**

Scripture: Psalms 123—125
The Story: Psalms 123—125 (Today read the commentary first; then read the three psalms)

Our help is in the name of the Lord, who made heaven and earth (Ps. 124:8).

"A Mighty Fortress Is Our God"

The Berkeley Version reports that during the 2,300 bombings of the island of Malta during World War II, Psalm 124 was the favorite scripture of the defenders as they gathered for prayer.

Today's three psalms belong together—a kind of trilogy of trust. Barnes titles them "The Rising Tide of Faith." In 123 we see "A Prayer for Mercy"; in 124 "God the Protector"; and in 125 "The Security of God's People" (TEV).

In Psalm 123 we are taught to place our confidence in the sole Source of our help. "As the eyes of slaves look to the hand of their master, as the eyes of a maid look to the hand of her mistress, so our eyes look to the Lord our God" (v. 2, NIV). Perhaps these figures are foreign to us. We might say, "As my frightened child snuggles close to me for protection, so I draw close to the Lord."

Psalm 124 lifts the tide of faith still higher. David reminds us that God is more than our sole Source of help—He is our completely adequate Source. The *Good News Bible, Today's English Version* puts verses 1-3 into an incisive question: "What if the Lord had not been on our side? Answer, O Israel!" The reply is an honest confession from every one who has been attacked by Satan: "If the Lord had not been on our side when our enemies attacked us, then they would have swallowed us alive." But God was there! "Our help comes from the Lord, who made heaven and earth" (TEV).

In Psalm 125 the rising tide crests as it lifts our spirits into the peace and security of the presence of God. "As the mountains are round about Jerusalem, so the Lord is round about his people from henceforth even for ever" (v. 2).

Trust opens the heart to the entrance of strength that comes only from God. The trustful man draws steadiness from the calm of God; my steadfastness is based on His strength and on His promise: "The mountains shall depart, and the hills be removed; but my kindness shall not depart from thee, neither shall the covenant of my peace be removed, saith the Lord" (Isa. 54:10). With Luther I sing:

> *A mighty fortress is our God,*
> *A bulwark never failing.*

255

Scripture: Psalms 126—128

Today's scripture gives opportunity to reflect on what God has done for us, and how good it is to walk with Him. These three psalms are the third trilogy in the 15 "songs of ascent" (Psalms 120—134). Barnes titles them "Return and Restoration." He interprets them as dealing with the return from Babylonian captivity (126), the rebuilding (127), and the repeopling (128) of Jerusalem (BBC, 3:407).

The Story: Psalms 126—128

The Lord has done great things for us, and we are filled with joy (Ps. 126:3, NIV).

Songs of Joy

How good it is to return home after we have been away for a long time! But how much more blessed to return if we had been forcibly detained and God had specially intervened to bring us home again. With Israel we want to sing, "The Lord has done great things for us, and we are filled with joy."

How good it is to know that if we trust in God and hang in there, He will bring us out to a place of rejoicing. "They that sow in tears shall reap in joy. He that goeth forth and weepeth, bearing precious seed, shall doubtless come again with rejoicing, bringing his sheaves with him" (126:5-6).

How good it is to discover our dependence upon God's help—and to learn to rest in Him! "Unless the Lord builds a house, the builders' work is useless. Unless the Lord protects a city, sentries do no good. It is senseless for you to work so hard from early morning until late at night, fearing you will starve to death; for God wants his loved ones to get their proper rest" (127:1-2, TLB).

How good it is to enjoy the blessings of family—wife and

children! They stand with us in our best endeavors; they stand beside us when pressures come. And if we have not found this special blessing, we are still not alone. We have a Heavenly Father and we have the family of God. We can still sing our song of joy: "Blessed are all who fear the Lord, who walk in his ways" (128:1, NIV).

> *Praise God, from whom all blessings flow:*
> *Praise Him, all creatures here below:*
> *Praise Him above, ye heav'nly host.*
> *Praise Father, Son, and Holy Ghost.*

▼

Scripture: Psalms 129—131
The Story: Psalm 130:1-8

I am waiting for the Lord; my soul is in expectation, and In His word do I hope (Ps. 130:5, NBV).

The Language of Devotion

How different would be the prayers and songs of the church if we had no written scripture! The Bible profoundly shapes the spirit and language of our worship. I recall a recent testimony expressed in the words of Ps. 103:1-2: "Bless the Lord, O my soul: and all that is within me, bless his holy name. Bless the Lord, O my soul, and forget not all his benefits."

Recently in personal Bible reading I felt that God gave me words of consolation for a friend in the church who had experienced deep tragedy: "May God our Father and the Lord Jesus Christ give you grace and peace. . . . He helps us in all our troubles, so that we are able to help those who have all kinds of troubles, using the same help that we ourselves have received from God. Just as we have a share in Christ's many sufferings, so also through Christ we share in his great help" (2 Cor. 1:2, 4-5, TEV).

257

In any Christian church today the hymnal would be poverty-stricken without concepts and language direct from the Bible. In the Old Testament, many of the psalms were used in the worship in essentially the form that we have them today. In British churches it is still common to sing the psalms in public worship.

As worshipers approached the Temple in Jerusalem they sang Psalm 130. Today, as we come to our prayer time there can be no better preparation than the words of the Psalmist:

"I am waiting for the Lord; my soul is in expectation, and in His word do I hope.

"My soul is looking for the Lord more than watchmen for the morning; yes, more than watchmen for the morning.

"O [soul], hope in the Lord, for with the Lord there is lovingkindness, and with Him is abundant redemption.

"He Himself will redeem [us] from all [our] iniquities" (Ps. 130: 5-8, NBV).

▼

Scripture: Psalms 132—134

These psalms are the last of 15 psalms of ascent, used in the Temple worship.

The Story: Psalm 132:1-18

I will not rest or sleep, until I provide a place for the Lord (Ps. 132:4-5, TEV).

Like Father, like Son

Today is not Father's Day, but any day is appropriate to reflect on how faith in God passes from parent to child.

In Psalm 132 God's man had come into God's house to praise and pray. There he recalled how the faithfulness and devotion of his forefather David made possible his own contact with God that day. In gratitude he prayed, "Lord, remember David . . . how he . . . vowed unto the mighty God of Jacob . . . I will not give sleep to mine eyes, or slumber to mine eyelids, until I find out a place for the Lord" (vv. 1-2, 4-5).

As you worship today, does your mind go back to the example of a faithful father or a godly mother? Last week I heard a friend tell of his boyhood experience. Across the years this man has contributed more than 20 percent of his income to the work of God. He testified: "When I was a teenager, I saw my father mortgage our home to help pay for a church where we could worship God. And I never got away from it."

From my own scrapbook come these lines written in my teens. I quote them, not as examples of good poetry, but as proof that a godly father makes an impact on his sons.

> *Calm and serene I behold thee,*
> *With manhood graven in every line;*
> *And wonder at thy noble bearing,*
> *O wonderful father of mine.*

> *It was ever thy noble example*
> *That caused thy sons to do right.*
> *It was ever thy wonderful manhood*
> *That spurred them on in life's fight.*

> *May our kind Heavenly Father grant*
> *That the reward of thy life may be*
> *Sons who are upright and noble,*
> *Sons who are worthy of thee.*

If perchance I have not been blessed with godly parents, I want my children to fare better than I. Through me, I want them to see Christ and be drawn to Him.

> *I may never get earth's glory,*
> *I may never gather gold;*
> *Men may count me as a failure*
> *When my business life is told.*
> *But if he who follows after*
> *Is a Christian, I'll be glad,*
> *For I'll know I've been successful*
> *As that little fellow's dad.*
>
> —AUTHOR UNKNOWN

Scripture: Psalms 135—137

Psalm 135 is exclusively a prayer of praise. The Psalmist praises God for choosing His people, verse 4; for His creative power, verses 5-7; for His control in history, verses 8-12; and for His supremacy in the universe, verses 13-18.

Psalm 136 is a litany. Use it today as a responsive prayer. Let one read the occasion for thanksgiving in each verse, and all respond with deep appreciation, "for his mercy endureth for ever."

The Story: Psalm 137:1-6

Praise the Lord; for the Lord is good: sing praises unto his name (Ps. 135:3).

"The Lord's Song in a Strange Land"

Psalm 137 was written during the Exile or at its close. It vividly portrays the mood of God's people heartsick for their homeland. After a wearisome march of 900 miles on foot these exiles from Judah were relocated near Babylon. There King Nebuchadnezzar expected them to begin life again.

In their captivity and dispersion the Jews often held their religious meetings on the banks of rivers (see Acts 16:13). On this occasion they gathered for worship "by the rivers of Babylon." They had brought their harps, and were prepared to sing "the songs of Zion." But the heartbreak was too much. The words and tunes recalled a flood of memories of the wonderful days that used to be; and they could not go on with their service.

"How shall we sing the Lord's song in a strange land?" It is the cry of a discouraged people. Here is a very human reaction—but it is not God's will for us. He wants to help His people rise above their disappointments. Though cut off from some happy past, we need not be cut off from God. His help is always available—anywhere.

"How shall we sing the Lord's song in a strange land?" By remembering that no land is strange to Him. Wherever we find ourselves, our Lord is at home there. And where He is can become a good land for us.

> *Anywhere! Anywhere! Fear I cannot know.*
> *Anywhere with Jesus I can safely go.*
> —JESSIE B. POUNDS

▼

Scripture: Psalms 138—140
The Story: Psalm 139:1-18, 23-24

Your hand will guide me, and your right hand will hold me fast (Ps. 139:10, NIV).

Secure in God

Psalm 139 has been acclaimed by Rabbi Aben Ezra as "The crown of all the psalms." David marvels that God knows all things, and that He is everywhere present.

We rest secure in the awareness of a God who is always near. Whittier knew this confidence when he prayed:

> *I know not where His islands lift*
> *Their fronded palms in air;*
> *I only know I cannot drift*
> *Beyond His love and care.*

In verse 3 David reminds us, "You are familiar with all my ways" (NIV). Jesus tells us, "Even the very hairs of your head are all numbered. Fear not therefore" (Luke 12:7). If some small concern is big enough to be a problem for me, it is big enough for His attention.

Just as God's knowledge penetrates to the very core of our being, so His presence follows us wherever we go. This always-present Heavenly Father is a great comfort to His obedient child. In verse 7 the question is not, "How can I escape God?" Rather, it is, "Can I ever get into any place where God's help is not immediately available?" The glad answer is no. If I go up to heaven, the Father is there. If I die and go to the grave *(sheol)*, I am still in His care. If I could fly as fast as the rays of the morning sun, God's Spirit would get to my destination first. He would be there when I arrived, be there to guide me in what I should do, and to hold me steady if I should falter.

David's devotion comes to its climax in verses 23-24. Here is the hunger of the human spirit to be like God. Here is the desire to be cleansed from all sin. It is a prayer of trust because I am willing for God to see me as I really am. Therefore I pray:

> *Search me, O God, and know my heart today.*
> *Try me, O Savior; know my thoughts, I pray.*
> *See if there be some wicked way in me;*
> *Cleanse me from every sin, and set me free.*
> —J. EDWIN ORR

Scripture: Psalms 141—143
The Story: Psalms 141:1-4; 143:5-10

Show me the way I should go, for to you I lift up my soul (Ps. 143:8; all quotes from NIV).

God's Help for My Discouragement

How long has it been since, in some discouraging moment, your heart sent to God a quick cry for help? The need for assistance is universal. And this urgent call is the theme of these three psalms. In them we discover ways to find help.

God's ministries to us are as varied as our personalities and as relevant as our needs. He has ways of speaking to the human spirit, in every time of need, but He does not always answer in the same way.

The surest route to divine help is to ask for it. God is more ready to help us than we are to respond to a call from our child. David sets the example when in distress he prays, "O Lord, I call to you; come quickly to me." The Bible encourages us, "Come near to God and he will come near to you" (James 4:8). Because He invites me, I come; I come asking Him to help me.

God loves me even if I have done wrong. But I have greater confidence in approaching Him when I have sincerely tried to do His will. Therefore every day I pray, "O Lord; keep watch over the door of my lips. Let not my heart be drawn to what is evil." I offer the prayer that Jesus taught us to pray: "Lead us not into temptation, but deliver us from the evil one" (Matt. 6:13).

Daily companionship with the Father keeps me so close to Him that He is near when emergencies arise. David prays, "May my prayer be set before you . . . like the evening sacrifice. . . . Let the morning bring me word of your unfailing love, for I have put my trust in you" (141:2; 143:8).

Our walk with God is life's most basic partnership. When we identify with Him, we see our own lives come to fulfillment in the success of His work. In that partnership our hearts cry, "Set me free . . . that I may praise your name. Then the righteous will gather about me because of your goodness to me" (142:7).

In God we find direction for the way that we should take; and in Him we find courage to persist until we reach the goal.

"Show me the way I should go, for to you I lift up my soul. . . . When my spirit grows faint within me, it is you who know my way" (143:8; 142:3).

▼

Scripture: Psalms 144—145

Yesterday our three psalms were prayers of petition. In contrast, Psalms 144 and 145 are prayers of praise.

The Story: Psalm 145:1-21
      Today, read the comments first, then read the scripture. If two or more persons are involved in worship, read Psalm 145 responsively. Let the leader read verse 1 and others respond by reading verse 2, and so on.

Every day will I bless thee; and I will praise thy name for ever and ever (Ps. 145:2).

Thank You, Lord

Thank You, Lord, for help in my work. You helped David, the general of the armies, but You are equally ready to help me at the office (144:1-4).

    Thank You, Lord, for responding when trouble came my way. "I will sing a new song to you . . . [because you] deliver and rescue me" (144:9-11, NIV).

    Thank You, Father, for children and for grandchildren to bless our lives and to carry forward our dreams (144:12).

    Thank You for food to eat, and for security from foreign oppressors. "Blessed are the people whose God is the Lord" (144:13-15, NIV).

    "Every day will I bless thee; and I will praise thy name for ever and ever" because You are God and You are "worthy of praise."

    Thank You, Lord, for the impulse to tell others about Your love—for those who told me; and for my opportunities to share with others.

    Thank You, Father, for Your readiness to forgive. I have needed Your mercy often, and You have given generously.

    I rejoice in Your good plan for the world, for our happiness here, and for Your promises for the world to come.

Thank You, Lord, for Your concern for the hungry, and for Your provision of food.

Thank You, Lord, that You are on the side of right against wrong. In this, let me always fight by Your side.

"I will always praise the Lord; let all his creatures praise his holy name forever" (Ps. 145:21, TEV).

▼

Scripture: Psalms 146—150

Our readings for today are known as the "Hallelujah Psalms." Each begins and closes with the Hebrew *Hallelu-Yah,* "Praise the Lord." From early times they have been used in the morning synagogue service.

The Story: Psalms 146; 148

Praise the Lord, O my soul. I will praise the Lord all my life (Ps. 146:1-2, NIV).

Praise the Lord

Psalm 146 reminds us, "Blessed is he whose help is the God of Jacob, whose hope is in the Lord his God" (v. 5, NIV). In six short verses the Psalmist recalls 10 blessings that call for our praise. God is the Maker of heaven and earth, and He is faithful in His care for us. He helps all who are oppressed, and provides food for the hungry. God frees those who are in bondage, and gives sight to the blind. The Lord lifts us when we are bent with burdens, and He supports us in every desire to do right. He watches over the alien; He sustains the fatherless and the widow.

In response my heart sings, "Praise the Lord, O my soul. I will praise the Lord all my life."

In Psalm 148 we find a ringing call to worship God, our Creator, who is worthy of praise. Wm. J. Kirkpatrick has paraphrased the psalm and set the words to music. My heart joins him in the song:

> Hallelujah! Praise Jehovah!
>   From the heavens praise His name.
> Praise Jehovah in the highest;
>   All His angels, praise proclaim.
> All His hosts, together praise Him—
>   Sun, and moon, and stars on high.
> Praise Him, O ye heav'n of heavens,
>   And ye floods above the sky.

These five psalms of praise are a fitting conclusion to "The Hymnbook of the Bible." For this book and for every blessing recorded in it my heart sings:

> Praise God, from whom all blessings flow:
> Praise Him, all creatures here below:
> Praise Him above, ye heav'nly host.
> Praise Father, Son, and Holy Ghost.

▼

☐ WEEK 26, FRIDAY   PROVERBS

The Book of *Proverbs*, like the Books of Job and Ecclesiastes, is described as wisdom literature. In 2:6, Solomon declares: "The Lord grants wisdom! His every word is a treasure of knowledge and understanding" (TLB). Because it is God who offers such wisdom, the wise man accepts and follows it. E. Stanley Jones has somewhere described this life-style as "finding and following the grain of the universe instead of living at cross-purposes with it."

Scripture: Proverbs 1—3
The Story: Proverbs 2:1-15

The Lord gives wisdom, and from his mouth come knowledge and understanding (Prov. 2:6, NIV).

Wisdom for Today

What God says makes good sense. Because this is true, it is mine to listen—and that listening must go to the very core of my being. To *receive* God's words is to hear them, to become aware of what He means. *Hiding* His commandments within the heart is to think about them, to reflect on them. To *incline* to wisdom is to grasp its meaning with approval and acceptance. When I incline, I acknowledge God's Word to be true.

To apply my heart to understanding means responding with my whole being. My mind acknowledges God's Word to be true. My moral judgment says it is right—that is the way life ought to be. My emotions respond affirmatively—I want to do the right and avoid the wrong. Then my will enters the response; I choose what my mind says is true, what my conscience acknowledges to be right, and what my feelings incline me to do.

Today God's Word tells me how I may find the wisdom He offers: "If thou seekest her as silver, and searchest for her as for hid treasures; then shalt thou understand the fear of the Lord, and find the knowledge of God" (2:4-5). But if I am indifferent toward God, I do not find Him. All of the really good things in life call for effort. To succeed in business, in art, or in homemaking requires a desire for achievement and the application of energy. If all of the other good things call for us to give our best, how much more should the search for God's truth demand that we seek for her as for silver?

> When God speaks, the high mountains tremble;
> When God speaks, the loud billows roll;
> When God speaks, my heart falls to listening;
> And there is response in my soul.*
> —CARLTON C. BUCK

With Solomon, I pray today for the enlargement and fulfillment of God's gracious gift:

"*Give . . . thy servant an understanding heart . . . that I may discern between good and bad*" (1 Kings 3:9).

*Copyright 1936. Renewed 1964 by Lillenas Publishing Co.

Scripture: Proverbs 4—7
The Story: Proverbs 4:4-18

Do not forsake wisdom, and she will protect you; love her, and she will watch over you (Prov. 4:6, NIV).

What Does It Mean to Be Wise?

Dr. J. B. Chapman was fond of saying, "Serving God is best in the long run—and it is the long run that we are on." To be wise is to make the choice that I will be happiest with when I look back on my decision. We cannot always know that our decisions are right because we do not know everything; but in moral choices God's Word offers us good guidelines.

✔ "Keep my commands and you will live," the Bible exhorts. (NIV). To be wise is to do what I believe God wants me to do.

✔ To be wise is also to do what I know to be right even when it is hard. God's Word urges, "Though it cost all you have, get understanding" (NIV). In moral decisions, to take the hard way is almost always to choose the right way.

✔ Verses 11-12 remind us that to act wisely today makes the going easier tomorrow: "I guide you in the way of wisdom and lead you along straight paths. When you walk, your steps will not be hampered; when you run, you will not stumble" (NIV).

✔ To be wise is to follow the path that leads to an ever brighter and happier tomorrow. That is the good promise of God's Word: "The path of the just is as the shining light, that shineth more and more unto the perfect day" (4:18).

Even in the far distant past God revealed to His servant the wonder of human life when lived in partnership with the Heavenly Father. Today I join that wise man in his song of praise:

"Blessed is the man who finds wisdom, the man who gains understanding, for she is more profitable than silver and yields better returns than gold. She is more precious than rubies; nothing you desire can compare with her. Long life is in her right hand; in her left hand are riches and honor. Her ways are pleasant ways, and all her paths are peace. She is a tree of life to those who embrace her; those who lay hold of her will be blessed" (Prov. 3:13-18, NIV).

My heart echoes:

> God's way is the best way,
> God's way is the right way.
> I'll trust in Him always,
> He knoweth the best.*
> —LIDA SHIVERS LEECH

▼

☐ WEEK 27, SUNDAY   PROVERBS

Scripture: Proverbs 8—10
The Story: Proverbs 8:22-31

I was appointed from eternity, from the beginning, before the world began (Prov. 8:23, NIV).

Who Is This Wisdom?

"The Lord created me first of all, the first of his works, long ago.
I was made in the very beginning, at the first, before the world began.
I was born before the oceans, when there were no springs of water.
I was born before the mountains, before the hills were set in place, before God made the earth and its fields or even the first handful of soil.
I was there when he set the sky in place, when he stretched the horizon across the ocean, when he placed the clouds in the sky, when he opened the springs of the ocean and ordered the waters of the sea to rise no further than he said.
I was there when he laid the earth's foundations.

269

I was beside him like an architect, I was his daily source of joy, always happy in his presence—happy with the world and pleased with the human race" (TEV).

Let us place this Proverbs passage beside John 1:1-4: "In the beginning was the Word, and the Word was with God and the Word was God. He was with God in the beginning. Through him all things were made; and without him nothing was made that has been made. In him was life, and that life was the light of men" (NIV).

Can we read these tributes without believing that both describe our Lord?

Whether we hear it in the Wisdom of Proverbs or in God's full revelation of himself in Jesus, the call to Wisdom is our invitation to Christ. God's New Testament messenger echoes and amplifies Wisdom's invitation: "The Spirit and the bride say, Come. And let him that heareth say, Come. And let him that is athirst, come. And whosoever will, let him take of the water of life freely" (Rev. 22:17).

With Charlotte Elliott, my glad heart responds:

"O Lamb of God, I come! I come!"

▼

□ WEEK 27, MONDAY   PROVERBS

Scripture: Proverbs 11—15

The first nine chapters of Proverbs give us some fairly lengthy discourses, each unfolding a unified theme. But in the main section of the book (chaps. 10—22) we find 375 short sayings that give us varied counsels for successful living. The compiler of the book did not attempt to group these truths under any plan or organization. Each stands on its own merit as counsel to the reader.

From your reading today and tomorrow underline in your Bible several of these insights that you have proved true in your own experience.

The Story: Proverbs 13:9, 21; 12:7; 14:26-27; 12:28
(in this order)

In the way of righteousness there is life; along that path is immortality (Prov. 12:28; all quotes from NIV).

The Way of Life

The wisdom sayings of Solomon include a wide range of brief comments on human interests. However, when he deals with the great issues of a fulfilled life, he repeats important counsels. Of these issues none is more crucial than our commitment always to choose God's revealed way.

In contemporary America we read much about a pluralistic society, and freedom to choose one's own life-style. But under God, we are permitted pluralism and freedom only within the boundaries that His wisdom has set. To live within these boundaries brings fullness of life and lasting happiness to us and to our children. To stray beyond them results in frustration. To stubbornly persist outside of them brings ultimate separation from God. Of these priority truths, Wisdom speaks again and again so that we may not plead ignorance.

"The light of the righteous shines brightly, but the lamp of the wicked is snuffed out."

"Misfortune pursues the sinner, but prosperity is the reward of the righteous."

"Wicked men are overthrown and are no more, but the house of the righteous stands firm."

"He who fears the Lord has a secure fortress, and for his children it will be a refuge. The fear of the Lord is a fountain of life, turning a man from the snares of death."

In life's ultimate choice there are not many ways—only two: "I have set before you life and death, blessings and curses. Now choose life, so that you and your children may live and that you may love the Lord your God, listen to his voice, and hold fast to him" (Deut. 30:19-20).

With the Psalmist my spirit is drawn to wisdom, and my heart responds to God's call:

"I have chosen the way of truth; I have set my heart on your laws" (Ps. 119:30).

Scripture: Proverbs 16—23
The Story: Proverbs 19:1-17

He who is kind to the poor lends to the Lord, and he will reward him for what he has done (Prov. 19:17; all quotes but last from NIV).

Counsels to the Comfortable and to the Poor

Most of us best express our loyalty to the Lord by the way we earn and spend our money. Wisdom therefore knows that we need guidance, whether rich or poor—or in the middle.

What counsel does God give to us regarding the needy?

★ It is wicked to be callous: "He who mocks the poor shows contempt for their Maker; whoever gloats over disaster will not go unpunished" (17:5).

★ God is pleased for us to be generous: "He who is kind to the poor lends to the Lord, and he will reward him for what he has done" (19:17).

★ Wealth can give us a false feeling of security and lessen our sense of dependence on God: "The wealth of the rich is their fortified city; they imagine it an unscalable wall" (18:11).

★ Unrestrained desire for wealth can corrupt the home: "A greedy man brings trouble to his family" (15:27).

★ To seek to gain wealth by injustice or force violates the will of God: "Better a little with righteousness than much gain with injustice" (16:8).

What does God's Word say to us if we are poor?

★ Poverty with honor is not life's greatest evil: "Better a little with the fear of the Lord than great wealth with turmoil. Better a meal of vegetables where there is love than a fattened calf with hatred" (15:16-17).

★ God is concerned with our need: "The Lord tears down the proud man's house but he keeps the widow's boundaries intact" (15:25).

★ Be honest: "Better to be poor than a liar" (19:22).

★ Don't be a beggar: "A poor man is shunned by all his relatives—how much more do his friends avoid him!" (19:7).

It is not right for us to avoid a man who is in need. But it is a human tendency to back away from someone who is always asking a favor. To keep my hand out for help is to alienate those who know me.

Today I join in the wise prayer of Agur:

"Give me neither poverty nor riches . . . lest I be full, and deny thee . . . or lest I be poor and steal, and take the name of my God in vain" (Prov. 30:8-9).

Scripture: Proverbs 24—31

Chapters 30—31 appear to be the work of writers other than Solomon. Nothing further is known of Agur the son of Jakeh, or of King Lemuel. They may have been, like Job and Balaam, non-Israelites who had come to know the God of Israel's faith. More significant than their identities is that their words were considered worthy of inclusion in the Book of Proverbs.

The Story: 27:1; 28:1, 5; 29:25; 30:4-5

Fear of man will prove to be a snare, but whoever trusts in the Lord is kept safe (Prov. 29:25, NIV).

Highest Wisdom

A growing faith in God brings a joyful sense of security under every circumstance. This is life's supreme wisdom. But how often we miss it!

In 30:4 Agur reminds us that our trust in God is well founded. The words reflect God's challenge to Job: "Where were you when I laid the earth's foundation? Tell me, if you understand. Who marked off its dimensions? . . . Who shut up the sea behind doors when it burst forth? . . . Who endowed the heart with wisdom or gave understanding to the mind?" (Job 38:4-5, 8, 36, NIV). To all such queries an honest man must humbly reply with Job: "I know that you can do all things; no plan of yours can be thwarted" (Job 42:1, NIV).

In 30:5 we see the Father's goodness in revealing himself, and in His complete faithfulness: "Every word of God proves true" (TLB).

God's great power, supported by His faithfulness, "is a shield to those who take refuge in him" (30:5, NIV). Here is our part in finding help. His power and love are available. It remains only for us to trust Him.

Since it is God with whom we have to deal, why do we hesitate to trust? We believe that He is our personal Friend, that He loves us, and that He has made known His will concerning us. We believe that He is wiser than we, and that He is more powerful than all the forces that may oppose Him. We believe that He is more interested in our welfare than we are in ourselves.

If we believe all of this, why should we not trust Him completely? Today my spirit sings:

> 'Tis so sweet to trust in Jesus,
> Just to take Him at His Word;
> Just to rest upon His promise;
> Just to know, "Thus saith the Lord."
> —LOUISA M. R. STEAD

▼

□ WEEK 27, THURSDAY   ECCLESIASTES

In Ecclesiastes we think about the meaning of our world, and the values of human life. If Solomon was not the author, certainly much in the book reflects his experience.

We see repeated shifts from pessimism to faith and back again. The book represents the struggle of a soul with dark doubts, but despite his pessimistic moods, the author sees life as precious as a golden bowl (12:6). His final answer to the quest for meaning is, "Fear God, and keep his commandments" (12:13).

Scripture: Ecclesiastes 1—3
The Story: Ecclesiastes 2:18-23

To the man who pleases him, God gives wisdom, knowledge and happiness (Eccles. 2:26, NIV).

You Can't Take It with You

In our story the writer reflects on a life spent in getting and hoarding wealth. What bothers him most is that he must leave it "unto the man that shall be after me. And who knoweth whether he shall be a wise man or a fool?" (2:18-19).

History has often verified the truth underlying the writer's pessimism. Few sons prove as effective in preserving fortunes as their fathers were in gathering them. But these facts need not drive us to despair. They should rather guide us in how we earn our money, for what we spend it, and to whom we leave it.

If a man is so mad after wealth that "his heart taketh not rest in the night," it is "vanity" (2:23). A satisfying life is more important than amassing a fortune. The king could have used his wealth while he lived. He could have spent it to relieve the needs of his fellowman, and invested it for the advancement of the work of God. The Bible teaches us that money is not only to be saved. Money is primarily to provide for the needs of human life.

It is not wise for God's man to spend a lifetime earning money and then leave entirely to others the decisions on how to use it. Those who follow may not be committed Christians, or they may not be wise. Christian money management would say: (1) In a man's lifetime let him give and invest as generously as he accumulates. (2) If he has something to leave to his heirs, let him pray over

275

these decisions. (3) If there is no real family need, or if there is no Christian commitment to use money in Christian ways, let him leave it to God's work where he has invested during his lifetime.

Father, in all the getting and managing of my money, give me "wisdom, knowledge and happiness." In Jesus' name I ask it. Amen.

▼

Scripture: Ecclesiastes 4—6

How shall we interpret 5:5, "It is better not to vow than to make a vow and not fulfill it"? (NIV). Are we to understand that failure to respond to God is somehow acceptable? No. It is bad not to respond to God's voice in obedience. It is worse to promise obedience and then fail to keep our word. Best of all is to pledge and to pay. Vows made to God have power, when kept, to lift us to new levels of devotion and service; but a broken pledge jeopardizes our standing with Him and undermines our integrity.

The Story: Ecclesiastes 5:1-7

I know that it shall be well with them that fear God (Eccles. 8:12).

Reverence in Worship

Today's summary sentence from Ecclesiastes is "Fear thou God" (5:7). Here is supreme wisdom and an indispensable attitude in true worship.

This wholesome respect for God is the open door through which we come to Him. Bible reading tells us about God, but worship brings us into the Divine Presence where we fellowship with Him in a conscious communion. In worship we listen and respond to Him.

"Keep thy foot" (5:1) is sharply rendered by a current slogan, "Watch your step!" God is high and holy; therefore reverent awe is

276

always becoming in His presence. Isaiah sensed this mood and wrote: "I saw also the Lord sitting upon a throne, high and lifted up . . . the seraphims . . . cried [one] unto another . . . Holy, holy, holy is the Lord of hosts: the whole earth is full of his glory" (Isa. 6:1-3).

The Preacher also counsels, "Let not thine heart be hasty to utter any thing before God" (5:2). When we are honestly seeking to know God's will we need not feel pressed into any hasty decision. It is wise counsel to "take time to be holy. / Speak oft with thy Lord." If we keep open to Him and keep talking to Him about the issue, He leads us to a point of certainty.

My spirit joins the glad prayer of the Psalmist: "When thou saidst, Seek ye my face; my heart said unto thee, Thy face, Lord, will I seek" (Ps. 27:8).

> Silently now I wait for Thee,
> Ready, my God, Thy will to see.
> Open my ears, illumine me,
> Spirit divine!
> —CLARA H. SCOTT

▼

Scripture: Ecclesiastes 7—9
The Story: Ecclesiastes 7:1-12

Calmness can lay great errors to rest (Eccles. 10:4, NIV).

The Wisdom of Restraint

Today's chapters contain a group of proverbs held together by the common question, What makes good sense in our kind of world? We are invited to think practically about God's way of life—try it, and see for yourself that it is a good way.

Verses 1-4 point out that a serious approach to life is better than a flippant mood. Life is a business rather than a party. When we adopt this responsible attitude we make the best decisions and enjoy the best reputation.

It is wisdom to recognize that death is as much a part of life as birth. If we keep this in mind we make better decisions than if we forget it.

In verses 5-12 our Preacher counsels us against obstacles to right judgment. Rate yourself on each point, circling A, B, or C from the scale below. After each self-evaluation offer an appropriate prayer.

A. I usually do the right thing—for which I thank God.
B. I sometimes fail at this point—and I ask for forgiveness.
C. I am inclined to do the wrong thing in this situation—but by God's help I intend to change.

★ Don't take the wrong advice. Listen to dependable advisors, even when their counsel hurts (vv. 5-6). A B C

★ Don't let your judgment be warped by irrelevant issues. We sometimes make wrong decisions and say the wrong things because of emotional pressures (v. 7). A B C

★ Don't decide on the basis of immediate results. Make your decisions in view of long-range purposes (v. 8*a*). A B C

★ Don't be impatient. Persistent patience has resolved many a problem that would not yield to immediate pressure (v. 8*b*). A B C

★ Don't get upset. Frustration is always the enemy of clear thinking and sound judgment (v. 9). A B C

★ Don't complain about the times. Even if they are bad, complaining never helps resolve today's problems (v. 10). A B C

Father, teach me Your wisdom for my way.

> *I would be prayerful thro' each busy moment.*
> *I would be constantly in touch with God.*
> *I would be tuned to hear His slightest whisper.*
> *I would have faith to keep the path Christ trod.*
> —AUTHOR UNKNOWN

Scripture: Ecclesiastes 10—12
The Story: Ecclesiastes 11:9—12:7

Remember your Creator in the days of your youth
(Eccles. 12:1, NIV).

Age and Death Belong to Life

Life is a puzzle, but faith in God puts the four pieces together: (1) the energies and joys of youth, (2) the decline of strength in old age, (3) the certainty of death, and (4) our accountability to God

Wisdom reminds us that the wrap-up years are also a part of life. In all literature no one has pictured old age as movingly as Ecclesiastes:

"Remember your Creator in the days of your youth, before the days of trouble [aging] come and the years approach . . . when the keepers of the house [the lips] tremble, and the strong men [the legs] stoop, when the grinders [the teeth] cease because they are few, and those looking through the windows [the eyes] grow dim; when the doors to the street [the ears] are closed and the sound of grinding fades . . . when men are afraid of heights [of falling] and of dangers in the streets; when the almond tree blossoms [white hair] and the grasshopper drags himself along [short, shuffling steps] . . . Then man goes to his eternal home and mourners go about the streets" (12:1-5, NIV, explanations added).

But we remember some things that Ecclesiastes forgot. "If old age is unhaunted by too many regrets and fears, it may well be a gracious period of tranquility, with treasures of memory, the compensations of children's children, blessed comradeship of mind and spirit—and rest. Like the late afternoon of a summer's day, when the shadows have grown long but the light lingers. . . . It may indeed be more; it may be the season for reaping and storing the final harvest of life" (Atkins).

I heard a man of 80 pray at the funeral service for his 87-year-old friend: "Lord, we do not depend on the strength of our youth. 'Though our outward man perish, yet the inward man is

renewed day by day. . . . We look not at the things which are seen
. . . for the things which are seen are temporal; but the things
which are not seen are eternal'" (2 Cor. 4:16, 18).

At 77 my heart responds, Amen.

▼

If the Song of Songs seems too intimate for family
reading, omit these meditations and move on to
Isaiah. For a full study of the Song of Solomon see
the author's interpretation in BBC, 3:601-36.

Scripture: Song of Solomon 1—4
The Story: Song of Solomon 2:1-4, 8-13

**Arise, come, my darling; my beautiful one, come
with me** (Song of Sol. 2:13; all quotes from NIV).

A Song of True Love

The phrase *song of songs* is the Hebrew way of expressing super-
latives. It is a form comparable to Lord of lords and holy of holies.
To the writer, true love is the best song in the book!

Commentators are agreed that the Song of Songs is a poem
about love, but beyond this there are wide differences.

The three-character interpretation seems to be the best basis
for outlining and explaining the content. According to this interpretation, the young woman Shulamite (6:13) from Shunem was
the only daughter among several brothers belonging to a widowed
mother in northern Israel. The girl fell in love with a handsome
young shepherd and they became engaged.

Meanwhile King Solomon on a summer visit to the neighborhood was attracted to the Shulamite. She was abducted and
taken to the king's court at his summer home in the Lebanon
mountains. Here the king tried unsuccessfully to woo her. All of

Solomon's promises of jewels and prestige failed to win the girl's affection. She steadfastly declared her love for her country sweetheart.

Finally, recognizing the depth and noble character of her love, Solomon released the girl. Accompanied by her beloved shepherd, the Shulamite left the court and returned to her humble country home.

If this interpretation be accepted, the theme of the book is faithfulness in love rather than exclusively conjugal love. After the king's first proposal (1:8-11, 15, 17) and its rejection, the Shulamite was rewarded by a vision of her true love who sang for her a song of joy:

"Arise, my darling, my beautiful one, and come with me. See! The winter is past; the rains are over and gone. Flowers appear on the earth; the season of singing has come, the cooing of doves is heard in our land. The fig tree forms its early fruit; the blossoming vines spread their fragrance. Arise, come, my darling; my beautiful one, come with me" (2:10-13).

With appreciation for the Shulamite's faithfulness and with gladness for God's gift of human love, we remember a prayer from the marriage ritual:

Our Father in heaven, we thank You that You are love and that You have created us after Your image. We thank You for planting love of woman in the heart of man, and love for man in the heart of woman.

▼

☐ **WEEK 28, TUESDAY**　　　　**SONG OF SOLOMON**

Scripture: Song of Solomon 5—8
The Story: Song of Solomon 6:1-3; 8:5-7

Many waters cannot quench love; rivers cannot wash it away (Song of Sol. 8:7, NIV).

The Strength of Love

The last half of the Song of Songs deals with the triumph and joys of true love. The "daughters of Jerusalem" could not understand why any woman would reject the attentions of the king in preference for the love of a shepherd. They themselves had accepted Solomon's harem as a way of life, but they wanted to know who this shepherd was whom the Shulamite dared prefer to the king.

The Shulamite's response, "I am my beloved's, and my beloved is mine," faithfully foreshadows the Christian wedding vow, "and keep me only unto thee so long as we both shall live."

After 7:9, Solomon apparently made no further advances. Convinced at last that he could not win the Shulamite's affection—and perhaps shamed by her steadfast loyalty—he released her from custody. Thus God's Word reflects the encouraging truth that the influence of a good and strong person can steady a weaker one and save an impulsive individual from low living.

In 8:6-7 there is poetry of high order:

> Love is strong as death;
> Ardent love is retentive as the grave. . . .
> Many waters cannot quench love,
> Neither can the floods drown it:
> If a man would give all the substance
>   of his house for love,
> It would utterly be rejected (adapted from TLB).

Verse 8:14 is to be understood as a fragment of a song that the Shulamite had been accustomed to sing for her lover. "With this song the drama ends, and the two lovers, arm in arm, pass from the scene, conscious that true love has triumphed. She clings as a signet ring to his arm, and he knows that her love for him is 'strong as death'" (adapted from Terry).

And so closes this strange book. It is different from any other in the Bible; but it is in the Bible. It is a book about love between a man and a woman—one of God's gracious gifts to us. With the hymnwriter we join in the song:

> For the joy of human love . . .
> Lord of all, to Thee we raise
> This our hymn of grateful praise.
> —FOLLIOTT S. PIERPOINT

Scripture: Isaiah 1—3

The first verse of Isaiah's prophecy describes the contents: "This book contains the messages about Judah and Jerusalem which God revealed to Isaiah son of Amoz during the time when Uzziah, Jotham, Ahaz, and Hezekiah were kings of Judah" (TEV).

Isaiah, who ministered in Jerusalem about 740-700 B.C., was the greatest of the eighth-century prophets, including Jonah, Amos, Hosea, and Micah. His name means "The Eternal One is salvation"; he is sometimes called "the prophet of holiness." More than any other Old Testament prophet, God revealed to Isaiah the coming of Jesus Christ, the Messiah.

The Story: Isaiah 1:1-4, 15-20, 24-28

Come . . . let us walk in the light of the Lord (Isa. 2:5; all quotes from NIV).

I Am Glad for a Forgiving God

Chapter 1 serves as an introduction to the book. Here we see the prophet's poetic style and the major themes of his message. The eternal God is in the foreground of all Isaiah's thinking—the God who judges evil but extends great mercy to those who repent and turn from their sins. Today let us hear the man of God in his own words—and in his own style:

"Hear, O heavens! Listen, O earth!
For the Lord has spoken;

I reared children and brought them up,
   but they have rebelled against me. . . .
When you spread out your hands in prayer,
   I will hide my eyes from you;
even if you offer many prayers, I will not listen.
Your hands are full of blood;
   wash and make yourselves clean.
Take your evil deeds out of my sight!
Stop doing wrong, learn to do right. . . .
'Come now, let us reason together,' says the Lord.
'Though your sins are like scarlet, they shall be as white as
   snow;
though they be red like crimson, they shall be like wool.
If you are willing and obedient, you will eat the best from the
   land;
but if you resist and rebel, you will be devoured by the sword.
For the mouth of the Lord has spoken. . . .
'I will thoroughly purge away your dross
   and remove your impurities. . . .
Afterward you will be called
   The City of Righteousness,
   The Faithful City.'
Zion will be redeemed with justice,
   her penitent ones with righteousness."

I am glad for a forgiving God. Today my heart responds to the
prophet's plea:
   "Come . . . let us walk in the light of the Lord."

▼

☐ **WEEK 28, THURSDAY**   **ISAIAH**

Scripture: Isaiah 4—6
The Story: Isaiah 6:1-8

**Lo, this hath touched thy lips . . . thine iniquity is
taken away, and thy sin purged (Isa. 6:7).**

A Life-changing Encounter

Religious testimony is one of our most dependable and moving sources for understanding God's work in the human spirit. Isaiah here tells of the crisis that came to him in the year that King Uzziah died. It was the greatest spiritual influence of his life.

These moments when God breaks in on the soul are landmarks to which we turn with confidence and reassurance throughout all our years. Here in Old Testament times God did something remarkably parallel to the New Testament baptism with the Holy Ghost and fire.

Isaiah was already a man of God, a counselor to Judah's king and a prophet to her people. But God had a deeper experience for His servant.

The young prophet's final confidence was not to rest in any earthly king because his ministry was to span the reigns for four of them. God wants our trust so completely grounded in Him that no changing human events can shatter our faith.

Here in the Temple Isaiah stood face-to-face with the divine love and power. He lifted the need of his heart to God; in response, the seraph flew to him bearing a live coal from off the altar. Touching the prophet's lips, God's angel declared: "Lo, this hath touched thy lips . . . thine iniquity is taken away, and thy sin purged."

When we earnestly seek Him, God reveals himself in a new and fuller measure to those who already know Him. When we seek to share in the holiness of God, our Lord gives a new vision of himself, "high and lifted up." Those who have received the Holy Spirit in sanctifying power testify that this experience is the beginning of a deeper and more satisfying life with God.

With Margaret Harris we too may testify:

> *Blessed be the name of Jesus!*
> *I'm so glad He took me in.*
> *He's forgiven my transgressions;*
> *He has cleansed my heart from sin.*

Scripture: Isaiah 7—9

The war with Syria and Israel (734 B.C.) was one of the great crises of Isaiah's ministry. Aram, king of Syria, joined Pekah, king of Israel, and came against Jerusalem.

A frightened King Ahaz, barely 21 years old, decided to form a defense pact with powerful Assyria to the northeast. Isaiah saw that such an alliance would bring disaster to both Israel and Judah because Assyria was just waiting for an opportunity to send her army into Palestine.

Isaiah promised Ahaz that God would deliver Jerusalem if the young king would trust Him (7:3-9). In order to encourage the king, Isaiah offered to give him a sign from the Lord (7:10-11). Ahaz, however, had already decided to make the treaty with Assyria. He refused to ask for the sign. Isaiah then repeated the Lord's prediction of the early destruction of Aram and Pekah (7:13-16). He went on to describe the awful suffering that Assyria would inflict on Judah (7:17—8:22).

The Story: Isaiah 7:1-9

Be careful, keep calm and don't be afraid. Do not lose heart (Isa. 7:4, NIV).

In Whom Do I Trust?

Committing ourselves to trust and obey God, no matter what the circumstances, is the most important decision of our lives. This is what it means to put God's will first.

Such a commitment will not save us from crises and fear, but God promises to support us, and He helps us to make right decisions when the crises come.

Isaiah knew that God is in charge of our world no matter how threatening the circumstances. God will have the last word. If we trust and obey Him, we always come out better in the long run.

Isaiah tried to encourage this confidence in the young king when he prophesied: "This is what the Sovereign Lord says: 'It will not take place, it will not happen. . . . Within sixty-five years

Ephraim will be too shattered to be a people'" (vv. 7-8, NIV). The prediction was fulfilled 13 years later in 721 B.C. when Samaria fell.

Along with the assurance that God gives when we choose to obey, He warns of the consequences if we falter in following Him. "This is what the Sovereign Lord says . . . 'If you do not stand firm in your faith, you will not stand at all'" (v. 9, NIV).

From the human standpoint, Ahaz had reason to be afraid. Seeking aid from Assyria appeared to be a way out of his dilemma. But God sometimes leads us contrary to human wisdom. There are times when He says to us, "My thoughts are not your thoughts, neither are your ways my ways" (Isa. 55:8). At those hours, in whom do I put my trust?

Prayer for today:

Lord, help me to declare with the Psalmist, "In God have I put my trust" (Ps. 56:11). Then I shall be able to sing with him, "The Lord is my light and my salvation; whom shall I fear? the Lord is the strength of my life; of whom shall I be afraid?" (Ps. 27:1).

▼

Scripture: Isaiah 10—12
The Story: Isaiah 10:20-21; 11:1-5; 12:1-6

The Lord . . . is my strength and my song; he has become my salvation (Isa. 12:2; all quotes from NIV).

The God of Hope

Yesterday we saw Isaiah, the statesman, pointing the road to national well-being for Judah. Today we see Isaiah the theologian; his name means "God is salvation." In these chapters he reveals the hope there is for us in God's offer of redemption through Christ.

The prophet reminds us that we may live in a society that rejects God, but we can rise above that evil influence. As in rebellious Judah, today God has a faithful minority, a remnant of those who love and serve Him. This passage intertwines three gospel truths: (1) the universal offer of salvation, (2) personal freedom to accept or reject God's offer, and (3) the sovereignty of God that assures Him of a kingdom and a people even though many may reject His salvation.

From the doctrine of the remnant in chapter 10, Isaiah moves to God's plan for the Messiah in chapter 11. Out of a faithful remnant God will raise a Messiah for Judah and a Redeemer for the world. The prophet here describes our Lord as the Branch, a shoot that "will come up from the stump of Jesse."

In 10:33-34 Isaiah likened the destruction of Assyria to a forest of cedars that were cut down. This destruction was final because the cedar stumps would rot and die; but not so with God's people. In the Exile they, too, would be decimated. But God has an eternal plan, and in Judah He would have a faithful remnant. Like the oak tree whose life remains in the roots, there shall come forth a shoot, a Branch that will grow and reproduce the tree. The Messiah of Judah and the Savior of the World would come from this faithful remnant in the line of David. In prophetic vision Isaiah looked forward 800 years and saw Christ, the Branch, as the hope of all men who trust in God. That hope is still with us.

After a long spiritual struggle, a young Jewish woman put her faith in Jesus as the Messiah. In her newfound joy she exclaimed: "Oh, I see now! In Jesus we know all of God that we shall ever know, and in Jesus we have all of God that we can ever need!" And we have!

With Isaiah my heart sings:

"The Lord is my strength and my song; he has become my salvation."

▼

□ **WEEK 29, SUNDAY**   **ISAIAH**

Scripture: Isaiah 13—17

Isaiah held a place of influence in Judah comparable to our secretary of state. In this position he moved freely among kings and other international leaders. Isaiah was thus as close to international actions and motives as most of us are to our personal lives and family affairs.

Chapters 13—23 is a collection of international news releases written by Isaiah on different occasions, but they are not in chronological order. Some were beamed for foreign consumption—the prophet warned a neighboring nation of God's punishment for her violence. Most were written to encourage Isaiah's own people to serve God faithfully and to be confident in His promise of protection.

To help understand this section, locate the following countries on a Bible map of the Old Testament world; they are the peoples of whom Isaiah wrote in these chapters: Babylon, 13—14; 21; Assyria, 14; Philistia, 14; Moab, 15—16; Damascus, capital of Syria, 17; Egypt and Cush (Ethiopia), 18—20; Jerusalem, 22; and Tyre, 23.

The Story. Isaiah 17:1-14

You have forgotten God your Savior; you have not remembered the Rock, your fortress (Isa. 17:10; all quotes from NIV).

God of the Nations

J. B. Phillips has written a book with the intriguing title, *Your God Is Too Small.* He was not thinking of our prophet. Isaiah's God was Lord of the nations. From his home in Jerusalem, the prophet looked out across national boundaries. He saw more clearly than any before him that every nation is under the sovereign rule of a righteous God. When these nations do evil, God will punish them; but if they repent and turn to Him, He forgives and blesses them just as He forgave and blessed Judah.

Chapter 17 was written to encourage Judah during the threat of an invasion by the armies of her northern neighbors, Syria and Israel. These two tried to force Judah into an alliance against Assyria. Isaiah knew that this was not God's plan, and he encouraged his countrymen to stand firmly against it. If Judah would only obey God, the Lord would destroy her enemies and honor the nation's faithfulness.

Isaiah assures Judah that in the day God acts: "Damascus

[capital of Syria] will no longer be a city but will become a heap of ruins."

He pleads with his countrymen to place their trust in God: "Although the peoples roar like the roar of surging waters, when he rebukes them they flee far away, driven before the wind like chaff on the hills, like tumbleweed before a gale. In the evening, sudden terror! Before the morning, they are gone! This is the portion of those who loot us, the lot of those who plunder us" (17:13-14).

The glory of trusting God and experiencing divine deliverance is our renewed awareness that God is God. Isaiah reminds Judah and us: "In that day men will look to their Maker and turn their eyes to the Holy One of Israel" (17:7).

When we have known such deliverance, we sing with Martin Luther:

A mighty fortress is our God,
A bulwark never failing.

▼

Scripture: Isaiah 18—23
The Story: Isaiah 16:9-12; 19:11-15; 21:1-4

Turn away from me; let me weep bitterly. Do not try to console me over the destruction of my people (Isa. 22:4; all quotes from NIV).

Man of Compassion

Isaiah never pronounced a woe without adding a corresponding promise. Though he predicted the downfall of nations and pronounced judgment on sinful men, he wept for those who suffered.

"My heart cries out over Moab; her fugitives flee as far as Zoar" (15:5).

"I weep, as Jazar weeps, for the vines of Sibmah.

O Heshbon, O Elealeh, I drench you with tears!" (16:9).

God's man has compassion not only because of physical suffering; he mourns deeply for all who do not know the true God.

"My heart laments for Moab like a harp, my inmost being for Kir Hareseth.

When Moab appears at her high place, she only wears herself out; when she goes to her shrine to pray, it is to no avail" (16:11-12).

Isaiah felt deep concern for the common man deceived and misled by national leaders. In the prophecy against Egypt, he mourns:

"The officials of Zoan have become fools, the leaders of Memphis are deceived;

the cornerstones of her peoples have led Egypt astray. . . . they make Egypt stagger in all that she does" (19:13-14).

Even the message of destruction for Babylon, Judah's mortal enemy, makes the prophet ill.

"At this my body is racked with pain, pangs seize me, like those of a woman in labor;

I am staggered by what I hear, I am bewildered by what I see.

My heart falters, fear makes me tremble;

the twilight I longed for has become a horror to me" (21:3-4).

This man of God drew his human concern from the Lord whom he served. God declares, "'I hid my face from you for a moment, but with everlasting kindness I will have compassion on you,' says the Lord your Redeemer" (Isa. 54:8).

Today my heart prays for more of that spirit.

> *Give me a love that knows no ill;*
> *Give me the grace to do Thy will.*
> *Pardon and cleanse this soul of mine;*
> *Give me a heart like Thine.**
> —JUDSON W. VAN DEVENTER

Scripture: Isaiah 24—27
The Story: Isaiah 26:1-9

In that day they will say, "Surely this is our God; we trusted in him, and he saved us" (Isa. 25:9, NIV).

Hope for Dark Days

What do I do when life caves in around me? David asked the same question: "If the foundations be destroyed, what can the righteous do?" (Ps. 11:3).

God's answer is to lift our eyes above the foundations. He is our Source of hope in dark days: "The Lord is in his holy temple, the Lord's throne is in heaven: his eyes behold . . . the children of men. . . . the righteous Lord loveth righteousness; his countenance doth behold the upright" (Ps. 11:4, 7).

Apocalypse is a theological term. It describes those parts of the Bible that tell us about God's final defeat of evil, and the triumph of goodness. The Books of Revelation and Daniel are the larger apocalyptic writings, but today's four chapters from Isaiah have been called "the little apocalypse."

These revelations of God's plans for the end times talk about His judgment on sin, and about our release from tribulation, war, famine, and pestilence. They also speak of great moral conflict between God and evil spirits. That day of the Lord will bring unprecedented upheavals in the heavens and on earth. But these shaking foundations bring joy to God's people because they indicate that the day of the Lord's triumph is near. Apocalyptic passages therefore abound in praise for God's deliverance of the redeemed. Moffatt translates 24:16:

"From earth's far bounds the chorus sounds,
'Now glory dawns for upright men!'"

When my own private world is threatened by disaster, disease, or death, I lift my eyes to God. He created me, He stands above

292

human life, He offers His saving help to all who look to Him. Even when the foundations of the whole world seem to be crumbling, "I will fear no evil: for thou art with me" (Ps. 23:4).

Because God is with us, we join Isaiah in his praises: "Surely this is our God; we trusted in him and he saved us." We go even further and pick up the sevenfold chorus of New Testament saints:

"Salvation belongs to our God, who sits on the throne, and to the Lamb. . . . Amen! Praise and glory and wisdom and thanks and honor and power and strength be to our God for ever and ever. Amen!" (Rev. 7:10, 12, NIV).

▼

Scripture: Isaiah 28—29

In 29:1, *Ariel* is "the city where David dwelt." The word means "the lioness of God," and is here applied to Jerusalem.

The Story: Isaiah 28:1-3, 7-8; 29:13-16

Wine is a mocker, strong drink is raging: and whosoever is deceived thereby is not wise (Prov. 20:1).

When Rebuke Is Kindness

The true prophet must proclaim the whole counsel of God. The message of divine judgment is as much a part of the truth as is the message of God's love. Judah was on a collision course with disaster. Under these circumstances even a harsh word and a stunning blow are kindnesses when designed to save us from ruin. It is this kind harshness that we hear from God's Word today.

Drinking alcoholic beverages was a serious social evil in Isaiah's time, as it is in our own. One does not need to look further than the morning's newspaper stories or an alcoholic neighbor to document the evils of alcohol. He who succumbs to drunkenness

293

becomes a human tragedy, jeopardizes his home, endangers his job, and demoralizes his community. So prevalent was this debauchery that Isaiah wrote:

"Here in Jerusalem men reel with wine and stagger with strong drink. . . . They are befuddled with wine. . . . Their very visions are distorted. They stumble over their words and judgment" (Phillips).

In light of these tragedies, and in view of a man's responsibility for his Christian influence, who would quarrel with the position of an evangelical church that "the Holy Scriptures and human experience alike condemn the use of intoxicating drinks as a beverage. The manufacture and sale of intoxicating liquors for such a purpose is a sin against God and the human race. Total abstinence from all intoxicants is the Christian rule for the individual, and total prohibition of the traffic in intoxicants is the duty of civil government."

By God's help I mean to keep my life free from this sin—and from all sin. I also want to help make my community a place where it will be easy for others to be good and to serve God.

> *I would be true, for there are those who trust me.*
> *I would be pure, for there are those who care.*
> *I would be strong, for there is much to suffer.*
> *I would be brave, for there is much to dare.*
> —HOWARD ARNOLD WALTER

▼

☐ **WEEK 29, THURSDAY**   **ISAIAH**

Scripture: Isaiah 30—33
The Story: Isaiah 31:1-3, 5-8; 33:20-22

Trust ye in the Lord for ever: for in the Lord Jehovah is everlasting strength (Isa. 26:4).

Facing My Hardest Decisions

When the lives of others depend on our decisions we need help from God. Former President Jimmy Carter testifies, "I spent more time praying while I was president than at any other time in my life."

The choices that confronted King Ahaz and his advisor, Isaiah, were hard decisions. If Assyria invaded the country, Judah's army was too small to defend herself. On the other hand, if King Ahaz invited Egypt to become his ally against Assyria, Judah would become a battleground between the two superpowers. There were awesome dangers either way. God, however, had made His will clear to the prophet; and Isaiah would follow that guidance whatever the cost.

Thank God, I have never had to decide for war or peace; for a man's life or death. I have, however, had to make family decisions that involved the welfare of those whom I loved. What does a man do when he feels sure of the will of God for himself, but knows there are risks for others if he makes that decision?

It is here that high faith and courage are called for. But isn't that what following God means? If we could always foresee the outcome, and if the outcome were always bright, only crazy people would choose another course. To trust God in these crisis hours is to serve Him.

And so, my Father, I pray for wisdom and for courage. Show me what is right, and I will do it. Give me courage to trust You for the results of my decisions in my own life, and in the lives of those whom I love.

But in the national scene, what if Isaiah were the secretary of defense charged with the safety of 240 million Americans? Would he write: "Woe to those who go down to nuclear arms for help, who trust in the multitude of their bombs?" I do not know. I am sure he would write: "Woe to those who . . . do not look to the Holy One of Israel, or seek help from the Lord."

I pray for my president and for all who counsel him in his hard decisions. I pray that God shall give them the wisdom to know the right, and the courage to do it.

And, when I pray, God gives personal strength. Even if nuclear annihilation seems near, the Christian word is hope, and not fear. Jesus says, When threats even as large as hydrogen bombs "begin to come to pass, then look up, and lift up your heads; for your redemption draweth nigh" (Luke 21:28).

God is bigger than bombs. My faith lifts me above fear and frustration because:

"I am persuaded, that neither death, nor life . . . shall be able to separate us from the love of God, which is in Christ Jesus our Lord" (Rom. 8:38-39).

▼

☐ **WEEK 29, FRIDAY** **ISAIAH**

Scripture: Isaiah 34—35
The Story: Isaiah 35:1-10

The ransomed of the Lord shall . . . come to Zion with songs and everlasting joy upon their heads (Isa. 35:10).

God's Glad Tomorrow

Chapters 34 and 35 are two sides of the same coin. They speak of God's final destiny for the evil and of His rewards for the righteous. In 34 we see the dark picture of all peoples who finally reject God. By contrast, chapter 35 reveals the abundant life that opens to all who walk in God's way of holy living.

Isaiah sees that God's plan for our lives is as satisfying as a garden of lilies. The Psalmist also invites us to enjoy life's most fulfilling experiences when he urges, "O worship the Lord in the beauty of holiness: fear before him, all the earth" (Ps. 96:9).

Verses 3 and 4 tell of the strength and courage that God brings when life's hills are steep and we falter in our journey: "Strengthen the feeble arms, steady the tottering knees; say to the anxious, Be strong and fear not" (NEB).

In God's future for His people the ravages of illness will be healed: "Then shall the eyes of the blind be opened, and the ears of the deaf unstopped. Then shall the lame man leap like a deer, and the tongue of the dumb shall sing" (NBV).

Isaiah reaches the climax of this vision of the future when he shows us that God's planned way of life is "the way of holiness." Seven hundred years before Christ, he saw that God's way is a sinless way. "The unclean shall not pass over it . . . but the redeemed shall walk there" (vv. 8-9).

In verse 10 the prophet sings of homecoming. God has designed the way of righteousness for our safe-conduct to the celestial city. He has sent His Holy Spirit to be our Guide and Travel Companion. At journey's end, with Him, "the ransomed of the Lord will return. They will enter Zion with singing: everlasting joy will crown their heads. Gladness and joy will overtake them, and sorrow and sighing will flee away" (NIV).

On that glad day, I want to be there!

▼

Scripture: Isaiah 36—39

Chapters 36—39 constitute a historical section between the two major divisions of Isaiah's prophecies. Here in his own writings the prophet recounts stories of God's answers to his prayers that are officially preserved in the records of the kings of Judah (2 Kings 18:13—19:37; 2 Chron. 32:1-23).

The Story: Read all of chapters 36—37

Now, O Lord our God, deliver us from his hand, so that all the kingdoms on earth may know that you alone . . . are God (Isa. 37:20; all quotes from NIV).

God, Our Security

Where do I turn when threatened with utter ruin?

From outward appearances Jerusalem was doomed. Stronger

cities had fallen to the Assyrian armies. The enemy commander spoke in Hebrew and sought to destroy the morale of the listening people. He first asked (36:4-6), Is Hezekiah depending on help from Egypt? Those armies cannot save you because Assyrian forces stand between Egypt and Jerusalem. In 36:8 he taunted Judah's leaders: If Assyria gave you 2,000 horses, you could not put riders on them. Then in a final effort at intimidation the Assyrian declared: "The Lord himself told me to march against this country and destroy it" (36:10).

The cause seemed hopeless. But Hezekiah knew where to turn—he "went into the temple." In his public role as king, Hezekiah turned to the Lord. He would trust God in spite of enemies in Jerusalem, ready to blame him if God failed to deliver the city. He turned, as we must turn in crisis hours, to past experiences of God's help. He reminded himself that God had saved Israel in other difficult days, and that God was still able to deliver His people. Hezekiah next recalled that "God's got the whole world in His hands." He strengthened his faith by remembering, "You alone are God . . . You have made heaven and earth" (37:16).

And so, with his faith made strong by these memories, Hezekiah prayed his prayer and supported it with a devout purpose: "Now, O Lord our God, deliver us from his hand, so that all kingdoms on earth may know that you alone . . . are God."

Hezekiah had learned what Menno Simons, founder of the Mennonites, voiced over 2,000 years later. I join him in that prayer of faith:

"Who, dear Lord, ever came to Thee with a pious heart and was rejected? Who ever sought Thee and found Thee not? Who ever sought help with Thee and did not obtain it?"

▼

☐ **WEEK 30, SUNDAY**   **ISAIAH**

Scripture: Isaiah 40—41

The first half of Isaiah is largely a message of judgment, but chapters 40—66 are filled with hope for God's people. Chapters 40—48 picture Jehovah's triumph over idols and foretell Judah's deliverance from Babylonian captivity. Chapters 49—57 foresee redemption through God's Suffering Servant. In the last 9 chapters Isaiah shows us God's final triumph and the future glory of the sons of God.

The Story: Isaiah 40:1-2, 9-11, 28-31

Do not fear, for I am with you . . . I am your God. I will strengthen you and help you (Isa. 41:10, NIV).

I Relax in God's Care

Today Isaiah slaps me on the back. In street language he says to me: Hey man, remember who God is!

Thank you, Isaiah. I turn my mind away from circumstances and lift my eyes to heaven. I forget men and remember God.

My Father, You are not far off; Your power and love are here to help me. When I see You and Your resources, my confidence rises and my troubled spirit finds assurance. As I fix my mind on You, I relax and my heart is calmed.

The comfort that comes from turning to God is more than simply forgetting my troubles. It is, rather, seeing my circumstances in the light of God's power and His love. This blessed vision gives instant energy for my immediate need. It also brings to me a continuing flow of strength as times goes on.

When I am discouraged because men have misunderstood me, I am sure that God knows my heart. If I am beset by poverty, my spirit grows strong remembering Jesus' counsel: "Seek ye first the kingdom of God . . . and all these things shall be added unto you" (Matt. 6:33). When my spirit droops because the body is ill, I am revived knowing that God can heal this body, or in spite of sickness He can make my spirit strong. He gives help when death takes those whom I love, or when I myself face the dark shadows. He gives me faith to believe, "Yea, though I walk through the valley of the shadow of death, I will fear no evil" (Ps. 23:4).

In 40:31, the preposition *upon* may also be translated *for.* Here is blessed truth: "Those who wait *for* the Eternal shall renew their strength" (Moffatt). Sometimes I am weakened because I am not willing to wait. Impatiently I try to crowd God into my own schedule. When I insist that He must act now or never, I weaken my soul. I expose myself to the unnecessary anguish of thinking that God is neglecting my need.

Help me, Father, to wait for Your time—and in waiting to grow strong. Today I come with my need to relax in Your presence. Both today and tomorrow I shall wait for Your action. While I wait, breathe into my spirit Your strength for today; and give me joy in waiting patiently for Your full answer tomorrow. In Jesus' name. Amen.

▼

☐ **WEEK 30, MONDAY** **ISAIAH**

Scripture: Isaiah 42—44
The Story: Isaiah 42:1-7; 43:10-11, 18-19; 44:2-3

Here is my servant, whom I uphold, my chosen one in whom I delight; I will put my Spirit on him (Isa. 42:1; all quotes from NIV).

My Servant, and Servants

What does it mean to serve God? Our title comes from one of Isaiah's favorite terms. This word "servant" appears 20 times in chapters 40—53. It means a person at the disposal of another; one to carry out his will, to do his work, to represent his interests.

In *The Perpetual Servant,* Dr. P. F. Bresee explains: "The Servant was a *people* (Israel), then a *remnant* of a people, called, held, empowered, used by God; then a *Person,* the ripe fruitage of the people, in whom dwelt all the fullness of God."

Thus this Servant is God's Son, the Messiah. But in Him we see reflected the kind of character that God desires in all of us who seek to be servants of the Servant.

In Him, and in us who are like Him, there is the spirit of compassion for the broken: "A bruised reed he will not break, and a smoldering wick he will not snuff out" (42:3).

His example spurs us to diligent pursuit of all that is right and fair: "He will not falter or be discouraged till he establishes justice on the earth" (42:4).

In servanthood God gives new beginnings growing out of old failures: "Forget the former things; do not dwell on the past. See, I am doing a new thing! Now it springs up . . . I am making a way in the desert and streams in the wasteland" (43:18-19).

Have I been sinned against? Then forgiveness is life's best gift. This unconquerable, forgiving love shines brightest in the Servant of God: "I, even I, am he who blots out your transgressions, for my own sake, and remembers your sins no more" (43:25).

He who truly serves God is filled with the Spirit of God: "Here is my servant, whom I uphold, my chosen one in whom I delight; I will put my Spirit on him" (42:1).

Oh, to share in this life of God's Servant! Oh, to be filled with compassion, concerned for justice, bringing hope to shattered lives, forgiving those who have sinned, filled with the Spirit of God!

> *Oh, to be like Thee, Blessed Redeemer . . .*
> *Stamp Thine own image deep on my heart.*
> —THOMAS O. CHISHOLM

☐ **WEEK 30, TUESDAY**   **ISAIAH**

Scripture: Isaiah 45—48
The Story: Isaiah 48:1-6, 14-15, 17

I am the Lord your God . . . who directs you in the way you should go (Isa. 48:17; all quotes from NIV).

"I Am God, and There Is No Other"

For me it is not difficult to accept the foreknowledge of God and the predictive prophecy of His servant Isaiah.

I believe in miracles
For I believe in God.

Isaiah prophesied in Jerusalem about 740 B.C., but Cyrus reigned in Babylon 200 years later. How could the prophet know of events to occur in the life of a foreign king not yet born? Of himself, he could not. But when an all-wise God predicts the facts, they come true as surely as the sun will rise in the morning. Let the words of God speak for themselves.

"This is what the Lord says . . . of Cyrus, 'He is my shepherd and will accomplish all that I please; he will say of Jerusalem, "Let it be rebuilt," and of the temple, "Let its foundations be laid."' This is what the Lord says to his anointed, to Cyrus, whose right hand I take hold of to subdue nations before him" (44:24, 28—45:1).

"For the sake of Jacob my servant, of Israel my chosen, I call you by name [Cyrus] and bestow on you a title of honor, though you do not acknowledge me. I am the Lord, and there is no other; apart from me there is no God. I will strengthen you, though you have not acknowledged me" (45:4-5).

"Concerning things to come, do you question me . . . ? It is I who made the earth and created mankind upon it. My own hands stretched out the heavens; I marshaled their starry hosts. I will raise up Cyrus in my righteousness: I will make all his ways straight. He will rebuild my city and set my exiles free" (45:11-13).

Oh, my sovereign God, I rejoice in Your full knowledge and in Your supreme power. Your testimony is true: "I foretold the former things long ago, my mouth announced them and I made them known; then suddenly I acted, and they came to pass" (48:3).

Because You can foretell and guide the destiny of nations, Your love and power shall guide my life.

"Show me your ways, O Lord, teach me your paths; guide me in your truth and teach me, for you are God my Savior, and my hope is in you all day long" (Ps. 25:4-5).

▼

Scripture: Isaiah 49—51
The Story: Isaiah 49:1-13

I am the Lord; those who hope in me will not be disappointed (Isa. 49:23; all quotes from NIV).

When God Speaks

When God speaks, my heart falls to list'ning;
And there is response in my soul.
                    —CARLTON C. BUCK

From the New Testament we read, "In the past God spoke . . . at many times and in various ways, but in these last days he has spoken to us by his Son" (Heb. 1:1-2). Seven hundred years earlier, through Isaiah, God gave us this glorious prophecy of the Servant of the Lord. Let us listen to that thrilling word spoken first to His Old Testament people.

"You are my servant, Israel, in whom I will display my splendor. . . . to bring Jacob back . . . and gather Israel" (49:3, 5).

But this Messianic promise was too good to be restricted to Israel alone. Messiah is the Good News for us also, "It is too small a thing for you to be my servant to restore the tribes of Jacob and bring back those of Israel I have kept. I will also make you a light for the Gentiles, that you may bring my salvation to the ends of the earth. . . . Kings will see you and arise, princes will see and bow down, because of the Lord, who is faithful, the Holy One of Israel, who has chosen you" (49:6-7).

In any language it is difficult to say all that Jesus Christ can mean of joy and fulfillment for human life. Here Isaiah envisions those blessings in the language of God's help for exiles far from home.

"This is what the Lord says: 'In the time of my favor I will answer you, and in the day of salvation I will help you . . . to say to the captives, "Come out," to those in darkness, "Be free!" . . . He who has compassion on them will guide them and lead them beside springs of water. I will turn all my mountains into roads, and

my highways will be raised up. See, they will come from afar—
some from the north, some from the west, some from the region of
Sinim [Africa]'" (49:8-12).

As Isaiah envisions all that God intends to do for those who
trust Him, he bursts into a song of praise. Today my heart joins
him:

"Shout for joy, O heavens;
    rejoice, O earth;
    burst into song, O mountains!
For the Lord comforts his people
    and will have compassion on his afflicted ones" (49:13).

▼

☐ **WEEK 30, THURSDAY** ISAIAH

> *Scripture:* Isaiah 52—53
> *The Story:* Isaiah 52:13—53:12
>   If you memorize this passage it will
> deepen your love for Christ for the rest of your
> life. Only the outline below has been added to
> the NIV translation.
>
> **He was wounded for our transgressions, he was
> bruised for our iniquities . . . and with his stripes
> we are healed** (Isa. 53:5).

The Suffering Servant, Our Savior

Today we enter the holy of holies of the Christian faith. This last of
Isaiah's Servant Songs clearly pictures our suffering and serving
Christ. No comment can be as moving as the words of Scripture.

The Servant Exalted. "See, my servant will act wisely; he will be
raised and lifted up and highly exalted. Just as there were many
who were appalled at him—his appearance was so disfigured beyond that of any man and his form marred beyond human
likeness—so will he sprinkle many nations, and kings will shut

their mouths because of him. For what they were not told, they will see, and what they have not heard, they will understand."

The Servant Despised. "Who has believed our message and to whom has the arm of the Lord been revealed? He grew up before him like a tender shoot, and like a root out of dry ground. He had no beauty or majesty to attract us to him, nothing in his appearance that we should desire him. He was despised and rejected by men, a man of sorrows, and familiar with suffering. Like one from whom men hide their faces he was despised, and we esteemed him not."

The Servant Afflicted. "Surely he took up our infirmities and carried our sorrows, yet we considered him stricken by God, smitten by him, and afflicted. But he was pierced for our transgressions, he was crushed for our iniquities; the punishment that brought us peace was upon him, and by his wounds we are healed. We all, like sheep, have gone astray, each of us has turned to his own way; and the Lord has laid on him the iniquity of us all."

The Servant Slain. "He was oppressed and afflicted, yet he did not open his mouth; he was led like a lamb to the slaughter, and as a sheep before her shearers is silent, so he did not open his mouth. By oppression and judgment, he was taken away. And who can speak of his descendants? For he was cut off from the land of the living; for the transgression of my people he was stricken. He was assigned a grave with the wicked, and with the rich in his death, though he had done no violence, nor was any deceit in his mouth."

The Servant Satisfied. "Yet it was the Lord's will to crush him and cause him to suffer, and though the Lord makes his life a guilt offering, he will see his offspring and prolong his days, and the will of the Lord will prosper in his hand. After the suffering of his soul, he will see the light of life and be satisfied; by his knowledge my righteous servant will justify many, and he will bear their iniquities. Therefore I will give him a portion among the great, and he will divide the spoils with the strong, because he poured out his life unto death, and was numbered with the transgressors. For he bore the sins of many, and made intercession for the transgressors."

Seven times the prophet rings out the great spiritual truth that in God's plan of salvation the innocent must bear the burden of the guilty. They were *our* griefs that *He* bore; they were *our* sorrows which *He* carried; it was for *our* transgressions that *He* was wounded, and *our* iniquities for which *He* was bruised. The chastisement

305

was *His,* but the peace was *ours; His* were the stripes, but the healing came to *us. We* were the foolish sheep who went astray, and *He* was the Good Shepherd who searched through the night to find us and bring us back.

Ah, I am grateful for the shelter of that fold, and my heart yearns to share Christ's compassion for those who are yet astray!

▼

Scripture: Isaiah 54:1—56:8
The Story: Isaiah 55:1-13

Ho, every one that thirsteth, come ye to the waters (Isa. 55:1).

Come unto Me

"Thou hast made us for thyself, and our hearts are restless until they find their rest in Thee." Thus Augustine describes the spirit's unconscious search for the high destiny for which we were born. I am glad that our Creator is eager for us to find our highest happiness in fellowship with Him.

The gracious invitation of today's scripture arises directly out of the work of the Suffering Servant before whom we worshiped yesterday. Because He made "his soul an offering for sin," we are invited to come—and to come now. He who issues the invitation promises, "I will give unto him that is athirst of the fountain of the water of life . . . And let him that is athirst come. And whosoever will, let him take the water of life freely" (Rev. 21:6; 22:17).

God's invitation is as universal as if He had stopped at the end of those first three words—"Ho, every one." But because we have free choice, we find salvation only when we desire to know the Creator personally. When our desire is as keen as an unslaked thirst on a hot day, we are close to Him. With the Psalmist I cry, "As the hart panteth after the water brooks, so panteth my soul after thee, O God. My soul thirsteth for God, for the living God" (Ps. 42:1-2).

One early conscious step toward finding Him is to "incline thine ear." An evangelist friend exhorts us: "Give your soul half a chance. Expose yourself to the Spirit of God long enough to consider what He is saying to you." When we thus consider God's offer seriously, He has already drawn us halfway to himself. He assures us, "Hear, and your soul shall live."

Thank You, Father. Today my heart responds anew to Your gracious invitation:

> *Ho, ev'ry one that is thirsty in spirit!*
> *Ho, ev'ry one that is weary and sad!*
> *Come to the fountain; there's fullness in Jesus,*
> *All that you're longing for. Come and be glad.*
> —LUCY J. RIDER

▼

☐ **WEEK 30, SATURDAY**   ISAIAH

Scripture: Isaiah 56:9—59:21

The Story. Isaiah 57:13-21

"The Redeemer will come to Zion, to those . . . who repent of their sins," declares the Lord (Isa. 59:20; all quotes from NIV).

Our Forgiving God

I am glad that God is on the side of righteousness. When we are wrong we rightfully fear His judgment, but when we seek to do right we can count on His support. This is the reassuring truth which Isaiah declares today.

Sin always alienates us from God; the Bible declares it: "Your iniquities have separated you from your God; your sins have hidden his face from you, so that he will not hear. For your hands are stained with blood, your fingers with guilt. Your lips have spoken lies, and your tongue mutters wicked things" (59:2-3).

Sin always separates us from God, but repentance always brings Him near. "For our offenses are many in your sight, and our sins testify against us. Our offenses are ever with us, and we acknowledge our iniquities: rebellion and treachery against the Lord, turning our backs on our God, fomenting oppression and revolt, uttering lies our hearts have conceived" (59:12-13).

I am glad that God's final word is forgiveness and comfort for all who repent of their sins. "This is what the high and lofty One says—he who lives forever, whose name is holy: 'I live in a high and holy place, but also with him who is contrite and lowly in spirit, to revive the spirit of the lowly and to revive the heart of the contrite. I will not accuse forever, nor will I always be angry, for then the spirit of man would grow faint before me—the breath of man that I have created. . . .

"'I have seen his ways, but I will heal him; I will guide him and restore comfort to him, creating praise on the lips of the mourners in Israel. Peace, peace, to those far and near,' says the Lord. 'And I will heal them'" (57:15-16, 18-19).

Today my heart sings:

> *Oh, the joy of sins forgiv'n!*
> *Oh, the bliss the Blood-washed know!*
> *Oh, the peace akin to heav'n,*
> *Where the healing waters flow!*
> —H. H. HEIMAR

▼

□ **WEEK 31, SUNDAY**   **ISAIAH**

Scripture: Isaiah 60—62
The Story: 60:1-2, 5, 10, 15-20; 61:1-3

I delight greatly in the Lord; my soul rejoices in my God (Isa. 61:10; all quotes from NIV).

Joyful in Hope

God's Old Testament promises of hope for Israel foreshadow the personal blessings intended for us. All who put their faith in Him are strengthened by an ever-recurring hope. Isaiah is saying, Think of the best time you ever had in your whole life; that is the kind of joy and happiness God intends to bring to His people. Let us rejoice in that hope today.

"Arise, shine, for your light has come, and the glory of the Lord rises upon you. See, darkness covers the earth and thick darkness is over the peoples, but the Lord rises upon you and his glory appears over you. . . . You will look and be radiant, your heart will throb and swell with joy. . . .

"Though in anger I struck you, in favor I will show you compassion. . . . I will make you the everlasting pride and the joy of all generations. . . . Then you will know that I, the Lord, am your Savior, your Redeemer, the Mighty One of Jacob. . . . I will make peace your governor and righteousness your ruler. No longer will violence be heard in your land, nor ruin or destruction within your borders, but you will call your walls Salvation and your gates Praise.

"The sun will no more be your light by day, nor will the brightness of the moon shine on you, for the Lord will be your everlasting light, and your God will be your glory. Your sun will never set again, and your moon will wane no more; the Lord will be your everlasting light, and your days of sorrow will end. . . .

"The Spirit of the Sovereign Lord is on me . . . He has sent me to bind up the brokenhearted . . . to comfort all who mourn, and provide for those who grieve in Zion—to bestow on them a crown of beauty instead of ashes, the oil of gladness instead of mourning, and a garment of praise instead of a spirit of despair."

Our prophet here struggles to express truth that is too big for words, but we know what he is talking about. With J. G. Crabble our hearts sing:

> He gives me joy in place of sorrow,
> He gives me love that casts out fear;
> He gives me sunshine for my shadow,
> And "beauty for ashes" here.

309

Scripture: Isaiah 63—66
The Story: Isaiah 63:7-9; 65:9-14

I will tell of the Lord's unfailing love; I praise him for all he has done (Isa. 63:7, TEV).

I Am Grateful to God

It is nine o'clock, Monday morning, August 13. Mrs. Harper just walked into the study to remind me of what we both knew well. On July 30 the surgeon had removed a part of my left lung. She said:

"Just two weeks ago this morning at this hour they were about two-thirds of the way through with your surgery. You don't look as though something that drastic had happened to you—and I am grateful to God."

I join her in that spirit of gratitude. "I will tell of the Lord's unfailing love; I praise him for all he has done."

In our second scripture passage Isaiah reminds us that God was displeased with His people because they lived as though He were dead. They did not recognize His care for them, nor were they grateful for it. Verse 11 makes their failure clear: "You . . . forsake me . . . who worship Gad and Meni, the gods of luck and fate" (65:11, TEV). They attributed their blessings to good luck and their troubles to some blind destiny. But that is not the kind of world in which we live; God is deeply grieved when we cut ourselves off from Him by this wrong attitude.

In these final chapters of the book, Isaiah warns passionately of the tragedies that we bring on our lives when we forget God: "I was ready to answer my people's prayers, but they did not pray. I was ready for them to find me, but they did not even try" (65:1, TEV).

Just as fervently God speaks through Isaiah to extend His

310

steadfast love to all who hear and respond: "I tell you that those who worship and obey me will have plenty to eat and drink . . . They will be happy . . . They will sing for joy . . . Anyone in the land who asks for a blessing will ask to be blessed by the faithful God" (65:13-14, 16, TEV).

With hearts full of praise we join the testimony of the faithful of all ages, "But now, O Lord, thou art our father; we are the clay, and thou our potter; and we all are the work of thy hand" (Isa. 64:8). I am grateful to God.

> O Thou in whose presence my soul takes delight,
> On whom in affliction I call,
> My Comfort by day and my Song in the night,
> My Hope, my Salvation, my All!
> —JOSEPH SWAIN

▼

Scripture: Jeremiah 1:1-3; 8:18—9:26; 36:1-32
The Story: Jeremiah 1:1-3; 8:18-22; 36:1-8

His word was in mine heart as a burning fire shut up in my bones, and I was weary with forbearing, and I could not stay (Jer. 20:9).

Meet Jeremiah and His Messages

We can always learn something from a man who walks with God, so let's get acquainted with one of the greatest of God's Old Testament prophets.

Jeremiah lived 125 years later than Isaiah; he was born about 646 B.C. in Anathoth, three miles northeast of Jerusalem. His father, Hilkiah, was a village priest. Though a Levite by birth, Jeremiah seems never to have served as a priest; instead God called him to be a prophet. He never married (see 16:1-5).

Jeremiah's ministry was not that of a village pastor, rather he was spiritual counselor to a nation. On issues of domestic policy and in times of international crisis God revealed to him how He wanted His people to respond.

Early in his career Jeremiah probably lived in Anathoth, appearing publicly in Jerusalem only in connection with the great religious festivals. Later he moved to Jerusalem. His ministry spanned 39 years, including the reigns of the last five kings in Jerusalem: Josiah, Jehoahaz, Jehoiakim, Jehoiachin, and Zedekiah.

Jeremiah's work might have seen a glorious fulfillment if he could have led his people to follow God's will. But he could not. He was constantly frustrated by indifferent people and cowardly kings. In his disappointments he was so often crushed that he became known as "the weeping prophet."

The Book of Jeremiah is neither a consecutive history, nor an organized series of sermons. It is more like miscellaneous messages preached by the prophet on historic occasions. Perhaps chapter 36 tells us how and why these revelations from God were put together in the book.

The messages are not always in chronological order, but always there is a man of God who saw a need among His people— and always he heard in his soul the Word of God for that need.

As I read Jeremiah my prayer is,

> Lord, speak to me, that I may speak
> In living echoes of Thy tone;
> As Thou hast sought, so let me seek
> Thy erring children lost and lone.
> —FRANCES R. HAVERGAL

▼

☐ WEEK 31, WEDNESDAY   JEREMIAH

Scripture: Jeremiah 1; 20
The Story: Jeremiah 1:4-10

The Lord ... said to me, "I am giving you the words you must speak" (Jer. 1:9; all quotes from TEV).

When God Gives a Hard Task

It is a high moment in life when we are confronted by God, when we know that He has singled us out and revealed His will for us.

Sometimes God's call is exciting and we respond with joy. More often, because the call is new it appears threatening. It was a hard task that lay before 19-year-old Jeremiah. He was a timid youth, and God gave him a job that called for courage. He was a teen who yearned for acceptance, but God sent him to oppose his peers. He was affectionate and loved people, but God sent him on a lifelong task of denouncing the evils of his neighbors.

Is there in this man's experience some pattern for us to follow? Three good responses are silhouetted from these scriptures.

✔ In verse 6 we see human fear, but in spite of fear an acceptance of God's will. At first came the flood of natural reluctance: "I don't know how to speak; I am too young." Our excuses may not be the same, but they spring up just as spontaneously—and they are usually no better. Jeremiah, however, calmed his fears by submitting them to God. Perhaps he could not speak fluently, but he knew when God was speaking to him.

✔ In verses 7 and 8 there is the assurance that comes from God when we begin to obey. He says, Don't concentrate on your weakness; fix your faith in My Word and depend on My power. "I the Lord have spoken."

✔ To those who depend upon God's direction and power, He gives influence in His kingdom. To Jeremiah He said: "Today I give you authority over nations and kingdoms to uproot and to pull down, to destroy and to overthrow, to build and to plant" (v. 10).

Ah, there is joy in partnership with God! It may be difficult, but let us accept the task He has for us today.

> God hath not promised skies always blue,
> Flower-strewn pathways all our lives through . . .
> But God hath promised strength for the day,
> Rest for the labor, light for the way.*
> —ANNIE JOHNSON FLINT

*Used by permission of Evangelical Publishers, a Division of Scripture Press Publications, Ltd.

Scripture: Jeremiah 2—3; 10
The Story: Jeremiah 3:6-15

Come back to me. I am merciful and will not be angry . . . Only admit that . . . you have rebelled against the Lord, your God (Jer. 3:12-13; all quotes from TEV).

The Evil of Forsaking God

Jeremiah 2 to 10 records a series of warnings and entreaties given to Judah over a period of 40 years. The common theme is Judah's failure to follow God, and the tragedies that follow from this failure. It is not pleasant reading—but it is true.

The worst sin is to shut God out of our lives. When He is excluded we expose ourselves to every possible evil. It is this sin of ignoring God that Jeremiah charged against his people.

God had made himself known. He had brought Israel and Judah out of Egypt and settled them in the land of promise. But Israel had forgotten God, and had turned to idolatry. God punished her by letting Assyria take the 10 tribes captive in 721 B.C. Now a century later Judah was following a similar path to frustration and destruction.

Today, idolatry seems far removed from us. When asked if he had broken the Ten Commandments, a young man flippantly replied, "Well, at least I haven't made any graven images." But idolatry is more than an ancient sin; it involves our allegiance to God.

Many of Israel's prophets describe idolatry as adultery—a wanton forsaking of one's first love, surrendering faithfulness for uncontrolled passion, living a human life on the level of animal instinct. Jeremiah cries that Israel's passion for false gods makes them "like well-fed stallions wild with desire, each lusting for his neighbor's wife" (5:8).

But the prophet does more than speak out forcefully against forsaking the Lord. He appeals to man's God-given reason: "People of Israel, listen to the message that the Lord has for you. . . . Do not

follow the ways of the other nations . . . The religion of these people is worthless. . . . idols . . . can cause you no harm, and they can
do you no good" (10:1-3, 5).

Idolatry is rejecting God; it is the ultimate sin; it is life's worst
tragedy. But even this deepest sin need not destroy us. The God of
steadfast love pleads: "Come back to me. I am merciful and will not
be angry . . . Only admit that . . . you have rebelled against the
Lord, your God."

My chastened heart replies, *"Lord, I'm coming home."*

▼

Scripture: Jeremiah 4; 6

To understand Jeremiah's repeated references to "the north" look
in your Bible at a map of ancient Bible lands. It was the army of
Babylon that finally destroyed Jerusalem—and Babylon is almost
due east. But between them lay 500 miles of almost uncrossable
Arabian Desert. To reach Palestine, armies from the east traveled
northwest along the Fertile Crescent formed by the Euphrates and
the Tigris rivers. Then from Carchemish they turned south toward
Jerusalem. Thus Judah's immediate threat was always from the
north.

The Story: Jeremiah 4:5-8, 13-18

What will they do when it all comes to an end?
(Jer. 5:31; all quotes from TEV).

Disaster from the North

Have you ever had to persist in a right policy when most of your
associates disagreed with your goals? If so, you can understand
Jeremiah. For 40 years he carried the sad burden of predicting the
destruction of his beloved Judah. At the beginning of his ministry
he wrote:

"The Lord asked me, 'Jeremiah, what do you see?' . . . I answered, 'I see a pot boiling in the north, and it is about to tip over this way.'

"He said to me, 'Destruction will boil over from the north on all who live in this land, because I am calling all the nations in the north to come. . . . I will punish my people because they have sinned'" (1:11-16).

How does a man get along with his neighbors when he predicts defeat for his own nation, and victory for her enemy? That is not the way to "win friends and influence people"! Judah's rulers maligned Jeremiah and threw him in jail more than once. But in a prophet's position the important question is not, What is pleasant to hear? The bottom line must be, What is true?

God's man was faithful to God's truth though it tore his spirit to shreds: "My heart has been crushed . . . I mourn; I am completely dismayed. . . . Why . . . have my people not been healed?" (8:21-22).

Early in his ministry Jeremiah asked the tragic question in our text, "What will they do when it all comes to an end?" He lived to see the sad answer: "Nebuchadnezzar came with all his army and attacked Jerusalem . . . They set up camp outside the city . . . and kept it under siege . . . when the famine was so bad that the people had nothing left to eat, the city walls were broken through. . . . While Zedekiah was looking on, his sons were put to death; then Nebuchadnezzar had Zedekiah's eyes put out, placed him in chains, and took him to Babylon" (2 Kings 25:1-4, 7).

Ah, it is true. "The wages of sin is death." But thank God, we need not serve that master.

"The gift of God is eternal life through Jesus Christ our Lord" (Rom. 6:23).

▼

☐ WEEK 31, SATURDAY   JEREMIAH

Scripture: Jeremiah 5; 7
The Story: Jeremiah 5:1-5, 25-29

My people . . . have forsaken me the fountain of living waters, and hewed them out cisterns, broken cisterns, that can hold no water (Jer. 2:13).

God's Second Commandment

From our text C. H. Waggoner drew the inspiration for his lyric:

> *I had found no satisfaction*
> *In the fleeting joys of earth;*
> *I had hewed me broken cisterns*
> *That had mocked me by their dearth.*

There is an unfailing cause-and-effect relationship between forgetting God and the host of social evils that spoil our human happiness and frustrate wholesome life together. When a man forsakes God, he is likely to prey on his neighbor.

Jeremiah charged his God-forgetting people: "Evil men live among my people; they lie in wait like men who lay nets to catch birds . . . they have set their traps to catch men. . . . they have filled their houses with loot. . . . There is no limit to their evil deeds. They do not give orphans their rights or show justice to the oppressed" (5:26-28, TEV).

At one point Jeremiah accepted the view that sin is due to ignorance, and that crime comes only from the ghetto: "I thought, 'These are only the poor and ignorant. They behave foolishly; they don't know what their God requires, what the Lord wants them to do'" (5:4, TEV). But experience taught him better. It was not only the ignorant and the poor who sinned. He discovered that "all of them have rejected the Lord's authority and refused to obey him" (ibid.).

It is not chiefly deprivation that makes a man take advantage of his neighbor. It is sin—the sin of selfishness in a man who has rejected God's second commandment. It is this commandment, "Thou shalt love thy neighbour as thyself," that assures social justice.

Forgetting God destroys the fabric of a wholesome society. It was true in Judah; it was true in Goldsmith's England; it is true anywhere in God's world:

> *Ill fares the land, to hastening ills a prey,*
> *Where wealth accumulates, and men decay.*

Scripture: Jeremiah 11—13
The Story: Jeremiah 11:1-10

**Obey my voice, and do . . . according to all which
I command you: so shall ye be my people, and I
will be your God** (Jer. 11:4).

Our Covenant-keeping God

Why would an evangelical group choose for a name The Evangelical Covenant church? Why do some Protestant groups describe their doctrinal position as *covenant theology?* Perhaps as we explore this passage we shall find the answers.

Our story is sometimes titled "Jeremiah and the Covenant." Five times God speaks of His covenant with His people. Webster defines this word as "a formal, solemn, and binding agreement: a compact." Understanding God's compact is important because it describes the fundamental moral relationship between Him and us.

Most covenants, or contracts, are drawn up between equal parties. The unique fact in God's covenant with us is that He is God and we are men. He had no obligation to us, but He took the initiative in offering us love and salvation. He counsels us, "Obey my voice . . . so shall ye be my people, and I will be your God."

Covenant theology emphasizes God's love for us. It also underlines the conditions that He has set if we are to enjoy His blessings. These conditions and man's failure to observe them are here the deep concerns of Jeremiah.

In verse 2 God challenges His people, "Listen to the terms of the covenant" (TEV). Then in verse 8 is the sad commentary, "I . . . commanded them to keep the covenant, but they refused. So I brought on them all the punishment described in it" (TEV). Without observing the terms of the covenant there is no salvation. But this obedience is within our power. The covenant requirements are conditions that we can meet if we will.

When we obey, we find that God is faithful. The Bible declares, "Know therefore that the Lord thy God, he is . . . the faithful God, which keepeth covenant and mercy with them that love him and keep his commandments to a thousand generations" (Deut. 7:9). In response our spirits rejoice:

> Great is Thy faithfulness! Great is Thy faithfulness!
> Morning by morning new mercies I see;
> All I have needed Thy hand hath provided.
> Great is Thy faithfulness, Lord, unto me!*
> —THOMAS O. CHISHOLM

▼

☐ WEEK 32, MONDAY   JEREMIAH

Scripture: Jeremiah 8; 14
The Story: Jeremiah 14:1-10, 19-22

None of the idols of the nations can send rain; the sky by itself cannot make showers fall. We have put our hope in you, O Lord our God, because you are the one who does these things (Jer. 14:22, TEV).

How Does God Punish Evil Men?

The theme of chapters 8 and 14 is God's judgment upon sin and sinners. Jeremiah wrote chapter 14 during a time of devastating drought in Judah. He declared the lack of rain was God's punishment on the people for their sins. Are we to believe that this is a universal truth? Is every natural disaster a punishment from God?

To this question Jesus says we must answer no. In Luke 13:1-5

He deals specifically with the issue. "Those eighteen, upon whom the tower in Siloam fell, and slew them, think ye that they were sinners above all men that dwelt in Jerusalem? I tell you, Nay: but except ye repent, ye shall all likewise perish."

God usually operates providentially by natural law. He sends His "rain on the just and on the unjust" (Matt. 5:45). When drought comes, godly farmers often suffer with the ungodly.

Shall we then conclude that Jeremiah was wrong? Does God never punish sin by bringing suffering into our lives?

On the contrary, we know that sin always brings loss and sorrow. To every listening sinner Jesus said, "Except ye repent, ye shall all likewise perish" (Luke 13:5). God is trying to draw us to himself. If we do not respond to His love, He sometimes sends harm and loss in order to awaken us and to save us from eternal punishment. He loves us too much to let us lose our souls easily.

When tragedy strikes, what is the right response to God? If we have tried to be faithful to Him, we can echo the prayer of verse 9, "Surely, Lord, you are with us! We are your people; do not abandon us" (TEV).

If we have been careless or rebellious, the prayer of Jeremiah for his people is the response for which God is yearning: "Even though our sins accuse us, help us, Lord, as you have promised. We have turned away from you many times; we have sinned against you. You are [our] only hope" (14:7-8, TEV).

To such a sincere prayer, God responds: "I alone know the plans I have for you, plans to bring you prosperity and not disaster, plans to bring about the future you hope for. . . . You will seek me, and you will find me because you . . . seek me with all your heart" (Jer. 29:11, 13, TEV).

Thank You, God, for Your mercy.

Scripture: Jeremiah 15—17; 20

In 17:5-8, Jeremiah gives us a short poem contrasting the ways of the wicked and the righteous. Notice how similar the structure and the ideas are to Psalm 1.

> *The Story:* Jeremiah 15:10-21 (Jeremiah's mood comes through most clearly in a modern translation, especially in TEV)

Lord, you are the one who protects me and gives me strength; you help me in times of trouble (Jer. 16:19; all quotes from TEV).

Self-pity Is No Good

In my study Bible, alongside of verses 10-21, I had once written, "Even God's man can miss God's way"—and we can. For a time Jeremiah got out of the will of God, and he did it through self-pity. In chapter 20 also, the prophet complains to the Lord.

If ever a man had a right to feel sorry for himself, Jeremiah did. He lived in such desperate days that God asked him not to marry and raise a family—to do so would only bring tragic suffering to the innocent children. In times of invasion, siege, and surrender of cities life cannot be carried on as usual. But even in those desperate times God's man cannot afford the luxury of complaining and feeling sorry for himself.

Self-pity is forbidden because it does no good. Even when circumstances are hard as were Jeremiah's, they are made still worse when we begin to feel sorry for ourselves. And the worst conditions that life can bring are made more tolerable by putting our faith in God and by exercising courage for the future.

I think Jeremiah told us about his complaints in order to show us how God rebuked him. When he complained, he disappointed God and got out of God's will. In response the Lord said to him, "If you return, I will take you back . . . If instead of talking nonsense you proclaim a worthwhile message, you will be my prophet again" (15:19).

Self-pity quickly takes us out of God's will, and our Father chastises us for the failure. But isn't it like Him to spend only one verse rebuking us and using two verses (20-21) to promise forgiveness and strength? In such hours we join in Jeremiah's glad testimony: "Lord, you are the one who protects me and gives me strength; you help me in times of trouble."

Why should we ever feel sorry for ourselves when God has promised so much? "I will bless the person who puts his trust in me. He is like a tree growing near a stream and sending out roots to the water. It is not afraid when hot weather comes, because its leaves stay green; it has no worries when there is no rain; it keeps on bearing fruit" (17:7-8).

Praise for today:

Thank You, Father, for saving us from self-pity. Thank You for the help that always comes in hard times when, without complaining, we sincerely put our trust in You.

▼

☐ WEEK 32, WEDNESDAY   JEREMIAH

Scripture: Jeremiah 18—19; 21
The Story: Jeremiah 18:1-6; 19:1-3, 11

Behold, as the clay is in the potter's hand, so are ye in my hand (Jer. 18:6).

Four Pictures in Clay

From Jeremiah's home in Anathoth, God told him to go visit the village potter. There He would reveal to the prophet messages to proclaim to Judah. But those lessons were not for Judah only. From that visit, Jeremiah paints four pictures that show us how God deals with the human spirit.

In the first we see how completely our lives depend upon the sovereign will of God: "Behold, as clay is in the potter's hand, so are ye in my hand." God gives us some freedom of choice. In other areas He keeps the controls in His own hands as completely as a potter determines what he will do with a piece of clay. How long we shall live is decided by God—not by us. The Bible tells us a "man also knoweth not his time" (Eccles. 9:12).

The second picture is in verse 3: "Then I went down to the potter's house, and, behold he wrought a work on the wheels." God means well by us. As the potter takes a shapeless lump of clay and fashions it into a beautiful vase, so God wants to make our lives useful and beautiful. Jesus said, "I am come that [you] might have life, and that [you] might have it more abundantly" (John 10:10).

Our lives are like clay in that God can mold us and shape us into His own image. Unlike clay, however, we must decide if we will let Him do His good work.

If we reject His appeal, the third picture in verse 4 shows us what may happen. "The vessel that he made of clay was marred in the hands of the potter; so he made it again another vessel, as seemed good to the potter to make it." As long as life lasts, God offers us second bests—even though we have refused His first plans. His second bests are never as satisfying and fulfilling as His first choices. But even a third best with God is infinitely better than a completely wasted life.

This brings us to Jeremiah's fourth picture. "Thus saith the Lord of hosts; Even so will I break this people . . . as one breaketh a potter's vessel, that cannot be made whole again" (19:11). The time comes when even God must give up the effort to salvage our lives. But that time comes only after we keep on refusing to accept His love and help.

What are the lessons from clay? Christ asks, Is your life yielded to Me? If not, will you yield it now? Don't wait until it is half wasted. Don't wait until it is hardened and broken. Trust Me now to make your life happy and useful.

Our yielding spirits can only respond:

> Have Thine own way, Lord! Have Thine own way!
> Thou art the Potter; I am the clay.
> Mold me and make me after Thy will,
> While I am waiting, yielded and still.
> —ADELAIDE A. POLLARD

Scripture: Jeremiah 22—23
The Story: Jeremiah 22:6-7, 15-16, 24-27
The Lord knoweth the way of the righteous: but the way of the ungodly shall perish (Ps. 1:6).

God Requires Righteousness

The theme that ties these two chapters together is the special responsibility for righteous living required of persons in places of influence.

In chapter 22 Jeremiah writes of four kings who reigned during his years as a prophet: Josiah, Jehoahaz (Shallum), Jehoiakim, and Jehoiachin (Jeconiah). These messages were probably given at different times, but put together in chapter 22 because of their common theme.

In 23:9-40 Jeremiah speaks to the false prophets. It was possible for this class of religious leaders to thrive in Judah because the people had a high regard for one who professed to speak in God's name. The prophets whom Jeremiah denounced were probably paid from the royal treasury. This would make it difficult for them to be critical of the king's policies.

These false leaders promised peace and safety even to those who despised God. They told the people that no evil would come upon them even though they had forsaken the law of God and were mistreating their fellowmen.

Jeremiah knew that the Holy One of Israel could not countenance such falsity and unfairness. God does not punish men easily; He values each one of us too highly for that. But He will not allow His affection for us to interfere with our growth in righteousness. And He will not permit us to injure our fellowman without punishment.

We see the tension in God's heart when He cries: "To me,

324

Judah's royal palace is as beautiful as the land of Gilead and as the Lebanon Mountains; but I will make it a desolate place where no one lives" (22:6, TEV). In verse 24 the same anguish shows through: "The Lord said to King Jehoiachin . . . 'As surely as I am the living God, even if you were the signet ring on my right hand, I would pull you off'" (TEV).

In spite of His great love for us—rather, because of that love—God requires righteousness of all who wish to find happiness here and life eternal hereafter.

Prayer for today:

"Teach me, Lord, what you want me to do, and I will obey you faithfully; teach me to serve you with complete devotion" (Ps. 86:11, TEV).

▼

☐ **WEEK 32, FRIDAY**   **JEREMIAH**

Scripture: Jeremiah 24—26
The Story: Jeremiah 24:1-10

They shall be my people, and I will be their God: for they shall return unto me with their whole heart (Jer. 24:7).

When It's Good to Look Bad

Truth that is obvious in nature is not always clear in human nature. Jeremiah could see immediately which figs were good, but God had to tell him who were better off, the captives in Babylon or the people living in their Jerusalem homes.

In 597 B.C. Nebuchadnezzar laid siege to the city. Young King Jehoiachin (also called Jeconiah) soon surrendered, and Nebuchadnezzar deported the king with 10,000 upper- and middle-class Jews to Babylon. He appointed Jehoiachin's uncle, Zedekiah, king of Judah.

Who were better off, the exiled Jews in Babylon or the Jews in

Jerusalem? Human wisdom would say the folk at home—but God knew better.

The difference between the two groups lay in the responses they were making to God and to His dealings with them. In Jerusalem the people had the advantage of the Temple, the book of the law, and the faithful prophets. But they had closed their minds to the ways of God. In 18:12 they had stubbornly declared, "We will walk after our own devices." When we are blessed with every material and spiritual advantage, the surface appearance is good—but if we are rejecting God, it is bad to look good.

In Babylon, away from their homeland and cut off from the Temple, things looked bad for the exiles. However, as God counts goodness, our highest good lies in spiritual renewal that comes by listening to His voice. The Psalmist declares, "I had rather be a doorkeeper in the house of my God, than to dwell in the tents of wickedness" (Ps. 84:10).

It is good to look bad—if God has His rightful place in our lives. How blessed when God says of us: "My eyes will watch over them for their good . . . I will build them up and not tear them down; I will plant them and not uproot them. I will give them a heart to know me . . . They will be my people, and I will be their God" (24:6-7, NIV).

To that glad promise, my heart responds: Let it be so.

▼

☐ WEEK 32, SATURDAY   JEREMIAH

Scripture: Jeremiah 27—29

The common theme of these three chapters is Jeremiah's ministry beyond the boundaries of Jerusalem and Judah. In 27:1-11 the prophet sent word to five neighboring countries—Edom, Moab, Ammon, Tyre, and Sidon. They, like Judah, must submit to the rule of King Nebuchadnezzar of Babylon. To resist would be national suicide.

The Story: Jeremiah 29:1-14

Ye shall seek me, and find me, when ye shall search for me with all your heart (Jer. 29:13).

Do the Best You Know

Jeremiah had a message from God for Judah's neighboring nations, but his chief concern was for his own people exiled in Babylon 900 miles away. In 28:1 these events are dated in the "fourth year that Zedekiah was king" (594 B.C.). Five years earlier Nebuchadnezzar had besieged Jerusalem. During the siege young Jehoiachin succeeded his father as Judah's king. He soon surrendered the city to Nebuchadnezzar's army. The king, together with 10,000 of his people and much of Jerusalem's treasure were taken to Babylon (2 Kings 24:6-16).

Now, five years later, these exiles were eager to return. National zealots both in Jerusalem and in Babylon were agitating for further opposition against Nebuchadnezzar. But Jeremiah was in touch with God; and God had showed him the future. He knew that only a little later Nebuchadnezzar would come again; Jerusalem would be totally destroyed, and most of her people would join the 10,000 already exiled. Knowing these facts, Jeremiah wrote his letter (chap. 29) to the exiles in Babylon.

What does God want us to do when we are faced with difficult circumstances beyond our power to change? In verses 4-9 He seems to say, Do the very best you know how to do for the moment —and it will prove best in the long run.

Plan to live—Build houses, plant gardens, and eat the fruit of them.

Cultivate family life—Take wives, rear sons and daughters.

Under God, be good citizens—Seek the peace of the city where you are living. Pray for your community because in its peace you shall have peace.

Try to find God's will—Don't be deceived. Do not pay attention to worldly dreamers who are out of touch with God and His plans.

But how can we know which way is right when there are conflicting claims to truth? We have the Bible to guide us; let us consult it. We have the Holy Spirit to teach us; let us search for His will.

Prayer for today:
"*Lead me in thy truth, and teach me: for thou art the God of my salvation*" (Ps. 25:5).

▼

☐ WEEK 33, SUNDAY   JEREMIAH

Scripture: Jeremiah 30—32
The Story: Jeremiah 32:1-17

The Lord Almighty, the God of Israel, has said that houses, fields, and vineyards will again be bought in this land (Jer. 32:15; all quotes from TEV).

Put Your Money with Your Mouth

Zedekiah, Judah's last king, ruled 11 years. During the closing 18 months of his reign Jerusalem lay under siege by the armies of Babylon. For the preceding 38 years Jeremiah had prophesied that because of her sin Jerusalem would be destroyed and her people exiled. Now those tragic events were clearly on the horizon. The city would fall within 12 months.

But God's final word is hope. Therefore in chapters 30—31 Jeremiah reminded his people of the divine promises—God would restore them to their homeland. Even Israel which had already been in Assyrian exile for 150 years was given a promise (30:1—31:20). Also God had said after Jerusalem's punishment of 70 years in Babylonian exile, "People will again live in Judah and in all its towns."

During the siege Jeremiah was considered a traitor, and he had been imprisoned by the king. Even his family had turned against him. A cousin, Hanamel, came to taunt him in the courtyard where he was under house arrest. Hanamel said in effect:

"If you think property will again be valued by our people, let me sell you my field. I'll take the cash now; you can run the risk of

328

trusting God to restore the exiles and then find a buyer for the field. If you believe what you say God has promised, put your money where your mouth is."

It was a severe test; and God knows that we need special help in times of pressure. He forewarned Jeremiah by telling him that Hanamel would come—and He told Jeremiah what Hanamel would say. God's man is human enough that even a prophet feels more sure of God's leading after he sees the events take place! "So I knew that the Lord had really spoken to me."

But here was a man who had the courage to act on God's word. He knew it could not profit him personally because he was now 66 years old, and Judah would be in exile for 70 years. But God's man was ready to pay a price to demonstrate his faith in the divine promise: "I bought the field . . . and weighed out the money . . . I signed and sealed the deed . . . Before them all I said to Baruch, '. . . place them in a clay jar, so that they may be preserved for years to come'" (32:9-10, 13-14).

Prayer for today:

Lord, give me the faith and courage of Jeremiah. When I am sure You are speaking to me, let me prove my faith by putting my reputation and my money on the line. Amen.

▼

☐ **WEEK 33, MONDAY**   **JEREMIAH**

Scripture: Jeremiah 33—35
The Story: Jeremiah 33:1-3, 6-8, 14-17, 25-26

Call to me, and I will . . . tell you wonderful and marvelous things (Jer. 33:3, TEV).

Hope for Our World

Jeremiah was often compelled to predict destruction and dismay for his people. But he is also a prophet of hope because in this life God's word of judgment is always followed by His promise of forgiveness and restoration.

Today we look at Jeremiah's predictions of the coming Messiah. These prophecies were first given to the Israelites, and they spoke of a new day in Judah's national history. The captives in foreign countries would return and dwell safely in their own Promised Land.

But in a wider sense these promises, especially verses 14-26, are made to the whole world. Like other Old Testament prophets, Jeremiah foresees the glorious day when God will dwell in His fullness among His people. Jesus often referred to these messages of hope and applied them to himself.

In verse 16 the title "The Lord our righteousness" seems to refer to Jerusalem, but in the parallel passage the reference to Christ is clear: "'Behold, the days are coming,' declares the Lord, 'when I shall raise up for David a righteous Branch; and He will reign as king and act wisely and do justice and righteousness in the land. . . . and this is His name by which He will be called, "The Lord our righteousness"'" (Jer. 23:5-6, NASB).

Today we are privileged to look back on these events as history. With Isaiah we exult, "Unto us a child is born, unto us a son is given: and the government shall be upon his shoulder: and his name shall be called Wonderful, Counsellor, The mighty God, The everlasting Father, The Prince of Peace. Of the increase of his government and peace there shall be no end . . . The zeal of the Lord of hosts will perform this" (Isa. 9:6-7).

With Bernard of Clairvaux our hearts rejoice:

> O Hope of ev'ry contrite heart,
> O Joy of all the meek,
> To those who fall, how kind Thou art!
> How good to those who seek!

▼

☐ **WEEK 33, TUESDAY**   **JEREMIAH**

Scripture: Jeremiah 36
The Story: Jeremiah 36:1-7, 27-28, 32

The Lord said to me ... Write everything that I have told you ... so that they will hear everything that the Lord has said (Jer. 36:1-2, 6, TEV).

Let Us Give Thanks for Scripture

We sometimes think of the Scripture only as God's message. It is that, but it is more—it is His written message.

There were other men of God who served their times well, but we do not remember them or their teachings. Their messages were just as true as Jeremiah's, but the truth faded with the transient memories of men. Those prophets spoke the word of the Lord, but their inspired words fell silent in their graves.

Let us thank God for the written Word because it preserves the truth unchanged. From 626 B.C. God had been revealing His plans to Jeremiah, and the prophet had been preaching those plans publicly. Now 21 years later in 605 God said, "Write everything that I have told you from the first time that I spoke to you." It would be at least another 18 years before those predictions were fulfilled in the fall of Jerusalem. In those 18 years there would be two new kings and many new counselors. All of them needed to know accurately the truths that God had revealed. God said, "Write it so that they will hear everything that the Lord has said."

They needed to know—and we need to know. Let us thank God for writing, because through the written Word the Spirit of God speaks more clearly to the spirits of men. God said to Jeremiah, Write it, and "perhaps they will pray to the Lord and turn from their evil ways" (v. 7). How often the Holy Spirit illuminates to us a clear and personal message from the written Word. He uses a scripture to grip our minds with conviction. As we read, we are convinced that this is indeed the word of the Lord to us.

God has put His truth into writing to guide us accurately, to speak to us personally, to reveal His holy will for our lives.

O Word of God incarnate, O Wisdom from on high,
O Truth unchanged, unchanging, O Light of our dark sky:
We praise Thee for the radiance that from the hallowed page,
A Lantern to our footsteps, shines on from age to age.
                                        —WILLIAM W. HOW

Scripture: Jeremiah 36; 45
The Story: Jeremiah 36:4-8, 14-19, 21-26, 32;
45:1-5 (See the acrostic below)

Seek ye first the kingdom of God, and his righteousness; and all these things shall be added unto you (Matt. 6:33).

"Seekest Thou Great Things for Thyself?"

God often speaks to us most clearly as we see Him at work in the life of another. In Baruch's story we see God's concern for us as persons. As the Sovereign of the universe revealed the destinies for the nations of the East, He paused to give clear guidance to one discouraged man (Jeremiah 45).

We do not know much about Baruch, but the important facts are reflected in this personal acrostic.

B—idden to write and read God's words (36:4-7)
A—ccepted God's call to serve (36:8)
R—ead the scroll to the princes (36:14-19)
U—nsuccessful in his appeal to the king (36:21-26)
C—ontinued to write God's words for others to read (36:32)
H—onored with a special promise from God (45:1-5)

For 20 years this man was the devoted friend, secretary, and faithful attendant of Jeremiah. For this ministry he paid a price. His brother, Seraiah, served as a high official under King Zedekiah (Jer. 51:59-64). Baruch had good reason to believe that he, too, could have gained a responsible position in Judah's court. But those dreams were shattered when from Jeremiah's prophecy he learned early the tragic fate of his beloved country.

It was a struggle for Baruch to give up hope for a high government position. His difficult decision, like our own hard choices, was not made without hesitation. But God knows best, and He offers us His best in our circumstances—always. No man suffers real loss by listening to God and following His counsel.

It takes strength of soul to see one's work destroyed, and then to do the work over again. But God gave Baruch that strength. He accepted the tedious task of rewriting God's messages—"all the words of the book which Jehoiakim king of Judah had burned in the fire; and there were added beside unto them many like words."

Baruch's name means "blessed." One of our Lord's beatitudes seems spoken especially for him: "Blessed are ye, when men shall revile you, and persecute you . . . for my sake. Rejoice, and be exceeding glad: for great is your reward in heaven" (Matt. 5:11-12).

Prayer for today:

Thank You, Lord, for Baruch and for his faithfulness. Show me Your will for my life—and teach me to accept it thankfully.

▼

☐ **WEEK 33, THURSDAY**   JEREMIAH

Scripture: Jeremiah 37—40; 52
The Story: Jeremiah 37:3-10; 38:14-20

Obey . . . the voice of the Lord . . . so it shall be well unto thee, and thy soul shall live (Jer. 38:20).

Two Men in Tension

Today we see two men playing out their roles in history against the backdrop of the last days of Jerusalem in 586 B.C.

The times were tragic, and the choices were terribly hard for King Zedekiah who had to make the decisions. President Harry S. Truman once said of the Oval Office in the White House, "The buck stops here." So it was with Zedekiah.

Should he go along with his advisors? To a man they recommended a policy dictated by apparent national interest: Hold the city. Repel the invader. Fight to the last man.

It seemed to make sense—except for one fact. Whenever the

king sought to learn the will of God, he got a different message. There were forces at work in Judah that no human power could hold off. God kept saying: "I am going to give the city to the Babylonian army . . . Whoever stays on in the city will die . . . But whoever goes out and surrenders to the Babylonians will not be killed; he will at least escape with his life" (38:2-3, TEV).

Like every man whom God confronts, Zedekiah had to make a decision. He chose wrongly. He took what looked like the easy way out. But he failed to obey God.

Tragically, no man fails God alone. Someone else is always involved. Zedekiah's wrong choice led to the total destruction of the city and the Temple. It cost him the death of his sons and the exile of his people.

Jeremiah, too, had hard choices. Can a man's loyalty to God make him a traitor to his country? This was the heartbreaking dilemma that faced the prophet. When a man's own city is under siege he normally gives his full support to the resistance movements of his people. But God's man has one loyalty that stands above patriotism. If his ruler and country are wrong, a man must be loyal to God and to truth. The decision is hard—but it is right.

There are no exceptions. It is the only right counsel for prophets, for kings—and for commoners:

"Obey . . . the voice of the Lord . . . so it shall be well unto thee, and thy soul shall live."

▼

□ **WEEK 33, FRIDAY**   JEREMIAH

Scripture: Jeremiah 41—44
The Story: Jeremiah 42:1-11, 15-16; 43:1-7

Whether it pleases us or not, we will obey the Lord our God . . . All will go well with us if we obey him (Jer. 42:6, TEV).

Prayer and Obedience

Without these four chapters our knowledge of Bible history would be greatly impoverished. Only one verse elsewhere (2 Kings 25:26) tells us the final story of the people left in Judah in 586 B.C.

But we have here more than history. Shining through the story we see clearly some universal principles of prayer and obedience to God.

When we are in trouble, we pray. My professor at the state university was still active, though suffering from incurable tuberculosis. One morning he commented, "Don't ask me why we pray; we just do." The Jews in Judah proved the professor's point. They cried, "Once there were many of us; but now only a few . . . are left . . . Pray [to] the Lord" (TEV).

We need guidance. At the crossroads of decision we often need better judgment than our own. It was right for the people to ask, "Pray that the Lord our God will show us the way we should go and what we should do" (TEV).

It often takes time to discern God's will. Even a prophet reports that he could not immediately find God's guidance. He tells us, "Ten days later the Lord spoke to me" (TEV).

It is hard to obey God when we are afraid. God said, Stay in Judah; be not afraid. But because the people feared reprisal from their enemy, they declared: "You are lying. The Lord our God did not send you to tell us not to go and live in Egypt" (TEV)

We sometimes influence each other in disobedience. Jeremiah had a special word for the rebellious wives. Their husbands knew the women were wrong, but went along with them. In mutual defiance they declared, "We will not listen to what you tell us in the name of the Lord. We intend to . . . burn sacrifices to the queen of heaven . . . as we used to do" (44:16-17, NEB).

Prayer for today:

Lord, we sincerely pledge to You, "Whether it pleases us or not, we will obey the Lord our God." And give us grace to go one step further—help us to keep that promise.

Scripture: Jeremiah 46—51

Jeremiah's first duty was to Judah, but many places in the book we see his sense of obligation to other people also. That is the key to these six chapters; they are called Jeremiah's "Oracles Against Foreign Nations."

The kingdoms involved were Judah's neighbors, or sometimes more distant countries that had an impact on her life. In chapter 46 we read of the battle of Carchemish between Egypt and Babylonia. In 47—48 Jeremiah tells of God's judgment on Philistia and Moab. In 49 there are messages for Ammon, Edom, Damascus, Kedar, and Hazor. Elam lay east of Babylon. Her capital city, Susa (Shushan), was the summer home of King Xerxes and Queen Esther (Esther 1:2). Jeremiah's last long oracle (chaps. 50—51) was directed against Babylon.

The Story: Jeremiah 51:1-10

I selected you to be a prophet to the nations (Jer. 1:5; all quotes from TEV).

God of the Nations

From these ancient political prophecies what lessons can we learn about God's character and concerns?

God is always fair. He says, "I will not let you go unpunished; but when I punish you, I will be fair. I, the Lord, have spoken" (46:28).

God punishes arrogance. To Moab He said, "You trusted in your strength and your wealth . . . now even you will be conquered" (48:7). And of Babylon He decreed, "You are filled with pride, so I, the Sovereign Lord Almighty, am against you" (50:31).

Some of God's judgments are final. He said of Babylon, "Never again will people live there, not for all time to come" (50:39). "That country will become a pile of ruins where wild animals live" (51:37). To this day Babylon is only a ghost town of ancient ruins.

God's Word is sure. The prophets were so certain of God's revelations to them that they often spoke of things in the future as though they were already present. In 595 B.C., Jeremiah wrote of Babylon's fall 60 years later: "Babylonia hammered the whole world to pieces, and now that hammer is shattered!" (50:23).

God teaches us compassion. He does not enjoy administering judgment even when it is necessary—and He would teach us to be like Him. Jeremiah, like our Lord, could feel sorrow even for his enemies. He sobs, "My heart mourns for Moab and for the people . . . because everything they owned is gone" (48:36).

God is Lord of the nations. He requires justice, mercy, and worship. When nations forget, He sends judgment. In our own day it is fitting that we as a people should pray with Kipling:

> *Judge of the nations, spare us yet,*
> *Lest we forget—lest we forget.*

▼

Scripture: Lamentations 1—2
The Story: Lamentations 1:1-5; 2:5-7

The Lord has brought her grief because of her many sins (Lam. 1:5; all quotes from NIV).

Understanding God's Judgments

Not all human suffering comes because of sin, but sin always brings suffering.

The five chapters of Lamentations are Jeremiah's poems of anguished reflection on the fall of Jerusalem, and on the sins which brought those judgments on his people.

When God permits us to suffer as a result of our sins, why does He do it? What shall we do about it?

We lament our situation. Jeremiah sighs for Jerusalem: "The roads to Zion mourn, for no one comes to her appointed feasts. All her gateways are desolate, her priests groan, her maidens grieve, and she is in bitter anguish" (1:4).

337

Our sins bring regrets. "In the days of her affliction . . . Jerusalem remembers all the treasures that were hers in the days of old. . . . You have dealt with me because of all my sins. My groans are many and my heart is faint" (1:7, 22).

We know that God permits it. "The Lord has brought her grief because of her many sins. . . . My sins have been bound into a yoke; by his hands they were woven together. They have come upon my neck and the Lord has sapped my strength. He has handed me over to those I cannot withstand" (1:5, 14).

God lets moral cause and effect take their course. "He has withdrawn his right hand at the approach of the enemy" (2:3).

In honesty, we recognize that we are at fault. "She did not consider her future. . . . The Lord is righteous, yet I rebelled against his command. . . . I am in torment within, and in my heart I am disturbed, for I have been most rebellious" (1:9, 18, 20).

When we accept our responsibility and acknowledge our sin, we are in position to accept God's forgiveness and restoration. Then we confess honestly with the Psalmist:

"It was good for me to be afflicted so that I might learn your decrees" (Ps. 119:71).

▼

☐ **WEEK 34, MONDAY**   **LAMENTATIONS**

Scripture: Lamentations 3—5
The Story: Lamentations 3:9; 5:9-22; 3:19-33 (in this order)

Turn thou us unto thee, O Lord, and we shall be turned; renew our days as of old (Lam. 5:21).

What Do I Do When I'm Down?

The people of Judah were in desperate straits—but no man is hopeless who turns to God for help. The Bible encourages us, "Is any among you afflicted? let him pray" (James 5:13). Sustained by faith in the goodness of God we may echo Jeremiah's prayer for attention: "Remember, O Lord . . . consider, and behold" (5:1). We are confident that if only God sees our concern and our repentance, He will come and save us.

One of the tragedies of sin is that others often suffer for our wrongdoing. It is a sign of true penitence when we recognize our own responsibility for suffering brought on by sinful choices. Because Judah had sinned, the women of Jerusalem and the maids in outlying towns had been ravished by the conquering armies. Because of the sins of a whole nation, her princes had been tortured and her elders dishonored. Because Judah rejected God's will, her young men were put to slave labor turning an enemy's mills, and her children fell under oppressive slave burdens meant for mature men.

It was sin that took the "elders . . . from the gate"—and with them, the administration of justice for which they were responsible. Sin took music from the young and stole joy from the hearts of all. Finally, the sin of the people had thwarted and destroyed the work of God; Mount Zion, the center of their worship, had become so desolate that wild animals roamed there.

The people of Judah had hit bottom, but they remembered to pray: "Turn thou us unto thee, O Lord, and we shall be turned."

Judah's world had fallen into ruins, but God still stood tall. He is the God of mercy who means good and not evil to men. Though He punishes evil, the intent of that punishment is to turn us from sin and its sorrow to the loving fellowship of a Heavenly Father. Of such fellowship my heart sings today:

> Pardon for sin and a peace that endureth,
> Thy own dear presence to cheer and to guide;
> Strength for today and bright hope for tomorrow—
> Blessings all mine, with ten thousand beside!*
> —THOMAS O. CHISHOLM

Ezekiel was a younger contemporary of Jeremiah and prophesied during Judah's exile. Nebuchadnezzar, king of Babylon, first invaded the land in 606 B.C. He captured Jerusalem and carried away several outstanding young men, including Daniel. Thus began the 70 years of captivity. Eight years later, in 597, Nebuchadnezzar attacked again, taking into exile another 10,000 prisoners, including Ezekiel.

At that time Zedekiah was made a puppet king in Jerusalem, but he soon revolted. The king of Babylon then invaded a third time. After a siege of three years the Babylonians captured Jerusalem in 586 B.C. They destroyed the city, the Temple, and the kingdom, killing or deporting most of the people.

During the fifth year of Ezekiel's Babylonian captivity, he was called to be a prophet. His name means "one whom God sustains." Ezekiel proclaimed God's warnings and hope to his fellow Jews both in Babylon and in distant Judah. He served God and his people at least until the middle of Judah's 70 years of captivity. Although we know nothing of his last days, it is said he was murdered in Babylon by a Jewish prince whom he had convicted of idolatry.

Because Ezekiel often uses figurative language we must sometimes look behind the allegories in order to understand the literal meaning of his words.

Scripture: Ezekiel 1—3
The Story: Ezekiel 1:1-3; 2:1-5; 3:16-21

I have made thee a watchman unto the house of Israel (Ezek. 3:17).

Prayer for a Pastor

In our church elections we call a pastor to the local congregation, but it is God who calls him to the ministry. There is always an element of mystery about this choice. Ezekiel was only one among "the captives by the river Chebar." There was no reason known to him why he should have been chosen.

Among us five brothers one was to become a schoolteacher, one a government worker, one a lawyer, and one a soldier. Why did God lay His hand upon the fifth to be a preacher? We do not know. But from among the others, God called him and charged him to proclaim God's Word to men.

Sometimes the call comes dramatically; at other times, without fanfare. But in that call God makes himself so real that one cannot doubt "the hand of the Lord was there upon him."

The pastor hears God's voice when he is called to preach; and ever after, his business in life is to listen for the voice of God. That Voice speaks to him concerning his own conduct and gives him guidance for the church. Sometimes the voice of the Spirit is so clear that a man knows he is right even when others are sure he is wrong. Ezekiel had such an experience when he wrote, "The Spirit entered into me when he spake unto me."

It is glorious to speak for God when men hear His warning and repent. But it is harrowing to follow in the prophet's steps and try to arouse men who reject the truth. Then the pastor must fall back on God's word to Ezekiel: "When I say unto the wicked, Thou shalt surely die . . . if thou warn the wicked . . . thou hast delivered thy soul" (3:18-19). When a man does this, he knows that he is clear before God, but still his heart is broken; even as the heart of God himself breaks when His people persist in evil and destroy themselves.

Today I join in the prayer of Frances Havergal for her pastor on a Sunday night:

"Rest him, O Father! Thou didst send him forth with great and glorious messages of love; but Thy ambassador is weary now, worn with the weight of his high embassy. Now care for him, as Thou hast cared for us in sending him, and cause him to lie down in Thy fresh pastures, by Thy streams of peace."

341

Scripture: Ezekiel 4—7
The Story: Ezekiel 4:1-3; 7:1-9
You will know that I am the Lord (Ezek. 6:7; all quotes from NIV).

In the Hour of Catastrophe

God's Word deals with truth. Chapters 4 to 24 give us Ezekiel's prophecies against Jerusalem. They were written in Babylon but dealt chiefly with conditions in Judah. The 10,000 exiles had been away from Jerusalem for five years. They were restless and eager to return. Both in Jerusalem and in Babylon young firebrands agitated for revolt. In mercy, God revealed to Ezekiel that even in Babylon the Jews were better off than they would be at home.

Only one who has lived through the siege and fall of a great city can understand today's scripture. I have been spared that tragedy, but reading of the fall of Berlin has given me some appreciation for the facts.

In our story God's prophet was instructed to make a symbol of the fate that was to overtake the Jews' beloved city. The clay tile would be a tablet about 24 by 12 inches, commonly used in Babylon for writing. On this tile Ezekiel was to draw a sketch of Jerusalem. Around the city he was to picture the besieging army. Forts were shown, such as besiegers would use to protect themselves from counterattack. Mounds of earth were pictured. These would let attackers climb high enough to shoot over the walls or to scale them. The battering rams were for breaking through the walls.

Finally the prophet was to set on edge an iron baking griddle to depict an impenetrable wall between the city and the attackers. There was no way of escape for the inhabitants of Jerusalem. Ezekiel was also told to ration his food and water to indicate that famine would accompany the siege (4:10-11).

God makes no mistakes. These symbols were set up in the home of Ezekiel in Babylon. In 2 Kings 25:1, 3-4, 7 we read of their sad fulfillment in Jerusalem: "Nebuchadnezzar . . . encamped outside the city and built siege works all around it. . . . By the ninth day of the fourth month the famine in the city had become so severe that there was no food for the people to eat. Then the city wall was broken through . . . They killed the sons of Zedekiah before his eyes. Then they put out his eyes, bound him with bronze shackles and took him to Babylon."

God was here dealing with Judah, but Ezekiel's message is relevant today. In my hour of confrontation I bow to God's will. With Mrs. C. H. Morris I repent:

> My stubborn will at last hath yielded;
> I would be Thine, and Thine alone;
> And this the prayer my lips are bringing,
> "Lord, let in me Thy will be done."

Scripture: Ezekiel 8—11
The Story: Ezekiel 8:1-5; 9:3-6; 11:13-20

I have been a sanctuary for them in the countries where they have gone (Ezek. 11:16, NIV).

With God, We Are Never Hopeless

In yesterday's reading, Judah's plight seemed hopeless. In today's chapters those blighting forces are still at work, but with God, we are never hopeless.

Six years after Ezekiel's exile, God showed him the destroying idolatry that was rampant among His own people in Judah. Idols were set up in the very Temple that had been dedicated to Jehovah. In view of Judah's sin, Ezekiel sighs: "Ah, Sovereign Lord! Will you completely destroy the remnant of Israel?" (11:13, NIV). We rejoice that God's answer is no. He always has a faithful remnant.

Ezekiel here echoes God's earlier revelation to Isaiah: "In that day the remnant . . . will return, a remnant of Jacob will return to the Mighty God" (Isa. 10:20-21, NIV). This remnant is a kind of "holy seed," a spiritual kernel of the nation which will survive impending judgment and become the germ of the people of God. The remnant will be blessed of God and made a blessing. In this there is hope. A host of people may fail, but some will always remain true; from them God's kingdom shall take root, grow again, and spread across the world.

There is hope also in the forgiving and sustaining love of God. "This is what the Sovereign Lord says: Although I sent them far away among the nations and scattered them among the countries, yet . . . I have been a sanctuary for them in the countries where they have gone" (11:16, NIV).

God spoke through Ezekiel to comfort this band of exiles. They yearned for Jehovah's Temple but felt themselves deprived of any spiritual help because they were far from His house. Here we see an early dawning of the glorious truth that God is everywhere available to those who seek Him. The true house of God is wherever He meets our spirits. Jesus made this crystal clear: "The hour cometh, when ye shall neither in this mountain, nor yet at Jerusalem, worship the Father. . . . the true worshippers shall worship the Father in spirit and in truth" (John 4:21, 23). Today I kneel before Him.

> *Break Thou the bread of life, Dear Lord, to me,*
> *As Thou didst break the loaves beside the sea.*
> *Beyond the sacred page I seek Thee, Lord;*
> *My spirit pants for Thee, O living Word!*
> —MARY A. LATHBURY

☐ **WEEK 34, FRIDAY**   **EZEKIEL**

Scripture: Ezekiel 12—16
The Story: Ezekiel 12:1-2; 14:1-6, 21-23; 16:59-63

I will establish my covenant with you, and you will know that I am the Lord (Ezek. 16:62, NIV).

Thinking About God's Judgments

God will not willingly allow us to destroy our lives and lose our souls. He puts roadblocks along the paths to hell. However, just as He stopped short of completely destroying Judah, so in His earthly punishments He stops short of final justice; He gives us opportunity to repent and to rebuild our lives.

God's goal is to win us. Ezekiel prophesied in Babylon, but he beamed these messages to the sinful of Jerusalem. The judgments were terrifying, but all were designed to draw Judah back to God. He cannot save us, however, unless we acknowledge Him as Lord. Nine times in these five chapters Jehovah declares His loving purpose: "You will know that I am the Lord."

God is fair. He judges us according to our knowledge of right and wrong. Judgment was pronounced first against Judah's prophets (chap. 13); they, more than others, knew the requirements of God. Even in life's final judgment, fairness prevails. Jesus tells us: "That servant, which knew his lord's will, and prepared not himself . . . shall be beaten with many stripes. But he that knew not, and did commit things worthy of stripes, shall be beaten with few stripes" (Luke 12:47-48).

Sins of the spirit grieve God most. Idolatry in Judah was open and public. But in the Jewish community of Babylon some tried to conceal their disloyalty to God. To such secret sinners He declares: "When any Israelite sets up idols in his heart . . . I the Lord will answer him myself in keeping with his great idolatry. . . . Therefore . . . Repent! Turn from your idols and renounce all your detestable practices!" (14:4, 6, NIV).

The sin of ingratitude. In chapter 16 Ezekiel tells an allegory to paint the dark picture of Judah's sin. Like a generous benefactor, God found Israel as a helpless newborn babe. He cared for her through childhood, nurtured her in youth, and provided for her an honorable marriage. But a thankless Judah chose to ignore all of this and turned to a life of shame. Shakespeare writes: "How sharper than a serpent's tooth it is to have a thankless child." If ingratitude wounds a human parent, how much more the heart of God!

345

Father, when I read about Your judgments, remind me that Your mercies are greater. You wound only in order to heal.

"I will extol thee, O Lord, for thou hast lifted me up . . . weeping may endure for a night, but joy cometh in the morning" (Ps. 30:1, 5).

▼

☐ **WEEK 34, SATURDAY**   **EZEKIEL**

Scripture: Ezekiel 17—19

Chapter 17 is a political allegory describing the treachery of Judah's King Zedekiah when he broke his pledge of allegiance to Babylon and formed an alliance with Egypt. Chapter 19 follows as a poem of lament for the fate of Judah's princes who suffered because of this treachery. Sandwiched between is chapter 18, one of the great theological messages of the Bible.

The Story: Ezekiel 18:1-9, 25-27, 30-32

If a wicked man turns away from all the sins he has committed . . . and does what is just and right, he will surely live (Ezek. 18:21, NIV).

I Am Responsible

The exiles in Babylon had given up hope of an early return to their homeland, and the prevailing mood was a deep pessimism. They blamed their plight on the sins of their fathers. This attitude was crystalized in a widely quoted proverb: "The fathers have eaten sour grapes, and the children's teeth are set on edge" (18:2). From such false teaching God seeks to set us right. "By my life! says the Lord the Eternal, you must never quote that proverb again in Israel!" (18:3, Moffatt).

When we do business with God we must face up to our personal responsibility. Ezekiel forcefully reminds us that each one stands before God on the same basis. The man who turns from righteousness to wickedness shall surely die. But Ezekiel also brings to us the wonder of the gospel message: "When the wicked man turneth away from his wickedness . . . he shall surely live."

Personal sin is the only cause for which we suffer the judgment of God; and personal righteousness is the sole basis upon which we gain His favor. The circumstances of life influence our choices, but they do not determine our decisions. In the inner citadel of the soul we decide whether or not we will repent and turn from sin.

By the help of God we can make the choice that brings a new heart and a new spirit. It will not do to blame our failure on poor parents, an unfair God, or an unchangeable fate. We have the power to decide. God declares, "I have no pleasure in the death of him that dieth . . . wherefore turn yourselves, and live" (18:32).

Father, today I face squarely the most serious responsibility of my life.

> A charge to keep I have,
> A God to glorify;
> A never-dying soul to save,
> And fit it for the sky.
> —CHARLES WESLEY

▼

☐ WEEK 35, SUNDAY   EZEKIEL

Scripture: Ezekiel 20—24

Today's chapters contain a group of prophecies dated in 590 B.C. Nebuchadnezzar's attack on Jerusalem began that year; after some three years under siege the city fell in 586.

From Babylon, Ezekiel sadly recounts Israel's earlier deliverance from Egypt and her perverse addiction to idolatry. Chapter 21 foresees the coming destruction and describes Babylon as God's sword to destroy Judah. In chapter 23 Ezekiel compares Israel and Judah to two adulterous sisters, Oholah and Oholibah. He uses strong language to portray the degradation and utterly perverse conduct of immoral persons who seem to have no sense of the evil of their behavior.

Chapter 24 was written on the day that Nebuchadnezzar laid siege to Jerusalem. The prophet pictures his home city as a corroded cooking pot burning up over a fierce fire. There is nothing left worth salvaging.

The Story: Ezekiel 24:15-27

I sought for a man among them, that should . . . stand in the gap before me for the land, that I should not destroy it (Ezek. 22:30).

Be Strong

How does a man responsible for his people's faith share tragic news with them? How does he tell his congregation terrible truths and at the same time help them to maintain their faith in God? Only he who, by God's help, has risen above great suffering can do that. So Ezekiel agonized in his personal Gethsemane.

God came to this suffering pastor and said: Ezekiel, I am about to let you pass through the deepest sorrow of your life. Your lovely wife will die suddenly. (She was probably no more than 35.) "With one blow I am about to take away from you the delight of your eyes" (24:16, NIV).

Then came God's deeper discipline. He said, In your sorrow do not follow the customs of your people and give vent to expressions of extreme mourning, as though God had forgotten and forsaken you. Your heart will be broken, but quietly show your people that God can sustain and give peace to those who suffer life's deepest tragedies.

Thus Ezekiel learned the meaning of his own name, "God will strengthen." He recounts in heroic simplicity his obedience to the divine will. "At even my wife died; and I did in the morning as I was commanded" (24:18). From thenceforth Ezekiel could testify in the words of another of God's great shepherds, "I bear in my body the marks of the Lord Jesus" (Gal. 6:17).

Today I, too, would draw closer to my Lord. With Washington Gladden I pray:

> O Master, let me walk with Thee
> In lowly paths of service free.
> Tell me Thy secret; help me bear
> The strain of toil, the fret of care.

348

Scripture: Ezekiel 25—28

The prophecies in today's reading were written about two years after the fall of Jerusalem. From his home in Babylon and from talk in the streets, Ezekiel knew about the next plans for the armies of Nebuchadnezzar. Judah had fallen; now her near neighbors could not escape Babylon's thrust for world conquest. See an Old Testament Bible map to locate Ammon, Moab, Edom, Philistia, Tyre, Sidon, and Egypt.

The Story: Ezekiel 25:15-17; 28:1-8

Forgive us our sins; for we also forgive every one that is indebted to us (Luke 11:4).

Some of God's Guidelines

What can we learn from this record of God's impending judgment on international policies? Perhaps it will help us to remember that national policies are but the lengthened shadows of decisions made by men like ourselves.

Ezekiel understood the mind of God. He knew that God does not overlook persistent and unconfessed sins in men or in nations.

The Lord is never pleased when I rejoice in the misfortune of another. Ammon's joy in the fall of Judah exposed a lack of compassion; it revealed a spirit contrary to God's command, "Thou shalt love thy neighbour as thyself" (Lev. 19:18).

God is against unfaith and atheism. Moab said the Lord's people were no better off than men who had no faith in Him. Such an attitude opens our lives to destruction as surely as it opened "the flank of Moab" (25:9, NIV) to the enemy's attack.

God asks us to forgive our enemies and to surrender our grudges —especially within the family. Edom had descended from Jacob's brother, Esau, and there was longstanding animosity between the two peoples. But God knows that grudges destroy both men and nations. He asks us to give them up—or we must suffer the sad consequences. Perhaps because vengeance is doubly destructive, God here gives us two warnings against it; Philistia would also be punished for her spirit of revenge.

The sin of Tyre was the sin of pride. When we feel self-sufficient and sense no need of God, He bids us remember the inevitable law of the moral world: "Pride goeth before destruction, and a haughty spirit before a fall" (Prov. 16:18).

Father, I ask You to expose every wrong spirit in me and in my people. Forgive our lack of love; forgive our failures of faith; forgive us the anger we have nursed, and the pride that shuts You out of our lives.

"Forgive us our sins; for we also forgive every one that is indebted to us." In Jesus' name. Amen.

▼

☐ WEEK 35, TUESDAY   EZEKIEL

Scripture: Ezekiel 29—32

Yesterday Ezekiel dealt with the lesser nations surrounding Judah. Today he prophesies the humiliation of Egypt, the second great world power of his day.

The 27th year of Ezekiel's exile (29:17) is the latest of his prophecies known to us. Most of the predictions in these chapters, however, were made earlier, only 10 or 12 years after he arrived in Babylon. The prophecies dealt with God's judgment against Egypt. But they may have been intended chiefly for Judah's ears to discourage them from expecting help from Egypt during the siege of Jerusalem.

As a warning to Egypt and a reminder to Judah, chapter 31 describes the destruction of Assyria, an earlier powerful empire that had fallen before the armies of Babylon.

The Story: Ezekiel 30:1-4, 8-12

Then they will know that I am the Lord (Ezek. 30:26, NIV).

Thinking About God's Sovereignty

In these four chapters, 18 times we encounter the phrase "the Lord God." The NIV translates it "the Sovereign Lord." What does this description tell us about God?

Sovereignty means supreme authority, or absolute power. Ezekiel thus reminds us that when we are dealing with God we either fight against an invincible foe, or we have on our side an unbeatable ally.

God has the last word in every controversy with man. When I fight Him to the bitter end, it is the end of me—and it is bitter! Wisdom bids me, Don't start a fight you can't win.

When the sovereign God is against me, I am rightly afraid. But, oh, the joy when I know He is on my side! With David I can then testify, "By thee I have run through a troop; and by my God I have leaped over a wall" (Ps. 18:29).

From God's viewpoint, however, it is not enough to have absolute power. His supreme purpose is to save us from sin and to help persons find fulfillment. To achieve that, He must make us aware of His great power and of His love for us. Seven times in these seven prophecies we read of God's eternal purpose for man: *"They shall know that I am the Lord God."*

I am glad that He is God, the Sovereign Lord. I am glad that He has won my love and my allegiance.

> *Joyful, joyful, we adore Thee,*
> *God of glory, Lord of love;*
> *Hearts unfold like flow'rs before Thee,*
> *Opening to the sun above.*
> —HENRY VAN DYKE

▼

☐ **WEEK 35, WEDNESDAY**   **EZEKIEL**

Scripture: Ezekiel 33—34
The Story: Ezekiel 34:11-16

351

I will seek that which was lost, and bring again that which was driven away, and will bind up that which was broken, and will strengthen that which was sick (Ezek. 34:16).

Our Redeeming God

I am glad that God is not frustrated by our backgrounds. Jim came from a home with a divorced father and an angry, unforgiving mother. These are not the seedbeds from which we expect lives devoted to Christ. But God sought him out. Jim gave his life to Christ and has served for 20 years as a missionary. Together with a godly wife he is rearing three children sincerely seeking to follow Christ. This is the work of our redeeming God.

Ezekiel here pictures God's care as the work of a faithful shepherd. A sudden tempest has swept down during the night upon the unprotected flock. In the darkness and in the storm the sheep have been scattered; they are hungry, wounded, and frightened.

But now it is morning. The night is past. The Good Shepherd is out in the hills seeking every sheep that needs help. It is God himself who gathers His flock and safely folds them. Whatever evil has befallen us can be removed by the ministry of our Shepherd. Those who were scattered by the storm shall be brought back; the lost shall be found; those far from the home of the Father shall return "to their own land"; the hungry sheep driven to the wilderness lowlands shall be fed "in a good pasture, and upon the high mountains of Israel"; those who are weary shall lie down to rest.

Our text describes with surpassing beauty God's purpose for all who have been hurt by sin and misfortune: "I will seek that which was lost, and bring again that which was driven away, and will bind up that which was broken, and will strengthen that which was sick."

I have found it so! In this life,

> *He gives me joy in place of sorrow;*
> *He gives me love that casts out fear;*
> *He gives me sunshine for my shadow,*
> *And "beauty for ashes" here.*
>
> —J. G. CRABBLE

And there is more! He is in charge of even greener pastures beyond this life. Therefore I rejoice with multitudes of the redeemed:

"Surely goodness and mercy shall follow me all the days of my life: and I will dwell in the house of the Lord for ever" (Ps. 23:6).

▼

Scripture: Ezekiel 35—36

After 586 B.C. the exile community in Babylon had been greatly enlarged by the captives taken when Jerusalem fell. Chapters 33—48 come from the last period of Ezekiel's ministry and were addressed to this larger community.

The Story: Ezekiel 36:24-36

I will put my spirit within you, and cause you to walk in my statutes, and ye shall keep my judgments and do them (Ezek. 36:27).

A Cleansed and Purified People

Because God offers hope, Ezekiel's message finds a responsive chord in our hearts today. God's immediate promise was that the exiles should be restored to their homeland. But even for Israel there was more than physical restoration in view. Here we see the full ministry that God plans for the spirit of man. His children shall be a cleansed and purified people.

In Israel's worship those who had sinned were to be made ceremonially clean by sprinkling water upon them. But here it is God himself who cleanses our defilement. He promises, "Then will I sprinkle clean water upon you, and ye shall be clean." I am grateful for His grace of forgiveness that takes away the guilt of sin.

In this redeeming work among the exiles, Israel was purged of her idolatry. Never again was idol worship a problem in the nation.

When our sins are forgiven, they too are past and forgotten. God promises, "I will forgive their iniquity, and I will remember their sin no more" (Jer. 31:34).

Our Lord's forgiveness is gracious, but His work in our lives is not finished when sin is pardoned. Forgiveness is the beginning of a new life; but to enable us to live that life God plans to give a new nature. It is this full salvation of which Ezekiel here speaks. Earlier the prophet had exhorted God's people to get "a new heart and a new spirit" (18:31). But here God declares that He will give us His own Spirit: "I will give you a new heart and put a new spirit in you . . . I will put my Spirit in you and move you to follow my decrees and be careful to keep my laws" (36:26-27, NIV).

Thank You, Father, for every good gift that You send. You created me and gave me life. You forgave my sins and filled me with Your Holy Spirit. I can think of no greater blessing than that "Ye shall be my people, and I will be your God."

In the college chapel we used to sing a chorus of commitment and confidence. It comes back to me today as a foundation for my faith:

> *I know the Lord will make a way for me;*
> *I know the Lord will make a way for me.*
> *If I live a holy life, shun the wrong and do the right,*
> *I know the Lord will make a way for me.* *

*Copyright 1942 by Nazarene Publishing House. Renewed 1970. Used by permission.

▼

☐ **WEEK 35, FRIDAY**   **EZEKIEL**

Scripture: Ezekiel 37—39

Adam Clarke writes that chapters 38—39 contain the most difficult prophecy in the Old Testament. Who Gog and Magog were has never been established to the satisfaction of Bible students. Some think the prophecy was fulfilled when Alexander the Great conquered Palestine 200 years later. Others have identified the country of the "north parts" (38:15) as Persia, Syria, Scythia, or Russia.

Perhaps the best explanation is to regard these chapters as dealing with the end of the world. In Rev. 20:7-9, John refers to Ezekiel's prophecy. There the end times are clearly the topic being discussed.

Gog seems to represent all the evil powers that will oppose God's people in the future. The prophecy is clear that our God is on the side of the righteous. He will protect them and will thwart the plans of even their most powerful enemies.

The Story: Ezekiel 37:21-28

My dwelling place will be with them; I will be their God, and they will be my people (Ezek. 37:27, NIV).

The Promise of His Presence

To exiles in a foreign land the words of our story must have been music to lift their spirits. God, who had been punishing them, promised "a covenant of peace." They who had been scattered abroad heard the message: "I will bring them into their own land." Their beloved Temple had been destroyed, but God promised, "I will . . . set my sanctuary in the midst of them for evermore." They felt that Jehovah had forsaken them, but now He assures them, "I will be their God, and they shall be my people."

These gracious promises were first fulfilled only 50 years later when the Babylonian exiles returned to Jerusalem, rebuilt the city, restored the Temple, and began new life as a nation. But we believe these promises have a still wider fulfillment in the future.

To identify chapters 38—39 with the end of the world is supported by the Messianic prophecies in chapter 37. The statement "my servant David shall be their prince for ever" can only be true of the final reign of Christ as "King of Kings and Lord of Lords" (see Rev. 19:16). The promise, "I will . . . set my sanctuary in the midst of them for evermore" must include God's fellowship with His people throughout eternity.

These are the times of which John later wrote: "I saw a new heaven and a new earth: for the first heaven and the first earth were passed away. . . . And I heard a great voice out of heaven saying, Behold, the tabernacle of God is with men, and he will dwell with them, and they shall be his people, and God himself shall be with them, and be their God" (Rev. 21:1, 3).

In gratitude for these promises and for the glad prospects of the future, I can only join the triumphant throng who sing:

"Alleluia; Salvation, and glory, and honour, and power, unto the Lord our God" (Rev. 19:1).

▼

☐ WEEK 35, SATURDAY   EZEKIEL

Scripture: Ezekiel 40—48 (Optional reading)

Much in these last nine chapters of Ezekiel does not seem relevant for today's Bible reader. In the 25th year of Ezekiel's captivity, and 14 years after the fall of Jerusalem, these visions came to the prophet. In another 50 years the exiles would be returning to Jerusalem. They would need to rebuild their national life, and they would need guidance.

Ezekiel begins where God begins—with our religious needs. In chapters 40—43 he gives blueprints for rebuilding the Temple. Chapter 44 revives God's special arrangement for the ministries of Jewish priests and Levites—but also introduces a new person, the Prince, who is the nation's political leader. Chapters 45—48 deal chiefly with reallocation of Palestine among the 12 tribes, the Prince, and the Temple area.

I have called these chapters optional reading because as far as we know most of the provisions were never carried out when the Jews returned. The Temple was rebuilt, but it followed the earlier plans of Solomon's Temple. Also, the allocation of the land to the tribes was never implemented.

Perhaps God gave these visions primarily to inspire hope in the exiles. Through Ezekiel, God was telling them that once again they would be His own people, in their own land, with His presence among them.

The Story: Ezekiel 47:1-12

I will live among them forever (Ezek. 43:9; all quotes from NIV).

God in the Midst

Ezekiel's last message is the message of the entire Bible. God has made a covenant with His people—and we are His people when we love and obey Him. His purpose is to save us from sin, to live in us, to love us, to bring abundant life here, and to assure us of eternal life hereafter.

With God there is always high hope for the future. The river that Ezekiel saw flowing from the Temple is the picture of God's ever-enlarging work through the Church. The prophet writes:

"I saw a great number of trees on each side of the river. . . . Swarms of living creatures will live wherever the river flows. . . . Fruit trees of all kinds will grow on both banks of the river. Their leaves will not wither, nor will their fruit fail. Every month they will bear, because the water from the sanctuary flows to them. Their fruit will serve for food and their leaves for healing" (47:7, 9, 12).

The work of God which Ezekiel foresaw in the future, John also saw in a vision looking back from the perspective of eternity:

"Then the angel showed me the river of the water of life, as clear as crystal, flowing from the throne of God and of the Lamb down the middle of the great street of the city. On each side of the river stood the tree of life, bearing twelve crops of fruit, yielding its fruit every month. And the leaves of the tree are for the healing of the nations. No longer will there be any curse. The throne of God and of the Lamb will be in the city, and his servants will serve him. They will see his face, and his name will be on their foreheads. There will be no more night. They will not need the light of a lamp or the light of the sun, for the Lord God will give them light. And they will reign for ever and ever.

"The angel said to me, 'These words are trustworthy and true'" (Rev. 22:1-6).

The last word of Ezekiel's prophecy is, "The name of the city from that time on will be: THE LORD IS THERE" (48:35).

Thank you, Ezekiel, and thank you, John. God gave you the message, and I believe it. I believe it so deeply that I commit my life to that faith.

All that I need He will always be,
All that I need till His face I see,
All that I need thro' eternity.
Jesus is all I need. *
— JAMES ROWE

▼

☐ WEEK 36, SUNDAY   DANIEL

Like Ezekiel, Daniel was a prophet of the Exile. His life spanned the entire 70 years of Jewish captivity in Babylon. He was probably no more than 12 or 15 years old when deported among the first Jewish captives. For 75 years Babylon was his home. Near 90 years old when Cyrus permitted the return of the Jews, age would have prevented him from making the trip.

While Ezekiel's ministry was directed to the Jewish community, Daniel served God as a prime minister in the court of Babylon.

Scripture: Daniel 1—2
The Story: Daniel 2:1-30

Praise be to the name of God for ever and ever; wisdom and power are his (Dan. 2:20, NIV).

Trust in God Always

The stature of the man can often be seen in the behavior of the boy. Daniel, the prophet who stood before kings, is foreshadowed in Daniel, the boy who spoke to the king's servant. Still in his teen years Daniel made a decision to serve God; it set the course for all of his life.

Eating the king's food meant compromising his faith in God, therefore "Daniel purposed in his heart that he would not defile himself with the portion of the king's meat, nor with the wine which he drank" (1:8).

The same faith in God is seen in interpreting Nebuchadnezzar's dream. The king had a disturbing night, and he either forgot or pretended to forget his dream in order to test the ability of his counselors. He called the astrologers and asked them to tell him both what he had dreamed and what the dream meant. The magicians rightfully protested that no king had ever asked such an impossible thing from his wise men. Arrogantly the king insisted that they meet his demands or forfeit their lives. When the magicians failed, the king ordered all the wise men of Babylon destroyed.

On their mission, the executioners came for Daniel and his friends. But this young man of faith dared to trust God. He sent word that if Nebuchadnezzar would give him a little time he would tell the king what he had dreamed and what the dream meant. Daniel and his three friends prayed earnestly because the lives of men were at stake. "Then was the secret revealed unto Daniel in a night vision."

For every answered prayer in time of deep need, I join Daniel in his thanksgiving:

"Praise be to the name of God forever and ever; wisdom and power are his. He changes times and seasons; he sets up kings and deposes them. He gives wisdom to the wise and knowledge to the discerning. He reveals deep hidden things; he knows what lies in darkness, and light dwells in him.

"*I thank and praise you, O God of my fathers: You have given me wisdom and power, you have made known to me what we asked of you*" (2:20-23, NIV).

▼

Scripture: Daniel 3—6
The Story: Daniel 4:19-27

I praised the Most High; I honored and glorified him who lives forever (Dan. 4:34; all quotes from NIV).

One Good Life

He was only a displaced Jew, but he was the servant of God. He moved the world for good through his ministry to four heathen kings. Today we measure Daniel's influence by listening to the prayers of Nebuchadnezzar, whose dream Daniel interpreted, and who was touched by Daniel's life.

When Daniel's three Hebrew companions were spared in the furnace, Nebuchadnezzar proclaimed: "Praise be to the God of Shadrach, Meshach and Abednego, who has sent his angel and rescued his servants! They trusted in him and defied the king's command and were willing to give up their lives rather than serve or worship any god except their own God. Therefore I decree that the people of any nation or language who say anything against the God of Shadrach, Meshach and Abednego be cut into pieces . . . for no other god can save in this way" (3:28-29).

A little later Nebuchadnezzar sent a testimony of faith across his empire: "To the peoples, nations and men of every language, who live in all the world: May you prosper greatly!

"It is my pleasure to tell you about the miraculous signs and wonders that the Most High God has performed for me. How great are his signs, how mighty his wonders! His kingdom is an eternal kingdom; his dominion endures from generation to generation" (4:1-3).

After Nebuchadnezzar's seven years of insanity which Daniel had foretold, we read the king's declaration of praise: "At the end of that time, I, Nebuchadnezzar, raised my eyes toward heaven, and my sanity was restored. Then I praised the Most High; I honored and glorified him who lives forever. His dominion is an eter-

nal dominion; his kingdom endures from generation to generation.
. . . He does as he pleases with the powers of heaven and the
peoples of the earth. No one can hold back his hand or say to him:
'What have you done?'

"Now I, Nebuchadnezzar, praise and exalt and glorify the
King of heaven, because everything he does is right and all his
ways are just. And those who walk in pride he is able to humble"
(4:34-37).

*My Father, I do not minister to kings or presidents. But grant that
some life may be moved toward You because I have passed his way. In
Jesus' name I ask. Amen.*

▼

Scripture: Daniel 7—8; 11—12

After prophesying during the 43 years of Nebuchadnezzar's reign,
Daniel lived another 25 years under three other Babylonian kings.
He must have been at least 85 when he read the handwriting on
the wall that foretold the fall of Babylon and the death of King
Belshazzar. In the new empire of Persia, Daniel's ministry continued under Darius and Cyrus. During these years God revealed
to him the visions of the near and far future that we read today.

The Story: Daniel 7:1-14

**I looked, and there . . . was one like a son of man,
coming with the clouds of heaven. . . . He was
given authority, glory and sovereign power . . .
His dominion is an everlasting dominion that will
not pass away (Dan. 7:13-14, NIV).**

The Meaning of Prophecy

I would like to know more about these prophecies. Daniel himself
asked: "My lord, what will the outcome of all this be?" (12:8, NIV).
To our inquisitive minds God seems to reply as to Daniel, "Go your

way . . . because the words are closed up and sealed until the time of the end" (12:9, NIV). I would like to know more, but I am grateful for all that God has revealed to us through His servant.

Some of these prophecies were fulfilled during the 500 years between Daniel's death and the birth of Christ. The "four winds" symbolize the whole world. The four "beasts" represent four world powers that arose and fell in succession. In prophetic writings the "horns" symbolize military strength; the "wings" speak of swiftness, and the "eyes" of intelligence. From secular history we recognize here the wars between the two great powers of Persia and Greece—a conflict that threatened the Jews who had resettled in Palestine. I am glad that God gave His people some forewarning of their external dangers, and some assurance that He was still in control of their national destiny.

I am grateful for other prophecies whose fulfillment extends to our times, and beyond. Isaiah predicted the birth of Jesus, which was fulfilled: "Unto us a child is born, unto us a son is given" (9:6). Daniel foretells Christ's second coming, in which we believe: "Before me was one like a son of man, coming with the clouds of heaven" (7:13, NIV).

To be forewarned is to be forearmed. I am glad that God has alerted us to the persecution that His people may face at the end of time. In our lifetimes thousands in other lands have died for their faith. Prophecy warns us of yet harder times to come. Evil powers "will speak against the Most High and oppress his saints and try to change the set times and the laws" (7:25, NIV).

But in spite of the worst our enemies can do, God declares that His people shall finally be victorious. Satan's "power will be taken away and completely destroyed forever. Then the sovereignty, power and greatness of the kingdoms under the whole heaven will be handed over to the saints, the people of the Most High. His kingdom will be an everlasting kingdom, and all rulers will worship and obey him. This is the end of the matter" (7:26-28, NIV).

I don't understand all of it, but I like the way it ends—and I believe it is true. Dr. Roy Swim writes of 12:9-13: "God has His work among men to do. *Many shall be purified and made white, and tried.* True, *the wicked shall do wickedly . . . but the wise shall understand.* Let not those who trust in God fret. 'No man knoweth the hour' (Matt. 24:36), but in God's good time, when it is required, the meaning will come clear. *Blessed is he that waiteth*" (BBC).

Scripture: Daniel 9—10
The Story: Daniel 9:1-19

We do not make requests of you because we are righteous, but because of your great mercy (Dan. 9:18; all quotes from NIV).

I Pray for Another

In intercessory prayer we are most like our Lord who laid down His life for others.

Father, teach us to use Your channel of grace that brings life to another through our prayers on their behalf. And thank You for Daniel who gives us a model to follow.

Interceding is a self-forgetful ministry. Daniel writes: "I turned to the Lord God and pleaded with him in prayer and petition, in fasting, and in sackcloth and ashes" (9:3). We do not deny ourselves in order to persuade God to answer our prayers. But self-denial reflects our readiness to bear another's burden.

Do I have a deep concern for the salvation of someone whom I love? Or for a neighbor? Perhaps through failure of my influence I bear some measure of responsibility. Daniel recognized that his people had sinned, and that he was one of them. He testifies: "I prayed to the Lord my God and confessed . . . We have sinned and done wrong. We have been wicked and rebelled; we have turned away from your commands and laws" (9:4-5).

We pray most effectively when we get beyond our personal interest in the answer. When our concern merges most completely with God's desires, we interecede most perfectly. Then we pray with Daniel: "Now, our God, hear the prayers and petitions of your servant. For your sake, O Lord, look with favor . . . Give ear, O God, and hear; open your eyes and see the desolation . . . We do not make requests of you because we are righteous, but because of your great mercy. O Lord, listen! O Lord, forgive! O Lord, hear and act! For your sake, O my God, do not delay, because your city and your people bear your Name" (9:17-19).

When we pray in this spirit, God gives us what we ask—or He will give us something better. From intercessory prayer we arise with a new sense of fellowship with God himself.

> *O Thou in whose presence my soul takes delight,*
> *On whom in affliction I call,*
> *My Comfort by day and my Song in the night,*
> *My Hope, my Salvation, my All!*
>
> —JOSEPH SWAIN

▼

☐ WEEK 36, THURSDAY   HOSEA

Hosea was one of God's prophets to the Northern Kingdom. Preaching before 721 B.C., he is one of the eighth-century prophets, contemporary with Jonah, Amos, Isaiah, and Micah. Hosea cried out chiefly against the evils of idolatry and prophesied God's judgment against the nation. He may have been taken into exile by the Assyrians when Samaria fell in 721 B.C. In spite of his ringing reminders of God's imminent judgment against sin, Hosea was the first of the prophets to proclaim the nature of Jehovah in terms of love.

Scripture: Hosea 1; 3
The Story: Hosea 1:2-11; 3:1-5

Go, show your love . . . again . . . Love . . . as the Lord loves the Israelites (Hos. 3:1, NIV).

Show Your Love Again

George Matheson, a young English minister, was engaged to be married. When his financée learned that a disease would soon leave George blind, she broke their engagement. Out of his heart-break, he went home and wrote our immortal hymn, "O Love That Wilt Not Let Me Go."

However we may understand the story of Hosea and Gomer, one message is clear: It is better to love than not to love. It is better to keep on loving than to begin hating. When Hosea had every reason to give up on an unworthy Gomer, God counseled him, "Go, show your love to your wife again . . . Love her as the Lord loves the Israelites."

Our human way is to love another because she is lovely and responsive. God's way is to love because she needs His love. A friend married a woman with a son born out of wedlock. There was some friction between husband and wife; also between step-father and son because the boy was not his child. But he, and all of us, need to remember that every child needs love. And the one for whom love does not come easily often needs an extra supply. That is why God counsels each of us who is tempted to give up, "Go, show your love again."

Unselfish love may not solve every problem in strained human relationships, but love will solve the problem better than any other action.

God used the example of His love for Israel to help Hosea find a happier marriage. He also used the prophet's genuine love for Gomer to help him understand God's love for Israel and for us.

It is always better to love than not to love. We believe it! When we try it, we are glad that we did. When love succeeds, we heal the strained relationship and rejoice in God's wise counsel. Even if love fails, we have the consciousness that we have followed God's advice. We know the joy of His approval, and we are better persons.

It is God's love that has saved us—and daily helps us. Today I yield myself anew to be shaped by the Savior.

> *O love that wilt not let me go,*
> *I rest my weary soul in Thee.*
> *I give Thee back the life I owe,*
> *That in Thine ocean depths its flow*
> *May richer, fuller be.*
> —GEORGE MATHESON

Scripture: Hosea 2; 4—6
The Story: Hosea 2:13-20

The word of the Lord that came to Hosea (Hos. 1:1; all quotes from NIV).

Let's Listen to Hosea

When God speaks, we do well to listen. Seldom has He had a better communicator than Hosea. With the passion and words of a poet, this prophet declares God's judgment and love; man's sin and redemption. His words have become proverbs for all who read the English Bible.

The God who woos our souls promises: "I will betroth you to me forever; I will betroth you in righteousness and justice, in love and compassion. I will betroth you in faithfulness, and you will acknowledge the Lord" (2:19-20).

He who depends on truth for the success of His work sighs, "My people are destroyed from lack of knowledge. . . . you have rejected knowledge" (4:6).

In every conversation where men discuss the impact of influence, we hear the echo of Hosea, "Like people, like priests" (4:9).

When men have sinned to the point of no return, even God himself must bow His head in sorrowful failure: "Ephraim is joined to idols; leave him alone!" (4:17).

When our repentant spirits hear God's invitation, Hosea gives words to express our longing: "Come, let us return to the Lord. He has torn us to pieces but he will heal us; he has injured us but he will bind up our wounds. . . . Let us acknowledge the Lord; let us press on to acknowledge him. As surely as the sun rises, he will appear; he will come to us like the winter rains, like the spring rains that water the earth" (6:1, 3).

Of the swift and terrible consequences of sinning, Hosea sighs: "They sow the wind and reap the whirlwind" (8:7). But of God's good plan for us he exhorts, "Sow for yourselves righteousness, reap the fruit of unfailing love, and break up your unplowed ground; for it is time to seek the Lord, until he comes and showers righteousness on you" (10:12).

Today I rejoice in God's final word to the repentant sinner: "I will heal their waywardness and love them freely, for my anger has turned away from them" (14:4).

Thank You, God, for loving us. And thank you, Hosea, for telling us of His love.

▼

Scripture: Hosea 7—10
The Story: Hosea 9:1-3, 7, 15-17

It is time to seek the Lord, until he comes and showers righteousness upon you (Hos. 10:12; all quotes from NIV).

What Is Wrong with Wrong?

Try reading Hosea 7—10, marking each verse with S for sin, J for judgment, or R for restoration. My own tally comes out: sin, 27; judgment, 35; restoration, 2.

Why come down so hard on evil? What is so wrong with wrongdoing? In clear language Hosea shows us.

✔ It is sin that keeps our lives from healing and wholeness: "Whenever I would restore the fortunes of my people, whenever I would heal Israel, the sins of Ephraim are exposed" (7:1).

✔ I can never be right with God while trying to hide an unconfessed sin from Him: "They do not realize that I remember all their evil deeds" (7:2).

✔ Sin is as treacherous as a defective weapon upon which my

367

life depends: "They do not turn to the Most High; they are like a faulty bow" (7:16).

✔ The further we go in sin, the worse it gets: "They sow the wind and reap the whirlwind" (8:7).

✔ Sin always ends in utter futility: "The stalk has no head; it will produce no flour. . . . Ephraim is blighted, their root is withered, they yield no fruit" (8:7; 9:16).

✔ God knows that sin is self-destructive. He has therefore sworn that we shall not get away with it: "The days of punishment are coming, the days of reckoning are at hand. . . . Because of their sinful deeds I will drive them out of my house" (9:7, 15).

But that need not happen. God's prediction of judgment on sin is always followed by His appeal to repent and be saved. "Stop doing wrong, learn to do right! . . . 'Come now, let us reason together,' says the Lord. 'Though your sins are like scarlet, they shall be as white as snow'" (Isa. 1:16, 18).

"It is time to seek the Lord until he comes and showers righteousness upon you." Today my heart responds:

> *Just as I am, and waiting not*
> *To rid my soul of one dark blot,*
> *To Thee whose blood can cleanse each spot,*
> *O Lamb of God, I come! I come!*
> —CHARLOTTE ELLIOTT

▼

☐ WEEK 37, SUNDAY HOSEA

Scripture: Hosea 11—14
The Story: Hosea 11:1-4; 14:1-9
    In 14:2, for "calves of our lips" (KJV), read "our sacrifices of praise."

I am living and strong! I look after you and care for you. I am like an evergreen tree, yielding my fruit to you throughout the year. My mercies never fail (Hos. 14:8, TLB).

God Is Good

God is great, God is good;
And we thank Him for our food.

How much richer our lives would be if we ordered them by the truth of this children's simple table grace. Hosea's prophecies have shouted the story of man's disobedience and the certainty of divine judgment. But he never lets us forget that God is good.

How much happiness has come to us just by being born human persons? Today Hosea reminds us of these birthright blessings. In 11:1 we see that God has been with us from birth; He gave life and a happy childhood. He created us in His own image, called us His sons, and showered us with His love.

In verse 3 we are reminded that God gave the ability to learn what we need to know. He has encouraged us, like a fond parent supporting a baby just learning to walk. He daily preserves our lives by the immunity system of the body and by the healing processes that begin immediately to restore cuts and bruises.

When we are unkind, God is still kind to us. When we are unlovely, He loves us. When we make trouble for ourselves, He lifts the yoke of guilt and hurt. When we are hungry, He feeds us.

He gives all of these blessings without our even asking; but He offers much more when we recognize His love and return it.

There is special revelation of His good way for us to go. "I spoke to you repeatedly by the prophets; I multiplied visions for you, and by the prophets I appealed to you in parables" (12:10, NBV). Now, in Christ He has more clearly "spoken unto us by his Son" (Heb. 1:2).

When we resist God's will, He reminds us of our ingratitude and folly: "You are against me, against your helper" (13:9, NIV).

In God's care we do not fear death. In return for our love and obedience He promises, "I will ransom them from the power of the grave; I will redeem them from death. Where, O death, are your plagues? Where, O grave, is your destruction?" (13:14, NIV).

With Hosea I remember God's goodness, and my heart joins with the Psalmist:

"Bless the Lord, O my soul: and all that is within me, bless his holy name" (Ps. 103:1).

Scripture: Joel 1—3
The Story: Joel 1:1-4; 2:12-14, 25, 28-29
**Return to the Lord your God, for he is gracious
and compassionate, slow to anger and abounding in love** (Joel 2:13; all quotes from NIV).

Turn from Your Sin

Has some calamity ever brought me face-to-face with my responsibility to God? If so, I can appreciate the Book of Joel.

In the days of King Josiah an invasion of locusts devastated
Judah. Did God send the locusts as punishment for the sins of the
people? Joel says that He did. In the New Testament, however, Jesus
teaches us that these natural calamities fall on the good as well as
on the evil. But in the same breath He warns, "Except ye repent, ye
shall all likewise perish" (Luke 13:1-5).

We believe that God does sometimes hurt us with suffering,
and chill us with fear to remind us that we are ignoring Him. And
we are sure that God may use even what He does not send to
remind us of our need to repent. This is the message of Joel.

Has God reminded me through some tragedy that I have
sinned against Him? Whatever the reminder, the right response is
clear: "Return to the Lord your God, for he is gracious and compassionate, slow to anger and abounding in love . . . Who knows but
that he may turn and have pity and leave behind a blessing"
(2:13-14).

Have I gone so far in sin that my life is deeply scarred, and
others have suffered because of my failure? If so, God has a personal promise for me: "I will repay you for the years the locusts
have eaten . . . and you will praise the name of the Lord your God,
who has worked wonders for you" (2:25-26).

The way of repentance leads on to the paths of hope and to

the joys of a new life. None is excluded because he is too old or too young. None is barred because of social standing or sex differences: "I will pour out my Spirit on all people. Your sons and daughters will prophesy, your old men will dream dreams, your young men will see visions. Even on my servants, both men and women, I will pour out my Spirit in those days" (2:28-29).

My glad heart responds to the message of Joel. I testify that what the prophet promises is true:

> There is welcome for the sinner,
> And more graces for the good.
> There is mercy with the Saviour,
> There is healing in His blood.
> —F. W. FABER

Scripture: Amos 1—3
The Story: Amos 2:6—3:2

Surely the Sovereign Lord does nothing without revealing his plan to his servants the prophets (Amos 3:7; all quotes from NIV).

Let's Meet Amos

"A dull rumble of thunder rolled out of the desert of Tekoa. Out of the desert in the voice of a man. Bearded, brawny, afire, Amos was God's thunder prelude to the gathering storm" (Frank S. Mead).

Amos was a shepherd living in Tekoa. He became God's prophet to Israel in her center of idol worship at Bethel. Here was no weeping Hosea. There are times when God uses His servants with gentle spirits. But they are not the men for the hour when the house is on fire and immediate action is needed.

For all his loud voice, God gave Amos a keen understanding of men. From 1:3 to 2:5, before he exposed Israel's own evils, the prophet took his hearers on a tour of the sins of their neighbors: Damascus, Gaza of the Philistines, Tyre, Edom, Ammon, and Moab. The crowd cheered him on. Coming closer to home the preacher exposed the sins of Judah, and the crowd grew uneasy. Where would the finger of judgment point next?

Amos did not keep his Israelite hearers waiting: "This is what the Lord says: 'For three sins of Israel, even for four, I will not turn back my wrath. They sell the righteous for silver, and the needy for a pair of sandals. They trample on the heads of the poor as upon the dust of the ground and deny justice to the oppressed'" (2:6-7).

Israel's sins were especially offensive to God because she had enjoyed such great opportunities to do better. He declared: "You only have I chosen of all the families of the earth; therefore I will punish you for all your sins" (3:2).

Where do I stand before God and the message of His prophet? Are there sins in my life that need to be confessed and forsaken? Are there evils in my land that need to be exposed and remedied?

Father, I open my heart to the voice of Your Spirit. I join the Psalmist in his commitment to You:

"I will listen to what God the Lord will say; he promises peace to his people, his saints—but let them not return to folly" (Ps. 85:8).

▼

☐ **WEEK 37, WEDNESDAY**   AMOS

Scripture: Amos 4—6
The Story: Amos 4:12; 5:4-6, 14-15

Seek good, not evil, that you may live. Then the Lord God Almighty will be with you (Amos 5:14; all quotes from NIV).

Our Seeking God

Nothing but sin separates us from God; but sin always does. That is why He is so insistent that we recognize Him as God. Israel was guilty of social injustice, but her real sin was refusing to do the will of God. If only He can get us to listen to Him and follow His law, our unfair treatment of others will cease, and we shall find eternal life. That is why He is so persistent in His efforts to win us.

The seeking God woos us, hoping to win our love and loyalty. Through Amos He pleads: "Seek me and live; do not seek Bethel, do not go to Gilgal, do not journey to Beersheba. For Gilgal will surely go into exile, and Bethel will be reduced to nothing. . . .

"Seek good, not evil, that you may live. Then the Lord God Almighty will be with you . . . Hate evil, love good; maintain justice in the courts. Perhaps the Lord God Almighty will have mercy on the remnant of Joseph" (5:4-5, 14-15).

When we do not respond to His love, God sometimes puts pressure on us. To a resisting, rebellious people the seeking God laments: "'I gave you empty stomachs in every city and lack of bread in every town, yet you have not returned to me,' declares the Lord. . . .

"'People staggered from town to town for water but did not get enough to drink, yet you have not returned to me,' declares the Lord.

"'Locusts devoured your fig and olive trees, yet you have not returned to me,' declares the Lord. . . . 'Therefore this is what I will do to you, Israel, and because I will do this to you, prepare to meet your God'" (4:6, 8-9, 12).

Father, if I have rebelled, I confess my pride. If I have sinned, forgive and restore. With the returning prodigal I sing:

> *Out of my sickness into Thy health,*
> *Out of my want and into Thy wealth,*
> *Out of my sin and into thyself,*
> *Jesus, I come to Thee.*
> —WM. T. SLEEPER

▼

□ WEEK 37, THURSDAY   AMOS

Scripture: Amos 7—9
The Story: Amos 7:1-9; 9:11-15

The Lord said, "Look, I am setting a plumb line among my people" (Amos 7:8, NIV).

I Will Restore

The character of a man is often revealed by the things against which he revolts. Amos showed true spiritual insight in his condemnation of material extravagance and physical self-indulgence—beds of ivory, lavish feasting, sensual music, alcoholic stimulants, and expensive perfumes for the body. God is always against selfishness and self-centered living.

Not many preachers, however, would get by with calling the society women of their congregations big, fat cows. But Amos wasn't counting on his salary that week; and a desperate situation called for violent language. In words so uncouth that they shocked the hearers, he shouted:

"Listen to this, you cows of Bashan, you women in high Samaria, you who defraud the poor and are hard on the needy, who tell your husbands, 'Let us have wine to drink!' As sure as I am God, the Lord Eternal swears, your day is coming" (4:1-2, Moffatt).

But we can take thunder from a man of God who is concerned for our souls; and Amos loved his people. Even his name means "burden bearer." With all of his blasting and predictions of destruction, Amos was a prophet of redemption. His final word in the book is a promise of hope.

"'In that day I will restore David's fallen tent. I will repair its broken places, restore its ruins, and build it as it used to be' . . . 'The days are coming,' declares the Lord, 'when the reaper will be overtaken by the plowman and the planter by the one treading grapes. New wine will drip from the mountains and flow from all the hills. I will bring back my exiled people Israel; they will rebuild the ruined cities and live in them. They will plant vineyards and drink their wine; they will make gardens and eat their fruit. I will plant Israel in their own land, never again to be uprooted from the land I have given them,' says the Lord your God" (9:11, 13-15, NIV).

With the Psalmist my heart responds:

"Thou, O Lord, art a God full of compassion, and gracious, long-suffering, and plenteous in mercy" (Ps. 86:15).

Scripture: Obadiah
The Story: Obadiah 1-21

Deliverers will go up on Mount Zion . . . And the kingdom will be the Lord's (Obad. 21; all quotes from NIV).

Thinking About God's Justice

The Book of Obadiah sounds negative, but the picture is no darker than the destiny of all who persist in opposing God and His people.

The prophecy reflects conditions in 586 B.C. after the fall of Jerusalem. It contains a warning to Moab but was probably meant to encourage the scattered remnants of Judah.

The Edomites, descendants of Esau, lived in the mountainous area south of the Dead Sea. Petra, the capital city, lay in a deep valley surrounded by 200-foot cliffs. It was accessible only through a 12-foot rift between sheer rock walls. The Edomites, an irreligious people, lived for food, spoils, and vengeance. They were clever, ruthless, and scheming—the very opposite of God's desire for His people.

In this brief message the prophet gives us clear insight into four profound elements in the righteousness of God.

✔ Vengeance does not belong to man, but the scales of justice must eventually be balanced in a moral world. And God will do it. He declares: "The pride of your heart has deceived you . . . Though you soar like the eagle and make your nest among the stars, from there I will bring you down" (vv. 3-4).

✔ God is against all who run roughshod over a weaker neighbor. "Because of the violence against your brother Jacob, you will be covered with shame; you will be destroyed forever" (v. 10).

✔ A righteous God does not permit us to remain idle spectators when we could relieve suffering. He charges Moab: "You stood aloof while strangers carried off his wealth and foreigners entered his gates and cast lots for Jerusalem" (v. 11).

✔ Righteousness does not permit us to gloat over a man who is hurting. God says: "You should not look down on your brother in the day of his misfortune, nor rejoice over the people of Judah in the day of their destruction" (v. 12).

I am glad that God has reserved to himself the right to judge and to punish. But I am also glad that He has determined that justice shall prevail. All evil shall finally come to an end. Only the righteous shall enjoy His kingdom. I believe it.

> *God is not dead, nor doth He sleep;*
> *The wrong shall fail, the right prevail,*
> *With peace on earth, goodwill to men.*
> —H. W. LONGFELLOW

▼

☐ **WEEK 37, SATURDAY**   **JONAH**

Scripture: Jonah 1—2
The Story: Jonah 2:1-10

In my distress I called to the Lord, and he answered me (Jonah 2:1; all quotes from NIV).

God Loves Me

When I say *Jonah,* what is the first word that comes to mind? Did you think of the *whale?* So did I. But when we really understand this book our response will be, *God's love.* Jonah failed more than once, but God did not give up on him.

The Israelites were God's chosen people, objects of His special love. But He chose them not primarily to privilege. God chose Israel in order that through their faith He might save others.

This divine yearning for the salvation of all men was "the

word of the Lord" that came to Jonah when God said to him, "Arise, go to Nineveh." The command was clear, but Jonah simply could not—or would not—do it. He tried to run away.

Francis Thompson describes the persistently pursuing Spirit of God as "the Hound of heaven." Seldom have the Lord's actions to reclaim a man been revealed more clearly than in His striving with Jonah. God sent the storm, the compassionate sailors, the great fish, the spirit of repentance; and then He brought Jonah safely to land.

Even though temporarily disobedient to God, a man cannot cut himself off completely from habits that righteous living has built into his life. Jonah still had his honesty. When questioned, he readily admitted who he was and what he had done; he would not lie. The prophet still had his sense of fairness—he would die for his own sin rather than let others suffer on his account. Also, he had found help in prayer too many times to refuse to call on God in his hour of trouble.

Chapter 2 is a psalm of praise written by Jonah after God had delivered him. In his prayer there is a good pattern for us. (1) Petition when in need: "In my distress I called to the Lord." (2) Confidence in God's mercy: "When my life was ebbing away, I remembered you, Lord." (3) The promise of obedience: "What I have vowed I will make good. Salvation comes from the Lord."

When we recall the story of Jonah, let us remember more than the whale.

> For the love of God is broader
> Than the measure of man's mind;
> And the heart of the Eternal
> Is most wonderfully kind.
> —F. W. FABER

▼

☐ **WEEK 38, SUNDAY**   **JONAH**

Scripture: Jonah 3—4
The Story: Jonah 3:1—4:10

**You are a gracious and compassionate God, slow
to anger and abounding in love** (Jonah 4:2, NIV).

God Loves All People

Haskell Miller notes, "The first and biggest whale that swallowed
this unhappy man was race prejudice." God loves all people—and
He wants us to share that spirit. I am glad that God was better than
Jonah. I am glad that no matter how deeply we have sinned, He
freely forgives us when we repent.

After the first day of Jonah's preaching, it appears the Nine-
vites became disturbed. And well they might. This convincing
prophet was predicting that the capital city of Assyria would be
destroyed within six weeks. The king himself set the example of
repentance—proclaiming a fast, wearing sackcloth, and sitting in
ashes. Heathen that he was, he had some faith in a forgiving God:
"Who can tell if God will turn and repent, and turn away from his
fierce anger, that we perish not?"

We do God's will most perfectly when His thoughts become
our thoughts—when our attitudes toward men become like His
compassionate love for them. It was at this point that Jonah failed.
He obeyed God to the letter in his preaching, but he lacked the
compassion of God.

When Nineveh repented, God spared the city but Jonah grew
angry. Now for the first time we are told why Jonah disobeyed God
and tried to flee to Tarshish. God was better than Jonah was willing
to become: "I knew that thou art a gracious God, and merciful,
slow to anger, and of great kindness." The prophet had praised
God for sparing his own life, but now was angry because God
showed compassion toward others.

But God is a patient Teacher. He still tried to break through
Jonah's wrong attitude and help him see human need as God sees
it. We do not know if He ever fully succeeded. The last word of this
blind and angry man was, "I do well to be angry"—angry because
God was compassionate!

I am glad that God's word is the last word in this book—it
points us to the kind of persons He wants us to be: "Should not I
feel grief over . . . persons who cannot discriminate between their
right hand and their left . . . ?" (NBV).

We who seek to follow Him can only respond with T. O. Chisholm:

>*Oh, to be like Thee! full of compassion,*
>*Loving, forgiving, tender, and kind,*
>*Helping the helpless, cheering the fainting,*
>*Seeking the wand'ring sinner to find.*

▼

☐ WEEK 38, MONDAY   MICAH

Scripture: Micah 1—4

Micah, like his contemporary prophets Isaiah and Amos, has much to say about God's anger against injustice and oppression. But because we have reflected on those truths recently, we turn our thoughts to Micah's equally relevant prophecies of God's coming kingdom.

The Story: Micah 4:1-7

We will walk in the name of the Lord our God for ever and ever (Mic. 4:5).

Peace on Earth

Under what conditions will Micah's prophecy become a reality? We believe that God's purpose for men is peace—but we live in a warring world. What, then, is our hope for the peace of which God here speaks?

The message was first addressed to Judah under the dark clouds of invasion and captivity. But the words point us beyond those ancient days to a time when God's purpose for all men shall be more fully realized. These Messianic prophecies certainly spoke of the birth of Jesus; but just as surely they point beyond His first advent to a day that we have not yet seen. Let us hear Micah's straightforward predictions in 20th-century English.

"In the last days Mount Zion will be the most renowned of all the mountains of the world, praised by all nations; people from all over the world will make pilgrimages there.

"'Come,' they will say to one another, 'let us visit the mountain of the Lord, and see the Temple of the God of Israel; he will tell us what to do, and we will do it.' For in those days the whole world will be ruled by the Lord from Jerusalem! He will issue his laws and announce his decrees from there.

"He will arbitrate among the nations, and dictate to strong nations far away. They will beat their swords into plowshares and their spears into pruning-hooks; nations shall no longer fight each other, for all war will end. There will be universal peace, and all the military academies and training camps will be closed down.

"Everyone will live quietly in his own home in peace and prosperity, for there will be nothing to fear. The Lord himself has promised this" (4:1-4, TLB).

Here is the peace that shall be ushered in when Christ returns to reign. We of the strife-torn 20th century can only fervently echo Paul's prayer: *"Our Lord, come!"* (1 Cor. 16:22, RSV).

▼

☐ WEEK 38, TUESDAY   MICAH

Scripture: Micah 5—7
The Story: Micah 5:2-5; 6:6-8; 7:18-19
   It appears that 5:3 is a prophecy of the suffering and salvation of the Jewish people as their destiny relates to the universal work of Christ.

As for me, I keep watch for the Lord, I wait in hope for God my Savior; my God will hear me (Mic. 7:7; all quotes from NIV).

"He Will . . . Shepherd His Flock"

I am grateful for the messages of Micah. Seven hundred years before Christ was born, God revealed three profound truths to His prophet.

God is forgiving. "Who is a God like you, who pardons sin and forgives the transgression of the remnant of his inheritance? You do not stay angry forever but delight to show mercy. You will again have compassion on us; you will tread our sins underfoot and hurl all our iniquities into the depths of the sea" (7:18-19).

God asks us to walk with Him in love and mercy. "With what shall I come before the Lord and bow down before the exalted God? Shall I come before him with burnt offerings, with calves a year old? Will the Lord be pleased with thousands of rams, with ten thousand rivers of oil? Shall I offer my firstborn for my transgression, the fruit of my body for the sin of my soul?

"He has showed you, O man, what is good. And what does the Lord require of you? To act justly and to love mercy and to walk humbly with your God" (6:6-8).

God has sent His Son to be our Savior. "But you, Bethlehem Ephrathah, though you are small among the clans of Judah, out of you will come for me one who will be ruler over Israel, whose origins are from of old, from ancient times. . . . He will stand and shepherd his flock in the strength of the Lord, in the majesty of the name of the Lord his God. And they will live securely, for then his greatness will reach to the ends of the earth. And he will be their peace" (5:2, 4-5).

In light of these truths I rejoice with David: "The Lord is my shepherd; I shall lack nothing. He makes me lie down in green pastures, he leads me beside quiet waters, he restores my soul. He guides me in the paths of righteousness for his name's sake. . . . Surely goodness and love will follow me all the days of my life, and I will dwell in the house of the Lord forever" (Ps. 23:1-3, 6).

Scripture: Nahum 1—3
The Story: Nahum 1:1-3; 3:7-11, 18-19

The Lord is good, a refuge in times of trouble. He cares for those who trust in him, but with an overwhelming flood ... he will pursue his foes (Nah. 1:7-8, NIV).

Understanding Nahum

For whom is the Lord jealous? Against whom does He take vengeance? To understand Nahum we must learn the answers to these questions.

Nahum lived in Judah; he prophesied there after Micah but before Jeremiah. In his time the great military threat to Palestine was the Assyrian Empire, with her capital city of Nineveh. A century earlier God had been gracious to this heathen land; He sent Jonah to preach to them. The people repented and God spared the city, but that repentance did not last. Only 30 years later the Assyrian armies laid siege to Samaria and destroyed the Jews of the Northern Kingdom. For the next 75 years Assyria constantly menaced Judah. The threat was relieved only when Nahum's prophecy came true, and Nineveh was destroyed by the Babylonian armies in 612 B.C.

Does Nahum seem obsessed with God's plans to punish Nineveh? Let us remember that the prophet's people were living under threat of national extinction. I am glad that God plans judgment for those who are the sworn enemies of the righteous.

The name Nahum means "comforter." It is encouraging to know that when we are on God's side, He is on our side. I am glad that He is jealous for the people who serve Him: "The Lord is good, a refuge in times of trouble. He cares for those who trust in him."

When we reflect on God's determination that evil must be destroyed, we are glad that the Lord who is "great in power" is also "slow to anger" (1:3). He sent Jonah to warn Nineveh before He revealed His awful vengeance in the days of Nahum.

But in the universal conflict between good and evil, one must finally prevail; the other must perish. We are glad that the Sovereign God is on the side of good, and that He stands against all that is evil.

We cringe at God's ultimate verdict against the wicked: "Nothing can heal your wound; your injury is fatal" (3:19, NIV). We cringe, but it is God's mercy that warns us of the outcome; it is His love that bids us avoid that consequence.

I can love a God who is "not willing that any should perish, but that all should come to repentance" (2 Pet. 3:9).

▼

Scripture: Habakkuk 1—3
The Story: Habakkuk 1:1-3, 13; 2:1-3, 14; 3:2, 17-18

The just shall live by his faith (Hab. 2:4).

God's Answer to My Why

When unreasonable pressures build up, reasonable persons ask why. Why must I be helpless in the face of injustice? Why are the wicked better off than the righteous?

Habakkuk lived about 600 B.C. just before the Exile to Babylon. His little book gives us: (1) the questions of a good man, (2) the wise counsel of a good God, and (3) the triumph of faith over frustration.

The first question he put to God was, Why don't You do something about the evils in Judah? "How long, O Lord, must I call for help, but you do not listen? . . . Why do you make me look at injustice? Why do you tolerate wrong?" (1:2-3; all quotes from NIV).

When God showed Habakkuk that He was going to use Babylon to punish Judah for her sin, the prophet's bafflement deepened.

He told God: "Your eyes are too pure to look on evil; you cannot tolerate wrong. Why then . . . are you silent while the wicked swallow up those more righteous than themselves?" (1:13).

When I am perplexed, do I listen to my doubts, or do I go to a place of prayer where God can talk to me? The prophet shows us the right procedure: "I will stand at my watch and station myself on the ramparts; I will look to see what he will say to me, and what answer I am to give to this complaint" (2:1).

God never fails us when we come with sincere questions. He bids us remember that although His answer be delayed, He is God, and He is committed to His righteous people. If I believe Him, my faith will bring me through. Read again 2:2-4, 14.

When I am open "to see what he will say to me," God brings understanding and reassurance. He says to my troubled whys: "Turn your thoughts from what you cannot understand to the eternal truths of which you are sure." When His answer takes possession of my spirit, I can join Habakkuk in his glad song of certainty:

"Though the fig tree does not bud and . . . though the olive crop fails and the fields produce no food . . . yet I will rejoice in the Lord, I will be joyful in God my Savior" (3:17-18).

Thank You, Lord, for Your answer to Habakkuk—and to me. Amen.

▼

☐ **WEEK 38, FRIDAY**   **ZEPHANIAH**

Scripture: Zephaniah 1—3
The Story: Zephaniah 1:14—2:3

Seek righteousness, seek humility; perhaps you will be sheltered on the day of the Lord's anger (Zeph. 2:3; all quotes from NIV).

I Want to Be Ready

David asks a question to which every man and woman must find the answer: "Who may ascend the hill of the Lord? Who may stand in his holy place?" (Ps. 24:3).

In this short prophecy Zephaniah refers 25 times to "the day of the Lord." Among the Hebrews there was a widespread belief that God would appear in the near future and bring some great victory to them. The prophets knew that God did not automatically bless His chosen people. What the day of His visitation brought would depend on how they had lived. It would be a day of blessing for the righteous but a day of terror for the wicked.

How can we be comfortable in the presence of God? To guide us to that answer Zephaniah describes some of the things that God is for and the things that He is against.

God is for goodness and against wickedness. "The wicked will have only heaps of rubble . . . I will bring distress on the people and they will walk like blind men, because they have sinned against the Lord" (1:3, 17).

God is against backsliding. "I will cut off from this place . . . those who turn back from following the Lord and neither seek the Lord nor inquire of him" (1:4, 6).

God opposes the indifferent: "I will . . . punish those who are complacent . . . who think 'the Lord will do nothing either good or bad'" (1:12).

God resists the proud. Of Moab, Zephaniah hears the Lord say, "This is what they will get in return for their pride . . . The Lord will be awesome to them when he destroys all the gods of this land" (2:10-11).

God rejects the rebellious. "Woe to the city of the oppressors, rebellious and defiled! . . . She does not trust in the Lord, she does not draw near to her God" (3:1-2).

Jesus said "the day of the Lord" would be like a shepherd dividing the sheep from the goats. The prophet therefore exhorts us: "seek righteousness, seek humility; perhaps you will be sheltered on the day of the Lord's anger" (2:3).

Father, I want to be ready for that day. I want to hear You say to me: "Do not fear . . . The Lord your God is with you, he is mighty to save" (3:16-17). Then shall I come before You with thanksgiving and come into Your presence with joy.

Haggai and Zechariah were studied in their historical context, during the rebuilding of the Temple in Jerusalem after the Exile, about 520 B.C.

Malachi ("My Messenger") preached to the Jews in Judah 70 years later, just before Nehemiah returned and rebuilt the walls. His prophecy is the last book of the Old Testament but does not record the last events. The issues with which he dealt were similar to the problems faced a few years later by Ezra and Nehemiah.

Malachi's style is more like a probing teacher than a proclaiming prophet. He gives voice to questions in his listeners' minds, then reminds them of facts that push them to right conclusions.

Scripture: Malachi 1—4
The Story: Malachi 2:17—3:10
Guard yourself in your spirit, and do not break faith (Mal. 2:16; all quotes from NIV).

Five Probing Questions

The issues that threatened godly living in 450 B.C. seem sharply relevant to our 20th century.

Am I giving God my best? (1:6-8) We no longer offer animal sacrifices as did these ancient Jews, but we must bring our best to God. Paul writes to New Testament Christians, "I urge you, brothers, in view of God's mercy, to offer [yourselves] as living sacrifices, holy and pleasing to God" (Rom. 12:1). Nothing less than placing our all upon the altar is worthy of God, and nothing less will secure His unreserved blessing upon our lives.

Does my homelife honor God? (2:14-16) Malachi gives us one of the strong Bible injunctions for lifelong marriages: "The Lord is acting as the witness between you and the wife of your youth, because you have broken faith with her, though she is your partner, the wife of your marriage covenant. Has not the Lord made them one? In flesh and spirit they are his. And why one? Because he was seeking godly offspring. So guard yourself in your spirit and do not break faith with the wife of your youth. 'I hate divorce,' says the Lord God of Israel."

Am I paying God's tithe? (3:7-12) If we do not support the work of God, it is because our hearts are far from Him. We do not believe that His cause is as important as the things for which we spend our money. If we have been failing at this point, God gives us His gracious offer of renewal: "Return to me and I will return to you."

Does my faith in God hold firm when things go wrong? (3:14-15) God is forever concerned with good, and He is opposed to all that is evil. When righteousness seemed not to pay off immediately, men of Judah complained, "What did we gain by carrying out his requirements? . . . Certainly the evildoers prosper, and even those who challenge God escape." There is no greater blasphemy than this—to defame a holy God by charging Him with indifference to wrong.

Am I living for God's future? (4:1-2) We never rightly understand God's plan if we think only of today. God's servant counts on God's future. Malachi here points us to the Christian's final hope: "Surely the day is coming . . . All the arrogant and every evildoer will be stubble, and that day . . . will set them on fire . . . But for you who revere my name, the sun of righteousness will rise with healing in its wings."

I want to be ready for that day.

THE END OF THE OLD TESTAMENT

Matthew, Mark, and Luke are called Synoptic Gospels: all three tell the story of Jesus in a similar way. Mark is believed by some to have been written first, and Matthew and Luke both could have borrowed materials from Mark; but each one was definitely a writer on his own.

For our meditations, I have tried to avoid duplication and to select materials unique to the Gospel from which they are drawn.

Scripture: Matthew 1—4
The Story: Matthew 1:18-25

He did what the angel of the Lord had commanded him (Matt. 1:24; all quotes from NIV).

When Believing Is Hard

The New Testament opens with a miracle of God and the obedience of a woman and a man. This blending of divine revelation and human faith always brings tension. But that blend lifts our lives to the heights God has planned for us.

Jesus came to bring to us God himself clothed in human flesh. The angel said to Mary, "The Holy Spirit will come upon you, and the power of the Most High will overshadow you. So the holy one to be born will be called the Son of God" (Luke 1:35).

This was the miracle—and Mary accepted her role of obedience. "I am the Lord's servant . . . May it be to me as you have said." But she had not told Joseph—or he could not believe her story.

Just as God chose Mary to be the mother of our Lord, He also chose Joseph to be head of the family and father in the home. For this role Joseph had sterling qualities. He was both a righteous man and a kind person. It would be wrong to overlook Mary's apparent sin, but he was too kind to carry out the law and stone her for infidelity. He must divorce her, but it would be done as kindly as possible. He believed that

> Kindness is to do and say
> The kindest thing in the kindest way.

God, however, had planned yet another miracle for the care of His Son. In Joseph's troubled sleep, an angel appeared with assurance and instruction: "Joseph, son of David, do not be afraid to take Mary home as your wife, because what is conceived in her is from the Holy Spirit. She will give birth to a son, and you are to give him the name Jesus, because he will save his people from their sins" (1:20-21).

How different life looked when Joseph wakened! Agonizing doubts vanished with the night. Instead of dreading that Mary's child would be the offspring of shame, there came a divine certainty; in this experience, both he and she were to be servants of God. All the answers were not yet clear, but Joseph knew the duty that lay before him. His obedience was as swift as it was glad. He believed; and faith lifted the burden from him.

I am glad that it is always thus when God speaks and I obey.

▼

☐ **WEEK 39, MONDAY**   **MATTHEW**

Scripture: Matthew 5

Chapter 5 opens a long teaching section in Matthew's Gospel.

The Story: Matthew 5:38-48

Love your enemies . . . that ye may be the children of your Father which is in heaven (Matt. 5:44-45).

The Way of Love

Jesus asks us to consider, What is the right way to treat a person who has done us wrong? The natural response is revenge; he hurt me, so I'll hurt him as much as I can. In the Old Testament God took the first step toward making us like himself in fairness and justice. He says: No more retaliation than the hurt you received. You must not kill a man for putting out your eye. Justice says, No more than "an eye for an eye, and a tooth for a tooth." That is certainly better than vengeance unlimited.

But in the New Testament Jesus bids me go further than justice. "I say unto you, Love your enemies, bless them that curse you, do good to them that hate you, and pray for them which despitefully use you, and persecute you; that ye may be the children of your Father which is in heaven."

If I really want to live in God's way, I must forget some injuries done to me. I can't even get even! I am not permitted to return a little evil for a lot of evil. Instead, when I have been wronged I am told to love the one who hurt me. I must bless him who curses me, do good to the man who hates me, and pray for the people who don't like me.

That seems hard, but Jesus says it is right. It is right because love is always better than hatred; forgiveness is better than to go on fighting. Someone must break the vicious circle of resentment and retaliation. That's the way Jesus did it. That's the way God wants it. With the help of His Holy Spirit, I'll strive for it.

But if you are like me, you can't think of an enemy who has set out to hurt you. How then can we put this principle to work today? Ah, yes. Love; bless; do good; pray.

Thank You, Lord, for that answer. I can think of someone who needs a little extra love today. I can bless someone by giving him the benefit of the doubt; I can credit him with right motives. There is some good that I can do for someone before sundown. There is someone for whom I can pray.

Master, teach me to follow Your way of love today. Amen.

Scripture: Matthew 6—7
The Story: Matthew 6:1-18

Your Father who sees in secret will reward you
(Matt. 6:6, RSV).

We Do It for God

Almsgiving, praying, and fasting were highly regarded among the Jews; so, also, are they among Christians. A loving concern for the needy, also prayer and self-denial for the work of God are high-level Christian virtues. But doing them from wrong motives spoils them.

Jesus warns us, "Beware of practicing your piety before men in order to be seen by them" (6:1, RSV). The key issue is "in order to be seen by them." If we give publicly in order to impress others with our generosity, Jesus says esteem of others is all we get. Such giving is better than failing to be generous, but it is not yet Christian.

The essence of Christlikeness is making God important in our lives. What we do as Christians is a love service offered to Him. Our best giving is when only He knows about it. Our best prayers are the conversations between Him and us alone. Our most Christian self-denial is a secret known only to God and us.

This is not to deny the importance of example, challenge, and human influence in the church. Generous giving has stimulated others to give; sincere public prayers have moved other persons to draw closer to God; known self-denial has encouraged more self-less service by others.

The point at issue is the motive. To perform our Christian duties in order to impress others is unchristian. To perform those same duties publicly when appropriate, and to be glad for any encouragement they give to others, is right. But even this is danger-ous because being well thought of by others can so easily lead us to being religious in order to be well thought of.

Today I want my Christian duties to be done only because of

my love for God. For this day, let them be between God and me alone. Today I want to forget myself and my needs. I want to put first in my prayer what Jesus put first:

"Our Father which art in heaven, Hallowed be thy name. Thy kingdom come. Thy will be done in earth, as it is in heaven. Amen."

▼

Scripture: Matthew 8—9
The Story: Matthew 9:18-31

Believe ye that I am able to do this? (Matt. 9:28).

What Miracle Do I Need?

That is the right question. We could have asked, What miracle am I hoping for? What miracle am I expecting? For what miracle do I have faith? All are appropriate questions, but the first seems to be the most promising route to God's blessings. We have needs, and our Lord has compassion. He wants to help us.

Do I believe Christ can do for me what I need? Even if it is something extraordinary? Even if it calls for the supernatural? Then these two chapters should help us. In them Matthew lists half of the 20 miracles recorded in his entire Gospel; 3 are given in the 13 verses we have read. If the miracle I need is no greater than curing an incurable hemorrhage, or healing blind eyes, or raising a little girl from the dead—Christ can do it!

What is my part in my miracle? From these accounts the human need seems to come first. Christ then asks us to believe in His power and to trust His compassionate love. In 5 of these 10 miracles Jesus asked people about their faith; or He told them that they had their miracle because they had faith in Him.

Even so, it is God's power that performs the miracle. My faith does not have to be perfect. I may be blessed with a miracle in spite of great human weakness. William Barclay points out that the ruler of the synagogue had an *imperfect motive;* he came to Jesus only as a last resort. The woman with the incurable hemorrhage had an *immature faith;* she looked for some kind of magic in touching His robe. The two blind men had an *incorrect theology;* they looked to Jesus as "the Son of David," the common Jewish phrase for a military Messiah.

Barclay concludes: "It does not matter how we come to Christ. No matter how inadequately and how imperfectly, His love and His arms are open to receive us. . . . It is not how we come that matters; it is that we should come at all; because He is willing to accept us as we are, and He is able to make us what we ought to be."

Lord Jesus, You know the miracle I need. I believe You can do it. I come with my need. Amen.

▼

☐ WEEK 39, THURSDAY   MATTHEW

Scripture: Matthew 10—12

In Matt. 10:5 6, the restriction of gospel ministry to the Jews was only a temporary rule. Israel must first be given opportunity to accept their Messiah. After Pentecost the Gentiles would be evangelized (BBC).

The Story: Matthew 9:35—10:8

Freely you have received, freely give (Matt. 10:8, NIV).

Penetrate Your World*

Three days ago we read Jesus' word to His followers: "Ye are the salt of the earth" (Matt. 5:13). Whatever salt is applied to, it invariably penetrates. Our Lord is saying to us who follow Him, "You, My followers, are the salt which simply must permeate and penetrate society if it is to have health and stability."

What Jesus said there in a figure, He says literally elsewhere: "As my Father hath sent me, even so send I you" (John 20:21). He was moved with compassion for human need. He says to us in simple, uncomplicated language, "Go, preach . . . Heal the sick . . . cast out devils: freely ye have received, freely give."

He asks no more of me than He asked of himself. He calls me to the same service. He sends me to similar situations. He intends that I shall contribute to the health and well-being of my little world.

But how can I go? I go as He went—in communion and in cooperation with the Father. In one prayer meeting we were preparing for our forthcoming revival services. We were told that every effort for Christ must begin with prayer. And it must. But in the benediction God's servant said, "Lord, I do not pray as a way of getting out of things; I pray as a way of getting involved in them." And I do.

The uniqueness of Christianity is our willingness to be lost in giving ourselves for the common good. We must be prepared to lose our lives, laying them down in self-giving for the sake of others.

Christ calls me to serve, but I do not do it alone. He and I are in this together. He has promised never to leave me on my own. His Spirit is with me—always.

No matter what my calling may be in life, no matter what career God has put me in, no matter what contribution I can make, we do it together. It is Christ in me, and I in Him. But I am involved.

> *O Master, let me walk with Thee*
> *In lowly paths of service free.*
> *Tell me Thy secret; help me bear*
> *The strain of toil, the fret of care.*
> —WASHINGTON GLADDEN

*Adapted from W. Phillip Keller, *Salt for Society,* 94-97.

Scripture: Matthew 13—15

Matthew 13 has been titled "Parables by the Sea." In it we find five of Jesus' teaching stories. Here also is the Master's answer to the question, "Why do you speak . . . in parables?" (v. 10, NIV). Other groups of Jesus' parables are found in Matthew 21—22; 24—25; and in Luke 14—16.

The Story: Matthew 13:1-8, 18-23

Other seed fell on good soil, where it produced a crop—a hundred, sixty, or thirty times what was sown (Matt. 13:8, NIV).

Sow the Seed

Yesterday Jesus sent us out to witness to our world. Today He forewarns us against discouragement and reminds us of the rich rewards.

It was time for barley sowing. Perhaps a farmer on the hillside in full view of the crowd on the lakeshore gave Jesus opportunity to make His message graphic.

"Hearken," said Jesus to focus attention. Then, with a gesture toward the farmer on the hill, He began: "Behold, a sower went forth to sow."

When the Master interpreted the parable, He said the seed was the Word; the sower was he who spread the message; the four different soils were those who heard the Word.

Some seed fell on the hard-packed pathway unbroken by the plow. Here it never had a chance to grow. Such soil speaks of the hardhearted who never give the gospel a chance to take root in their spirits.

The stony ground speaks of shallow lives. These are they who backslide soon after they accept Christ. They receive the Word with gladness, but the truth does not penetrate deeply enough into their lives. They respond with enthusiasm but not with deep persuasion and determination.

In the third soil the failure was sadder. The earth was soft and rich. The seed took root and grew. But the thorns grew there also and choked out the good life. Jesus tells us plainly what these spiritual thorns are: (1) "the cares of this world," (2) "the deceitfulness of riches," and (3) "the desires for other things" (cf. Mark 4:19, NIV).

But there is also the good soil. It is he who hears the Word, allows it to grow in his heart, and permits no competing desires to thrive unchecked. In such lives the seed of the Spirit brings a rich harvest.

The farmer got no crop in three out of four places that he sowed. But Jesus assures us that even so, such work is not useless. If we keep sowing, some witness will fall on the good ground. When it takes root, what a harvest! Even the poorest result is worth 30 times the effort put forth. And one receptive life may produce 100 more!

Promise for today:

Be sure that nothing you do for him is ever lost or wasted (1 Cor. 15:58, Phillips).

▼

☐ **WEEK 39, SATURDAY**   **MATTHEW**

Scripture: Matthew 16—18
The Story: Matthew 17:14-21; Mark 9:17-29
All things are possible to him that believeth (Mark 9:23).

Jesus Asks Me for Faith

There is no more moving experience in life than to see a parent who has a defective child. And there is no more moving scene in the Bible than this father who came to Jesus. According to Mark's account our Lord did not at once cast out the demon because He would first strengthen the father's faith.

Recently a friend testified: "It is easier for me to say, *Thy will be done,* than it is to say, *Lord, I believe.*" Often faith does not come easily, but it is needed. There is no way that God can give us the gifts of faith except through our belief. In some way that we do not fully understand, our attitudes of unbelief restrict the power of God. Without our exercise of faith, He cannot do for us what He otherwise would do to heal our hurts.

Even while the boy lay writhing on the ground, the Master turned to the father as the most likely one in whom He could kindle faith. Jesus asked, "How long has he been afflicted?" The question was designed to increase the father's sense of need—and it worked. When the father remembered how much his child had suffered, he implored: "If thou canst do anything, have compassion on us, and help up." But there was a damaging question mark in his voice, and it reflected the deeper doubt in his mind. Before Christ's power could save the child, the father's unbelief must be removed.

Our Lord then turned the responsibility back to the father: "All things are possible to him that believeth." When the distraught father saw that the life of his child depended on his own attitude of faith, he made the supreme effort. He "cried out, and said with tears, Lord, I believe; help thou mine unbelief."

Must my faith always be perfect to get from Christ what my heart yearns for? The answer is no. The father's faith was not perfect—but it was enough. Christ gave him the desire of his heart; He healed his child.

> Simply trusting ev'ry day,
> Trusting through a stormy way;
> Even when my faith is small,
> Trusting Jesus, that is all.
> —EDGAR PAGE STITES

Scripture: Matthew 19—20
The Story: Matthew 19:16-22

If you want to be perfect, go, sell your possessions ... Then come, follow me (Matt. 19:21, NIV).

Follow Me

At some point in the Christian life Christ confronts each of us with a watershed spiritual choice. From that point onward our walk with Him grows richer and deeper, or love for the world begins to take over.

Somewhere on Jesus' last journey to Jerusalem, this eager young man came running to learn from Him the deepest secret of the Christian life. He was already doing all that he knew to please God: He kept the commandments, and he had faith enough to come to Jesus for some deeper experience with God. Our Lord did not question the young man's testimony but pointed out to him God's plan for full sovereignty of our lives: "If you wish to go the whole way, go, sell your possessions ... and come, follow me" (NEB).

Jesus had previously asked Peter and John to give up their fishing boats; He now asked this young man to give up his farms. The Master was getting His followers ready for Pentecost, and He offered the same opportunity to the rich young ruler. Had he accepted Christ's offer, there could have been 121 Christians filled with the Holy Spirit in the Upper Room.

But when the young man heard the conditions, "he went away sad." His property meant more to him than obeying the call that Christ placed upon him. His desire for God's best was not deep enough to carry him past his self-interest. He was not ready to make Christ Lord of his life.

God fills us with himself when we go one step further than the rich young ruler went. The Holy Spirit fills me when I say yes to all that Christ asks me to do. Am I ready to follow His ultimate challenge, "Come, follow Me"?

O Jesus, I do not draw back.

> *My life, my love, I give to Thee,*
> *Thou Lamb of God, who died for me.*
> *Oh, may I ever faithful be,*
> *My Saviour and my God!*
> —RALPH E. HUDSON

▼

Scripture: Matthew 21—23
The Story: Matthew 21:1-9

Blessed is he who comes in the name of the Lord! Hosanna in the highest! (Matt. 21:9, NIV).

Your King Comes to You

Mary anointed our Lord on Saturday evening in Bethany. On Sunday, Jesus made His way into Jerusalem. We call the day Palm Sunday because the people cut palm branches and spread them on the road to honor Jesus in the way they would honor a king. We call it the Triumphal Entry because for a few brief hours the throngs hailed Jesus as their Messiah, shouting, "Hosanna to the Son of David!"

Our Lord was facing the Cross, only five short days away. But the Cross was not the end of the road; it was rather a triumphal arch opening the way for us into the kingdom of God. It is fitting that Palm Sunday should be a celebration in honor of Him who opened wide the gates of heaven.

Christ had drawn the multitudes to himself. It was for only a few brief hours in Jerusalem, but that glad throng is a symbol of the redeemed host who will one day stand before Him again with palms in their hands—a host that "no man can number." I want to be among them.

In Jerusalem Jesus was King for a day, but I have enthroned Him King of my life. I join that unnamed disciple from Bethphage who freely released his animals when he learned the Lord needed them. I join those joyful followers who stripped off their cloaks to honor Him. I join the glad throng spreading palm branches to beautify His pathway and to pledge their loyalty. My heart sings today: "Hosanna to the Son of David: Blessed is he that cometh in the name of the Lord; Hosanna in the highest."

> *Jesus, my King, my wonderful Saviour,*
> *All of my life is given to Thee.*
> *I am rejoicing in Thy salvation,*
> *Thy precious blood now maketh me free.*
> —J. M. HARRIS

▼

□ **WEEK 40, TUESDAY**   **MATTHEW**

Scripture: Matthew 24
The Story: Matthew 24:36-44

Therefore be ye also ready: for in such an hour as ye think not the Son of man cometh (Matt. 24:44).

Jesus Is Coming Again

Our church choir gave a rendition of the cantata *Jesus Is Coming Again.* At the close of the service, in his exhortation the pastor said, "There is nothing more certain than the second coming of Christ. Are you ready for His return?"

His question made me reexamine my own attitude toward this Bible truth. Jesus himself says, "Therefore be ye also ready: for in such an hour as ye think not the Son of man cometh."

Through faith in Christ, I believe that I am ready for His coming; I am not afraid. But am I as alert and as involved as Christ wants me to be?

The unexpected return of our Lord today would find some of my loved ones and some of my friends unprepared to meet God. Has my belief in the reality of Christ's return moved me to pray for them? To warn them in love of their jeopardy in not being prepared?

But belief in the Second Coming holds more than jeopardy. The Bible teaches that there is a better day for God's people in the future. Our final salvation and God's ultimate plan for us is yet to come. When my spirit reaches out for more of God, Christ says to me, "Let not your heart be troubled: ye believe in God, believe also in me. . . . I go to prepare a place for you. And if I go and prepare a place for you, I will come again, and receive you unto myself; that where I am, there ye may be also" (John 14:1-3).

The Bible says, "The Lord himself shall descend from heaven with a shout . . . and the dead in Christ shall rise first: then we which are alive and remain shall be caught up together with them in the clouds, to meet the Lord in the air: and so shall we ever be with the Lord. Wherefore comfort one another with these words" (1 Thess. 4:16-18).

Jesus is coming again! I believe it. I want that glorious truth and that blessed hope to make my life different today. From my heart I respond.

"Amen. Even so, come, Lord Jesus" (Rev. 22:20).

▼

☐ WEEK 40, WEDNESDAY   MATTHEW

Scripture: Matthew 25
The Story: Matthew 25:1-13

Stay awake and be prepared, for you do not know the date or the moment of my return (Matt. 25:13, TLB).

Am I Ready?

Tuesday afternoon of Holy Week Jesus left the Temple area where He had been teaching. With the disciples He moved across the Kidron Valley and up the western slope of the Mount of Olives. When they had found a spot to rest, the disciples asked Him: "What will be the sign of your coming and of the end of the age?" (24:3, NIV). In chapters 24—25 Jesus answered their questions and warned them to be ready.

Chapter 25 has been called "Three Parables of Preparedness." The central truths are: (1) Be ready in your personal relationship with God; (2) Be busy doing the work of Christ; (3) Be concerned, as Jesus was, for the people around you.

An effective personal evangelist confronts us with the question: "Have you come to the place in your spiritual life where you know for certain that if you were to die tonight you would go to heaven?" Jesus himself puts the question to us with equal directness: "If I were to return tonight, are you sure you would be ready for My coming?"

In the parable, the bridegroom is Christ; the 10 virgins are you and me—the Church, the intended Bride of Christ. Jesus' obvious warning is that not all who hope to join in the Marriage Supper will be admitted. The crucial question is, Am I ready?

What is the essential preparation? What is the extra oil that the wise had but the foolish lacked? In both the Old and the New Testaments oil is used as a symbol for the Holy Spirit.

It was Tuesday afternoon when Jesus gave this parable to His disciples. Thursday evening He told them at length about His plan to send the Holy Spirit to them; and He prayed, "Father . . . sanctify them" (John 17:17).

O Jesus, I am sure I need all of the grace that You died to provide for me. I cannot borrow this relationship with God from anyone else. I open my life to You for the answer to Your prayer for me.

Fill me with Your Holy Spirit now—and continually fill me every day and every hour. Thus by Your death and by Your Gift I am assured that I am Yours—and I am ready. Amen.

Scripture: Matthew 26—28
The Story: Matthew 28:1-10

He is not here; he has risen (Matt. 28:6, NIV).

He Is Risen!

Alleluia! Jesus Christ is risen!

So what? This question is not to be flippant about the day that I hold sacred, nor to cheapen our celebration of Easter. It is to ask, What difference has the risen Christ made in my life?

It is difficult to sort out my personal answers, because from birth He has been doing good things for me. The earliest, I know only because my parents have told me. But I remember when I was eight, the Holy Spirit spoke to me about my sins. There was a deep conviction that wrong things needed to be made right. Under the guidance of a Christian mother I confessed my sins and asked Christ's forgiveness. Something happened in my heart. I knew that the world's Redeemer had become my Savior.

At 18 I became conscious of a hunger to be filled with the Holy Spirit whom Jesus had promised to send to His followers. He would change their lives in ways that would make them true disciples of our Lord. For me, the crucial question was, Would I preach? Would I share with others what Christ was doing in me, and what He wanted to do for them? I finally agreed that I would try if He would help me. I have not always been as faithful to Him as I wish I had been—but He has been completely faithful to me.

On a flight to Hawaii, three of the plane's four engines went out. The pilot alerted passengers that he was descending to a lower altitude. The only hope was that in the heavier air at sea level he might be able to keep airborne. A dozen times the plane faltered, but each time the pilot maneuvered to gain a little altitude—and flew on.

At the airport, desperately short of power, the plane made a frighteningly rough landing—but a safe one. Grateful passengers pressed toward the cockpit and the pilot. The first man spoke for all:

"Sir, we are ready to fly with you under any circumstances, at any time, anywhere in the world."

That is my glad testimony to the risen Lord. For 77 years He has made my life safe, and rich, and full.

Alleluia! Jesus Christ is risen!

▼

Scripture: Mark 1—4
The Story: Mark 2:1-12

When Jesus saw their faith, he said to the paralytic, "Son, your sins are forgiven" (Mark 2:5, NIV).

The Faith of Five

Christ comes to people through people. No account in the Bible pictures this truth more dramatically than our story for today. The needy man was paralyzed and poor. But he had one life-preserving asset—four faithful friends.

It was probably Peter's house which had the roof so unceremoniously torn up. If so, Peter would have been seated near Jesus as He spoke. The worried host kept glancing up as he heard muffled sounds overhead. Out of the corner of his eye he caught sight of the first small hole that appeared in the roof, and the first debris that began to filter down.

Jesus must have stopped speaking and looked up as all eyes moved to the ceiling above His head. Then He caught sight of the pallet just as it came through the roof. At the corners of the open hole, barely three feet away, He looked into the eyes of four eager men as they lowered their friend into His presence.

"When Jesus saw their faith," He performed the twin

404

miracles—forgiveness and healing. Was it the faith of the four friends, or the faith of the paralytic? Both. The faith that Christ saw was the faith of all five.

Had the paralytic asked his friends to bring him to Jesus, or did they first come to him encouraging him to accompany them? We do not know. But with his initiative and their help, or with their initiative and his willingness, there was faith enough to get him to Jesus. Any man who comes willingly to Christ has faith enough for a miracle.

But this man would never have made it without the faith of his friends. Even if he had desperately wanted to come, he would never have got to the door without their help.

How many paralytics are among my neighbors? My acquaintances at work? How many know nothing of Christ's power? How many need my encouragement and faith before Christ can see and respond?

Prayer for today:

> Open my mouth and let me bear
> Gladly the warm truth ev'rywhere;
> Open my heart and let me prepare
> Love with Thy children thus to share.
> —CLARA H. SCOTT

Scripture: Mark 5—7
The Story: Mark 7:14-23

From within, out of the heart of men, proceed evil thoughts ... covetousness, wickedness, deceit (Mark 7:21-22).

Evil Acts Come from an Evil Heart

Jesus often turned the thoughts of His listeners to the fact that a carnal heart is the source of sin—that evil acts are caused by an evil condition in man's spirit. Paul Rees says the following inventory of an uncleansed heart "reads like a sewer inspector's report."

"From within, out of men's hearts, come evil thoughts of lust, theft, murder, adultery, wanting what belongs to others, wickedness, deceit, lewdness, envy, slander, pride, and all other folly. All these vile things come from within; they are what pollute you and make you unfit for God" (7:21-22, TLB).

Elsewhere our Lord asks: "How can ye, being evil, speak good things? for out of the abundance of the heart the mouth speaketh. A good man out of the good treasure of the heart bringeth forth good things: and an evil man out of the evil treasure bringeth forth evil things" (Matt. 12:34-35). When we sense wrong attitudes, the Master urges us, "Cleanse first that which is within . . . that the outside . . . may be clean also" (Matt. 23:26).

Dr. B. F. Neely writes, "Carnality is that which rises up and tries to open the door every time the devil knocks from without." We can have clean lives only when we deal with this inner troublemaker. Through the cleansing of the Holy Spirit, we must get rid of the traitor at the door.

At our human best we are still prone to fall short of holy living. Should this not make us hunger for all the resources of the Spirit that God can give?

Prayer for today:

"Create in me a clean heart, O God; and renew a right spirit within me" (Ps. 51:10).

▼

Scripture: Mark 8—10
The Story: Mark 10:13-16

Let the little children come to me, and do not hinder them (Mark 10:14, NIV).

Seeing Children as Jesus Saw Them

Sunday School Sam sez:

> *If you can keep those kids in class,*
> *Take courage, harried teacher;*
> *For though they squirm and wiggle now,*
> *They'll pay tomorrow's preacher.*
> —HELEN TEMPLE

When in Rome, we visited St. Peter's Cathedral at the hour for a papal audience. Pope Pius was carried slowly down a center aisle on a dais borne on the shoulders of four men. Mothers pressed eagerly against the restraining ropes to hold out small children for his blessing. At intervals the pontiff reached out and placed his hands on a baby's head. Devout Catholic parents went home with a lifetime memory—and a story to repeat with wonder to their child.

How much more blessed the child who has come into contact with the Master himself! We hear His words in our scripture today: "Let the little children come to me, and do not hinder them."

✔ What does His admonition say to us? Do we bring our children to Jesus when we pray together? Do we discover there:

> *Just when I need Him, Jesus is strong,*
> *Bearing my burdens all the day long.*
> —WM. C. POOLE

✔ Do we bring some neighbor child to Jesus when our car goes to Sunday School?

✔ Does some other parent's child in the church see Jesus more clearly when we call the child by name? When we know him well enough to chat with him about his hobby or his school?

✔ Do we pray for, and give support to, the church's ministry with children? Do we thus open doors of influence through which some child may come into His presence?

Thank You, Heavenly Father, for the children. . . . Give them a sense of belonging, in the family, in the church, and with their friends. And may they feel at home with You in the beautiful world that You have made. Amen.

—ELIZABETH B. JONES

Scripture: Mark 11—13
The Story: Mark 12:28-34

Love the Lord your God with all your heart and with all your soul and with all your mind and with all your strength (Mark 12:30, NIV).

What Does God Want Most from Me?

The Jewish rabbis divided the law into 365 prohibitions—as many as the days of the year. To keep in mind all those details was a dreary task. When this scribe asked which was the most important, Jesus answered: "Love the Lord your God with all your heart." We need not remember 365 precepts if we are sure that we love God supremely—and love our fellowman sincerely.

If our duty to God were expressed in deeds, we could not say it in a single word; no one act can include all that is implied. But the essence of our relationship to Christ is found in an attitude of the spirit.

What does it mean to love God with all the heart? At least this must be true: Our love for Him is to be supreme. Other loves and loyalties may enrich life as long as they are in harmony with our love for God; but they must not draw us away from Him. Am I ready to lay aside the things that conflict with His will for me? Am I willing to suffer what He permits to come my way? That is to love Him with my whole heart. And this includes my thinking.

Our service for God was never intended to shackle the mind. In the Old Testament quotation three words are used: love God with your *heart, soul,* and *might* (*might* can be translated *strength*). Jesus enlarged the trio to a quartet, adding the word *mind.* When God is first in life I use my mind for His tasks.

To love Him with the whole mind is to push aside every thought that I would be embarrassed to share with Him. When I love Him with my mind, I also begin to see that Christ is concerned with all of the decisions of my life. I often ask, What do You want me to do?

To love God with all my strength is to put energy behind my faith. It is to put at God's disposal my time, my money, my talents, my influence. This attitude and commitment is what God wants most from me.

Do I really love God with all my heart? Only He knows the answer. But the question sends me to my knees. With bowed head my subdued spirit replies:

> What shall I give Thee, Master?
> Thou hast giv'n all for me.
> Not just a part, or half of my heart,
> I will give all to Thee.
> —HOMER W. GRIMES

▼

Scripture: Mark 14—16
The Story: Mark 14:60-65; 15:6-20, 25-39 (Today, read first the comments, then read the scripture and linger a while in prayer)

My soul is exceeding sorrowful unto death: tarry ye here, and watch (Mark 14:34; all other quotes from NIV).

It Was for Me

Today we enter the holy of holies as we follow our Savior from Gethsemane to Calvary and to death. I would grant His desire for companionship and support: "Stay ye here, and keep watch."

14:60-65. The prophet wrote, "He was despised and rejected by men" (Isa. 53:3). Jesus' own people were the first who tried to destroy Him. In an illegal night trial the high priest framed Him with a dilemma question. Caiaphas knew that the Master's answer to the question, "Are you the Christ?" would convict Jesus in the minds of the court. The strategy worked. "They all condemned him as worthy of death. Then some began to spit at him; they blindfolded him, struck him with their fists, and said, 'Prophesy!'"

15:6-15. The Roman ruler went along with his malicious subjects. Pilate knew "it was out of envy that the chief priests had handed Jesus over to him. . . . [But] wanting to satisfy the crowd, Pilate released Barabbas to them. He had Jesus flogged, and handed him over to be crucified."

15:25-32. "It was the third hour [9 A.M.] when they crucified him." Our Lord was placed upon the Cross as it lay on the ground. His outstretched arms were bound to the crossbar; nails were driven through His hands and feet. The 10-foot Cross was then raised and set in the prepared hole. There our Lord hung exposed, in pain and thirst, until the end.

15:33-39. "At the ninth hour [3 P.M.] Jesus cried out in a loud voice . . . 'My God, my God, why have you forsaken me?'" With a loud cry He breathed His last. It was for me.

> Blessed Redeemer! Precious Redeemer!
> Seems now I see Him on Calvary's tree;
> Wounded and bleeding, for sinners pleading—
> Blind and unheeding—dying for me!*
> —AVIS BURGESON CHRISTIANSEN

▼

☐ WEEK 41, WEDNESDAY   LUKE

Scripture: Luke 1—3
The Story: Luke 1:26-38

I am the Lord's servant . . . May it be to me as you have said (Luke 1:38, NIV).

God Wants to Work Through Me

God most often works through persons. When He became flesh and lived as a man among men, He accomplished His plan through Mary. Without her cooperation He could not have come in the way He had chosen.

When God works through us He communicates His will to us; we must know what He wants us to do in cooperation with His plan. We cannot always predict how He will make His purposes known. There is, however, always a sense of awe and a certainty that it is God with whom we are dealing.

An angel appeared to Mary and spoke in an audible voice: "The angel went to her and said, 'Greetings, you who are highly favored! The Lord is with you.'" But even the appearance of Gabriel did not quiet her fears: "Mary was greatly troubled at his words and wondered what kind of greeting this might be" (1:28-29, NIV).

After God gets our attention, He does not leave us in the dark. He calmed Mary's fears, told her of God's favor, and explained the wonder of the Child who would be born to her. But there were still high hurdles. Would Joseph believe her? Would her friends and neighbors understand?

How old do we need to be to hear and obey the voice of God? In the East, girls usually married early. It is probable Mary was only in her late teens. Age is not really important in doing God's will. It depends not so much on maturity as on our sensitivity to His call and our readiness to obey. Elizabeth declared what is always true: "Blessed is she who has believed that what the Lord has said to her will be accomplished!" (1:45, NIV). Even a developing teen can say with Mary, "I am the Lord's servant. . . . May it be to me as you have said."

Such obedience always brings God's blessing. Mary sang: "My soul praises the Lord and my spirit rejoices in God my Savior, for he has been mindful of the humble state of his servant. . . . the Mighty One has done great things for me—holy is his name" (1:46-49, NIV).

My promise for today:

"Teach me, Lord, what you want me to do, and I will obey you faithfully" (Ps. 86:11, TEV).

Scripture: Luke 4—6
The Story: Luke 4:1-14

Our Father in heaven . . . lead us not into temptation, but deliver us from the evil one (Matt. 6:9, 13; all quotes from NIV).

Overcoming Temptation

Let him who has never been tempted, close the book. But he who has faced some dark night of the soul may here find help.

Our story is the record of Satan's attack on the Son of God. But in this account we find universal truths that teach us the ways of Satan, and our countermeasures from God.

✔ The Bible here teaches us that temptation comes to the strongest Christian. We never reach a place in this life where Satan cannot make some form of evil appealing to us.

✔ The devil also takes advantage of our human weakness to attack when resistance is low. He came to Jesus at the end of 40 days of fasting when our Lord was physically weak and desperately hungry. But God can give the needed strength if only we stand firm—and sincerely call for His help.

✔ Most temptations are suggestions to satisfy a proper desire in a selfish way. In the first appeal Satan says, If you are God's child, let Him pamper you—"Tell this stone to become bread." But serving God is not designed only to make life easier; rather it makes life rich and full. "Man does not live on bread alone." To seek the easy way in moral decisions is to yield to the tempter.

✔ Satan appealed next to human ego and ambition. He said to Jesus, "I'll let you fulfill your life's dreams—if you will only do it my way." But any way other than God's way is the wrong way.

✔ The last appeal was the most tricky: Ask God to make a great display of His power through you. But such a request is a sin of egotism—Show Your power through *me*. Jesus gave the reply that we must echo, "Do not put the Lord your God to the test."

Matthew tells us that when Jesus had resisted three times, "The devil left him, and angels came and attended him" (Matt. 4:11).

Prayer for today:

Father, in my hour of darkest struggle help me resist the enemy. Remind me that to the faithful, soon comes the song. In the Conqueror's name. Amen.

▼

Scripture: Luke 7—9
The Story: Luke 7:36-50

Only Luke records this story; perhaps he tells it because of his special interest in Jesus' attitude toward women. The story is not to be confused with a similar anointing of Jesus by Mary. This anointing took place early in Jesus' ministry, in Galilee. Mary anointed Jesus in Bethany, Saturday evening before the Crucifixion.

Her sins, which are many, are forgiven; for she loved much (Luke 7:47).

Finding Forgiveness

The oriental feast was served in a semiopen courtyard. Uninvited guests often came into the yard, stood about the walls and watched, or conversed. The guests normally reclined on mats or cushions. Leaning on one elbow, they used the other hand to help themselves to food on the table. Reclining thus, Jesus' feet were extended away from the table and were easily accessible to Ms. Forgiven Much—the only name by which we know her.

What brought her to Jesus? And how did she find forgiveness? These truths are clear.

She was a sinner. She knew it, and Simon knew it. The whole community knew it, because this was "a woman who had lived a sinful life in that town" (7:37, NIV). Our English translations describe her with the gentler word, sinner. But the original term is prostitute.

Somewhere this woman who had been involved in gross sinning, came into contact with Jesus Christ. By Him she had been aroused from her degradation. Some believe she had previously been forgiven and came now only to express her thanksgiving. However that may be, her deep love for Christ was her motivation.

Somehow she sensed that this love for Him must forever bring to an end the old sinful life. That awareness led to forgiveness. Her great penitence and a surging burst of love flowing from her heart seemed to sweep before it all the guilt of her transgressions. Here is a beautiful blending of love, penitence, and faith. Jesus said to her—and in similar circumstances, He says to all—"Her many sins have been forgiven—for she loved much. . . . 'Your sins are forgiven. . . . Your faith has saved you; go in peace'" (7:47-48, 50, NIV).

> Beautiful words, wonderful words,
> Wonderful words of Life!
> —PHILIP P. BLISS

▼

☐ WEEK 41, SATURDAY   LUKE

Scripture: Luke 10—12
The Story: Luke 12:22-34

Seek ye the kingdom of God; and all these things shall be added unto you (Luke 12:31).

A Credo for Today

"1. Just for today I will try to live as a child of God, through this day only and not set far-reaching goals to try to overcome all my problems at once. I know I can do something for 12 hours that would appall me if I felt that I had to keep it up for a lifetime.

"2. Just for today I will try to be happy. I will not dwell on thoughts that depress me. I will chase them out of my mind and replace them with happy thoughts.

"3. Just for today I will adjust myself to what is. I will face reality. I will try to change those things which I can change, and accept those things I cannot change.

"4. Just for today I will try to improve my mind. I will not be a mental loafer. I will force myself to read something that requires effort, thought, and concentration.

"5. Just for today I will exercise my soul in three ways: I will do a good deed for somebody—without letting them know it. I will do at least two things that I know I should do but have been putting off. I will not show anyone that my feelings are hurt; they may be hurt, but today I will not show it.

"6. Just for today I will be agreeable. I will look as well as I can, dress becomingly, talk softly, act courteously, and speak ill of no one. Just for today I'll not try to improve anybody except myself.

"7. Today I will have a program. I may not follow it exactly, but I will have it, thereby saving myself from two pests: hurry and indecision.

"8. Just for today I will have a quiet half hour to relax alone. I will reflect on God's love for me, on my behavior, and will try to get a better perspective of my life.

"9. Just for today I will be unafraid. I will gather the courage to do what is right and take the responsibility for my own actions. I will expect nothing from the world, but I will realize that as I give to the world, the world will give to me."

—Adapted from *Kansas City Star,* AUTHOR UNKNOWN

▼

☐ **WEEK 42, SUNDAY**   **LUKE**

Scripture: Luke 13—15
The Story: Luke 13:34-35; 19:41-44; read also
    Matthew 23:37-39

How often I have longed to gather your children together (Luke 13:34; all quotes from NIV).

Our Compassionate Christ

As the traveler rounded the southern shoulder of Mount Olivet, Jerusalem and the Temple, in all their glory, burst on his view. It was a scene that stirred the love and loyalty of every pious Jew. Centuries earlier the Psalmist exulted: "Walk about Zion, go around her, count her towers, consider well her ramparts, view her citadels, that you may tell of them to the next generation. For this God is our God for ever and ever; he will be our guide even to the end" (Ps. 48:12-14).

But in spite of this beauty, on Palm Sunday morning Jesus could only weep for the city. That sorrow came from an agony deep within His spirit. Some days earlier in Perea, He had cried out: "O Jerusalem, Jerusalem . . . your house is left to you desolate." Again on Tuesday morning of Passion Week the suffering tore at His heart (Matt. 23:37-39). He had come from the Father to fulfill for Jerusalem every good promise that God had given to His chosen people. But in ignorance and rebellion they were rejecting Him, bringing destruction on themselves and on their children.

Even before the Feast of the Passover, the rulers had determined to arrest and destroy Him. He knew that before another Sabbath they would succeed in their plot. Any other man would have been angry with these implacable enemies; he would have rejoiced that his tormentors would suffer for their evil deeds. But not the compassionate Christ. His love triumphed over hatred: "How often I have longed to gather your children together." From the Cross He prayed: "Father, forgive them, for they do not know what they are doing" (Luke 23:34).

I cannot comprehend such love, but my heart is drawn by it. *O Master, pour into my heart Your spirit of forgiveness and love.*

> *Let the beauty of Jesus be seen in me,*
> *All His wonderful passion and purity.*
> *O Thou Spirit divine, All my nature refine,*
> *Till the beauty of Jesus be seen in me.*
> —ALBERT ORSBORN

Scripture: Luke 16—18
The Story: Luke 18:1-8

Jesus told his disciples ... that they should always pray and not give up (Luke 18:1, NIV).

It Pays to Pray

One Wednesday evening in prayer meeting a young mother testified she had proved it pays to pray. Said she:

"I've found that in my quiet times God gives me real help. Because I have two small children, my quiet times are not always quiet. *But I have given this time to God,* and in it He makes himself real to me."

Our Lord did not commend the unjust judge; nor did He say that God is like him. Rather, Jesus gives us a contrast. If even an unfair judge responds to a determined appeal, how much more will a loving Heavenly Father answer when we seek His help!

When we come to God we cannot predict the exact response that He will make—but of these things we are sure:

✔ God is there, and He is paying attention to us.

✔ He is a good Father; He wants us to have everything we need.

✔ God has the resources to help—and He knows what is best for us.

✔ If my earnest desire must be delayed or denied, He slips an arm around my shoulder and shares my hurt.

✔ The Heavenly Father invites us to pray; and Jesus encourages us to be persistent. He says, "Ask and it will be given to you; seek and you will find; knock and the door will be opened to you" (Luke 11:9, NIV).

417

Here is Jesus' own acrostic of urgency:

A sk

S eek

K nock

Asking shows our confidence in coming to God; *seeking* points to an earnest plea; *knocking* describes our urgent, sometimes desperate prayers.

Today I join the sincere cry of another:

O Thou by whom we come to God—
The Life, the Truth, the Way—
The path of prayer thyself hast trod;
Lord, teach us how to pray!
—JAMES MONTGOMERY

▼

☐ **WEEK 42, TUESDAY** LUKE

Scripture: Luke 19—20
The Story: Luke 19:1-10

The Son of Man came to seek and to save what was lost (Luke 19:10, NIV).

Caring as Jesus Cares*

Too often our understanding of Jesus' ministry to Zacchaeus is stunted by remembering only the little jingle:

Zacchaeus was a wee little man,
A wee little man was he.
He climbed up in a sycamore tree,
For the Lord he wanted to see.

Let us remember that on this day Jesus brought salvation to an entire household—and His action shows us how He did it. Our Lord was sensitive to an unspoken heart cry. Responding, He reached out in compassion to an unloved human being.

O Master, let me learn Your lesson from Jericho. Teach me to follow You in this caring ministry. Let me show to the lost the new purpose, new direction, and fulfillment that You can bring to their lives. Let me move close to the weak and faltering; to lift their hearts, fire their hopes, and transfer attention from their failings to our Father's faithfulness.

Let them see that our confidence comes not from the community of men, but from the goodness of God. Let their spirits soar with hope.

I would give them love. Not just soft, sentimental affection, but Your strong love of a laid-down life.

I would share what I have—time, thought, attention, care, strength, money—to brighten and excite the life of another. Let me inject some unexpected surprise of love into the lives of those who are less fortunate.

In daring concern and compassion I would reach out to befriend the friendless, to lend a touching hand to the despairing, to lift a saddened soul from loneliness.

> Oh! use me, Lord, use even me,
> Just as Thou wilt, and when, and where;
> In kindling thought and glowing word,
> Thy love to show, Thy life to share.
> —FRANCES HAVERGAL, adapted

*Adapted from W. Phillip Keller, *Salt for Society*, 111-13.

☐ WEEK 42, WEDNESDAY   LUKE

Scripture: Luke 21—22
The Story: Luke 22:7-20

This is my body given for you; do this in remembrance of me (Luke 22:19, NIV).

The Last Supper

God comes to us through remembering. At this Last Supper Jesus warned Peter that he would deny his Lord. Later that evening when it happened, Peter remembered what Jesus had told him. The memory broke his heart, led him to repent, and drew him back to God.

During the hours of this sacred Thursday evening, Jesus did two things to help you and me remember Him: (1) He promised to send the Holy Spirit to recall for us what He had taught, and (2) He instituted the Lord's Supper to remind us of what He had done.

The last two days before His crucifixion Jesus reserved for communion with His Father; for intimate fellowship and final instructions for His disciples. Wednesday He spent in quiet retirement at Bethany. Thursday afternoon He sent Peter and John to Jerusalem to arrange for their Passover meal together—probably at the home of Mary, the mother of John Mark.

The arrangements were made, and Luke tells us, "When the hour was come, he sat down, and the twelve apostles with him" (22:14). Our Lord's deep feeling for this hour is reflected in His opening sentence: "With desire have I desired to eat this passover with you before I suffer" (22:15).

At the Lord's table we accept the broken bread, remembering His words: "This is my body given for you; do this in remembrance of me."

Receiving the wine, our hearts are moved by His explanation: "This cup is the new covenant in my blood, which is poured out for you" (22:20, NIV).

At Communion we are reminded—and we remember:

> There is a green hill far away,
>   Without a city wall,
> Where the dear Lord was crucified,
>   Who died to save us all.
>
> We may not know, we cannot tell
>   What pains He had to bear;
> But we believe it was for us
>   He hung and suffered there.
>   —CECIL F. ALEXANDER

Scripture: Luke 23—24
The Story: Luke 24:13-36

Were not our hearts burning within us while he talked with us on the road and opened the scriptures to us? (Luke 24:32; all quotes from NIV).

Fellowship with the Living Lord

The Lord is risen indeed! Our joy is full as we recall the wonder of this truth for those early disciples—and for us.

Sometime during the Day of Resurrection Cleopas and his companion left their friends. Perhaps they were beating a retreat. He whom they had trusted to be the Messiah was dead. It was time to admit their mistake and drop the matter—so they left Jerusalem and journeyed to Emmaus.

Yet drop this matter they could not. "They were talking with each other about everything that had happened." When we turn our minds to Him, He draws near as He did on that first Easter Day. Perhaps the very doubting that troubled them brought Him to their aid. He comes when we need Him.

Moments in which our Lord reveals himself to us come to an end too soon if we do not put forth an effort to preserve them. But if, like Cleopas, we encourage the Heavenly Visitor, He will tarry. "So he went in to stay with them."

They were the hosts and He was the Guest. Normally one of them would have blessed the bread, broken it, and served Him. But as always, when we invite the risen Lord to share our lives, He becomes the Giver.

Somehow in that moment their eyes were opened. We cannot explain the miracle—perhaps they themselves could not. But they saw Him, and their uncertainties vanished in His presence. They were sure!

Now they understood that strange warmth of spirit which they had felt along the way—it was Jesus! Now they knew why the scripture had seemed so clear and so satisfying—it was the Lord!

We are glad for the proof of the empty tomb, we are grateful for the testimony of angels, we thank God for the record of Scripture. But all of these are something less than the glad assurance of His living presence. To know that, we must see Him—and we may!

He lives, He lives! Christ Jesus lives today!
He walks with me and talks with me along life's narrow way.
He lives, He lives, salvation to impart!
You ask me how I know He lives? He lives within my heart. *

—ALFRED H. ACKLEY

▼

☐ WEEK 42, FRIDAY   JOHN

Scripture: John 1—3

Today we read the first of seven miracles that John chose to show the deity of Jesus. The seven were: (1) Water Made Wine, 2:1-11; (2) Healing the Nobleman's Son, 4:43-54; (3) Healing the Crippled Man, 5:1-15; (4) Feeding the 5,000, 6:1-14; (5) Walking on the Water, 6:16-21; (6) Healing a Man Born Blind, 9:1-38; (7) Raising Lazarus from the Dead, 11:1-44.

The Story: John 2:1-11

Do whatever he tells you (John 2:5; all quotes from NIV).

A Gracious Miracle

George wakened on a Sunday morning with severe abdominal pain. His mother, a trained nurse, administered first aid. But suspecting acute appendicitis, she called the doctor. While waiting for him to come, the pain grew worse, and an eight-year-old boy implored: "Pray for me, Daddy. Pray for me."

His mother and I knelt by his bed and asked God to ease the pain. In just a few minutes it passed. The doctor came but could find no cause for the emergency. His diagnosis: "Perhaps gas pressure from the intestine."

Was the relief from pain a miracle or a coincidence? I cannot say for sure; but a boy of eight and his parents have always looked back to that Sunday morning with a deepening faith in God.

Are there days in our lives to which we look back and say, "It had to be God"? Those are the days!

The unnamed bridegroom of our scripture never forgot the first gracious miracle that Jesus performed in Cana of Galilee. And it was only the first one in this Gospel of miracles.

Sometimes John calls them *signs*. The Greek word is used 17 times in the book. Four times the KJV translates it *signs*, and 13 times as *miracles*. The NIV includes both ideas: "This, the first of his miraculous signs, Jesus performed in Cana of Galilee" (John 2:11).

And how do miracles happen? Jesus' mother knew; she told the servants, "Do whatever he tells you."

This first miracle was performed as a gracious act of love. The water was turned into wine to save a bridegroom from embarrassment and to make a bride's wedding day happier. But there were blessed consequences for the Kingdom: "[Jesus] thus revealed his glory, and his disciples put their faith in him." John himself says, "These signs are written in order that you may have faith that Jesus is the Christ, the Son of God, and that having faith you may have life in his name" (20:31, literal translation, BBC).

O Jesus, I thank You for those special times when You have revealed Your love and power in my life. Today I reaffirm my faith in You. Amen.

▼

Scripture: John 4—6
The Story: John 6:28-40

The work of God is this: to believe in the one he has sent (John 6:29; all quotes from NIV).

Why Do I Believe?

Matthew, Mark, and Luke teach us that Jesus was "truly man." John shows us that our Lord was "truly God." Yesterday we were moved to believe in Him through the wonder of a miracle. Today Jesus bids us broaden the base of our faith.

✔ He says, Believe in me, and you will not be disappointed: "Everyone who drinks this water will be thirsty again, but whoever drinks the water I give him will never thirst. Indeed, the water I give him will become in him a spring of water welling up to eternal life" (4:13-14).

✔ He bids us give credence to the testimony of others: "Many of the Samaritans from that town believed in him because of the woman's testimony, 'He told me everything I ever did'" (4:39).

✔ He reminds us that some accept His claim on simple faith in His word: "Because of his words many more became believers. They said to the woman, 'We no longer believe just because of what you said; now we have heard for ourselves, and we know that this man really is the Savior of the world'" (4:41-42).

✔ Sometimes we may be persuaded by a miracle of timing. Of the nobleman we read: "When he inquired as to the time when his son got better, they said to him, 'The fever left him yesterday at the seventh hour.' Then the father realized that this was the exact time at which Jesus had said to him, 'Your son will live.' So he and all his household believed" (4:52-53).

✔ Jesus bids us believe Him because of His work, because of the testimony of God, and because of the Bible: "The very work . . . which I am doing, testifies that the Father has sent me. And the Father who sent me has himself testified concerning me. . . . These are the Scriptures that testify about me . . . If you believed Moses, you would believe me, for he wrote about me" (5:36-37, 39, 46).

Are we concerned to know God's will? Are we sincerely asking, "What must we do to do the works God requires?" If so, we shall hear our Lord's reply: "The work of God is this: to believe in the one he has sent" (6:28-29).

It is enough, O Savior. "We believe and know that you are the Holy One of God" (6:69). With Thomas our hearts cry, "My Lord and my God!" (20:28).

▼

Scripture: John 7—9
The Story: John 7:14-17, 37-41; 8:12-16, 29-32

If you hold to my teaching, you are really my disciples. Then you will know the truth, and the truth will set you free (John 8:31-32, NIV).

Jesus Is Lord

Though we are in only the seventh chapter of John's Gospel, these events occurred barely six months before the Crucifixion. Opposition from the Pharisees was so strong that Jesus must be cautious about appearing in Jerusalem. But the time had now come when He must declare himself as the Son of God—and let the opposition burst in a fury.

The Feast of Tabernacles was celebrated in the fall of the year, commemorating the 40 years of Israel's wilderness wandering. Recalling God's gift of water from the rock, a procession of white-robed priests drew water from the Pool of Siloam, carried it in a golden vase to the Temple, and there poured it out as an offering of praise to God.

At that dramatic point in the feast, His voice vibrant with authority, Jesus cried: "If any man thirst, let him come unto me and drink" (7:37). The claim of that call could not be mistaken.

Another part of the feast was the festival of illumination. Two great golden lamps were lighted in the court of the women, recalling the pillar of cloud and fire. With this background, perhaps under the glow of these lights, the Master presented himself as the Answer to man's deep need. As the crowds recalled the guiding and protecting light of the pillar of fire, Jesus declared His divine Sonship: "I am the light of the world" (8:12).

The Pharisees were furious with His claim. But they were wrong; He was right. When Christ confronts the human spirit, lines are always drawn. We must accept His claims and own Him as Lord; or reject those claims and refuse Him the throne of our lives. There can be no neutrality in dealing with Christ—and my spirit wants none.

Joyfully I accept Christ's claim. Joyfully I shout, Jesus is Lord! Joyfully I sing:

> *Jesus, my Lord, I'll ever adore Thee,*
> *Lay at Thy feet my treasures of love.*
> *Lead me in ways to show forth Thy glory,*
> *Ways that will end in heaven above.*
> —J. M. HARRIS

▼

☐ WEEK 43, MONDAY   JOHN

Scripture: John 10—12
The Story: John 12:20-33

If any man serve me, let him follow me (John 12:26).

The Glory of the Cross

The setting of our scripture was in the Temple at Jerusalem, where Jesus taught the people in the court of the women on Tuesday of Passion Week. Here no Gentile was permitted, so the Greeks had to send word to Him.

426

The story is found only in John's Gospel. He tells it to introduce the discourse to the Greeks (12:23-36), the last recorded public message of Jesus. Here He sums up His claims to be the Savior of the World.

To live, we must give. Jesus sets the awesome alternatives before us with an illustration from the fields. If a grain of wheat refuses its destiny—if it fails to pass on the life it has been given—it faces the tragedy of unfruitful isolation; "it abideth alone."

The only reason for the existence of a grain of wheat is that it may sustain life—either to support the higher life of animals and men, or through dying, to multiply itself into still wider usefulness.

Is there any different reason for our lives? Were we not given eternal life in order to serve the high purposes of God's spiritual world? Jesus says to us: "If any man serve me, let him follow me; and where I am, there shall also my servant be: if any man serve me, him will my Father honour" (12:26).

This fellowship of giving is glorious—but it is also costly. As the shadow of the Cross deepened, our Master cried, "Now is my soul troubled." Here, as later in the Garden of Gethsemane, He had a moment of hesitation—and we love Him for it. When for a moment we hesitate before some difficult decision, we know that we are not different from our Lord.

But hesitation was not Jesus' final decision. He faced the issue and resolutely accepted His Father's will: "For this cause came I unto this hour. Father, glorify thy name."

O Jesus, You went resolutely to Your cross. Teach me the glory of mine—and keep me committed to it.

> *To the old rugged Cross I will ever be true,*
> *Its shame and reproach gladly bear.*
> *Then He'll call me someday to my home far away,*
> *Where His glory forever I'll share.* *
>   —GEORGE BENNARD

Scripture: John 13—15
The Story: John 15:1-11

These things have I spoken unto you, that my joy might remain in you, and that your joy might be full (John 15:11).

"Abide in Me"

Our scripture, unique to John's Gospel, is part of Jesus' last discourse to His disciples (chaps. 14—16). At 14:31 our Lord had said, "Arise, let us go hence." Leaving the Upper Room they made their way down into the Kidron Valley and up the slopes of Olivet to the Garden of Gethsemane. En route they probably passed a vineyard where laborers had pruned the vines during the day and were burning the dead branches after dark.

In the glow of those fires Jesus spoke of our relationships to Him. First there is the indispensable contact: "I am the vine, ye are the branches." Eternal life comes from Christ to us. First. Last. Always.

If we forget it we face the tragedy of the barren branch. There is no life apart from the Spirit of Christ. Apart from His abiding presence we wither, we become fruitless, and at last we are cut off and perish.

But He does not want that to happen. We are living branches. He assures us, "Ye are clean through the word which I have spoken unto you." To enjoy continuing life and fruitfulness, we need only abide in Christ and submit to the Father's pruning process. He trims off any life-style that is unlike himself. He transforms our spirits so that we produce the fruit of His Spirit.

And what is that fruit? The Bible lists nine of them (Gal. 5:22-23). Faith, meekness, and temperance reflect a right spirit toward God. Long-suffering, gentleness, goodness (and meekness) are Christlike attitudes that I can see in your life. Joy, peace, love (and faith) are life-building fruits that I experience in my own growing spirit.

Jesus says, "Abide in me." But how? Barclay gives this wise counsel: "There must be no day when we never think of Jesus and feel His presence. . . . For some few of us abiding in Christ will be a mystical experience which is beyond words to express. For most of us, it will mean a constant contact with Jesus Christ. It will mean arranging life, arranging prayer, arranging silence in such a way that there is never a day when we give ourselves a chance to forget Him" (*The Daily Study Bible*, 205).

O Savior:

> *I need Thy presence ev'ry passing hour.*
> *What but Thy grace can foil the tempter's pow'r?*
> *Who, like thyself, my guide and stay can be?*
> *Thro' cloud and sunshine, oh, abide with me!*
>   —HENRY F. LYTE

▼

Scripture: John 16—17

Our English word *paraclete* comes from the Greek *paracletos;* it means "advocate," "comforter," "consoler," "counselor," "helper," "intercessor." The Greek word is used in the New Testament to signify the Holy Spirit, who fulfills for the believer all of the offices mentioned (fn., NBV).

The Story: John 17:1, 6-20

Sanctify them through thy truth: thy word is truth
(John 17:17).

Our Deepest Need

Without John's Gospel we would have missed Jesus' Farewell Discourses (chaps. 14—17). In those last hours He comforted His disciples and told them about His gift of the Comforter. He wanted them to be filled with the Holy Spirit. It is His deep desire for all of us who follow Him. Let us listen to our Lord:

"If you love me, obey me; and I will ask the Father and he will give you another Comforter, and he will never leave you. He is the Holy Spirit, the Spirit who leads into all truth. The world at large cannot receive him, for it isn't looking for him and doesn't recognize him. But you do, for he lives with you now and some day shall be in you" (14:15-17, TLB).

"When the Father sends the Comforter instead of me—and by the Comforter I mean the Holy Spirit—he will teach you much, as well as remind you of everything I myself have told you" (14:26, TLB).

"I will send you the Comforter—the Holy Spirit, the source of all truth. He will come to you from the Father and will tell you all about me" (15:26, TLB).

"It is best for you that I go away, for if I don't, the Comforter won't come. If I do, he will—for I will send him to you. And when he is come he will convince the world of its sin, and of the availability of God's goodness, and of deliverance from judgment" (16:7-8, TLB).

At this point Jesus ceased talking to the disciples about God and began to talk to God about them—and about us.

"Holy Father, keep through thine own name those whom thou hast given me . . . I pray not that thou shouldest take them out of the world, but that thou shouldest keep them from the evil. . . . Sanctify them through thy truth: thy word is truth. . . . Neither pray I for these alone, but for them also which shall believe on me through their word" (17:11, 15, 17, 20).

Jesus knew—and in our best moments we know—that our deepest need is to be filled with the Holy Spirit of God.

> Holy Spirit, be my Guide.
> Holy Spirit, my door's open wide.
> Make me to know Thy will divine;
> Holy Spirit, be Thou mine!*
> —MILDRED COPE

▼

Scripture: John 18—21
The Story: John 21:15-25
What is that to thee? follow thou me (John 21:22).

Failure Forgiven

Through chapters 18; 19; and 20 John follows Matthew, Mark, and Luke in the story of Jesus' arrest, crucifixion, and resurrection. But in chapter 21 John alone tells us of Jesus' appearance to seven of the disciples by the Sea of Galilee.

Peter is the central character. His failure had been great. But God, who inspired the Scriptures, wanted us to know that our failures need not be final.

The Big Fisherman had boldly declared: "Though all men shall be offended because of thee, yet will I never be offended" (Matt. 26:33). Just hours later he denied his Lord. Earlier, when Jesus had promised, "Follow me, and I will make you fishers of men," Peter had left his nets and boats. But now he had gone back to the old life on the lake—and six of his fellow disciples had followed his bad example (21:2-3).

But Jesus doesn't give up on us when we fail Him. The angel at the empty tomb had sent a special message to the one who had fallen: "Go your way, tell his disciples *and Peter* that he goeth before you into Galilee: there shall ye see him" (Mark 16:7).

Now, at the lakeside, Jesus kept that promise. After breakfast our Lord gave assurance of forgiveness—and He gave guidance for future faithfulness. Peter had denied Him three times, so Jesus gave him the chance to wipe out those memories with three declarations of his love—and He gave him a job to do to express his love.

Still very human, Peter wanted to know if his cross was larger and heavier than the cross to be carried by another. Lovingly but faithfully, Jesus dealt with His disciple's frailty: "If I will that he tarry till I come, what is that to thee? follow thou me."

Jesus forgives. Jesus rebukes. Jesus teaches. Jesus does for us whatever we need done to keep us faithfully following Him. *Thank You, Lord, for Your faithfulness to me.*

> O Love that wilt not let me go,
> I rest my weary soul in Thee.
> I give Thee back the life I owe,
> That in Thine ocean depths its flow
> May richer, fuller be.
> —GEORGE MATHESON

▼

☐ WEEK 43, FRIDAY   ACTS

Scripture: Acts 1—2
The Story: Acts 1:1-9

Wait for the gift my Father promised . . . in a few days you will be baptized with the Holy Spirit (Acts 1:4-5; all quotes from NIV).

The Promised Blessing

Our story for today is both the introduction to the Book of Acts and the key to its contents. The book is called The Acts of the Apostles but is more truly described as the Acts of the Holy Spirit.

More than 40 days earlier than these events Jesus had promised to send the Comforter. In John 14—16 He gave the promise; in chapter 17 He prayed earnestly for its fulfillment in the disciples' lives, and in ours. Now in Acts we hear His command to tarry for the Holy Spirit. Here also we see the blessed results of the Spirit in the lives of His followers.

"He appeared to them over a period of forty days and spoke about the kingdom of God. . . . he gave them this command: 'Do not leave Jerusalem, but wait for the gift my Father promised, which you have heard me speak about. . . . In a few days you will be baptized with the Holy Spirit. . . . You will receive power when

the Holy Spirit comes on you; and you will be my witne
Jerusalem, and in all Judea and Samaria, and to the ends
earth'" (1:3-5, 8).

"When the day of Pentecost came, they were all together in
one place. Suddenly a sound like the blowing of a violent wind
came from heaven and filled the whole house where they were
sitting. . . . All of them were filled with the Holy Spirit" (2:1-2, 4).

That same day Peter testified: "'This is what was spoken by the
prophet Joel: 'In the last days, God says, I will pour out of my Spirit
on all people. . . . Even on my servants, both men and women"
(2:16-18).

"God has raised this Jesus to life, and we are all witnesses of
the fact. Exalted to the right hand of God, he has received from the
Father the promised Holy Spirit and has poured out what you now
see and hear" (2:32-33).

"When the people heard this, they were cut to the heart and
said . . . 'Brothers, what shall we do?' Peter replied, 'Repent and be
baptized, every one of you, in the name of Jesus Christ so that your
sins may be forgiven. And you will receive the gift of the Holy
Spirit. The promise is for you and your children and for all who are
far off—for all whom the Lord our God will call'" (2:37-39).

It is Christ's prayer for His people, and my heart responds:

> Breathe on me, Breath of God,
> Till I am wholly Thine,
> Until this earthly part of me
> Glows with Thy fire divine.
> —EDWIN HATCH

▼

☐ WEEK 43, SATURDAY   ACTS

Scripture: Acts 3—5

In 4:31, why does Luke tell us that Christians who had already
been baptized with the Holy Spirit at Pentecost were now "filled
with the Holy Spirit"?

Dr. Ralph Earle explains: "One is filled with the Holy Spirit when his heart is cleansed from all sin in the experience of entire sanctification (cf. 15:8-9). But Paul wrote to the Ephesian Christians, 'Be filled with the Spirit' (Eph. 5:18). Here the verb [means] 'Go on being filled with the Spirit' . . . There must be an initial filling. But this should be followed in the consecrated Christian's life by many fresh fillings of the Spirit for special service in the Kingdom" (BBC).

In chapter 5, how shall we understand the immediate and tragic judgment that fell on Ananias and Sapphira? God is usually more long-suffering with sinners.

We do not know all of the answers, but it is clear that this husband and wife tried to conceal selfish spirits under cover of an apparent full commitment to Christ. No deceit is worse. God's people need to know how serious it is to be dishonest in our devotion to God.

The result of this judgment was a blessing to the Church. Those who heard of these events developed a wholesome fear of God: a fear of trying to deceive Him; a fear of conspiring together against Him; a fear of trying to appear more devoted than was true. Who can tell how many have been saved from similar sins by the warning of this one example of New Testament judgment?

The Story: Acts 4:13-20

When they saw the courage of Peter and John . . . they were astonished and took note that these men had been with Jesus (Acts 4:13; all quotes from NIV).

Courageous for Christ

"Courage is fear that has said its prayers." Such courage for Christ comes from communion with Him and from being filled with the Holy Spirit whom He promised to send to us.

Before Pentecost Peter was so fearful that he denied his Lord. In Gethsemane "all the disciples deserted [Jesus] and fled" (Matt. 26:56). But now, only a few short weeks later, those who heard the preaching of these men marveled "when they saw the courage of Peter and John."

What made the difference? Luke knew; and he tells us: "Then Peter, *filled with the Holy Spirit,* said to them . . ." Increased courage

434

came through the baptism with the Holy Spirit in answer to their prayers and their obedience in waiting for Him.

After their first witnessing, Peter and John were threatened by the rulers; they were specifically warned to testify no more. But they, with others, went to prayer. It is a prayer that will bring courage to timid Christians today: "Now, Lord, consider their threats and enable your servants to speak your word with great boldness. Stretch out your hand to heal and perform miraculous signs and wonders through the name of your holy servant Jesus" (4:29-30).

Neal Dirkse tells of a young woman in his church who left a prayer meeting to go and witness for Jesus. Through her tears she confessed: "I'm scared to death, but this is what I was saved to do, and I intend to obey Christ."

If we have not been sanctified and lack courage to speak for our Lord, we may expect the baptism with the Holy Spirit to increase our courage. If we have been sanctified and still feel the need for greater courage in witnessing, the Holy Spirit will give courage in answer to our specific prayer and faith.

Today we join the prayer of an unnamed fellow Christian:

I would be prayerful through each busy moment.
I would be constantly in touch with God.
I would be tuned to hear His slightest whisper.
I would have faith to keep the path Christ trod.

▼

☐ **WEEK 44, SUNDAY**   **ACTS**

Scripture: Acts 6—8

In chapter 7, note how Stephen seeks to win his fellow Jews by a full account of their history under God (7:2-50).

The Story: Acts 8:26-40

We cannot help speaking about what we have seen and heard (Acts 4:20, NIV).

You Will Be My Witnesses

We become like Christ when, like Him, we seek the salvation of others. No act of worship draws us so close to God as the endeavor to share in His work of winning souls.

And this ministry of witnessing is for all of us. The Philip of our story was Philip the layman. He was at first given only a ministry to physical needs—selected to provide for the needy widows of the congregation. But Philip was a New Testament Christian who knew that our deepest needs are not physical. He was a layman who, like Stephen, was "full of faith and of the Holy Ghost" (6:5).

Sometimes God speaks to us about witnessing as clearly as He spoke to Philip: "Go to that chariot and stay near it" (8:29, NIV). But we must not limit our sharing of Christ to these urgent promptings of the Holy Spirit. Rather, our hearts should be so filled with the joy of the Lord that our routine contacts with people will provide occasions for sharing our experience of Christ.

In 8:4-5 the church in Jerusalem had suffered persecution, and many had fled from the city. In these unpromising circumstances "Philip went down to the city of Samaria, and preached Christ unto them." Here God's man was witnessing without the command of an angel or the special prompting of the Holy Spirit. He was among a people who needed the gospel, and he had what they needed. Those simple facts called forth his Christian testimony.

If we are faithful in using opportunities that are close at hand, God begins to use us in larger assignments. While Philip was busy in Samaria, the Lord sent an angel to show him a specific mission. Later the Holy Spirit himself told Philip what he was to do.

If we are faithful in witnessing for Christ, men and women will be saved. How Philip's heart must have thrilled when the Ethiopian said, "What doth hinder me to be baptized? . . . I believe that Jesus is the Son of God"!

Our Lord gave us His commission: "You will be my witnesses" (1:8, NIV). My heart responds, *Lord Jesus, by Your grace I will. Give me the burning spirit of those early Christians who said, "We cannot help speaking about what we have seen and heard." Help me to be a faithful witness and thus to become more like You, whom I love and whom I serve. Amen.*

Scripture: Acts 9:1-31

The story of Peter's ministry dominates the first 12 chapters of Acts, but 7:58—8:1 and 9:1-31 introduce Saul of Tarsus whose work is central in the second half of the book.

The Story: Acts 9:1-19

Brother Saul, the Lord—Jesus, who appeared to you . . . has sent me so that you may see again and be filled with the Holy Spirit (Acts 9:17, NIV).

How Does God Reveal Himself to Us?

The writer of Hebrews explains: "In the past God spoke to our forefathers . . . at many times and in various ways" (Heb. 1:1, NIV). He still has His chosen methods of revealing himself; Saul's experience is a kind of New Testament mirror for us.

God speaks through conscience. We cannot resist God and oppose righteousness without inner turmoil. Jesus said of the Holy Spirit, "When he comes, he will prove to the people of the world that they are wrong about sin and about what is right and about God's judgment" (John 16:8, TEV). The Holy Spirit thus works through man's conscience to make us uncomfortable when we go contrary to His will. In Saul's case, the risen Christ also confronted him on the road to Damascus: "Saul, Saul, why do you persecute me?" (Acts 9:4, NIV). He was not the first nor the last man whose mind has been troubled by the growing persuasion that he is not right with God.

God speaks with specific guidance. When we begin to listen to the voice of conscience, the Spirit shows us what to do. This man inquired, "Who are you, Lord?" and God told him three things: (1) "I am Jesus, whom you are persecuting"; (2) "Get up and go into the city"; (3) "You will be told what you must do" (NIV). Responding to

God's call always brings enough guidance for the next steps to find Him.

God speaks through faithful Christians. When our Lord finds a man seeking truth, He looks for a Christian to bring it. The instructions to Ananias were as clear as the guidance to Saul. After conquering his fears, this disciple became God's faithful messenger: "Then Ananias went to the house and entered it. Placing his hands on Saul, he said, 'Brother Saul, the Lord—Jesus, who appeared to you on the road as you were coming here—has sent me so that you may see again and be filled with the Holy Spirit'" (NIV).

We rejoice in the faithful ministry of our God who is always seeking to reveal himself and His will to us. Our spirits yearn to be used by Him in that ministry.

> Lord, speak to me, that I may speak
> In living echoes of Thy tone;
> As Thou hast sought, so let me seek
> Thy erring children lost and lone.
> —FRANCES HAVERGAL

▼

☐ **WEEK 44, TUESDAY**   **ACTS**

Scripture: Acts 10—11:18
The Story: Acts 10:1-23 (For the full story read all of 10:1—11:18)

Do not call anything impure that God has made clean (Acts 10:15; all quotes from NIV).

Letting Love Remove Barriers

God has planned for the Good News to spread from one person to another, but the gospel does not move freely where barriers keep man from man. To get the gospel from Jewish Peter to Gentile Cornelius, God had to crowd both of them. Maclaren writes: "Peter would never have dreamed of going with the messengers if he had not had his narrowness beaten out of him on the housetop, and Cornelius would never have dreamed of sending to Joppa if he had not seen the angel."

Sometimes the barrier is sheer physical distance. The Spirit could not talk to Peter effectively in Joppa about Cornelius in Caesarea. God's man had to get closer to know the heart hunger of this Gentile and to observe the workings of God's Spirit in his life. When we contact the same small circle of acquaintances day after day, we are seldom moved by the spiritual needs of other men. We are not close enough to be really aware of their hungers. Because the gospel does not have free course when men are far apart, the Spirit told Peter to go. The Holy Spirit still bids us go to a neighbor, take the gospel to the next town, go overseas to those who have never heard.

Even after Peter reached Caesarea the barriers were not all down, because Cornelius and his friends did not belong to Peter's culture. The Apostle acknowledged this barrier when he said, "You are well aware that it is against our law for a Jew to associate with a Gentile or visit him" (10:28). Sometimes it is easier to give the gospel than to give ourselves to men whose life-styles are different from ours. Those who took Peter to task (11:3) did not object to his spiritual ministry; rather they challenged his social fellowship: "You went into the house of uncircumcised men and ate with them."

Father, I pray that no difference of life-style shall keep me from freely sharing what You have done for me. Cleanse from my spirit every prejudice that contradicts the spirit of love. Let Your love flow freely through me today—and every day. In Jesus' name I ask it. Amen.

▼

☐ **WEEK 44, WEDNESDAY** ACTS

Scripture: Acts 11:19—14:28

Chapters 13—14 tell the story of Paul's first missionary journey. On a Bible map trace the route from Antioch (in Syria) to Salamis,

Paphos, Perga, Antioch, Iconium, Lystra, and Derbe; then the return journey: Lystra, Iconium, Antioch, Perga, Attalia, and Antioch (in Syria).

The Story: Acts 12:24—13:5

Set apart for me Barnabas and Saul for the work to which I have called them (Acts 13:2; all quotes from NIV).

God Calls and the Church Supports

In a recent church board meeting we granted a young woman a local preacher's license. We also recommended other young people to be granted minister's licenses by the district assembly. The pattern for this cooperation of the church in recognizing and encouraging God's call comes right out of the New Testament.

In Acts 9:15 the Holy Spirit said to Ananias concerning Saul: "Go! This man is my chosen instrument to carry my name before the Gentiles." God had called and the church was instructed to confirm and support.

In 11:25-26 Paul was fulfilling his call in Tarsus when the church opened a new place of ministry to him: "Then Barnabas went to Tarsus to look for Saul, and when he found him, he brought him to Antioch. So for a whole year Barnabas and Saul met with the church and taught great numbers of people."

Again we see the pattern in 13:1-3: "In the church at Antioch ... while they were worshiping the Lord and fasting, the Holy Spirit said, 'Set apart for me Barnabas and Saul for the work to which I have called them.' So after they had fasted and prayed, they placed their hands on them and sent them off."

I rejoice that our church follows this New Testament plan. "We recognize that the Head of the Church calls some to the more official and public work of the ministry. . . . The church, illuminated by the Holy Spirit, will recognize the Lord's call.

"When the church discovers this divine call, the proper steps should be taken for its recognition and endorsement, and all suitable help should be given to open the way for the candidate to enter the ministry" (*Manual*).

Thank You, Lord, for giving us a little part in nurturing and encouraging those whom You call to minister to Your Church.

> *Blest be the tie that binds*
> *Our hearts in Christian love;*
> *The fellowship of kindred minds*
> *Is like to that above.*
> —JOHN FAWCETT

▼

Scripture: Acts 15:1-35
The Story: Acts 15:1-20

It seemed good to the Holy Spirit and to us not to burden you with anything beyond the following requirements (Acts 15:28; all quotes from NIV).

Don't Let Differences Divide

Between Paul's first and second missionary journeys the Early Church resolved one of its most far reaching issues. The decision helped the Church become universal and Christian; had the decision gone the other way the movement could have lapsed into a Jewish sect. We rejoice in their right decision; and we also rejoice in the model here given to guide us in resolving differences that threaten to break Christian fellowship. What steps led them to success?

1. They brought the problem into the open and heard both sides. We are always ready to accept a contrary view more gracefully when we have been given full opportunity to present our own case.

2. The Early Church was willing to be guided by the facts. Peter showed that God had redeemed the Gentiles as completely as He had the Jews—and without their following the Jewish custom of circumcision: "God, who knows the heart . . . accepted them by giving the Holy Spirit to them, just as he did to us" (15:8).

441

3. Peter emphasized the common faith held by both Gentile and Jew: "We believe it is through the grace of our Lord Jesus that we are saved, just as they are." Fellowship is always strengthened when we focus on our big agreements instead of magnifying our small differences.

4. These early Christians were willing to accept the authority of the Scriptures. In them God had foretold the salvation of all peoples: "I will restore . . . that the remnant of men may seek the Lord, and all the Gentiles who bear my name, says the Lord" (15:16-17; see Amos 9:11-12).

5. Good Christians listen to reason and are amenable to the sanctified judgment of Christian leaders. The community followed the wisdom of their chosen representative: "It is my judgment, therefore, that we should not make it difficult for the Gentiles who are turning to God" (15:19).

Separation from false teachers is sometimes necessary to preserve the Christian faith. Christlikeness, however, is more often seen in our willingness to let Christian comrades differ from us and still maintain a fellowship of love. In the Church we are:

> *Elect from ev'ry nation,*
> *Yet one o'er all the earth;*
> *Her charter of salvation,*
> *One Lord, one faith, one birth.*
> —SAMUEL J. STONE

▼

☐ WEEK 44, FRIDAY   ACTS

Scripture: Acts 15:36—18:22

These chapters give us the account of Paul's second missionary journey. At Lystra, Timothy joined the party. On this first trip into the Western world Paul established at least three churches: Philippi, Thessalonica, and Corinth. To them he later wrote five of the New Testament Epistles.

From 16:10 we learn that Luke, the author of Acts, joined Paul's party in Troas. Earlier he wrote, "Paul and his companions traveled."

But in verse 10 he writes, "*We* got ready at once to leave for Macedonia" (NIV). From here on in the Acts, the "we" passages tell us when Luke was present.

The Story: Acts 15:36—16:10

So the churches were strengthened in the faith and grew daily in numbers (Acts 16:5; all quotes from NIV).

Finding Direction in Frustration

How do we serve God effectively when things do not go like we want them to? How do we find the will of God when doors of service close in our faces? From Paul's experiences at the beginning of this journey, God shows us some answers.

There was deep discouragement even in the planning stages. Was Paul too adamant in what he thought was right? In any case, he must have grieved deeply over having to reject the wishes of Barnabas and part company with his closest Christian friend and missionary colleague. No one likes to do that; but what is the right thing to do when it seems necessary?

Paul did not let disappointment defeat his purpose; he chose Silas as a partner and went ahead with the journey. Barnabas also persevered in missionary service—and in seeking to save a young man to the Christian ministry. In these Christlike responses there is right example and cause for joy.

Paul's second frustration arose from unknown elements in God's plan. First, he was "kept by the Holy Spirit from preaching the word in the province of Asia." Next, "they tried to enter Bithynia, but the Spirit of Jesus would not allow them to."

Sometimes we wish God would explain His plans earlier and more clearly—but for His own reasons He does not. What shall we do in these hours of uncertainty?

When we don't know what to do tomorrow, it is wise to do the best we know to do today. Paul did. Blocked on his left and on his right, he went straight ahead and came to Troas. There God was able to make the next move clear. As a result, the Christian gospel came to Europe; and from Europe the message came to North America and to you and me. In spite of Paul's frustrations, he

443

continued to follow God, and "the churches were strengthened in the faith and grew daily in numbers."

With William Cowper we may sing in our hours of frustration:

> *Ye fearful saints, fresh courage take.*
> *The clouds ye so much dread*
> *Are big with mercy, and will break*
> *In blessings on your heads.*

▼

Scripture: Acts 18:23—21:14

The heart of the third missionary journey was the three years that Paul labored establishing the church in Ephesus. From there he again visited the churches he had organized on the second journey in northern and southern Greece. En route home, he decided against stopping at Ephesus; it would be too hard to get away in time to reach Jerusalem by Pentecost. Instead, the party stopped at Miletus, some 30 miles from Ephesus, and Paul called for the elders of the church to meet him there.

The Story: Acts 20:17-38

I consider my life worth nothing to me, if only I may ... complete the task the Lord Jesus has given me (Acts 20:24; all quotes from NIV).

The Heart of a Pastor

In the presence of these beloved leaders of his Ephesian congregation, Paul laid his heart bare. It is an accurate portrait of every truly Christian pastor. No words of explanation can make the passage clearer or more moving.

"'You know how I lived the whole time I was with you, from the first day I came into the province of Asia. I served the Lord with great humility and with tears ... You know that I have not

444

hesitated to preach anything that would be helpful to you but have taught you publicly and from house to house. . . .

"'And now, compelled by the Spirit, I am going to Jerusalem, not knowing what will happen to me there. I only know that in every city the Holy Spirit warns me that prison and hardships are facing me. However, I consider my life worth nothing to me, if only I may finish the race and complete the task the Lord Jesus has given me—the task of testifying to the gospel of God's grace.

"'Now I know that none of you among whom I have gone about preaching the kingdom will ever see me again. . . . I have not hesitated to proclaim to you the whole will of God. Guard yourselves and all the flock of which the Holy Spirit has made you overseers. Be shepherds of the church of God, which he bought with his own blood. . . .'

"When he had said this, he knelt down with all of them and prayed. They all wept as they embraced him and kissed him. What grieved them most was his statement that they would never see his face again. Then they accompanied him to the ship" (20:18-20, 22-25, 27-28, 36-38).

Father, thank You for pastors who love their people sincerely, serve You faithfully, and accept Your will completely. Surely goodness and mercy shall follow them—and us whom they serve—all the days of our lives, and we shall dwell with You forever.

▼

Scripture: Acts 21:15—23:35
The Story: Acts 21:17-26

Make up your mind not to put any stumbling block or obstacle in your brother's way (Rom. 14:13, NIV).

Accommodation to Avoid Conflict

Paul could be more adamant than most men when he felt an important spiritual issue was in jeopardy. But the spirit of Jesus moved him to give up personal privilege when Christian fellowship was threatened by unnecessary contention.

When he arrived in Jerusalem, he was warmly received by all the church leaders. After hearing the report of God's gracious work among the Gentiles, James, leader of the Jerusalem church, reminded Paul that thousands of Jewish Christians still were zealous for keeping the laws of Moses. Because Paul taught that the Gentiles need not observe these laws, the Jews would be prejudiced against him. James, therefore, advised him to take part in a typically Jewish Temple ceremony with four other Christian Jews. This would tend to allay criticism and avoid conflict. The plan involved no compromise of Christian truth, so Paul agreed to it.

In this response he proved to be a genuine Christian teacher—living by what he preached. Earlier when counseling the Corinthians regarding eating meat offered to idols, the Apostle declared that he saw in this practice no violation of God's law. But he went on to push the Corinthians, and us, to the more important questions: Will such conduct be wise? Will it be the most helpful thing we can do? Will it strengthen our Christian neighbor? Increase our devotion to God? Build the church? These are the issues upon which the Christian decides his response to differences of opinion. To guide us, Paul sums up his own guideline for such Christlike conduct: "Let no man seek his own, but each his neighbor's good" (1 Cor. 10:24, ASV). Thank you, Paul, for showing us the right attitude.

We shall never go far wrong in human relations if we act out of genuine Christian love. Jesus made it clear that showing consideration for our fellowman is second only to love for God himself. I want to be like Jesus.

> *I have one deep, supreme desire,*
> *That I may be like Jesus.*
> *To this I fervently aspire,*
> *That I may be like Jesus.* *
> —THOMAS O. CHISHOLM

Scripture: Acts 24—26

The story for today is a snapshot of Paul taken about two years after the third missionary journey, and several years before his death. You will want to read all of chapters 24—26. It is a half hour of Christian biography.

The Story: Acts 25:13—26:1

I have had God's help to this very day, and so I stand here and testify to small and great alike (Acts 26:22; all quotes from NIV)

I Testify

Paul was a prisoner and would remain so most of the rest of his life. Although in bonds, pleading for his liberty, he put his Christian witness first.

"'King Agrippa, I consider myself fortunate to stand before you today as I make my defense . . . Therefore I beg you to listen to me patiently. . . .

"'It is because of my hope in what God has promised our fathers that I am on trial today. . . . O king, it is because of this hope that the Jews are accusing me. Why should any of you consider it incredible that God raises the dead?

"'I too was convinced that I ought to do all that was possible to oppose the name of Jesus of Nazareth. . . . I was going to Damascus with the . . . commission of the chief priests. About noon, O king, as I was on the road, I saw a light from heaven, brighter than the sun, blazing around me and my companions. We all fell to the ground, and I heard a voice saying . . . "Saul, Saul, why do you persecute me? It is hard for you to kick against the goads."

"'Then I asked, "Who are you, Lord?"

"'"I am Jesus, whom you are persecuting," the Lord replied. "Now get up and stand on your feet. I have appeared to you to appoint you as a servant and as a witness . . . I will rescue you from your own people and from the Gentiles. I am sending you to open their eyes from darkness to light, and from the power of Satan to God, so that they may receive forgiveness of sins and a place among those who are sanctified by faith in me."

"'So then, King Agrippa, I was not disobedient to the vision from heaven. . . . I preached that they should repent and turn to God and prove their repentance by their deeds. That is why the Jews seized me in the temple courts and tried to kill me. . . .

"'I am not insane, most excellent Festus . . . What I am saying is true and reasonable. The king is familiar with these things, and I can speak freely to him. . . . King Agrippa, do you believe the prophets? I know you do.'"

"Then Agrippa said to Paul, 'Do you think that in such a short time you can persuade me to be a Christian?'

"Paul replied, 'Short time or long—I pray God that not only you but all who are listening to me today may become what I am, except for these chains'" (Acts 26:2-3, 6-9, 12-21, 25-29).

Thank You, Father, for Your servant Paul and for every faithful Christian witness. Teach me to be one of them.

▼

Scripture: Acts 27—28

On a Bible map trace Paul's journey from Caesarea to Rome.

For the Apostle's account and response to his prison days in Rome, read his seven short prison letters—Colossians; Ephesians; Philemon; Philippians; 1 and 2 Timothy; Titus.

The Story: Acts 27:18-36

I believe God, that it shall be even as it was told me (Acts 27:25).

Man of Christian Courage

Strength is always better than weakness. Courage is always better than cowardice. Through faith in Christ, Paul found both of them.

Hear his testimony on a sinking ship in a storm at sea: "There stood by me this night the angel of God . . . saying, Fear not" (vv. 23-24).

Because of courage, born of his Christian faith, God's man was able to bring hope to others: "I exhort you to be of good cheer: for there shall be no loss of any man's life among you . . . for I believe God, that it shall be even as it was told me" (vv. 22, 25).

Why did Luke cut this man's story short at the end of chapter 28 when there was yet so much we would like to know? The best conjecture is that he planned to write another book dealing with Paul's last years but was prevented from doing so—perhaps by death.

Our last Bible information about Paul comes from 2 Timothy. In A.D. 64 the emperor Nero began an appalling persecution of the Christians. Paul had earlier been released from his first imprisonment, but was apparently arrested again and brought back to Rome. Traditions from the Early Church agree that he was tried, sentenced to death, and executed by beheading. One stroke of the executioner's ax, and Paul's earthly life was over.

But what a heritage of courage he left us! From a prison cell, perhaps the death sentence already passed on him, he wrote triumphantly: "I am now ready to be offered, and the time of my departure is at hand. I have fought a good fight, I have finished my course, I have kept the faith: henceforth there is laid up for me a crown of righteousness, which the Lord, the righteous judge, shall give me at that day" (2 Tim. 4:6-8).

But even on his way to execution Paul could not forget that the good news of Christ was meant for all of us. In one last gesture he threw his arms around the world and cried, "not to me only, but unto all them also that love his appearing" (2 Tim. 4:8).

Thank you, Paul, for that strong assurance. We follow in your footsteps. We too love His appearing. We shall continue to fight the good fight. We shall keep the faith. We shall join you there "at that day."

449

The Book of Romans is Paul's longest letter. He wrote from Corinth, about A.D. 55, near the close of his third missionary journey. After a trip to Jerusalem, the Apostle planned to visit Rome (15:22-29). The letter served as an introduction to Paul, and especially to his message.

In chapters 1—8 the Apostle explains the doctrine of salvation—both justification by faith and sanctification by the Spirit. Chapters 9—11 seek to explain why the Jews have not accepted the Christian faith. The next four chapters give us practical guidance for Christian living, followed by one of greetings.

Scripture: Romans 1—4

What to look for: chapter 1, verses 18-32, the sins of the Gentile world; chapter 2, sins of the Jews; chapter 3, there is no salvation from sin through mere formal observance of Old Testament law— obedience to God is important, but we are saved by faith; chapter 4, even Abraham pleased God because of his faith.

Do verses 3:10 and 23 mean that no Christian can live without sinning? No. At this point Paul is talking about fallen man apart from the grace of God. There is no man righteous before God until he accepts Christ. Before we accepted Christ, all of us had sinned and fallen short of God's will for us. We were in need of His salvation.

The Story: Romans 1:1-17

I am not ashamed of the gospel of Christ: for it is the power of God unto salvation to every one that believeth (Rom. 1:16).

Thank God for the Gospel

I am glad for the gospel; I thank God for every follower of Christ who is stirred to share that wonderful news with someone else.

What is this Good News? The gospel is God's plan to save us from the life-destroying sins of false worship, sexual perversion, greed, envy, and malice. I have seen the sad results of these sins in the lives of broken men and women. I thank God that He has saved me from their corruption and from their tragic consequences. If sin is working havoc in our lives today, Christ wants to forgive and heal us.

God's stern opposition to sin is no mere whim. He requires righteousness because He loves us. He knows that we cannot be fulfilled and happy apart from fellowship with Him, and apart from obeying His laws for life. Because sin ruins men and women, God is the sworn enemy of sin. I am glad that He is.

Has the oft-repeated story of salvation dulled the wonder of this great Good News? If so, let us restore the joy by remembering.

Can I recall the day when I knew I was guilty? When I had sinned against God and had deeply wronged another person? Do I remember the burden of condemnation when I knew that without God's mercy I was lost? Can I recall my confession?

> Just as I am, without one plea
> But that Thy blood was shed for me,
> And that Thou bidd'st me come to Thee,
> O Lamb of God, I come! I come!
> —CHARLOTTE ELLIOTT

In response to my faith God forgave my sin. I gladly testified with Paul—and that testimony rings true today: "Therefore being justified by faith, we have peace with God through our Lord Jesus Christ" (Rom. 5:1).

Oh, it is the Good News! Father, help me to share it with someone today. In Jesus' name I ask it. Amen.

▼

Scripture: Romans 5—8
The Story: Romans 8:1-16

The life-giving principles of the Spirit have freed you in Christ from the control of the principles of sin and death (Rom. 8:2, NBV).

Life in the Spirit

Jesus prayed that His followers might be filled with the Holy Spirit. Paul would breathe a deep Amen to that prayer. The truth of the Spirit-filled life, perhaps not clear to the Roman church, may have prompted Paul to write: "I long to see you, that I may impart unto you some spiritual gift, to the end ye may be established" (1:11). In today's 16 verses he speaks of the Spirit 15 times.

Chapter 7 reflects our deep need for entire sanctification. Paul testifies that apart from the work of the Holy Spirit, the human heart is carnal. This evil nature is a foreign element that enslaves the unsanctified spirit. Carnality works in opposition to our best interests as children of God, and frustrates our highest desires: "I can will what is right, but I cannot do it. For I do not do the good I want, but the evil I do not want is what I do" (7:18-19, RSV).

In misery, the unsanctified spirit cries, "O wretched man that I am! who shall deliver me from the body of this death?" (7:24). But Paul has found the answer in the glorious gospel of which he is not ashamed: "I thank God there is a way out through Jesus Christ our Lord" (7:25, Phillips).

Chapters 6—7 deal with the negative side of entire sanctification, but in chapter 8 we see the constructive work of the Holy Spirit. God's highest will for us is to be Spirit-filled and to live Spirit-led lives. "As many as are led by the Spirit of God, they are the sons of God" (8:14). The bottom line for the Christian is *life in the Spirit*. The Bible teaches no lower goal—and offers no higher gift of grace.

It is the indwelling Holy Spirit who keeps us free from sin (8:2). The Spirit gives life and peace (8:6). The blessed Holy Spirit brings assurance of salvation (8:14-16). It is He who aids us at every point of need. "The Spirit helps us in our weakness. We do not know what we ought to pray, but the Spirit himself intercedes for us with groans that words cannot express" (8:26, NIV).

I am thankful for the Holy Spirit whom Jesus promised to His followers.

> *Holy Spirit, be my Guide.*
> *Holy Spirit, my door's open wide.*
> *Make me to know Thy will divine;*
> *Holy Spirit, be Thou mine!**
> —MILDRED COPE

▼

☐ **WEEK 45, FRIDAY**   **ROMANS**

Scripture: Romans 9—11

In 9:14-18, did God harden Pharaoh's heart? Does God ever do anything to hinder a person from finding and obeying Him? No. See note at Exod. 7:13, page 31.

The Story: Romans 9:1-3; 10:1; 11:26-36

O the depth of the riches both of the wisdom and knowledge of God! how unsearchable are his judgments, and his ways past finding out! (Rom. 11:33).

Hang In There

What shall I do when God doesn't seem to be doing anything about my deepest concern?

This is the issue with which Paul wrestles in today's scripture. It is the pain that a Christian parent feels for a wayward child; the agony of a Christian wife for an unsaved husband: "Oh Israel, my people! Oh, my Jewish brothers! How I long for you to come to Christ. My heart is heavy within me and I grieve bitterly day and night because of you" (9:2, TLB).

What shall I do, when with bowed head I sit where Paul sat? God's answer is, Do what Paul did.

I maintain my concern. I keep my whole life committed as an instrument for God's use to answer my prayer. "When does a Christian stop praying for the salvation of non-Christians in the family? Never! But there comes a time when continuing a burden at the level which affects emotional and physical health is not to the glory of God. It may take more faith to commit a son or daughter into God's hands than it does to keep up a self-defeating, joy-reducing schedule of prayer which tends to forget the blessings of God and to downgrade the prayers which have been answered" (Leslie Parrott).

I try to see the situation from God's perspective. I may recall how long it took me to respond to His call—and how slowly my own life is being transformed into Christ's likeness. I reflect on God's concern, His love, and His power. I recognize and am grateful for every manifestation of goodness in the person for whom I pray. I focus on the foundations for faith. Here I find my best interim answers while waiting for God's full reply.

Having done all that I can do, *I commit myself and my loved one to the care of the Heavenly Father.* That is the right place for both of us. "How inexhaustible God's resources, wisdom, and knowledge are!" (Smith-Goodspeed). He knows more than I know. He is wiser than I. His love for my loved one is deeper than mine. "Shall not the Judge of all the earth do right?" (Gen. 18:25).

Today I do not see the way out of the dilemma. But I know that the way out is with God. I shall walk with Him. Together we shall find the answer to my deep desire—and to His.

▼

☐ WEEK 45, SATURDAY   ROMANS

> *Scripture:* Romans 12—13
> *The Story:* Romans 12:1-13
>
> **I plead with you therefore, brethren, by the compassion of God, to present all your faculties to him as a living and holy sacrifice acceptable to him** (Rom. 12:1, Weymouth).

I Will Give All

Father in heaven, today I come as Your child. Your mercies to me have been great. I am a follower of Your Son. In Him You have already made my life rich and full. But He promised that You would fill me with the Holy Spirit; He prayed for me that I might be sanctified. I yearn for that prayer to be answered in my life.

Just now I give myself to You. I give my life to You as completely as if my body were laid upon an altar and my life were to be taken as a sacrifice. I reserve no rights of my own; I withhold nothing that You desire.

I give You my all. But this commitment is a reasonable service because You love me. You accept my gift. You fill me with Your Holy Spirit. You give me back my sanctified self to walk in closer fellowship with You for all the rest of my days. You let me share in Your perfect love.

Transfused by that love, my life is already being transformed into Your image. I am losing the life-style of the world around me. I see more clearly how You wish me to live. I more quickly do Your bidding. By the power of the Holy Spirit I am enabled to do Your "good, and acceptable, and perfect will."

I no longer see myself as an independent ego. I am the child of God; created by Him; to be nurtured by Him. I am the brother of my fellowman, to help him when I can.

You have taught me that I have something to share. My gift can be a blessing to others. I have given myself wholly to You, now teach me to use my gift in a ministry to Your people. I give because of the faith and love You have given to me. I give simply, I give diligently, I give faithfully, I give cheerfully. By Your grace I shall keep on giving. I give because You have given to me. I give because I desire Your kingdom to come. I yearn for Your will to be done on "earth, as it is in heaven."

> *What shall I give Thee, Master?*
> *Thou hast giv'n all for me;*
> *Not just a part or half of my heart;*
> *I will give all to Thee.*
> —HOMER W. GRIMES

455

Scripture: Romans 14—16

In chapter 16 how could Paul greet by name 26 persons in Rome when he had never been there? The answer is mobility in the church. Priscilla and Aquila had been Paul's colleagues in Corinth. Epenetus (16:5) had been his "first convert to Christ in the province of Asia" (NIV). We assume the others were also persons whom he had met on his missionary journeys. They had migrated to Rome, and Paul knew they were now part of the Christian congregation there.

The Story: Romans 14:1—15:2

Make up your mind not to put any stumbling block or obstacle in your brother's way (Rom. 14:13, NIV).

Right Attitudes Toward Incidentals

In Paul's day Christians were divided over three issues: (1) Is it right to eat meat that has been offered to idols? (2) Should a Christian ever eat meat—or only vegetables? (3) Should Christians observe holy days that are sacred to the Jews? Paul felt that none of these actions was right or wrong in itself. These were decisions where Christians could differ and both be equally pleasing to God. They were incidentals. But when do such incidentals become important?

Lord Jesus, would You sit here with us today as we read Your Word and try to find Your answers to this question?

Read verse 1. Do I really accept my Christian brother who has odd ideas about serving You? Which is more important to me, his oddities or the fact that he is a fellow Christian honestly seeking to follow You?

Read verses 3, 10. Have I criticized his oddities to someone else in the church? Have I despised him for those strange views even if I have not talked about them to others? Forgive me, Jesus.

Read verses 5-8. Have I shaped my own life-style by consciously seeking Your will, or have I simply absorbed my attitudes and habits thoughtlessly from my past—whether good or bad? Am I living to please myself, or am I sincerely trying to "live unto the Lord"?

Read verses 14, 22-23. Have I tried to ignore my conscience when You were speaking to me? Has Your Holy Spirit convicted me of actions that are not pleasing to Him? Am I allowing something in my conduct or attitudes that condemns me? Please forgive me; I will change it.

Read verse 17. Father, am I guiding my life by Your priorities? When something seems questionable, do I ask, Is it right? If there is a difference with my brother, do I resolve it on the basis of greater peace in the church? In a questionable situation, do I ask, Will my decision and action bring joy as I look back on it?

Read verses 13, 16, 20-21. Have I considered my influence? Have I reflected on how my actions may affect others who are seeking to follow You? I really would not want to hurt someone for whom Christ died. If I have been careless about my influence, increase in me Your concern for the welfare of others.

Read verse 19. In tension-filled encounters, do I quickly seek my own way? Or do I consider first what will bring peace to the church and benefit to my brother?

Read verse 22. When there are differences, do I agitate the tension or let the friction quietly subside?

Thank You, Jesus, for spending this time with us and for reminding us again of Your way of love.

> *Lord, take my life, and make it wholly Thine;*
> *Fill my poor heart with Thy great love divine.*
> *Take all my will, my passion, self, and pride.*
> *I now surrender; Lord, in me abide.*
> —J. Edwin Orr

The Corinthian Letters

On Paul's second missionary journey he spent a year and a half in Corinth (A.D. 50-51). There he won converts to Christ and established a congregation. See the story in Acts 18:1-19.

These converts had come from a pagan environment of loose morals and intellectual pride. They were new Christians but often influenced by old habits and a worldly environment.

Four years after leaving Corinth, Paul was pastoring the new church in Ephesus, 300 miles across the Aegean Sea. Word reached him there concerning problems that threatened the life of the Corinthian church. He wrote the first letter from Ephesus, about A.D. 55; the second, a year later from Macedonia. In the letters he deals with problems of deep concern to Christian pastors and committed laypersons.

Scripture: 1 Corinthians 1—4
The Story: 1 Corinthians 1:1-10

I appeal to you, brothers, in the name of our Lord Jesus Christ ... that there may be no divisions among you (1 Cor. 1:10, NIV).

How Christ Heals Divisions

Paul might well have prayed the Southern preacher's prayer—for Corinth, and for us: "Yo' ain't what yo' ought to be; yo' ain't what yo' wants to be; yo' ain't what yo's gwine to be; but still, thank de good God, yo' ain't what yo' used to be."

In these four chapters Christ's Apostle must deal with a quarrelsome party spirit. In his impassioned appeal for a united church he does not ask for a deadening sameness of ideas. The rich variety that God has built into human personality is bound to cause differences of opinion. But in the great fundamentals of our Christian faith we are agreed; and in the lesser issues, our differences are not to be pressed to the point of broken fellowship. It was in this that the Corinthians had failed to be Christlike. Their differences had become quarrels.

Division destroys God's work. Therefore, it is a sin to bring division into a congregation over an issue that is not fundamental. Even in important differences it is a sin to quarrel. Christians may part and go their separate ways—but they must go in a spirit of love. Always Christian love must be present because love is the glory of the Church.

In *Screwtape Letters,* C. S. Lewis tells of one of the devil's emissaries. He was greatly disturbed because the man he was trying to damn had joined the church. The devil reassured his henchman that there was nothing to worry about if only the man could be kept aware of *the little things.* But, warned the devil, *Don't let him see the glory of the Church!*

God's Word admonishes us to forget lesser differences, and to fix our minds on the big agreement. Nine times in the first nine verses Paul turns our thoughts to Christ who died for us, and who yearns for deep fellowship among us.

How does the Lord want to heal our divisions?

> *Turn your eyes upon Jesus;*
>   *Look full in His wonderful face;*
> *And the things that divide will grow strangely dim*
>   *In the light of His glory and grace.* *
>   —HELEN HOWARTH LEMMEL, adapted

▼

☐ **WEEK 46, TUESDAY**   **1 CORINTHIANS**

Scripture: 1 Corinthians 5—8

In chapter 5 we see that Christian discipline is sometimes necessary to save a church. Chapter 7 discusses Christian management of the sex urge. For Paul's broader discussion of Christian marriage see Eph. 5:21—6:4.

The Story: 1 Corinthians 8:1-13

If eating meat offered to idols is going to make my brother sin, I'll not eat any of it as long as I live, because I don't want to do this to him (1 Cor. 8:13, TLB).

Guidelines to Goodness

Recently in our Sunday School class we faced a personal question: Am I personally involved in some debate over right and wrong? We agreed that the debate might be between Christians, as was the eating of meat offered to idols in Corinth. Or it might be in my own conscience: What ought I to do? In either case we are asking, What choices are Christian? How shall I guide my actions?

We agreed that these guidelines would help us:

Is my choice biblical? God's Word often gives clear guidance. The Bible says, "Thou shalt not commit adultery" (Exod. 20:14); therefore in chapter 5 Paul does not hesitate to expel a flagrantly immoral man from the church. Where the Bible speaks clearly on moral issues, I accept that rule for my Christian life.

Is it reasonable? Where the Bible does not speak, I may use my sanctified judgment. In 8:4-6 and 8, Paul presents facts to convince the mind. We know there is only one God; we need not, therefore, be troubled by irrational teachings about false gods.

Is it the judgment of the church? Where the Bible does not speak explicitly, the majority conscience of God's people is my best guide. Is it not reasonable that a Christian majority decision is likely to be closer to God's will than my individual judgment? This collective conscience is usually expressed in church rules—and Paul commends it as a safe guide: "If anyone wants to be argumentative about it, I can only say that we and the churches of God generally hold this ruling on the matter" (1 Cor. 11:16, Phillips).

Is it loving? Genuine love is our ultimate guideline to Christian choices. Love asks, How will the choice affect my brother? Love answers, If my choice injures my brother I will never do that again.

Is the choice easy or hard? Most of the moral decisions can be resolved correctly by asking God to give me courage to take the way that is hardest for me.

What does the Holy Spirit tell me? After prayerfully considering these guidelines, I may ask: Lord, what do You want me to do? As Christ's follower I am a Spirit-guided person. Jesus promised, "When he, the Spirit of truth, is come, he will guide you into all truth" (John 16:13).

Have I been filled with the Holy Spirit? Then I may turn to Him—and I do.

Spirit of God: "Just tell me what to do and I will do it, Lord. As long as I live I'll wholeheartedly obey" (Ps. 119:33-34, TLB).

▼

☐ **WEEK 46, WEDNESDAY**   **1 CORINTHIANS**

Scripture: 1 Corinthians 9—11

In chapter 9 Paul defends his actions as an Apostle of Christ. In chapter 10 he shows us how the Old Testament serves as a guide to New Testament Christians.

The Story: 1 Corinthians 11:23-28
> *In the middle of Paul's counsels for Co-rinth's problems and failures, we thank You, Lord, for these words that have blessed Your children for 20 centuries.*

Take, eat: this is my body, which is broken for you: this do in remembrance of me (1 Cor. 11:24).

"In Remembrance of Me"

Our purpose in the Christian life is to be faithful to Christ, to be guided by His counsel, to follow His example. Jesus did two things to help us continue as His faithful followers: (1) He sent the Holy Spirit to teach us; He "will bring glory to me by taking from what is mine and making it known to you" (John 16:14, NIV). (2) He established the Lord's Supper to help us remember.

There is strength in recalling what Christ has done for us. In Him "we have redemption through his blood, the forgiveness of sins, according to the riches of his grace" (Eph. 1:7). At the Communion table I remember that, through Christ, I am forgiven; I have become a child of God, and I have the supporting help of fellow Christians in the church.

In communion with Christ I recall my failures—but not to discouragement and defeat. Paul counsels us, "Let a man examine himself, and so let him eat of that bread, and drink of that cup." As I come to the Lord's table, I open my heart to His probing Spirit. If He shows me failure, I confess and repent and am forgiven. Then I "eat of that bread and drink of that cup" to my "soul's comfort and joy."

At the Lord's Supper I remember that Jesus suffered and died for me. My spirit is drawn to Him, my love burns with a steadier flame, and my devotion is deepened. Through remembering Him, I grow strong.

> We may not know, we cannot tell
>   What pains He had to bear;
> But we believe it was for us
>   He hung and suffered there.
> Oh, dearly, dearly has He loved,
>   And we must love Him, too;
> And trust in His redeeming blood,
>   And try His works to do.
>   —CECIL F. ALEXANDER

▼

☐ **WEEK 46, THURSDAY**   **1 CORINTHIANS**

Scripture: 1 Corinthians 12
The Story: 1 Corinthians 12:12-27

You are the body of Christ, and each one of you is a part of it (1 Cor. 12:27, NIV).

I Am Important to God

Today the big word in psychology is *self-image*. If my life is to be fulfilled I must feel needed; I must be important to someone. As a Christian I can be stunted and destroyed by wrong attitudes of self-depreciation and discouragement. Therefore God boosts my sense of self-worth. He assures me that He loves me, He needs me, He has a job that only I can do for Him.

I stand a little taller when I remember that my life and my service to others are important to God. My head comes up when the Bible assures me that I have been chosen especially for my place of service: "God put every different part in the body just as he wanted it to be" (18, TEV).

God needs many ministries in His work—and He needs mine! If He had needed only eyes He would have made the body just one big eye. But He didn't. Important as they are, eyes would have a difficult time without hands and feet. Every one of us belongs to Christ's Body, and every one is needed. The whole body suffers when a finger hurts. The whole life is endangered when just one tiny part of one small gland fails to do its appointed task. I am that important to God's work in someone's life.

God's Word warns me that there is to be no soul-destroying self-depreciation and self-pity in my life. Humility? Yes. Self-depreciation? No.

If I feel useless, it is because I am comparing my service with someone who seems to be more talented and important. But that attitude is not Christlike, and such thoughts wither the soul. I can find someone who needs me; in Christ's name I can help him in some way.

When I begin to serve, I become more Christlike and more worthy. Then God pours into my spirit His gift of feeling my worth to Him and my importance to other people.

Father, I pray not so much to feel worthy as to be worthy and to be of service to Your children.

Make me a blessing, O Saviour, I pray.
*Make me a blessing to someone today.**
                                          —IRA B. WILSON

Scripture: 1 Corinthians 13—14
The Story: 1 Corinthians 13:1-13
Love never fails (1 Cor. 13:8, NIV).

Paul Sings of Love

Father, thank You for Paul's hymn of love. Teach me to love more deeply as I read Your Word today.

"If I had the gift of being able to speak in other languages without learning them, and could speak in every language there is in all of heaven and earth, but didn't love others, I would only be making noise. If I had the gift of prophecy and knew all about what is going to happen in the future, knew everything about *everything,* but didn't love others, what good would it do? Even if I had the gift of faith so that I could speak to a mountain and make it move, I would still be worth nothing at all without love. If I gave everything I have to poor people, and if I were burned alive for preaching the Gospel but didn't love others, I would be of no value whatever.

"Love is very patient and kind, never jealous or envious, never boastful or proud, never haughty or selfish or rude. Love does not demand its own way. It is not irritable or touchy. It does not hold grudges and will hardly even notice when others do it wrong. It is never glad about injustice, but rejoices whenever truth wins out. If you love someone you will be loyal to him no matter what the cost. You will always believe in him, always expect the best of him, and always stand your ground in defending him.

"All the special gifts and powers from God will someday come to an end, but love goes on forever. Someday prophecy, and speaking in unknown languages, and special knowledge—these gifts will disappear. Now we know so little, even with our special gifts, and the preaching of those most gifted is still so poor. But when we have been made perfect and complete, then the need for these inadequate special gifts will come to an end, and they will disappear.

"It's like this: when I was a child I spoke and thought and reasoned as a child does. But when I became a man my thoughts grew far beyond those of my childhood, and now I have put away the childish things. In the same way, we can see and understand only a little about God now, as if we were peering at his reflection in a poor mirror; but someday we are going to see him in his completeness, face to face. Now all that I know is hazy and blurred, but then I will see everything clearly, just as clearly as God sees into my heart right now.

"There are three things that remain—faith, hope, and love—and the greatest of these is love" (TLB).

▼

Scripture: 1 Corinthians 15—16
The Story: 1 Corinthians 15:42-58

O death, where is thy sting? O grave, where is thy victory? . . . Thanks be to God, which giveth us the victory through our Lord Jesus Christ (1 Cor. 15:55, 57).

"But Now Is Christ Risen"

Faith for the future gives us strength for today. In our text it was as if Paul were already on the execution block. Gesturing to the executioner to hold the blow for a moment, he looks up at the ax and sings, "O death, where is thy sting?" He glances at the open grave and exults, "O grave, where is thy victory?" He then voices a prayer of praise for us all, "Thanks be to God, which giveth us the victory through our Lord Jesus Christ"—and motions for the ax to fall.

Death could not frighten this man because he knew that

465

Christ had conquered even death. If there be in our hearts any uncertainty about the resurrection of Jesus we are bereft: "Ah, if in this life we have nothing but a mere hope in Christ, we are of all men to be pitied most! But it is not so! Christ did rise from the dead" (15:19-20, Moffatt).

In the ceremony of the Passover the Jews presented a barley sheaf in the Temple, the first of the harvest. It was a sign of thankfulness and an expression of faith that the whole harvest would be gathered. Paul fittingly pictures the resurrection of our Lord "as the early ripe and early reaped sheaf, the pledge and prophecy of the whole ingathering." Eternal life is God's gift to all who belong to Him. "But now is Christ risen from the dead, and become the first fruits of them that slept." Because He lives, we too shall live.

Paul was no longer a young man. He had lived a strenuous life which had taken its toll of his physical vitality. He saw what all of us must recognize as life's sun moves toward midafternoon; our bodies have not been built for eternity. They shall perish; signs of decay may already be appearing.

But as the body grows weaker our spirits may grow stronger. As the ties that bind us to earth are loosened we feel the bonds of heaven grow taut. We are not to be cast adrift at the setting of the sun. Eternal life today is our strong assurance for tomorrow.

> *Because He lives, I can face tomorrow;*
> *Because He lives all fear is gone;*
> *Because I know He holds the future,*
> *And life is worth the living just because He lives.* *
> —WILLIAM AND GLORIA GAITHER

▼

☐ **WEEK 47, SUNDAY**   **2 CORINTHIANS**

Scripture: 2 Corinthians 1—3
The Story: 2 Corinthians 1:3-11 (Paul's message will be clearer if you read from a modern English version)

Thank God, the Father of our Lord Jesus Christ, that he is our Father and the Source of all mercy and comfort (2 Cor. 1:3, Phillips).

The God of All Comfort

Discouragement is one of our deepest dangers in the Christian life. Hope and courage are among the greatest blessings that come from God, our Father—and He wants us to share them with others.

It ain't so much the money . . . Keeps the old world turnin' 'round,
But just the liftin' up o' folks who fall upon the ground;
An' sometimes in the darkness to hear an humble cry
An' give the hand o' fellowship to a feller passin' by.

—A. E. B.

"Let us give thanks to the God and Father of our Lord Jesus Christ, the merciful Father, the God from whom all help comes!" (1:3, TEV).

Help me to remember "that I am able to comfort people who are in any distress by the comfort with which I myself am comforted by God" (1:4, Moffatt).

Thank You, Father, for the encouragement from Your servant who suffered so deeply: "You can be sure that the more we undergo sufferings for Christ, the more he will shower us with his comfort and encouragement" (1:5, TLB).

Teach us, Father, that any effort we make for You is blessed by You; and even any suffering that follows is therefore good. "We are in deep trouble for bringing you God's comfort and salvation. But in our trouble God . . . comforted us" (1:6-7, TLB).

Father, sometimes I shrink from the price my loved ones must pay because I follow You. But thanks for the deep persuasion that following You will also be best for them. Let my life say persuasively to each one: "We are . . . confident that if you have to suffer troubles as we have done, then, like us, you will find the comfort and encouragement of God" (1:7, Phillips).

Thank You, Father, for Paul's personal testimony: "I would like you to know about the distress which befell me in Asia, brothers. I was crushed, crushed far beyond what I could stand, so much so that I despaired even of life. . . . But this was to make me rely not

467

on myself but on God who raises the dead; he rescued me from so terrible a death, he rescues still, and I rely upon him for the hope that he will continue to rescue me" (1:8-10, Moffatt).

To You, the God of all comfort, I give praise today.

▼

Scripture: 2 Corinthians 4—6
The Story: 2 Corinthians 4:1-9

God ... made his light shine in our hearts, to bring us the knowledge of God's glory shining in the face of Christ (2 Cor. 4:6; all quotes from TEV).

When God Speaks to Me

It is Saturday morning. An urgent issue affecting the welfare of the church has been in the forefront of my mind for several days. My actions did not create the problem, but my decision is a significant factor in setting a policy. I have been in consultation with others who share responsibility for this policy, but we do not all see alike. Whatever decision is made, there will be some benefits and some losses to the church. I wish the issue were so clear that all would be in agreement—but they are not. A decision must be made, and I have been wishing someone else had that responsibility.

Before breakfast I spent a few devotional moments with the Bible. My current reading is from the *Good News Bible, Today's English Version.* As I began the fourth chapter of 2 Corinthians these were the first words that I read—and they were for me: "God in his mercy has given us this work to do, and so we do not become discouraged. ... we do not act with deceit, nor do we falsify the word of God. In the full light of truth we live in God's sight and try to commend ourselves to everyone's good conscience" (vv. 1-2).

At breakfast I shared my discovery with Mrs. Harper. She immediately responded: "That is just what I need for the problem that we have been having with several uncontrolled pupils in our

Primary Department. I want to tell my teachers, 'God in his mercy has given us this work to do, and so we do not become discouraged.'"

Thank You, Lord, for Your word to Mrs. Harper and to me.

This personal illumination of the Scripture is the work of the Holy Spirit. Sometimes the message comes without my initiative. More often God speaks in this direct way when I sincerely open my heart to Him. At these times I begin to read the Bible, asking, *Lord, what do You want to say to me?* This is my prayer today:

> *Break Thou the bread of life, Dear Lord, to me,*
> *As Thou didst break the loaves beside the sea.*
> *Beyond the sacred page I seek Thee, Lord;*
> *My spirit pants for Thee, O living Word!*
> —MARY A. LATHBURY

▼

Scripture: 2 Corinthians 7—9

Chapter 7 is the picture of a parent who has severely disciplined his son; he now gathers the sobbing child in his arms and assures him of a father's love.

In chapters 8—9 Paul writes of a money-raising project. He asked the Gentile churches to join him in raising and sending a substantial offering to help the poor in the Jewish churches of Palestine. In the earlier letter (1 Cor. 16:1-4) he had told the Corinthians about the project.

The Story: 2 Corinthians 9:6-15

Each man should give what he has decided in his heart to give, not reluctantly or under compulsion, for God loves a cheerful giver (2 Cor. 9:7, NIV).

The Blessings of Giving

God's grace includes all of His free gifts to us. Giving is our glad response to Him. Thank You, Father, for Your Word that shows how to use our money in ways that enrich our lives.

I am glad You have reminded us that giving to Your work is not money lost; it is money invested in ministries of deep concern to You. As we give generously to Your work, we never regret it. We are sure that "whoever sows generously will also reap generously" (NIV).

Since I am Yours, what is mine belongs to You. I gladly join these Christians of Macedonia who "gave themselves first to the Lord" (8:5, NIV). Because I have given myself wholly to You, I do not find it hard to put my money alongside of my life. I give most freely when I remember most fully what You have done for me.

I am grateful for Your reminder that I must be honest in estimating my ability to give. You do not ask for what I do not have. However, You do not permit me to give little when there is great need—and You do not bless me for a low level of giving when my resources increase. Thanks for Your reminder, "Whoever sows sparingly will also reap sparingly" (NIV).

Father, when I can't quite see how I shall give what You ask and still meet my financial obligations, I rest on Your Son's promise: "Seek ye first the kingdom of God, and his righteousness; and all these things shall be added unto you" (Matt. 6:33). I believe Your promise, made through Paul, "God is able to give you more than you need, so that you will always have all you need for yourselves and more than enough for every good cause" (9:8, TEV).

It is a glorious thing to be a Christian and to share in Christ's work. Today I join the Apostle's glad testimony of praise:

"Thanks be unto God for his unspeakable gift."

▼

Scripture: 2 Corinthians 10—13

These chapters deal with Paul's authority as an apostle. They include a refutation of charges made against him and his work in Corinth; they also give his testimony to show us how God was working in his life.

The Story: 2 Corinthians 10:7-18 (Read it in a
        modern translation; TLB and NIV are both
        good)

Let him who boasts boast in the Lord (2 Cor. 10:17; all quotes from NIV).

Can God Commend Me?

Self-defense may sometimes be necessary; it may sometimes be helpful; but defending oneself is never pleasant nor attractive. That is why Paul reminds us, "It is not the man who commends himself who is approved, but the man whom the Lord commends" (10:18).

What should we do when criticized or attacked? Perhaps Paul's model can help us.

Show love. Paul begins: "By the meekness and gentleness of Christ, I appeal to you" (10:1). He says in effect, "I am Paul, the pastor who labored among you for 18 months, the man who led you to Christ. I appeal to you in the spirit of our Savior and Lord." If any soft answer can turn away wrath, the answer of love is the one to use.

Be concerned for the welfare of the church. "Besides everything else, I face daily the pressure of my concern for all the churches. Who is weak, and I do not feel weak? Who is led into sin, and I do not inwardly burn?" (11:28-29).

Testify to God's help. "There was given me a thorn in my flesh, a messenger of Satan, to torment me. Three times I pleaded with the Lord to take it away from me. But he said to me, 'My grace is sufficient for you, for my power is made perfect in weakness.'

Therefore I will boast all the more gladly about my weaknesses, so that Christ's power may rest on me. . . . For when I am weak, then I am strong" (12:7-10).

Lift our vision to high goals. "Aim for perfection, listen to my appeal, be of one mind, live in peace. And the God of love and peace will be with you" (13:11).

Pray for your opposition. Paul seeks to close this breach of fellowship by a sincere prayer for those who opposed him: "May the grace of the Lord Jesus Christ, and the love of God, and the fellowship of the Holy Spirit be with you all" (13:14).

Can God commend us in our response to criticism? He can when we respond in love, in concern for His work, in testimony to His grace, in seeking His will, and in prayer for those who think we are wrong.

▼

Scripture: Galatians 1—3

In 3:6-9, Paul appeals to Old Testament truth because many to whom he wrote were Jews by birth—and all were being wrongly influenced by Judaizing teachers. See also 4:21-31.

The Story: Galatians 2:15—3:3 (Read in a modern translation)

Christ lives in me. And the real life I now have . . . is a result of my trusting in the Son of God, who loved me and gave himself for me (Gal. 2:20, TLB).

Life in Christ

Paul learned that Jewish teachers had visited the churches he had founded in Galatia—Antioch, Iconium, Lystra, and Derbe (Acts 12:14; 14:1, 5-6). The false teachers had almost convinced these new converts that in order to be Christians they must observe the

Jewish ceremonial laws. Paul knew he must give them—and us—clear guidance because no man's faith is secure if he accepts wrong answers to his questions.

Of these false teachers the Apostle writes: "They tried to get us all tied up in their rules, like slaves in chains. But we did not listen to them for a single moment, for we did not want to confuse you into thinking that salvation can be earned by being circumcised and by obeying Jewish laws" (2:4-5, TLB).

He appeals to faltering Galatian Christians: "I am amazed that you are turning away so soon from God who, in his love and mercy, invited you to share the eternal life he gives through Christ; you are already following a different 'way to heaven,' which really doesn't go to heaven at all. . . . you are being fooled by those who twist and change the truth concerning Christ" (1:6-7, TLB).

He tells us, "It was through reading the Scripture that I came to realize that I could never find God's favor by trying—and failing—to obey the laws. I came to realize that acceptance with God comes by believing in Christ" (2:19, TLB).

I am glad for this way to heaven through faith—by accepting God's whole plan of salvation through Christ.

✔ He forgives our sins when we ask to be forgiven.

✔ He pours into our forgiven hearts a spirit of love and complete trust. Because we trust Him, we believe the ways He chooses for us are best.

✔ Because we love Christ, we follow His law: "You shall love the Lord your God with all your heart . . . and . . . you shall love your neighbor as yourself" (Matt. 22:37-39, RSV).

✔ Because we love Christ supremely, we do what He asks us to do.

I am glad that Paul insisted on the truth, and I rejoice in that truth. With him I confess:

"The Lord Jesus Christ . . . died for our sins just as God our Father planned, and rescued us from this evil world in which we live. All glory to God through all the ages of eternity. Amen" (1:3-5, TLB).

▼

Scripture: Galatians 4—6

Paul's affliction (4:15) may have been poor eyesight. See 6:11, also 2 Cor. 12:7-9.

The Story: Galatians 5:13-25

If we live in the Spirit, let us also walk in the Spirit (Gal. 5:25).

"The Fruit of the Spirit Is . . ."

In Christ we are freed from Jewish law, but we are guided by the Spirit of God within. As we allow the Holy Spirit to fill us, our lives more and more resemble the spirit of Jesus.

The nine attractive fruits of the Spirit-filled life fall into three triads. The first three—love, joy, and peace—are feelings that flourish as our lives are yielded to the indwelling Christ.

I want to be filled with the *love* of Jesus. I want to be as compassionate a person as Christ wants me to be. *Father, fill me with a love like Yours.*

The fountain of my Christian *joy* has its source in God. When I am most sure of Him that fountain bubbles up in my spirit. I am glad that I belong to Christ. Just now I feel the joy of His presence.

My *peace* also comes from God. In His presence my worries no longer worry me. *Thank You, Father, for Your promise:* "The peace of God, which passeth all understanding, shall keep your hearts and minds through Christ Jesus" (Phil. 4:7).

The second group of graces are Christlike attitudes that surface in our relationships with others.

To be *longsuffering* is to have Jesus' spirit of patience. *Lord, let that fruit grow and ripen in me!*

Gentleness is love shown in small things and to small people. Today I shall pay loving attention to some child.

Goodness is love that has put on its working clothes. It is "seeking to do good to the bodies and souls of men; feeding the hungry, clothing the naked, visiting the sick and imprisoned, and ministering to the needy." My heart yearns for more of this fruit.

The last cluster of graces are the Spirit-nourished attitudes with which we face the problems of life.

Faith, or faithfulness, is the grace to keep walking with God when I am tempted to quit. *I thank You, Father, for every time You have given me courage to keep going.*

Meekness is the readiness to adapt myself to another person when I don't feel like it. *Teach me, Lord, to be flexible for You.*

Perhaps Paul listed *temperance* last because it is the most difficult to cultivate. It is self-control. In the Spirit-led life, temperance is disciplining myself in line with the leading of the Holy Spirit.

Father, at some point today, remind me to deny myself in order to be more like my Master. In Jesus' name I ask it. Amen.

▼

☐ WEEK 47, SATURDAY   EPHESIANS

Scripture: Ephesians 1—2

Ephesians was probably written as a circular letter to be read in the churches of Ephesus, Laodicea, and Colosse. See 1:15 and 3:2 where Paul indicates lack of acquaintance with those to whom he wrote. He would not have written this way if he were writing only for the Ephesians with whom he had recently labored. See also Col. 4:16 indicating Paul's use of circular letters.

How shall we understand the meaning of predestination in 1:5, 11, and elsewhere in the New Testament? In the original language these terms mean only "preplanned." They are the same words a surveyor used when he said, "We planned to erect the building at this place." To be predestined means only that God planned to save us through the work of Christ and our acceptance of Him.

The Story: Ephesians 1:3-7; 2:1-10

By grace are ye saved through faith; and that not of yourselves: it is the gift of God (Eph. 2:8).

Thinking About Our Salvation

Whenever we open the Word of God we stand in a holy place, but today we enter the holy of holies. Salvation from sin is God's supreme purpose for every man—and Christ's atonement is at the heart of our salvation.

No fact of Scripture is clearer than the awesome truth: "Christ died for our sins" (1 Cor. 15:3). Jesus came to conquer sin in human life. His atonement is the only method revealed in the Bible for dealing with this deep-seated problem. Christ's death and resurrection are God's way of reversing the tragedy caused by the fall of the human race. No words could present the truth more forcefully than Paul's declaration: "Because of his great love for us, God . . . made us alive with Christ" (2:4-5, NIV).

The Bible uses many figures to depict the devastation caused by sin, but no figure is stronger than the picture Paul paints. Man's alienation from God is called death. This spiritual death is at work in every unsaved person. At one time all of us lived in slavery to sin, and we "were by nature the children of wrath." Because of sin, we needed God's mercy; as slaves of sin we needed to be set free; as dead men, we needed Christ's resurrection power.

Salvation is offered because of our deep need, but more profoundly salvation begins in the purpose of God. The Father purposed to bring sinful men back to himself. In wisdom and love, God has made life for us possible through the suffering and death of His Son.

"Surely he hath borne our griefs, and carried our sorrows: yet we did esteem him stricken, smitten of God, and afflicted. But he was wounded for our transgressions, he was bruised for our iniquities: the chastisement of our peace was upon him; and with his stripes we are healed" (Isa. 53:4-5).

In response to God's love seen in Christ's sacrifice, our hearts can only reply:

> *Oh, dearly, dearly has He loved,*
> *And we must love Him, too;*
> *And trust in His redeeming blood*
> *And try His works to do.*
> —CECIL F. ALEXANDER

Scripture: Ephesians 3
The Story: Ephesians 1:15-19; 3:14-21

I . . . ask the God of our Lord Jesus Christ . . . to give you the Spirit (Eph. 1:16-17, TEV).

A Prayer for Us Christians

When Paul first visited Ephesus he inquired of the believers there, "Have ye received the Holy Ghost since ye believed?" (Acts 19:2). Because they had known only John's teaching, they were further instructed and given Christian baptism. Then under Paul's ministry "the Holy Ghost came on them."

The apostle felt this urgent need for Christians to receive the Spirit when he also wrote to the other churches where this letter was to be read. Twelve times he refers to the ministry of the Holy Spirit. That concern is at the heart of his two prayers for us Christians:

"Ever since I heard of your faith in the Lord Jesus and your love for all of God's people, I have not stopped giving thanks to God for you. I remember you in my prayers and ask the God of our Lord Jesus Christ . . . to give you the Spirit, who will make you wise and reveal God to you, so that you will know him. I ask that your minds may be opened to see his light, so that you will know what is the hope to which he has called you, how rich are the wonderful blessings he promises his people, and how very great is his power at work in us who believe" (1:15-19, TEV).

Again this pastor's heart turns to his most urgent concern in the second prayer: "I fall on my knees before the Father . . . I ask God . . . to give you power through his Spirit to be strong in your inner selves, and I pray that Christ will make his home in your hearts through faith. I pray that you may have your roots and foundation in love, so that you, together with all God's people,

477

may . . . be completely filled with the very nature of God" (3:14, 16-19, TEV).

To other Christians Paul had written: "The very God of peace sanctify you wholly . . . Faithful is he that calleth you, who also will do it" (1 Thess. 5:23-24). On that same note of confident faith, he closes his prayer for us: "To him who by means of his power working in us is able to do so much more than we can ever ask for, or even think of: to God be the glory in the church and in Christ Jesus for all time, forever and ever!" (3:20-21, TEV).

Father, may these prayers be answered in my life—and in the life of every believer. May we receive Your Holy Spirit, and so "be completely filled with the very nature of God."

▼

Scripture: Ephesians 4:1—5:20
The Story: Ephesians 5:1-20

Put on the new self, created to be like God in true righteousness and holiness (Eph. 4:24; all quotes from NIV).

Why Do We Serve Christ?

Peter admonishes us: "Always be prepared to give an answer to everyone who asks you to give a reason for the hope that you have" (1 Pet. 3:15). In our scripture story for today Paul gives us six!

V. 2. We serve God because we are grateful for the love He has shown by giving His Son for our salvation: "Christ loved us and gave himself up for us as a fragrant offering and sacrifice to God."

V. 3. We avoid the evils of sin because "these are improper for God's holy people." We have chosen the path that leads to life eternal. Because we have chosen that path, we adopt a life-style that is appropriate to it.

V. 6. Most of our reasons for serving God are positive; we

recognize that following Christ enriches our lives, increases our happiness, and gives us a sense of well-being. But in a moral world we also seek to avoid the penalties for wrongdoing. God is a righteous Father, and He does not tolerate unrighteous conduct in His children. "God's wrath comes on those who are disobedient." Let him who is wise avoid that wrath.

V. 8. We serve God because we have experienced the consequences of two life-styles. Once we were "in darkness." The deeds of those days left life fruitless and unfulfilled. It is shameful even to mention what we once did. But Christ has changed all that for us. Now we are "light in the Lord." The fruit of that light "consists in all goodness, righteousness and truth." Thank God, it was a good change! We would not want to go back.

Vv. 13-14. Because we now live in the light, we have nothing to hide. This freedom is such a release from guilt and depression that we can only join in the Apostle's glad exhortation to those who are yet in darkness: "Wake up, O sleeper, rise from the dead, and Christ will shine on you."

V. 18. We who follow Christ seek to live carefully and wisely, making the most of every opportunity to grow. To this end we seek to be "filled with the Spirit."

For these glad reasons we are "always giving thanks to God the Father for everything, in the name of our Lord Jesus Christ."

▼

□ **WEEK 48, TUESDAY**   **EPHESIANS**

Scripture: Ephesians 5:18—6:24
The Story: Ephesians 5:21—6:9

Submit to one another out of reverence for Christ (Eph. 5:21; all quotes from NIV).

Love in Every Relationship

God's Word urges us, "Be filled with the Spirit"—and His Spirit brings to us the spirit of perfect love. God counsels us to let love rule in every relationship with other persons.

In marriage? By all means! "Submit to one another out of reverence for Christ. Wives, submit to your husbands as to the Lord. . . . Husbands, love your wives, just as Christ loved the Church" (5:21-22, 25).

Does the admonition sound harsh to the wife tuned to the emancipation of women? Does submission seem a false teaching to the husband who assumes his authority is to be absolute? Where either attitude prevails, God would teach us the wisdom of love. Neither partner needs to fear submission in any relationship when Christlike love is the dominant atmosphere of the home. In such a marriage, every expectation from the partner is guided by love; and all major decisions are prayed over together. In this atmosphere, accepting the wishes of our partner is the path to happiness.

And love makes parent-child relationships smoother. I do not say placid, because some tensions are normal. But love always makes the relationships better than if love is missing. In *Your Teenager and You* Audrey Williamson writes:

"The teenager must understand that his respect for all the rules of the home is expected and required. If he fails to comply punishment must be forthcoming. . . . A plain talk in which the teenager is made to realize he has hurt or disappointed the parents is often the severest kind of punishment.

"Close the interview with prayer. It cements the bond of understanding and tempers justice with mercy. Keep the relationship between yourself and your children such that you can always pray together."

And what has God to say to us in our day when we no longer experience the roles of slave and master? There is still important truth in this passage. In all of our lives are there not difficult circumstances that we would not choose? And duties that we cannot avoid? In these hard assignments God says to us, "Serve wholeheartedly, as if you were serving the Lord . . . because you know that the Lord will reward everyone for whatever good he does" (6:7-8).

So, with Cecil Alexander we pray:

> *Jesus calls us. By Thy mercies,*
> *Saviour, may we hear Thy call,*
> *Give our hearts to Thy obedience,*
> *Serve and love Thee best of all.*

Scripture: Philippians 1—2
The Story: Philippians 2:1-11

Let this mind be in you, which was also in Christ Jesus (Phil. 2:5).

Christ Jesus, Our Lord

It is hard to be self-centered when we meditate on the unselfish spirit of Christ. Therefore, Paul asks us to imitate the love that made our Lord give up heaven's best.

"He always had the nature of God, but did not think that by force he should try to become equal with God. Instead of this, of his own free will he gave up all he had, and took the nature of a servant. He became like man and appeared in human likeness. He was humble and walked the path of obedience all the way to death—his death on the cross" (2:6-8, TEV).

Even though we can read the words, we cannot know the depth of their meaning. We can only dimly understand at what cost He came to make possible our salvation. We cannot rightly appreciate His humiliation—but we must try. He had everything that He most longed for—holiness, heaven, and unhindered union with the Father. Perhaps we can begin to sense that cost in the experienced anguish of losing a child. God gave His Son because there was no other good enough to save us.

The apostle uses a triple title to exalt the Son of God. The name *Jesus* reflects His work as Savior; *Christ* points to His coming as the Promised One of prophecy; *Lord* describes both His supreme position in the universe and the exalted place we give Him in our lives. With Avis Christiansen we lift our hymn of praise:

Oh, how I love Him, Saviour and Friend!
How can my praises ever find end!
Thro' years unnumbered on heaven's shore,
My tongue shall praise Him for evermore. *

And now that our hymn is sung, we would bow our hearts in prayer:

"Be ever more and more to us, Lord Jesus Christ, in all Thy answer to our boundless needs. . . . Let us come to Thee. Let us yield to Thee. Let us follow Thee. . . . And so through a blessed fellowship in Thy wondrous humiliation we shall partake for ever hereafter in the exaltations of Thy glory, which is the glory of immortal love" (H. C. G. Moule).

▼

Scripture: Philippians 3
The Story: Philippians 3:4-11

I count all things but loss for the excellency of the knowledge of Christ Jesus my Lord (Phil. 3:8).

The Fellowship of His Sufferings

Jesus and His disciples were making their way to Jerusalem for the last Passover—and the Cross. Mark tells us, "Those who followed were afraid." I too am sometimes fearful as I follow Jesus toward some of my crosses. I hesitate to join Paul's prayer: "I want to know Christ . . . and the fellowship of sharing in his sufferings" (3:10), NIV). Although it is a hard road, He goes before me, and He bids me follow.

If society is to be redeemed, if men and women are to be saved, we have our part to play in the great redemptive purposes of Christ. We, too, must be fully prepared to be offered up in sacrifice. This is no easy thing. We shun it. We prefer more pleasant activities.

But the Christian is a person prepared to be wiped out in order that others may be salvaged. In our crazy, chaotic society, if we would be of service we must be prepared to lay down our lives for others. This is not pious prattle. This is the tough, strong force of God's love at work in the world through us.

The apostle puts it candidly: "Jesus Christ laid down his life for us. And we ought to lay down our lives for our brothers" (1 John 3:16, NIV).

In His own special, wondrous way, God our Father calls each of us to serve that segment of society where our particular background, experience, personality, and training can be given in glad service. He does not ask me to try to save the whole of society. He does not suggest that any one of us can do it all. What He requires is that I be faithful where I am. He asks me to be alert and open to those who cross my path. He asks me to lay down my life for those immediately at hand.

All of this takes time. It calls for expenditure of enormous energy. It requires our willingness to be totally available to others.

We simply go out to love a dying world because God first loved us. We lay down our lives for others because Christ laid down His life for us. We go out to lift and cheer and restore because in wondrous care and compassion God's gracious Spirit does this for us.

O Christ my Lord, I follow You. I want to go with You—even in the fellowship of Your sufferings. This week help me to go a little further in giving my life for others, because You gave Your life for me. Amen.

(Adapted from W. Phillip Keller, *Salt for Society,* 137-43.)

▼

☐ **WEEK 48, FRIDAY**   **PHILIPPIANS**

Scripture: Philippians 4
The Story: Philippians 4:1-13

My God will meet all your needs according to his glorious riches in Christ Jesus (Phil. 4:19; all quotes from NIV).

Living with Christian Joy

As I began exploring this chapter today I discovered the record of another day when I had worked with it:

"I write today in a rather drab room of a second-class hotel. Outside the sky is overcast, and it has been spitting snow. I am 1,000 miles from loved ones and cannot get home until Thanksgiving morning.

"I was alone and tempted to feel sorry for myself, but as I turned to my task for the day I opened a well-thumbed Gideon Bible in the hotel room. There on the flyleaf I read this note penned by another in my circumstances: 'God bless whoever stops in this room. I have had three wonderful days here and God has blessed me. Read this Book and you too will be blessed.' I was!"

The letter to the Philippians has been called the Epistle of Joy. In four brief chapters Paul uses the words "joy" or "rejoice" 18 times. His radiant mood is reflected 11 more times in the words "peace," "thankfulness," "confidence," "comfort," "gladness," and "not afraid."

He exhorts us, "Rejoice in the Lord always. I will say it again: Rejoice! . . . Do not be anxious about anything, but in everything, by prayer and petition, with thanksgiving, present your requests to God" (4:4, 6).

Can we have real needs and yet not be anxious? Can we ask God to meet those needs and yet know a deep joy if we fail to get what we ask? God's answer is yes.

Anxiety and worry are killjoys, but we can conquer these twin enemies of the spirit. This victory comes to us, Paul declares, by going deeper with Christ. Our needs are real and our requests urgent. But more than immediate answers we want God's will for our lives. With every request we bring to Him, we know there are a thousand previous blessings for which we give thanks. By God's grace we can testify: "I have learned to be content whatever the circumstances. I know what it is to be in need, and I know what it is to have plenty. . . . I can do everything through him who gives me strength" (4:11-13).

Then it is that we begin to understand the gracious promise: "And the peace of God, which transcends all understanding, will guard your hearts and your minds in Christ Jesus."

> *I know I love Thee better, Lord,*
> *Than any earthly joy;*
> *For Thou hast given me the peace*
> *Which nothing can destroy.*
> —FRANCES HAVERGAL

▼

Paul dictated the letter to Colosse about the same time he wrote Ephesians and Philemon. The church had been founded by Epaphras (1:7), and the pastor apparently came to visit with Paul in Rome. While there he had been arrested. Because Epaphras could not return at once, Paul wrote to the Colossians to reassure them and to answer the questions Epaphras had raised.

Scripture: Colossians 1—2
The Story: Colossians 1:9-22

God was pleased to have all his fullness dwell in him (Col. 1:19, NIV).

"All Hail the Power of Jesus' Name"

Jesus Christ is the central Figure of our faith. In the Epistle to the Colossians we seek to understand and rejoice in who He is.

When we describe Christ as "the firstborn of every creature" we use language that the Jewish rabbis applied to God himself. Christ is "truly God." Instead of being only one of many created persons, Christ the Lord is high above them. "For by him were all things created . . . whether they be thrones, or dominions, or prin-

485

cipalities, or powers." Whatever exists in the whole universe, in heaven or on earth, "all things were created by him."

In Christ "we have redemption through his blood, even the forgiveness of sins." If we read the words casually they are only sounds, but when we repeat them thoughtfully our spirits fill with thanksgiving. A Man died for us. Ah, He was more than a man, He was the Son of God!

From our personal experience we confess: "Once [we] were alienated from God and were enemies in [our] minds because of [our] evil behavior. But now he has reconciled [us] by Christ's . . . death to present [us] holy in his sight, [pure and faultless]" (1:21-22, NIV).

With glad hearts we acknowledge "Jesus is Lord." This is our confession and the basis of our Christian life.

From the depths of our spirits we accept Christ as the Son of God. Because of this we seek:

to become "fruitful in every good work"
to increase "in the knowledge of God"
to find strength in "his glorious power"
to become "longsuffering with joyfulness"
to give "thanks to the Father, who has qualified [us] to share in the inheritance of the saints in the kingdom of light" (1:10-12, NIV).

> *All hail the pow'r of Jesus' name!*
> *Let angels prostrate fall.*
> *Bring forth the royal diadem,*
> *And crown Him Lord of all.*
> —EDWARD PERRONET

▼

☐ WEEK 49, SUNDAY   COLOSSIANS

Scripture: Colossians 3—4
The Story: Colossians 3:1-17

Christ is all, and is in all (Col. 3:11, NIV).

Christ Living in Me

Yesterday we focused on who Christ is. Today we reflect on how He transforms our lives. As a Christian pastor, Paul exhorts us. But our response is best expressed in a prayer. Let us begin with gratitude.

> *Thank You, Lord, for saving my soul;*
> *Thank You, Lord, for making me whole;*
> *Thank You, Lord, for giving to me*
> *Thy great salvation so rich and free.**
> —MR. AND MRS. SETH SYKES

Father, because You have raised me to new life in Christ, I want to be like Him. Help me to set my mind on the things that filled His mind. With another who hungered for righteousness I pray, "Let the words of my mouth, and the meditation of my heart, be acceptable in thy sight, O Lord, my strength, and my redeemer" (Ps. 19:14).

Make my separation from sin as final as death itself. By Your grace my sins have been forgiven and put behind me; by Your power the old sinful nature has been crucified with Christ. Now "I no longer live, but Christ lives in me. The life I live in the body, I live by faith in the Son of God, who loved me and gave himself for me" (Gal. 2:20, NIV). Because You live in me,

> *I desire that my life shall be ordered by Thee,*
> *That my will be in perfect accord.***
> —HALDOR LILLENAS

Give me compassion, kindness, humility, gentleness, and patience. Lord Jesus, You have forgiven me so much, teach me to bear with others, and to quickly forgive every grievance—imagined or real.

May Your love so fill my spirit that these fruits of the Spirit shall spring from my love-filled life as steadily and as naturally as water from a flowing fountain.

Father, let Your peace rule in my mind. Give me the assurance and contentment that come from knowing my life is pleasing in

Your sight. Let Your Word dwell in me. Fill my mind with Your truth. Teach me through "psalms, hymns and spiritual songs." Let whatever I do, "whether in word or deed," be done "in the name of the Lord Jesus." Then shall I joyfully give "thanks to God the Father through him" (3:15-17, NIV).

▼

☐ WEEK 49, MONDAY   1 THESSALONIANS

The Thessalonian letters are the earliest of Paul's Epistles. Both were written about A.D. 51, during the second missionary journey. Acts 17:1-10 and 1 Thess. 3:1-8 give us the background. Paul had preached in Thessalonica and had won a band of converts. Then persecution by the Jews had forced him to hurriedly leave the little congregation. During the next few months he moved to Berea, Athens, and Corinth. From Corinth Paul wrote to encourage and instruct these new Christians in Thessalonica.

Scripture: 1 Thessalonians 1—2
The Story: 1 Thessalonians 1:2—2:12

You became imitators of us and of the Lord . . . And so you became a model to all the believers (1 Thess. 1:6-7; all quotes from NIV).

The Power of a Model

One example is worth 1,000 words. It is true in education, and it is the way to best communicate the gospel. It is God's message to parents, Sunday School teachers, personal workers, and pastors—to all who seek to nurture another in the Christian faith.

Christlike example begins with Christ himself. Paul knew it—and we must never forget it. He commends these early Christians for "your work produced by faith, your labor prompted by love, and your endurance inspired by hope." That faith, that love, and that hope are all inspired by "our Lord Jesus Christ" (1:3).

Because Paul followed Christ, he was willing to put his life on the line as a model for the Thessalonians. After the Apostle left Thessalonica, his enemies sought to destroy his work through slander. To all this Paul replied in straightforward fashion:

"You know, brothers, that our visit to you was not a failure." Christ redeemed you! I was not seeking ease for myself; "with the help of our God we dared to tell you his gospel in spite of strong opposition." My message was not deceitful, unclean, or two-faced; you know what I preached. I sought no gain for myself; "we worked night and day in order not to be a burden to anyone while we preached the gospel of God to you" (2:1-3, 9).

It is a good thing to live a life above reproach and to be able to answer slander with the record. Paul gave us that kind of an example

Paul gave it, and the Thessalonians followed it. "You became imitators of us and of the Lord . . . And so you became a model to all the believers in Macedonia and Achaia" (1:6-7).

I pray that my example, too, may be a channel for God's grace.

> Make me a blessing; Make me a blessing.
> Out of my life may Jesus shine.
> Make me a blessing, O Saviour, I pray,
> Make me a blessing to someone today.*
> —IRA B. WILSON

▼

☐ **WEEK 49, TUESDAY**   **1 THESSALONIANS**

Scripture: 1 Thessalonians 4:1-12; 5:12-28
The Story: 1 Thessalonians 4:1-8; 5:12-24

God chose you to be saved through the sanctifying work of the Spirit (2 Thess. 2:13, NIV).

Scriptural Teaching

When John Wesley was challenged to defend his understanding of entire sanctification as a second work of grace, attainable by faith, in this life, he appealed to the Scriptures: "I tell you, as plain as I can speak . . . I found it in the oracles of God . . . when I read them with no other view or desire but to save my own soul." Several of these convincing evidences Wesley found in Thessalonians. We are grateful for this truth.

Paul writes, "This is the will of God, even your sanctification" (1 Thess. 4:3). The passage occurs in a paragraph where the Apostle is exhorting Christians to live pure lives. The immediate context, however, does not change the broader message. God's will is that every Christian shall experience this work of grace that shields him from sin—the sin of fornication and every other sin.

The Apostle closes the paragraph with a convincing appeal to live a life above sin: "God hath not called us unto uncleanness, but unto holiness. He therefore that despiseth, despiseth not man, but God, who hath also given us his holy Spirit."

In our key verse we see God's plan that our salvation is to be accomplished "through the sanctifying work of the Spirit."

In 1 Thess. 2:10 Paul describes God's sanctifying ministry in his own life: "You are witnesses, and so is God, of how holy, righteous and blameless we were among you who believed" (NIV). What God had done for him, Paul yearned to see experienced by all who have found Christ: "We pray most earnestly that we may see you again and supply what is lacking in your faith" (3:10, NIV). Again in 3:13 he prays that the Lord "may stablish your hearts unblameable in holiness before God."

He then closes his first letter to these new Thessalonian Christians with this earnest prayer: "May God himself, the God of peace, sanctify you through and through. May your whole spirit, soul and body be kept blameless at the coming of our Lord Jesus Christ. The one who calls you is faithful and he will do it" (5:23-24, NIV).

Thank You, Father, for this truth of Your Word. With Charles Wesley we pray:

> Come, Almighty to Deliver;
> Let us all Thy life receive. . . .
> Let us all in Thee inherit;
> Let us find that second rest.

490

Scripture: 1 Thessalonians 4:13—5:11
The Story: 1 Thessalonians 4:13—5:11

The Lord himself will come down from heaven . . . we who are still alive . . . will be caught up . . . to meet the Lord in the air (1 Thess. 4:16-17; all quotes from NIV)

The Second Coming of Christ

In answering questions for the Thessalonians Paul gave us the wording of our own statement of faith: "We believe that the Lord Jesus Christ will come again; that we who are alive at His coming shall not precede them that are asleep in Christ Jesus; but that, if we are abiding in Him, we shall be caught up with the risen saints to meet the Lord in the air, so that we shall ever be with the Lord." What does the Bible tell us about the Second Coming?

1. This glorious hope of all who believe in Christ rests on our faith in His redeeming work: "We believe that Jesus died and rose again and so we believe that God will bring with Jesus those who have fallen asleep in Him."

2. Christ's coming will be visible. John writes: "Look, he is coming with the clouds, and every eye will see him" (Rev. 1:7).

3. All Christians, both dead and living, will be caught up to meet the Lord. Paul tells us, "The dead in Christ will rise first. After that, we who are still alive . . . will be caught up with them in the clouds to meet the Lord in the air."

4. His coming will catch many by surprise who are not ready: "The day of the Lord will come like a thief in the night" (5:1). But though He comes unexpectedly, we who know Christ will not be caught unprepared. As faithful servants we shall be found doing His work and waiting His return.

5. Though our spirits are tuned for His coming today, we wisely plan for earthly needs as though we did not expect Him for 100 years. We do not unfit ourselves for life's responsibilities by presuming to know the day and the hour. This knowledge the Father has reserved for himself alone. Paul instructs all who would only idly wait, Go back to work: "Keep away from every brother who is idle . . . For even when we were with you, we gave you this rule: 'If a man will not work, he shall not eat'" (2 Thess. 3:6, 10).

6. We regard Christ's coming with joy because it marks the final success of God's purposes for the world.

Jesus' coming back will be the answer to earth's sorr'wing cry,
For the knowledge of the Lord shall fill the earth and sea and sky.
God shall take away all sickness and the suff'rer's tears will dry,
When our Saviour shall come back to earth again.

—JAMES M. KIRK

▼

☐ WEEK 49, THURSDAY   2 THESSALONIANS

Scripture: 2 Thessalonians 1—3
The Story: 2 Thessalonians 2:1-17

May our Lord Jesus Christ himself and God our Father . . . encourage your hearts and strengthen you in every good deed and word (2 Thess. 2:16-17; all quotes from NIV).

Facing the End

The Bible reveals two parallel truths regarding the time of Christ's second coming. Yesterday we saw that no man dares set a date for the end of the world; God alone knows His planned timetable. But today Paul talks about one of the signs by which Christians may be alerted.

Someone had quoted Paul to the Thessalonians as saying that Christ had already returned. In reply, he wrote that this could not be true because the man of sin had not yet appeared.

We do not know all that we would like to know about this sign of the end of the world, but these truths seem clear:

1. Paul describes this person as an end-time man consecrated to, and controlled by, Satan. He will lead the final rebellion of men against God. In the Epistles, John calls him the Antichrist.

2. He is Antichrist because he is against everything that Christ is for. He sets himself above God and rejects the truths revealed by God in Scripture.

3. This man of sin is a person who shall appear at the end of time, but he also represents an evil attitude now present in society—the spirit that rejects God and acts as if man knows more than God. It is the presence of this spirit that concerned John when he wrote: "You have heard that the antichrist is coming, even now many antichrists have come. . . . the man who denies that Jesus is the Christ. Such a man is the antichrist—he denies the Father and the Son" (1 John 2.18, 22).

4. We are sure that all rebellion against God is doomed to failure. The man of sin is no exception. Even now his influence is held in check by the Holy Spirit, and his power will be finally destroyed at the second coming of Christ. We rejoice that a righteous God is in control of the whole universe.

What then should our attitudes be as we face the end of our world—either by nuclear war or by the final conflict between God and Satan?

Paul writes, "We ask you, brothers, not to become easily unsettled or alarmed." We are sure that right is right, and that God is on the side of right. We rest secure in the God of whom Paul prays:

"May our Lord Jesus Christ himself and God our Father, who loved us . . . encourage your hearts and strengthen you in every good deed and word."

▼

☐ WEEK 49, FRIDAY   1 TIMOTHY

The little Books of Timothy and Titus are Paul's last letters. The Apostle wrote them to encourage and instruct two pastors, one in Ephesus and the other on the island of Crete. Though addressed to pastoral concerns, they give Christ's counsel to Christian disciples—both pastors and laymen.

Scripture: 1 Timothy 1—2

How shall we understand Paul's statement in 2:11-15 of the role of women in the church? Had we lived in Ephesus we might have agreed with Paul. If Paul lived in our day we think he could hold a different view. We believe that Christ calls both men and women into His service and ministry.

The Story: 1 Timothy 2:1-8

I thank Christ Jesus our Lord, who has given me strength (1 Tim. 1:12, NIV).

Teach Us to Pray

The Apostle was a man of God who put first things first. When he outlined for Timothy the ministries of the church, he began: "I urge, then, first of all, that requests, prayers, intercession and thanksgiving be made for everyone" (2:1, NIV). Of all the means by which we grow in the Christian life, none is more important than prayer. Bible reading tells us about God, but in true prayer we literally come into His presence. No amount of knowledge about God or service for Him can take the place of this intimate fellowship of communion.

Such a living relationship takes different forms. Paul here lists four of them. *Requests* may be prayers for averting evils of every kind. *Prayers,* in the original language, suggests petitions for the good things that we need—both spiritual and physical. *Intercession* is heartfelt prayer on behalf of others. *Thanksgiving* is the prayer of praise to God for His many blessings to us. We need all of them, but if our praying is chiefly asking favors of God, it reveals a one-sided spiritual life. Prayer that includes a wholesome proportion of praise to God, and intercession for others, reflects a well-balanced Christian experience.

When Paul calls for prayer for all men, he includes persons whom we find it hard to love. If there are strained relations between followers of Christ, mutual prayer will go far toward removing the strain. When we have been mistreated, prayer helps us to understand and to forgive. Sincere prayer always breaks down barriers in our own spirits. And to know that we are praying for him will go further than any other action in disarming and winning over an enemy.

When we pray, we are to "lift up holy hands." Maclaren writes: "A man will not pray over the counter of a saloon. A man will not pray over a sharp bargain. A man will not pray that God may bless his outbursts of anger or sensuality." Why? Because when we pray we bring ourselves into the presence of God, and no man is comfortable in His presence when there is known sin in his life. With David we come before God confessing, "I will wash mine hands in innocency, and would go about Thy altar, O Lord" (Ps. 26:6, NBV).

> O Thou, by whom we come to God,
> The Life, the Truth, the Way,
> The path of prayer thyself hast trod;
> Lord, teach us how to pray.
> —JAMES MONTGOMERY

▼

☐ WEEK 49, SATURDAY   1 TIMOTHY

Scripture: 1 Timothy 3—4

In the church of Paul's day local leaders were known by several titles. *Presbyter* or *elder* was used more in the Jewish churches; it signified mature age. In Gentile churches *bishop* and *deacon* were more common. The deacons were charged with temporal affairs: finance and care of the poor. The bishops were responsible for spiritual instruction and growth. In the church at Ephesus Timothy would be comparable to the pastor in our church.

The Story: 1 Timothy 4:4-16

Set an example for the believers in speech, in life, in love, in faith and in purity (1 Tim. 4:12, NIV).

Marks of Maturing Christians

In these two chapters Paul describes the qualities of Christian maturity that we expect from church leaders. But as children of God each of us may find here a pattern of Christlikeness toward which we strive. Phillips translates 4:7, "Take time and trouble to keep yourself spiritually fit."

In every area of the spirit our Lord asks us to be growing Christians: in speech, in general conduct, in love, in spiritual-mindedness, in faith, and in morals. All are important, but some are more important than others.

Next to loving God with all the heart, Christ asks us to show love to people.

The first opportunity is in the home. As we learn to adjust lovingly to each other in the family, we learn Christlike attitudes toward persons in the church. Paul says such a growing Christian in the home is "one who ruleth well his own house." Adam Clarke describes this parent as "one who has the command of his own house, not by sternness, severity, and tyranny, but . . . governing his household by rule, everyone knowing his own place, and each doing his own work."

Successful relationships with people—in the home and out of it—call for patience. He who follows Christ must pray for patience, and then work hard to answer his own prayers. Without patience we tend to become overaggressive, to produce friction, and to destroy fellowship. Those who follow Christ are not to be strikers—lashing out with verbal or physical violence; or brawlers—acting like quarrelsome men under the influence of liquor. "The servant of the Lord must not strive; but be gentle unto all men, apt to teach, patient" (2 Tim. 2:24).

In addition to patience, Paul counsels us, "Do nothing by partiality." Personal favoritism quickly destroys confidence in our Christian integrity. When members of any group think that rewards and opportunities are given to favorites instead of to those who are worthy, morale disappears. For this reason Paul urges growing Christians to be fair—to do "nothing by partiality" (5:21).

Today, I desire to be a maturing Christian. I join Charles Gabriel in his petition:

More like the Master is my daily prayer;
More strength to carry crosses I must bear;
More earnest effort to bring His kingdom in;
More of His Spirit, the wanderer to win.

▼

Scripture: 1 Timothy 5—6
The Story: 1 Timothy 6:6-19

Trust . . . in the living God, who giveth us richly all
things to enjoy (1 Tim. 6:17).

The Christian's Use of Possessions

Alexander Maclaren writes: "For a very large number of us, almost
the most important influence shaping our characters is the attitude
that we take in regard to . . . the getting and the distribution of
worldly wealth."

Maclaren learned this truth from Paul. The Apostle knew that
a self-centered attitude toward money could blight, and eventually
destroy, a man's soul. He also knew that the practice of Christ's
teaching regarding our stewardship of money would build spiritual life today and lead to eternal life tomorrow. How, then, do we
manage our money in relation to Christ's work?

The Christ-centered life does not separate us from the concerns of the physical world, but it puts material concerns in their
proper second place. Godliness comes first; it is followed by contentment. The original word signifies a sufficiency—enough of
material things for the support of life. Paul urges us, "Having food
and raiment let us be therewith content" (6:8). If we have God and
enough to eat and wear, what more should we seek?

We are not to withdraw from the physical world, but Christ
wants to free us from its excessive demands. When getting money
is our dominating motive we have become worldly; we are striving
for the wrong goal; we are not the kind of persons Christ asks us to

be. In verse 9, Phillips' translation makes clear why we are on the wrong track: "Men who set their hearts on being wealthy expose themselves to temptation. They fall into one of the world's traps, and lay themselves open to all sorts of silly and wicked desires, which are quite capable of utterly ruining and destroying their souls."

How, then, shall we manage the money that God permits us to control? "The Scriptures teach that God is the owner of all persons and things, that men are His stewards of both life and possessions . . . all His children should faithfully tithe and present offerings for the support of the gospel."

On the wall of David Livingstone's home hangs the motto that guided his Christian commitment: "I will value nothing that I possess except in relation to the kingdom of God."

Father, help me to make that my commitment today—my guideline for the earning, spending, investing, and sharing of the money that comes under my control. In Jesus' name I ask it. Amen.

▼

☐ **WEEK 50, MONDAY**   **2 TIMOTHY**

Scripture: 2 Timothy 1—2
The Story: 2 Timothy 1:3-8; 2:1-10

Fan into flame the gift of God, which is in you (2 Tim. 1:6, NIV).

"Be Strong . . . in Christ Jesus"

One morning I got out of bed reluctantly and dragged around slowly with the early tasks of the day. Then at family worship we read the story of Jeremiah. Mrs. Harper prayed: "Lord, we thank You for a prophet who wouldn't give up." Through God, her prayer gave me the resolution to move ahead with the assignments for the day.

In our service for Christ it is as important to keep going as it is to get started. If the devil cannot keep us out of the Kingdom he seeks to slow us to a standstill. Timothy was devoted but reticent. He was discouraged by vexing problems and may have considered resigning his duties. Paul felt it necessary to prod him: "As I urged you when I went to Macedonia, stay there in Ephesus" (1 Tim. 1:3, NIV).

How do we keep on keeping on when we feel like giving up? Sometimes strength comes from the prayers of a wife or the counsel of a friend. Because we ourselves have so often been helped by encouragement from another, we ought to watch for signs of weakening that call for our word of strength and cheer.

Timidity and fear are not sins, but they are tools that Satan uses to defeat us. Paul knew that "God did not give us a spirit of timidity." Negative feelings of reluctance and discouragement come from Satan. To rise above them God gives us "a spirit of power"—confidence that we can do what He asks of us. He gives us the spirit "of love"—a desire for the success of His work in the lives of people. He gives us "self-discipline"—the strength of will to make the right decision even when it seems hard.

In times of discouragement Paul counsels us to do what we know is right—and never mind how we feel! When feelings are about to flicker out, "Fan into flame the gift of God, which is in you." When tempted to give up, "Guard the good deposit that was entrusted to you—guard it with the help of the Holy Spirit who lives in us" (2:14).

Thank You, Father, for every help that You give when I am feeling low. Thank You for help to clear my mind, to strengthen my will, and to restore the joy of my salvation. Now I walk with a steadier tread.

▼

☐ **WEEK 50, TUESDAY**   **2 TIMOTHY**

Scripture: 2 Timothy 3—4
The Story: 2 Timothy 4:6-18

I know whom I have believed, and am persuaded that he is able to keep that which I have committed unto him against that day (2 Tim. 1:12).

A Courageous Christian

Second Timothy is the last letter that we have from the pen of Paul. After a period of freedom from prison, he was again under arrest in Rome, there awaiting the sentence of death. In this last letter he wrote:

"I am now ready to be offered, and the time of my departure is at hand. I have fought a good fight, I have finished my course, I have kept the faith: henceforth there is laid up for me a crown of righteousness . . . Do thy diligence to come shortly unto me . . . The cloak that I left at Troas with Carpus, when thou comest, bring with thee, and the books, but especially the parchments. . . . Do thy diligence to come before winter. . . . Grace be with you" (4:6-9, 13, 21-22).

He was a dying man but his thoughts were not of death. "Stir up the gift of God, which is in thee," he writes. "The things that thou hast heard of me . . . commit thou to faithful men, who shall be able to teach others also. . . . I charge thee therefore before God . . . Preach the word; be instant in season, out of season . . . watch thou in all things, endure afflictions, do the work of an evangelist, make full proof of thy ministry" (1:6; 2:2; 4:1-2, 5).

Only one thing really concerned Paul; it was that Christians should bear consistent, courageous witness to the salvation which they had found through faith in Jesus.

His last words are words of courage and confidence:

"At my first defense, no one came to my support, but everyone deserted me. May it not be held against them. But the Lord stood at my side and gave me strength, so that through me the message might be fully proclaimed and all the Gentiles might hear it. And I was delivered from the lion's mouth. The Lord will rescue me from every evil attack and will bring me safely to his heavenly kingdom. To him be glory for ever and ever. Amen" (4:16-18, NIV).

Thank You, Father, for Paul and for his ministry to us. Because of his example our spirits cry:

> *Lord, give us such a faith as this;*
> *And then, whate'er may come,*
> *We'll taste, e'en here, the hallowed bliss*
> *Of an eternal home.*
> —WILLIAM H. BATHURST

Titus was one of Paul's early converts. The apostle addresses him as "mine own son after the common faith" (1:4). Born of Gentile parents, he accompanied Paul to Jerusalem for the church council that dealt with Gentile observance of Jewish laws (Acts 15:1-31; Gal. 2:1, 3).

When Paul was released from his first Roman imprisonment, he made a missionary journey to Crete, taking Titus with him. After starting a number of churches, the apostle had to move on to other responsibilities before the work was well organized. He left Titus to "set in order the things that are [left undone], and ordain elders in every city" (1:5). To help Titus in this task, Paul wrote the letter.

Scripture: Titus 1—3
The Story: Titus 2:1-15

God wants us to turn from godless living and sinful pleasures and to live good, God-fearing lives day after day (Titus 2:12; all following quotes from TLB).

The Christian's Life-style

One of the serious problems in Crete was the deplorably low morality among the people. Because few of us are wholly exempt from these temptations, God guided Paul to write for every Christian pastor: "You must teach what is in accord with sound doctrine."

Students of human development speak of age-level learning tasks that face us as we mature. Paul recognized some specific Christian growth tasks for each of four groups in the church.

✔ "Teach the older men to be serious and unruffled; they must be sensible, knowing and believing the truth and doing everything with love and patience" (v. 2). Read it again. Any personal improvements needed?

✔ "Teach the older women to be quiet and respectful in everything they do. They must not go around speaking evil of others . . . but they should be teachers of goodness" (v. 3). Any ground for me to gain?

✔ "Train the younger women to live quietly, to love their husbands and their children, and to be sensible and clean minded, spending their time in their own homes, being kind and obedient to their husbands, so that the Christian faith can't be spoken against by those who know them" (vv. 4-5). Are there areas of need where the Holy Spirit probes me?

✔ "Urge the young men to behave carefully, taking life seriously. And here you yourself must be an example to them of good deeds of every kind. Let everything you do reflect your love of the truth and the fact that you are in dead earnest about it" (vv. 6-7). Is my example a good pattern for other Christians to follow?

When John Wesley wrote his mother about holy living, she gave him an ethical guideline that speaks to all of us: "Whatever weakens your reason, impairs the tenderness of your conscience, obscures your sense of God, or takes off the relish of spiritual things, whatever increases the authority of your body over your mind, that thing for you is sin."

Father, are there things in my life-style that You want to change? I open my heart to You; I promise to obey what You show me.

▼

☐ **WEEK 50, THURSDAY**   **PHILEMON**

Scripture: Philemon
The Story: Philemon 1-16

Your love has given me great joy and encouragement (Philem. 7, NIV).

502

Doing It Christ's Way

The Epistle of Paul to Philemon is a bit of private correspondence dealing with a personal matter. Yet it is rich in Christian teaching because a man of godly insight shows the Christlike solution to a serious problem.

Onesimus was a slave who had defrauded his master, Philemon, of Colosse, and had then run away, eventually finding his way to Rome. Some years earlier, Philemon had been converted under Paul's preaching (v. 19), perhaps in Ephesus, which was not far from Colosse. In the providence of God, Onesimus also came under Paul's influence and was converted in Rome. A bond of love grew between the two as the younger man ministered to the needs of the prisoner-apostle.

Eventually Onesimus' newfound happiness in Christ fell under a shadow. God had forgiven his sins, but there was restitution to make. He must go to his master and make right the wrongs of the past. Onesimus was understandably hesitant to return because he could be put to death for his theft and rebellion. Paul, too, was reluctant to let him go, but God's man knew the right thing must be done even when it is dangerous. He must have persuaded Onesimus that we never lose when we take Christ's way.

Paul also knew that Philemon would need to be convinced that Christ wanted him to freely forgive Onesimus. He therefore began his appeal by commending Philemon for his Christlike spirit of love "toward all saints."

Paul next reminded Philemon that following Christ makes better men. It is a different Onesimus who returns. When he ran away he was Philemon's slave; now he is Paul's son—born again by the Spirit of God under the ministry of the apostle.

Who knows, Paul writes, perhaps Onesimus was taken away from you for a time just so that he could come here to Rome, get converted, and then return to you. And, moreover, return not only for this life, but as a fellow Christian, to share heaven with you forever! Oh, Christ does make people different—different and better! Onesimus comes back a better servant, and more. He is now a brother beloved in the Lord; now not only a member of the household but also a member of "the church in thy house."

Was Paul's appeal successful? Tradition says that it was; that

Onesimus, a freed man, was eventually ordained bishop of the church in Ephesus.

Thank you, Paul, for showing us Christ's way.

> *God's way is the best way,*
> *God's way is the right way,*
> *I'll trust in Him always,*
> *He knoweth the best.* *
> —LIDA SHIVERS LEECH

▼

☐ WEEK 50, FRIDAY   HEBREWS

The Epistle to the Hebrews was written to Jewish Christians who were being persecuted for their faith. At the time, Christianity was not one of the recognized religions of the Roman Empire; Judaism was. It was tempting, therefore, to give up the Christian faith and take the easier way of Judaism. The writer sought to encourage those Christians to remain faithful. He shows that salvation through Christ is God's new plan; to return to Jewish faith would be backsliding.

The universal message is that Christ is God's supreme revelation to us. If we give up our faith in Him, we have lost all. But if we remain true, He will help us. "Let us therefore come boldly unto the throne of grace, that we may obtain mercy, and find grace to help in time of need" (4:16).

Scripture: Hebrews 1—3
The Story: Hebrews 1:1-14

He has spoken to us by his Son (Heb. 1:2, NIV).

504

Let's Think About Jesus

The poet gives voice to every Christian when he sings:

Jesus is all the world to me:
My Life, my Joy, my All.

The early Christian who wrote the Book of Hebrews felt the same way about Jesus. In this first chapter he joins us in worship and praise as he recalls who our Lord is and what He does.

✔ Let us praise Christ because He is God's clearest Word and His highest Revelation to us. "In the past God spoke . . . in various ways, but in these last days he has spoken to us by his Son" (1:1-2, NIV).

✔ Let us glory in Christ, the Creator. Through Him God "made the universe . . . O Lord, you laid the foundations of the earth, and the heavens are the work of your hands. They will perish, but you remain . . . You will roll them up like a robe; like a garment they will be changed. But you remain the same, and your years will never end" (1:2, 10-12, NIV).

✔ Let us rejoice because when we know Jesus we understand who God is. "The Son is . . . the exact representation of his being" (1:3, NIV). Because we belong to Jesus, we are comfortable in the presence of God.

✔ Let us be glad that through Jesus we have "purification for sins" (1:3, NIV).

Is there some deep stain that once brought shame to the conscience and tragedy to our lives? Then let us rejoice in God our Savior. "He is the one who died to cleanse us and clear our record of all sin, and then sat down in highest honor beside the great God of heaven" (1:3, TLB).

✔ Let us join the Father and the angels in worship. The Father says, "'You are my Son . . . I will be his Father, and he will be my Son' . . . When God brings his firstborn into the world, he says, 'Let all God's angels worship him'" (1:5-6, NIV). My heart responds:

We'll join the everlasting song,
And crown Him Lord of all!

▼

Scripture: Hebrews 4—6
The Story: Hebrews 4:9-16

Let us then approach the throne of grace with confidence, so that we may receive mercy and find grace to help us in our time of need (Heb. 4:16; all quotes from NIV).

Our Approachable God

One Sunday morning at our open altar, the pastor invited any worshiper with a special concern to join him at the front during the pastoral prayer. My neighbors were among those who came. I joined them because I thought I knew their deep concern. Their hearts ached for a grown daughter who was in danger of making a wrong decision.

Is there some unsolved problem in my life today? A problem that gives deep concern? If so, the Chief Pastor himself invites me to come to Him with that need—because He is our approachable God.

The text shows three clear steps for our coming. The first is simply an exhortation to action: *Let us come;* and let us do it now. To hold back is to disregard His invitation. Verse 6 reminds us of those who "did not go in because of their disobedience." Always our coming should be prompt. When we need God's help, the time is now: "Today, if you hear his voice"—come.

The second step is to *come with faith:* "Let us then approach the throne of grace with confidence." Elsewhere the writer tells us: "Anyone who comes to him must believe . . . that he rewards those who earnestly seek him" (Heb. 11:6). Has He helped me before? Do I believe He can help me today? I know that He can. I come to express my faith in Him. I come with confidence.

God's Word further assures us that *he who comes, finds.* Our coming is to find His mercy—because we do not deserve His gifts. We come expecting only grace—His unmerited favor.

Today in my time of need I come to find His help.

O Hope of ev'ry contrite heart,
O Joy of all the meek,
To those who fall, how kind Thou art!
How good to those who seek!
—BERNARD OF CLAIRVAUX

▼

☐ **WEEK 51, SUNDAY**   **HEBREWS**

Scripture: Hebrews 7—9
The Story: Hebrews 7:23-28; 8:7-13

A better hope is introduced through which we draw near to God (Heb. 7:19, NBV).

Thank You, God

It is hard to let go of something good, even to receive something better. That was the struggle of Jewish Christians, reflected in these chapters. God had greatly blessed the Hebrews through the promises to Abraham, the laws of Moses, and the sacrifices required of Old Testament people. It was the best religion in the world. Even today many of those blessings are part of our Christian worship. But in Christ, God had planned something better for His people. I like the new plan better.

I think we get better leaders. God now calls His preachers for each generation instead of men entering the ministry because their fathers were preachers. An inherited priesthood was weaker.

I am glad that I no longer need a priest as a go-between. I can come to God directly in the name of Christ. There is a blessed and personal fellowship when I can come to God and say, *Father.*

It is good that I do not need to wait a whole year for the high priest to come before God in the holy of holies. I can bring my offerings of praise when His Spirit moves me. I can confess my failure when it occurs. I can know immediately the joy of forgiveness and the wonder of restored fellowship.

I am glad that I no longer need to depend on symbols; my experience of God is personal and real. He is a Spirit; He brings my spirit into tune with His own so that I "worship him in spirit and in truth" (John 4:24).

I am glad that no animal needs to die to secure forgiveness for my sin. Jesus shed His own blood once for all—for all persons and for all times. That is a better sacrifice.

I am glad "He is able to save to the uttermost those who come to God through Him" (7:25, NBV). There is no limitation here. Through the work of Christ all sin can be put away—our sinful dispositions as well as committed sins. "Wherefore Jesus also, that he might sanctify the people with his own blood, suffered without the gate" (Heb. 13:12).

Thank You, God, for Your new plan of salvation. Thank You for the better hope through which we may now draw near to You.

> *Thank You, Lord, for saving my soul;*
> *Thank You, Lord, for making me whole;*
> *Thank You, Lord, for giving to me*
> *Thy great salvation, so rich and free.**
> —MR. AND MRS. SETH SYKES

▼

☐ **WEEK 51, MONDAY**   **HEBREWS**

Scripture: Hebrews 10—13
The Story: Hebrews 11:32—12:2

Seeing we also are compassed about with so great a cloud of witnesses ... let us run with patience the race that is set before us (Heb. 12:1).

We Belong to a Great Company

In Christian comradeship there is strength. During an afternoon camp meeting sermon Dr. T. W. Willingham testified to the power of fellowship: "I have gone too far to go back. I have Christian friends all across the country who expect me to be true to God. There are old schoolmates who knew me as a Christian; there are young people to whom I have preached; my wife and children are counting on me. I dare not fail them by failing God."

We Christians gather strength, not only from those now with us; we also gather from those who have gone before. The saints of the ages look down on us from "the city of the living God, the heavenly Jerusalem." Those who watch include "an innumerable company of angels," and myriad saints who make up "the general assembly and church of the firstborn" (12:22-23).

From that vast host the writer points out a few familiar faces. Samson is among them because despite his weakness and failures, he obeyed the promptings of the Spirit of God. Jephthae is there in spite of an immoral mother and a bad beginning.

And look! Witnesses are there whose spiritual needs are like yours and mine. There is a mother who had deep needs; through faith she "obtained promises" that those needs would be met. There is a young man who was powerfully tempted to do wrong, but through faith he "wrought righteousness." And see, there are two whose moral fiber was weak, but they trusted God, and "out of weakness were made strong." My Christian father and mother are there. Can you see yours? They all smile encouragement to us.

We belong to a great company, but our final confidence is in "Jesus, the author and finisher of our faith." If the spectators watch with eager yearning, our Lord literally runs with us. He knows the course because He once ran the race. When we stumble, His heart beats faster until we run with steady stride again. When we press on with firm pace, He thrills with us in our faithfulness.

> *O Jesus, I have promised*
> *To serve Thee to the end;*
> *Be Thou forever near me,*
> *My Master and my Friend.*
> —JOHN E. BODE

In James we have a pastor-friend concerned with the nitty-gritty of daily Christian living. A half-brother of Jesus, he was converted only after the Resurrection, but rose to leadership of the church in Jerusalem (see Acts 15:13; Gal. 1:19; 2:9). As leader of the church, James wrote to encourage Christians scattered by the persecutions. The letter was intended to be read in one congregation and then passed on to another—a general Epistle.

Scripture: James 1—2
The Story: James 1:2-18

Blessed is the man who perseveres under trial, because when he has stood the test, he will receive the crown of life that God has promised to those who love him (James 1:12, NIV).

Courage, My Friend

We are given no choice as to whether we shall have trials. Probably God could not trust us to choose what is good for us!

We cannot decide whether to have tests, but we can choose what shall be our attitude toward them. James counsels us, "When all kinds of trials and temptations crowd into your lives, my brothers, don't resent them as intruders, but welcome them as friends!" (1:2, Phillips). He who achieves spiritual victories must fight battles of the spirit.

But being glad because you hurt is a difficult assignment! Is it possible? Yes, when we realize that those hurts are the means that God uses to help us grow into the likeness of Christ. James bids us remember that hard times "come to test your faith and to produce in you the quality of endurance. But let the process go on until that endurance is fully developed, and you will find you have become men of mature character" (1:3-4, Phillips).

When God enables us to triumph, the tests of life are rich in the fruits that they bear: patience, prayer, increased faith, and steadiness. As these Christlike virtues increase we become more like our Master; one day we shall be fitted to "receive the crown of life, which the Lord hath promised to them that love him."

And so, Father, I ask for the wisdom that You promise—the wisdom to trust and keep faith in You in spite of my trials. And even when the burdens are heaviest, do not let all of my energy be spent in sheer endurance.

Teach me to find joy in the Lord; joy in spite of burdens; deep happiness because I know the loads cannot crush me; an overwhelming sense of fellowship with You as You carry the heavy end of the load; real joy because through these trials I share in the fellowship of Christ's sufferings and am being fashioned into His likeness.

With Paul, I want to testify, "Most gladly therefore will I rather glory in my infirmities, that the power of Christ may rest upon me" (2 Cor. 12:9). In Jesus' name. Amen.

▼

☐ **WEEK 51, WEDNESDAY** **JAMES**

Scripture: James 3—5
The Story: James 4:1-10

How shall we understand verse 5? Most modern translators agree that the verb "dwelleth" is the word used in the New Testament to indicate the presence of the Holy Spirit. *The Living Bible* therefore interprets it: "The Holy Spirit, whom God has placed within us, watches over us with tender jealousy."

Draw nigh to God, and he will draw nigh to you. Cleanse your hands, ye sinners; and purify your hearts, ye double minded (James 4:8).

"He Gives Us More Grace"

God wants us to be Christlike persons. It is His goal for us from the day we are born. When we were converted, He forgave our sins and regenerated our spirits. He yearns over this new life, prodding us if we begin to drift back into sin: "Don't you know that friendship with the world is hatred toward God?" (4:4, NIV).

In our quest for Christlikeness, it is not enough to have clean hands. God wants to give us pure hearts. He wants us to be wholly His own, to be filled with a deep and abiding love for himself.

Eager as He is, God cannot create in us this perfect love until we ourselves seek for such a devoted spirit. We are urged to exert ourselves in order to receive His grace: "Submit yourselves," "Resist the devil," "Draw nigh to God," "Cleanse your hands," "Purify your hearts," "Humble yourselves." If we receive this greater grace, we must act.

However, if we will but come, He has grace to meet our needs. God resists the proud because as long as we have confidence in the worth of our own unspiritual, worldly attitudes, as long as we think them satisfactory, God can do no more for us. But He gives grace to the humble, because then we know that our spirits have been wrong. If in humility we draw near to God and ask Him to purify our hearts, "He gives us more grace" (4:6, NIV).

It is ours to ask, it is God's to give; ours to come, God's to cleanse; ours to surrender, God's to purify. Whatever our need, if we draw near, "He gives us more grace." Because He yearns for our love, we yearn to respond.

> *Out of unrest and arrogant pride,*
> *Jesus, I come; Jesus, I come.*
> *Into Thy blessed will to abide,*
> *Jesus, I come to Thee.*
> —WILLIAM T. SLEEPER

▼

First and Second Peter were written by the Apostle to Christians in five provinces of Asia Minor. These believers may have included converts of Paul who had founded churches there. Following Paul's example, Peter sought to give continued apostolic counsel. The first letter encourages Christians to be faithful in the face of persecution; the second warns them against false teachers. The warning against heresy in 2 Pet. 2:1—3:3 is paralleled in Jude 4-19.

Scripture: 1 Peter 1—3
The Story: 1 Peter 1:13-23

Your faith and hope are in God (1 Pet. 1:21; all quotes from NIV).

Committed Christian Living

Discouragement is one of our deepest dangers. The Christian life calls for moral conduct above the average—and it takes courage to be different. Always in our moments of weakness, Satan is ready to suggest: What is the use? Aren't you only human? Why make the effort to do right when it is hard? Why try to live God's way when most of those around you think those standards are foolish?

But when we are tempted to forsake the way, God's Word exhorts us to endure. Peter reminds us that our hope is in God, and our citizenship is in heaven. We are only temporary sojourners here in enemy country—and we are never free from the threat of attack and defeat. "Therefore, prepare your minds for action; be self-controlled; set your hope fully on the grace to be given you when Jesus Christ is revealed."

In chapter 1 Peter calls us to live a holy life, then in chapters 2—3 he spells out some of the attitudes that are sometimes difficult. He admonishes: Since your souls have been purified by the

Spirit of God, "See that ye love one another with a pure heart fervently" (1:22).

Even after we have been sanctified wholly we must cultivate the graces of Christian love. In 2:1 Peter makes the character of that love very specific. We are to put out of our lives forever all ill will, all deceit, all envy, and all evil speaking. A cleansed heart is thus the road to victorious living. In 3:8-9 we are told that holy living calls us to be united in purpose, to be sympathetic, merciful, and courteous. We may not return evil for evil, but rather bless those who injure us. Holy living means a spirit of goodwill which we steadfastly refuse to surrender—a genuine love toward all men under all circumstances.

Father, Your way for me is sometimes hard—but I know it is right and good. Cleanse my spirit, strengthen my will, and I shall find joy as I walk with You.

▼

☐ WEEK 51, FRIDAY   1 PETER

Scripture: 1 Peter 4—5
The Story: 1 Peter 4:1-2, 12-14, 19; 2:21-23 (in this order)

Rejoice, inasmuch as ye are partakers of Christ's sufferings (1 Pet. 4:13).

Expect to Pay a Price

Every worthwhile thing in life costs effort. A holy life cannot be attained without investing in it. God's own struggle against sin cost the Father His only Son. If our Lord himself could not defeat sin without suffering, we must not count on all joy and no work.

The human spirit requires struggle if we are to gain moral strength. Therefore an easy religion is dangerous to the soul. In the Old Testament, Araunah offered to give David an altar and animals for his sacrifice. The king wisely replied, "No. I will pay you for it. I will not offer to the Lord my God sacrifices that have cost me nothing" (2 Sam. 24:24, TEV).

It is a high New Testament call that asks us to share in Christ's suffering. But we who have set out to follow Him have placed our feet on a high way. Isaiah calls it the highway of holiness. Sure, there are difficulties to be encountered and burdens to be borne, but they are only passing problems. This is the highway home! It is along this route that "the ransomed of the Lord shall return, and come to Zion with songs and everlasting joy upon their heads: they shall obtain joy and gladness, and sorrow and sighing shall flee away" (Isa. 35:10).

Peter wisely helps us forget our burdens by remembering Jesus. We seek to follow in the footsteps of Him "who did no sin, neither was guile found in his mouth: who, when he was reviled, reviled not again; when he suffered, he threatened not: but committed himself to him that judgeth righteously." God's Apostle reminds us, If you will just think about Jesus for a little while, being patient under pressure won't be a problem anymore today!

O my Savior, You suffered for me. Teach me to bear the strain of a holy life.

> I shall not fear the battle
> If Thou art by my side,
> Nor wander from the pathway
> If Thou wilt be my Guide.
> —JOHN E. BODE

▼

☐ **WEEK 51, SATURDAY**　　　　　　**2 PETER; JUDE**

Scripture: 2 Peter 1—3; Jude
The Story: 2 Peter 1:1-11

His divine power has given us everything we need for life and godliness through our knowledge of him who called us (2 Pet. 1:3, NIV).

Understanding Christian Holiness

Peter is concerned to share with us his best wisdom for successful Christian living. In eight words he sums up that counsel: "You ought to live holy and godly lives" (3:11, NIV). But what is Christian holiness?

Verses 3-4 tell us that holiness is God's provision for full salvation; He has "given us everything we need for life and godliness."

Among our Lord's "very great and precious promises" is, first, His promise to save us from sin: "Behold, I stand at the door, and knock: if any man hear my voice, and open the door, I will come in to him" (Rev. 3:20). There is the further promise to sanctify His people by filling us with His Holy Spirit: "Wait for the gift my Father promised . . . you will be baptized with the Holy Spirit" (Acts 1:4-5, NIV). Faith in God, and accepting these salvation gifts by faith is necessary "for life and godliness." But that is not all.

Everything we need for a full salvation includes the additions to faith. In a prayer meeting our pastor said, "We get ourselves in trouble if we worship the experience more than the daily life."

Filled with the Holy Spirit, we are daily enabled to live godly lives. We listen to the instruction of the Spirit; we remember Jesus' example; in prayer we find strength to choose right. Thus we daily add to our faith.

Our knowledge grows as we read the Bible and as we obey the Spirit's leading. Self-control comes as we depend on the Spirit's power.

Perseverance flows from determination and from reliance on the resources of the indwelling Holy Spirit. The godliness that we seek is simply to become more like Jesus. When we pattern our lives after Him, we grow in our concern for others.

And undergirding all is love—a deep, moving love for God, and a genuine, caring love for persons around us. Through His love we "escape the corruption in the world caused by evil desires," and through His love in us we "participate in the divine nature" (1:4, NIV).

Oh, to be like Thee! Oh, to be like Thee,
Blessed Redeemer, pure as Thou art!
Come in Thy sweetness, come in Thy fullness;
Stamp Thine own image deep on my heart!
—THOMAS O. CHISHOLM

First John is not a typical letter. It is more like a short essay on Christian doctrine. The Apostle writes as a pastor seeking to nourish the spiritual life of his people. Here we find Christian teaching about sin, confession, atonement, cleansing, and assurance of salvation. These are basic truths, essential to fellowship with God and to a life of perfect love.

Scripture: 1 John 1—4
The Story: 1 John 3:19-24; 4:12-16

We know that we live in him and he in us (1 John 4:13; all quotes from NIV).

Christian Assurance

Aunt Julia attended a church where they taught predestination. She went to her pastor and asked him, "Can I be sure that I belong to Christ?" He answered, "I feel certain about myself, but I cannot tell you that you can be sure." A seeker after Christ deserves a better answer than that from her pastor.

We need to be certain. If we are not sure, our hearts are troubled; we are disturbed and uneasy. God wants His true children to be at rest, to feel confident, to know that we are loved and secure in Him. That is why the Apostle can write: "We know that we live in him and he in us." And John is careful to tell us how we can know. Christian assurance is like a river that is fed by six tributary streams.

✔ The first is a conscious knowledge of God in Christ. "If anyone acknowledges that Jesus is the Son of God, God lives in him and he in God. And so we know and rely on the love God has for us" (4:15-16).

✔ A second source of assurance is obedience. "If anyone obeys his word, God's love is truly made complete in him. This is how we know we are in him: Whoever claims to live in him must walk as Jesus did" (2:5-6). "Those who obey his commands live in him, and he in them" (3:24).

✔ Flowing close to the stream of obedience is the refreshing assurance of a clear conscience: "Dear friends, if our hearts do not condemn us, we have confidence before God" (3:21).

✔ The Lord whom we serve is a God of righteousness. "Dear children, do not let anyone lead you astray. He who does what is right is righteous . . . This is how we know who the children of God are" (3:7, 10).

✔ Now John points us to a fifth tributary: "We know that we have passed from death to life, because we love our brothers" (3:14). "If we love each other, God lives in us and his love is made complete in us" (4:12).

✔ Writing after the Day of Pentecost, John knew the blessed assurance that comes from being filled with the Holy Spirit. "We know that we live in him and he in us, because he has given us of his Spirit" (4:13).

With joy we testify: "How great is the love the Father has lavished on us, that we should be called children of God! And that is what we are! . . . Dear friends, now we are children of God, and what we will be has not yet been made known. But we know that when he appears, we shall be like him" (3:1-2).

Thank You, Lord, for John and for his message of assurance.

▼

☐ **WEEK 52, MONDAY**   **2 JOHN; 3 JOHN**

Second and Third John are brief pastoral notes, probably written from Ephesus where the aged Apostle was living in semiretirement.

From a nearby church he had received a heartwarming report of their Christian growth. He responded with the note of appreciation and encouragement found in 2 John.

Third John is addressed to a generous Christian layman, Gaius. It appears the Apostle had sent out missionaries carrying letters of commendation to the congregations. Diotrophes, the carnal pastor of this church (perhaps Pergamos), refused to accept them; he even turned out of the church those who entertained the missionaries. John commends Gaius for his hospitality and in verse 11 perhaps suggests that the evil Diotrophes should be replaced by the good Demetrius as pastor of the church.

Scripture: 1 John 5; 2 John; 3 John
The Story: 3 John 1-14

Dear friend . . . It gave me great joy to have some brothers come and tell about your faithfulness to the truth (3 John 3, NIV).

Christian Fellowship

There is a blessed tie that binds together the people of God. When receiving members into the church the pastor says, "The privileges and blessings which we have in association together in the Church of Jesus Christ are very sacred and precious. There is in it such hallowed fellowship as cannot otherwise be known."

Gaius was more than just another Christian; he was one of John's converts. The fellowship ran deep. In similar circumstances Paul wrote to Timothy as "my own son in the faith" (1 Tim. 1:2). Such a bond of affection can be fully understood by one who has led another to Christ.

Where there is mutual Christian love, it is easy to give and to accept suggestions for the furtherance of Christ's work. God's leader does not hesitate to call a generous layman to still further generosity for the sake of the Kingdom. He said in effect:

Gaius, it was noble of you to help these servants of God. The church appreciates what you have done. Now such workers are to come your way again. Can we count on your assistance? I urge you to do this, because in so doing "we may work together for the truth" (v. 8, NIV).

Verses 13-14 are some of John's last words that have been preserved for the Church. What the Apostle could not write, he hoped presently to say to them. Though now perhaps too infirm to walk alone, the grand old saint yet hoped to make one more trip to tell the church the way of love, and to make further plans for the promotion of the gospel. Whether he made the trip we do not know. His closing word is: "Peace be to thee. Our friends salute thee. Greet the friends by name."

If he did not see them on earth, he met them shortly at the side of the river of life and communed with them face-to-face. There, members of the Christian fellowship meet to part no more forever.

Blest be the tie that binds
Our hearts in Christian love;
The fellowship of kindred minds
Is like to that above.
—JOHN FAWCETT

▼

☐ **WEEK 52, TUESDAY**   **REVELATION**

Scripture: Revelation 1—3
The Story: Revelation 1:4-6, 12-18

The seven churches in chapters 2—3 were located in the western part of Asia Minor, now Turkey. The virtues and faults of these churches were common to other congregations of the 1st century—and the 20th. The living Lord commends, admonishes, and holds out hope to His people wherever they assemble in His name.

In verse 4 "the seven spirits" probably allude to the Holy Spirit in His complete ministry. In Scripture, seven is often used to imply perfection or completion.

To him who loves us and has freed us from our sins by his blood . . . to him be glory and power for ever and ever! (Rev. 1:5-6; all quotes from NIV).

Our Living Christ

The Christ whom we worship is more like this vision of John on Patmos than like Jesus of Galilee. There He carried the limitations of humanity. Now He is the King of Kings.

Who is this living Lord? He is *Jesus Christ*, the promised Messiah. He is *the faithful witness* to God's goodness, power, and love. He is *the firstborn from the dead*, assuring us of life everlasting. As Lord of history He is *the ruler of the kings of the earth*. One with God the Father, He is *the Alpha and the Omega*—our present Savior, our past Redeemer, our future Lord and Leader. He loved us without measure. Through His death on Calvary He *has freed us from our sins by his blood* (see 1:5, 8).

In symbols strange to us, but filled with profound meaning, John describes the glories of the strong Son of God. The *robe* speaks of the dignity of a king; the *golden sash* is an emblem like the stars on the collar of a five-star general. The *white hair* reflects maturity and wisdom, as the *blazing eyes* show that nothing is hidden from Him. The *feet of bronze* depict strength, and His *voice* is as impressive as the thunder of the sea. His *hand* holds the destiny of the Church, and His *sharp sword* protects her against every foe. To see *his face* is to find the joy of a glorious sunrise, and to know the warmth of the noonday sun (see 1:13-16).

We join in John's three doxologies of adoration and praise to this living Christ and glorious Savior: "To him who loves us . . . and has made us to be a kingdom and priests to serve his God and Father—to him be glory and power for ever and ever!" (1:5-6).

"To him who sits on the throne and to the Lamb be praise and honor and glory and power, for ever and ever!" (5:13).

"Salvation belongs to our God, who sits on the throne, and to the Lamb" (7:10).

In language more familiar to us we sing:

> *Jesus, my King, my wonderful Saviour,*
> *All of my life is given to Thee.*
> *I am rejoicing in Thy salvation.*
> *Thy precious blood now maketh me free.*
> —J. M. Harris

521

Scripture: Revelation 4—5

A spirit of devotion must flow from a fountain of understanding. As you read chapters 4—5, and later on in the book, translate John's terms (NIV) as follows:

Twenty-four elders means the Church, all of God's redeemed people.

Four living creatures (beasts) represent the whole universe, all nature.

The scroll contained God's plan for our lives and for the whole of creation.

The Lion of the tribe of Judah and the *Lamb* are Bible names for Christ.

The *seven horns* mean complete power; the *seven eyes* are perfect wisdom; the *seven spirits* represent the fullness of the Holy Spirit of God.

When you encounter these symbolic terms, substitute the translations above, and discover how much more meaningful the text becomes.

The Story: Revelation 4:1-11 (Today, read the comments first, then read the scriptures with a spirit of thanksgiving and praise)

Worthy is the Lamb, who was slain, to receive power and wealth and wisdom and strength and honor and glory and praise! (Rev. 5:12, NIV).

"Worthy Is the Lamb"

If I could stand before the throne of God, what would I see? How could I describe it so that those who had not seen would get a picture of it? This was John's privilege and assignment.

Beginning with chapter 4 we move from a vision of the churches on earth to scenes in heaven at the end of time. Here John saw all of creation and redeemed men from all ages gathered to worship God. Chapter 4 focuses on God the Creator, but in chapter 5 we see our exalted Christ, the Lamb slain from the foundation of the world.

In 4:3 John caught a vision of awesome beauty. Of this first glimpse of God on His throne, Phillips translates: "His appearance blazed like a diamond and topaz, and all around the throne shone a halo like an emerald rainbow."

Beyond its beauty, John saw heaven as a place of praise and worship. He writes of all created beings there: "Day and night they never stop saying: 'Holy, holy, holy is the Lord God Almighty, who was, and is, and is to come'" (4:8, NIV).

When creation sings its glad praise, God's redeemed people "fall down before him who sits on the throne, and worship him who lives for ever and ever. They lay their crowns before the throne and say:

'You are worthy, our Lord and God, to receive glory and honor and power, for you created all things, and by your will they were created and have their being'" (4:10-11, NIV).

In chapter 5 heaven sang a new song. They turned from rejoicing in creation to praise for redemption. All nature and all the redeemed of earth sang in praise of our Christ:

"You are worthy to take the scroll and to open its seals, because you were slain, and with your blood you purchased men for God from every tribe and language and people and nation. You have made them to be a kingdom and priests to serve our God, and they will reign on the earth" (5:9-10, NIV).

Then John heard more than 100 million angels join in the glad chorus. I don't understand it all, but I don't want to miss any of it. I want to join them when they sing:

"Worthy is the Lamb, who was slain, to receive power and wealth and wisdom and strength and honor and glory and praise!" Hallelujah!

▼

Scripture: Revelation 6—9

How shall we understand the numbers in 7:1-8? The 144,000 is considered by some as a symbolic figure meant to represent all of God's people—both from Israel and from the Gentiles. The identical figures of 12,000 from each tribe suggest what John says explicitly in verse 9—God has faithful followers in every tribe and nation.

The Story: Revelation 7:9-17

These are they which came out of great tribulation, and have washed their robes, and made them white in the blood of the Lamb (Rev. 7:14).

Salvation and Safety in God

Chapters 6, 8, and 9 paint a picture of the final terrible consequences of sin. There come times when even sinners who seem well off discover the evil of their ways: "The kings . . . the princes, the generals, the rich, the mighty . . . hid in caves and among the rocks . . . They called to the mountains and the rocks, 'Fall on us and hide us from the face of him who sits on the throne and from the wrath of the Lamb!'" (6:15-16, NIV).

But in the midst of these seven seals of judgment on an evil world, and within the sound of the seven trumpets announcing plagues on those who do wickedly, there is a great hope. In chapter 7 John shares his vision of security for God's people. Verses 1-8 tell of an angel who "put a seal on the foreheads of the servants of our God" (v. 3, NIV). The mark on God's people recalls the blood of the lamb sprinkled on the doorposts to protect the Israelites in Egypt. When death stalks the land, those protected by God's seal are perfectly safe. Even here on the earth in the midst of the terrible calamities of the last days, John saw that there was safety in God and in Christ.

But security in this world is only a foregleam of the eternal blessedness that God has prepared for all who follow Him. We

Christians sometimes seem in a minority here, but in heaven John was shown "a great multitude, which no man could number, of all nations, and kindreds, and people." They are "before the throne of God, and serve him day and night in his temple ... the Lamb which is in the midst of the throne shall feed them, and shall lead them unto living fountains of waters: and God shall wipe away all tears from their eyes."

With the poet, I affirm, "It will be worth it all when we see Jesus." By God's grace I mean to be among that number. I want to join in their glad chorus:

"Salvation to our God which sitteth upon the throne, and unto the Lamb. . . . Blessing, and glory, and wisdom, and thanksgiving, and honour, and power, and might, be unto our God for ever and ever. Amen."

▼

Scripture: Revelation 10—14

In 11:2 and 13:5 we find references to 42 months. In 11:3 and 12:6 there are references to 1,260 days. Three and a half days are mentioned in 11:9, 11. Finally in 12:14 there is the expression "a time, and times, and half a time." These terms give rise to the understanding of three and a half years so often encountered in time charts of the last days.

The Story: Revelation 10:5-11; 11:15-18

We give thanks to you, Lord God Almighty ... because you have taken your great power and have begun to reign (Rev. 11:17, NIV).

"The Kingdom of Our Lord and of His Christ"

Wrong is wrong, and right is right. Our minds revolt when wrong triumphs over right. Our hearts tell us that God must be on the side of goodness, and that wrong cannot finally prevail. With James Russell Lowell we first agonize, and then our faith asserts itself:

> *Truth forever on the scaffold,*
> *Wrong forever on the throne.*
> *Yet that scaffold sways the future,*
> *And behind the dim unknown*
> *Standeth God within the shadows*
> *Keeping watch above His own.*

What our troubled spirits yearn for, the Bible declares is true.

In 10:7 *the mystery of God* is heaven's plan that eventually righteousness shall prevail and wrong shall be put down. The dominant note of the end times of Revelation is that God's purposes are now about to be fully achieved. The angel "swore by him who lives for ever and ever . . . 'There will be no more delay!'" (v. 6, NIV).

The little scroll represents God's plan for the ages. He will protect and exalt the righteous. That is sweet as honey. But God's moral law also banishes those who persevere in wickedness. That makes our spirits ache. We regret its tragedy for the finally impenitent. But the tragedy need not be; that is the Good News of *the mystery of God.* The secret of the little scroll is: "God so loved the world, that he gave his only begotten Son, that whosoever believeth in him should not perish, but have everlasting life" (John 3:16).

The last times of Revelation are times of finally putting an end to injustice and evil. We cannot gloat over the destruction of any conscious being—but we must agree to the rightness of God's decision in "destroying those who destroy the earth" (11:18, NIV).

We can only say Amen to God's ultimate plan: "The time has come for judging the dead, and for rewarding . . . your saints and those who reverence your name, both small and great" (v. 18, NIV).

With subdued spirits, we join the heavenly chorus:

"We give thanks to you, Lord God Almighty, who is and who was, because you have taken your great power and have begun to reign."

Evil shall be no more!

Scripture: Revelation 15—17
The Story: Revelation 15:1-4; 16:5-7

Great and marvelous are your deeds, Lord God Almighty. Just and true are your ways, King of the ages (Rev. 15:3; all quotes from NIV).

Songs of the Redeemed

Revelation is a partial description of what will take place when God finally breaks into human history and sets up His eternal kingdom. At that point evil shall be completely conquered and removed from our world. Just before John's vision of God's last great judgments on the wicked of the earth, he was shown the people of God rejoicing in heaven in the presence of their Savior. He had made them "victorious over the beast and his image and over the number of his name. They held harps given them by God and sang the song of Moses the servant of God and the song of the Lamb."

John likened their triumph to the rejoicing Israelites as they stood on the safe shore of the Red Sea after divine deliverance from their mortal enemy. Even now we join in their glad praise:

"The Lord is my strength and my song; he has become my salvation. He is my God, and I will praise Him, my father's God, and I will exalt him. . . .

"Who among the gods is like you, O Lord? Who is like you—majestic in holiness, awesome in glory, working wonders? . . .

"In your unfailing love you will lead the people you have redeemed. In your strength you will guide them to your holy dwelling. . . .

"You will bring them in and plant them on the mountain of your inheritance—the place, O Lord, you made for your dwelling, the sanctuary, O Lord, your hands established. The Lord will reign for ever and ever" (Exod. 15:2, 11, 13, 17-18).

But today we know even more of the grace of God than was known by the rejoicing people under Moses. We have been redeemed by the blood of the Lamb. Therefore we add His song:

"Great and marvelous are your deeds, Lord God Almighty. Just and true are your ways, King of the ages. Who will not fear you, O Lord, and bring glory to your name? For you alone are holy. All nations will come and worship before you, for your righteous acts have been revealed" (15:3-5).

Our rejoicing spirits join in the benediction of Revelation: *"Amen! Praise and glory . . . be to our God for ever and ever. Amen!"*

▼

Scripture: Revelation 18—20
The Story: Revelation 18:19-24; 20:11-15

Blessed are those who are invited to the wedding supper of the Lamb! (Rev. 19:9, NIV).

I Intend to Be There

We find many ways to classify people, but God finally uses only two. The Bible declares, "The Lord knoweth the way of the righteous: but the way of the ungodly shall perish" (Ps. 1:6). In the Revelation, God shows us clearly the final separation of those two ways.

It is not pleasant to contemplate the fate of the unrighteous— but it is profitable to reflect awhile if we may thereby avoid it.

In chapter 18 we are shown the end of a godless civilization. The city is called Babylon, but almost certainly it refers to Rome, the great enemy of first-century Christians. Sin's destruction carries with it the ruin of all the values that we hold most precious. For the finally unrighteous, there are no more harpists; sin silences the music of life. The joy of meaningful work is lost. The grinding of the hand mills and other familiar sounds of the home disappear. The lights go out. Love and happy marriages are no more. When God is left out, these good things are not enough to fulfill life. Without His touch our human values fail; and without His blessing, sin eventually destroys all of them.

In contrast to chapter 18, John's vision in chapter 20 deals with our personal destinies. Human life is enriched by social relationships with other persons, but our eternal hope rests on personal decisions. We are born into the world one by one, and we shall face the judgment one by one. John testifies, "I saw the dead, great and small, standing before the throne, and books were opened" (v. 12, NIV).

Our lives are concerned with what is written there. The Bible says, "The dead were judged according to what they had done as recorded in the books" (NIV).

But the crucial record is our relationship to Christ. The Judge looks to see if my name is found in the book of life. It will not be written there if I have rejected Christ here. But, O glorious thought! If my name is in that book, beside it will be my invitation to the wedding supper of the Lamb.

There, by His grace, I shall join that great multitude. They sounded to John "like the roar of rushing waters . . . shouting:

'Hallelujah! For our Lord God Almighty reigns. Let us rejoice and be glad and give him glory!'" (19:6-7, NIV).

Scripture: Revelation 21—22
The Story: Revelation 21:1-7, 22-27

Now the dwelling of God is with men . . . They will be his people, and God himself will be with them and be their God (Rev. 21:3, NIV).

"A New Heaven and a New Earth"

Columbus set sail by faith and discovered a new world, but before that discovery there were many trials. His mutinous men were ready to turn back after they had sailed for weeks on uncharted seas. But at last there were birds overhead, bits of vegetation floating in the water—signs of a country. Then came the glad cry: "Land ahead!"

We, too, journey in faith seeking a better country. We have not seen that land, but there is evidence that it is not far. God has revealed a glimpse of its glories to our lookout, John the Beloved. In these last chapters of Revelation he shouts, "Land ahead!"

That land is God's land. As John Wesley lay on his deathbed he cried out, "The best thing of all is that God is with us." Always we have needed Him; always He has been near; but always His presence has been less than complete. When we have finished with the limitations of this life we shall know Him better. There "the dwelling of God is with men, and he will live with them. They will be his people" (NIV).

Even now God lives with us and His blessed presence eases the shocks of life. He walks with us here and shares our burdens. Because He is with us the tears are less scalding, death is no longer terrifying, sorrow is turned to joy, our crying is hushed, and our pain is eased. If the earnest of His presence can do this for us now, what will it be when we see Him! "He will wipe every tear from their eyes. There will be no more death or mourning or crying or pain, for the old order of things has passed away" (21:4, NIV). Ah, what wonder that the angel urged John, saying, "Write: for these words are true and faithful" (v. 5).

This is the new heaven and the new earth. How beautiful "that the last page of Revelation should come bending around to touch the first page of Genesis." Man, who because of his sin was driven from the tree of life, may at last have free access to that tree.

"The Spirit and the bride say, 'Come!' And let him who hears say, 'Come!' Whoever is thirsty, let him come; and whoever wishes, let him take the free gift of the water of life" (22:17, NIV).

I am coming.

Lord, I care not for riches, neither silver nor gold.
I would make sure of heaven; I would enter the fold.
In the book of Thy kingdom, with its pages so fair,
Tell me, Jesus my Saviour, Is my name written there?
—MARY A. KIDDER